Complexity, Institutions and Public Policy

Complexity, Institutions and Public Policy

Agile Decision-Making in a Turbulent World

Graham Room

Professor of European Social Policy, University of Bath, UK

Edward Elgar

Cheltenham, UK • Northampton, MA, USA

Published by
Edward Elgar Publishing Limited
The Lypiatts
15 Lansdown Road
Cheltenham
Glos GL50 2JA
UK

Edward Elgar Publishing, Inc.
William Pratt House
9 Dewey Court
Northampton
Massachusetts 01060
USA

A catalogue record for this book
is available from the British Library

Library of Congress Control Number: 2011925739

MIX
Paper from
responsible sources
FSC
www.fsc.org   FSC® C018575

ISBN 978 0 85793 263 1 (cased)

Typeset by Servis Filmsetting Ltd, Stockport, Cheshire
Printed and bound by MPG Books Group, UK

Contents

Figures, tables and boxes

FIGURES

TABLES

BOXES

Preface

The ideas presented here are ones with which I have wrestled for more than a decade. Nevertheless, the bulk of the work was undertaken during a two year Research Fellowship from the UK Economic and Social Research Council (Award RES-063-27-0130) during 2008–10. I am enormously grateful to the Council; without their support the rather ambitious project in which I found myself involved would have been quite impossible. I am also grateful to the University of Bath for freeing me from other duties during this period.

In this book I have ventured far from my core academic specialism. Without the advice and support of colleagues in other fields, such a journey would not have been possible. I have been fortunate in being able to draw on a variety of inter-disciplinary work underway within my own institution in particular, but also that of colleagues elsewhere.

Colleagues in my own Department to whom I am especially grateful include Louise Brown, Ian Butler, Ian Gough, Nick Gould, Jane Millar, Tess Ridge and Antonis Roumpakis. Ruth Birchall and Amilcar Moreira read the whole manuscript and gave me detailed and invaluable comments. Colleagues elsewhere in the University to whom I am indebted include Glynis Breakwell and Ian Jamieson, Stuart Reynolds and Matthew Wills (Biological Sciences), Julian Padget (Computer Sciences), John Powell and Richard Vidgen (Management), Nick Britton, Chris Budd and Stephen Pring (Mathematical Sciences), Mike Owen (Mechanical Engineering), Dick James (Physics) and Richard Velleman (Psychology).

Ian Stewart and Jack Cohen (University of Warwick Mathematics Institute) helped me greatly in making sense of the mathematics of complex systems.

Colleagues at Oxford University who read and commented on portions of the book include John Goldthorpe, John Odling-Smee and J.L.H. Thomas. Jean Boulton (Cranfield School of Management), Colin Crouch (University of Warwick) and Max Stewart of Decomplexity Associates (http://www.decomplexity.com) did likewise.

Jason Potts (University of Queensland) kindly made available to me a pre-publication copy of his 2008 study with Kurt Dopfer, *The General Theory of Economic Evolution* (London: Routledge).

This book is about policy. I benefitted from discussion of its ideas with, among others, Tony Clayton (UK Office of National Statistics), Audrey MacDougall (Scottish Government), Eric Marlier (EU Social Protection Committee Indicators Working Group) and Jean-Paul Tricart (DG Employment, European Commission).

A version of the material in Chapter 12 previously appeared in the journal *Policy Studies* (Room, 2011).

I am grateful to Oxford University Press for permission to include Table 12.1. Professor Hawoong Jeong at the Korea Advanced Institute of Science and Technology kindly provided Figure 11.1.

Graham Room
University of Bath
September 2010

1 Introduction

The research in which I have been engaged for many years has made me increasingly dissatisfied with conventional approaches within social policy studies to the conceptualisation and measurement of dynamic change. In complex and rapidly changing societies we are not well equipped as researchers to offer critical illumination and advice for policy-makers and the wider public.[1] However, my wider reading suggests that there are approaches in adjacent fields of enquiry that can and should be harnessed to policy analysis in general, social policy analysis in particular, and it is to this task that this book is devoted.

This opening chapter summarises my dissatisfaction in relation to mainstream social policy research; indicates in what sense we need a new policy analytics; and anticipates some of the intellectual tools and resources on which the study as a whole will draw.

1.1 THE UNSATISFACTORY STATE OF POLICY ANALYSIS

1.1.1 Poverty and Social Exclusion

I have over a long period undertaken research in the area of poverty and social exclusion, including involvement in various European programmes of research and evaluation. Recent decades have seen an impressive body of such research: all, to a greater or lesser extent, undertaken in the context of global economic restructuring, welfare 'recalibration' and concerns about social polarisation. This is a turbulent world that calls for appropriate tools of dynamic analysis.

For many scholars, the way forward, in terms of dynamic analysis, lies in the longitudinal analysis of household circumstances through cohort and panel studies (Leisering and Walker, 1998; Goodin et al., 1999). Sustained investment in such data sets – and ensuring their comparability cross-nationally – has been a major achievement of the social science community and government during recent decades. They can tell us how far household circumstances at one period are associated with household circumstances at some earlier period. Nevertheless, if such associations exist, they are mediated by the institutions and policies that are operative in the society concerned. Thus, for example, it is easy to demonstrate that redundancy and unemployment are in general associated with subsequently lower levels of income. However, redundancy is not a randomly distributed event: it is the result of a decision by an employer who is pursuing certain strategic goals, within particular labour market conditions and employment regulations. The consequences of redundancy for household financial circumstances then depend on the rules governing redundancy payments, the generosity of social security benefits and the opportunities for retraining (Gallie et al., 1994).

If such data sets, referring to persons and households, allow inferences to be drawn about these institutional processes, in general they are no more than that: intuitively plausible inferences. Yet to understand these processes is of central importance, if we are to draw policy lessons, because public policy reform typically involves re-shaping the strategic environment of key institutional actors. We need to understand how the strategies of key institutional decision-makers are shaped by public policy, and how these then affect particular categories of individuals and households.

This is not all. Individuals and households themselves pursue active strategies vis-à-vis these various institutions: shaping them, resisting them, by-passing them, extracting benefit from their operations. They may also mobilise and form alliances, so as to give their individual strategies greater chance of success. Those who are victorious on one institutional terrain – education, housing, labour market and so on – are then in a stronger position to continue the struggle on other terrains. They are also better placed to challenge the welfare settlements that protect the circumstances of different categories of household. This is of course the familiar 'Matthew principle'. It tends to produce self-reinforcing feedback loops: these may be of particular significance for processes of social inclusion and exclusion, if they enable some social groups to prosper while sending others along catastrophic downward trajectories. William Julius Wilson's studies of urban disadvantage in Chicago provide a classic example (see, for example, Wilson, 1987).

We need to study the strategic goals of the individual and the household, the resources and techniques at their disposal, the investments they make in new skills and resources, and relevant aspects of the broader environment on which they depend. We need to model and to measure the interactions of strategic decision-makers and households within institutional contexts that are themselves contested. These interactions may involve feedback loops and cumulative change: these require analysis as dynamic systems. This may be of particular significance for investigations into social inclusion and exclusion, where these dynamic interactions send some households and communities along catastrophic downward traject-ories, with the institutions that support them being progressively degraded.

In general, the longitudinal national data sets that have been established do not allow us to say much about these social, political, economic and insti-tutional dynamics and the larger changes in political economy within which they unfold. As a tool for analysing the dynamics of social change they are therefore of rather limited value. So are the policy recommendations that researchers can derive from them, except insofar as they draw also on other qualitative studies, and studies at the local level, so as to provide additional insights into the institutional dynamics to which I have referred.

1.1.2 Social Dynamics of the Knowledge Economy

During 2001–04 I led a team within the EU Framework 5 research pro-gramme. This was concerned with evaluating the statistical indicators being used to track the development of the new 'knowledge economy': ranging across its social, technological, economic and organisational aspects (Room, 2005a). Here again, it seemed necessary to recognise the dynamic and turbulent processes involved and to select indicators accordingly.

One thing was immediately apparent. Policy-makers place great weight on indicators that track the diffusion of the new information technologies across a society (Rogers, 2003): for example, the proportion of enterprises, or universities or households who have adopted a particular technol-ogy (Figure 1.1). These indicators show how far a given technology has reached even the least reachable. Far fewer indicators are available of the 'leading edge' of innovation: the entrepreneurs or 'first movers' who forge

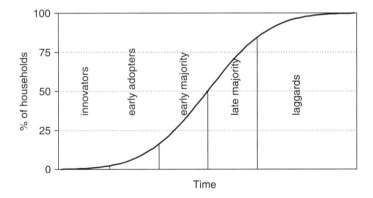

Figure 1.1   Diffusion of technologies

new combinations of technology, organisation and skill within enterprises and who provide the impetus to wider socio-economic transformation.[2]

From a social policy standpoint, maybe this does not matter. Maybe we are not interested in the first movers, only in the 'last movers': in this particular case, the contours of the so-called digital divide, regularly re-shaped by new waves of technological change, and threatening new lines of social polarisation. However, this would surely be short-sighted. Social, economic and technological processes are dynamically coupled systems: if we do not understand the dynamics of the first movers, neither will we understand the fate of the last movers.

So what of these first mover processes? This research revealed *inter alia* that processes of 'take-off' into the new knowledge economy cannot be triggered solely by particular levels of research and development (R&D) expenditure or by the application of particular investments in information and communication technology (ICT). Dynamic innovation is a more complex process, involving interactions between technological investment, organisational change, entrepreneurship and workforce development at the level of the enterprise (Pettigrew et al., 2003: Part 2). It also depends upon the impetus and support offered by national – and international – 'innovation systems'. Nevertheless, indicators of these first mover processes – the dynamics that generate innovation – are as yet only rudimentary. So also are the indicators that policy-makers might use to track the consequences of these first mover processes for last movers and for social polarisation across the wider society.

These observations are not new. For example, the Organization for Economics Cooperation and Development (OECD, 2003: Ch. 3) provides a review of recent studies which demonstrate the importance of these firm-level interactions for innovation and take-off: it suggests how data sets may be linked so as to developing appropriate indicators. Such indicators could illuminate more adequately the trajectories of socio-economic transformation along which policy-makers aspire to direct their societies. For the moment, however, this remains largely unexplored territory.

1.2   A NEW POLICY ANALYTICS

From these two strands of my previous work there arise the central questions with which I seek to engage in this book. First, how can we best conceptualise these dynamic processes of socio-economic change: processes that involve interactions between agents (households, enterprises and so on) and institutions: processes that may result in 'downward' trajectories of exclusion but also those which catalyse 'upward' trajectories of 'take-off'? Second, how can we model these dynamics empirically, as processes that are endogenous rather than merely the response to exogenous shocks? Third, what analytical tools – including indicators – can be made available to policy-makers for the purpose of monitoring and steering these processes of transformation? The book is ultimately to be judged by reference to these latter, policy-related questions, even if, in order to answer them, I devote the initial chapters to problems of conceptualisation. I therefore start with some comments about the world of the policy-maker.

How can public policy-makers make good decisions? What counts as a good decision? And having made it, how can they check just how good it turned out to be? There are of course many answers to these questions. In some form or other they are at the centre of most books on policy-making. One answer that is current today is that good policy decisions are evidence-based decisions. Such decisions are good in two senses. First, they select policies that are likely to be effective. Second, with evidence to back them up, they can expect to command public support.

The paradigm case of evidence-based intervention is that of the randomised controlled medical trial. On the basis of this gold standard, a spectrum of methodologies and approaches has been elaborated to cope with less controllable interventions. The gold standard assumes that evidence about interventions can be gathered and analysed on the basis of *ceteris paribus*: other things are equal or unaffected and serve as no more than context to the intervention itself. Insofar as the intervention has side effects, these are limited in scope and identifiable and can thus be included in the evaluation of the evidence. Equipped with such evidence, the public policy-maker can institute an appropriate intervention in the socio-economic functioning of society.

However, the appropriateness of this approach depends on how we conceive of the terrain on which public policy-makers find themselves. If the gold standard is the controlled medical trial, one metaphor that may be useful is that of the putting green. On this uniform terrain, where all local perturbations have been flattened, the golfer can apply the putter to the ball in a simple expression of Newton's laws of motion. True, the eye may reveal that there is a gentle slope, although in any self-respecting golf club this will be a uniform one, for which a slight angling of the stroke will suffice to compensate. The golfer may also misjudge the degree of friction that the well-manicured grass offers: but in this case some increase or decrease in the force with which the ball is struck will again suffice. The policy-maker, equipped with reliable evidence and the mantra of *ceteris paribus*, can confidently institute an intervention with a force and towards a target that can similarly be expected to be a winner.

However, the real world of policy-making is perhaps less like a putting green than a game of crazy golf: and a game of crazy golf, moreover, that is played on the 'bouncy castles' that are now commonplace in children's playgrounds. Now the landscape is far from uniform: there are hills, valleys and obstacles; worse still, as the ball is struck and proceeds on its course, its weight modifies the topology of the golf course itself. In such a world, is evidence-based policy-making even possible? If not, what answers can be given to the questions with which we started, concerned with good policy decisions?

One way to summarise this world of valleys, hills and malleable topographies is to say that it is non-linear. However, there are many types of non-linearity and not all of them pose major problems for evidence-based policy-making.

A medicine which has proved effective in clinical trials may nevertheless have non-linear effects on patients. There may be a threshold effect: below a certain level of dosage, the medicine has no beneficial consequences. At the opposite end of the scale, it may be that increasing the dose beyond a certain point fails to increase the benefit to patients: it reaches a plateau. The medicine in question thus has a non-linear profile in relation to dosage and effectiveness. This does not, however, affect the *ceteris paribus* assumption, nor does it undermine the ability of the experimentalist to pronounce on the effectiveness of the medicine at various levels of dosage.

A second medicine may have various side effects – physical, motivational and so on. These may in turn have consequences for the medical outcomes of interest, reducing or reinforcing these outcomes. These secondary effects mean that the relationship between intervention and particular outcomes is no longer a simple and direct one. Nevertheless, providing that these secondary effects follow reliably from the initial intervention, and do not spill out in ways that undermine the broader *ceteris paribus* assumptions within which the clinical trial is nested, evidence-based assessment of the medicine in question again remains possible.

A third medicine may, however, set a variety of secondary effects in motion, whose effects on the outcomes of interest depend also on other factors that are outside the control of the experimentalist: for example, the attitudes and actions of family members of the trial subjects, in relation to these secondary effects. If such family members respond in predictable ways and if these responses are such as to dampen down the secondary effects, the validity of the clinical trial is to some extent restored. If, however, family members respond in a variety of different ways, which for the moment at least are beyond the capacity of the experimentalist to understand or predict, and if, moreover, these responses affect the secondary effects in quite different ways, then the clinical trial is seriously undermined.

This is the type of non-linearity with which I am concerned in this book. It involves feedback loops which bring into play a variety of actors who set about re-shaping the policy intervention in light of their own strategic objectives. I do not say that such non-linearity is a significant feature of all policy domains, only that it is true of some: including, I suggest, those with which this chapter started. This is policy-making played out on a bouncy castle, whose topography is itself being continually transformed, as a result of these policy interventions and the efforts of a wider array of actors to anticipate and re-shape the policy terrain.

However, non-linearity is not the only problem. On each putting green, the contest is renewed as though for the first time. True, the player who, on reaching the final green, lags many holes or strokes behind, may feel so demoralised as to be unable to summon up a final display of competitive courage. Nevertheless, the topography of the final green is not itself affected by the unequal struggles on the preceding holes. The same is hardly true in public policy-making. No policy is made on a *tabula rasa*: any policy is an intervention in a tangled web of institutions that have developed incrementally over extended periods of time and that give each policy context its own specificity. This history shapes the constraints and the opportunities within which policy interventions can then unfold. Policy terrains and policy effects are path dependent.

Nevertheless, to acknowledge non-linearity and path dependency does not necessarily mean that good policy decisions based on sound and reliable evidence are impossible under these conditions. On the contrary, it is precisely to assess the scope for such policy-making, even off the 'gold standard' of the controlled medical trial, that this book has been written.

1.3   PATH DEPENDENCY AND POLICY ANALYSIS

This book will have much to say about path dependency. For the moment we offer just a few comments (for a good overview, see Mahoney, 2000).

One commonly used illustration of path dependency couches it in terms of probabilities. An urn (the so-called Polya urn) contains balls of two different colours. Each time a ball of one colour is drawn out, slightly more of the other are left in the urn, and so it is slightly more likely that one of the other colour will be drawn next time. The cumulative numbers resulting from successive withdrawals are likely to approximate the initial proportions in the urn. If, however, the ball initially drawn is returned to the urn, along with an additional ball of the same colour, before the whole process is repeated, the chances of the same colour being drawn a second time are reinforced, as are the chances that this colour becomes progressively dominant. Thus the initial random draw tends to send the contents of the urn along a self-reinforcing course: we have path dependency and 'first mover' advantage. This is a 'random walk' but on a surface where the initial choice 'tilts' the topography and makes more likely continuing movement in the same direction (Crouch, 2005: 76).

Ebbinghaus and Crouch explore such path dependency in directions that are central to our own endeavour. Ebbinghaus (2005) distinguishes what he sees as two very different forms of path dependency: on the one hand, the 'road juncture', the fateful choice between alternative paths at a road junction; on the other hand, the 'trodden trail', the pathway that by virtue of repeated use becomes the 'taken for granted' low cost option for everyone. However, while these are indeed logically distinct, they correspond to the two elements that together make for path dependency in the case of the Polya urn. On the one side there is first mover advantage: which colour is drawn out first. On the other is the process of reinforcement, as additional balls of that same colour are added to the urn. As we shall argue in later chapters, while these two forms of path dependency may, as Ebbinghaus argues, be quite different in principle, it is when they co-exist in practice that processes of path dependency become particularly powerful. This key insight underpins the analytical toolkit that we seek to build in the course of this study.

The Polya urn involves some simple algorithms. The person who draws the successive balls is neither required nor allowed to make any strategic judgements and choices. However, Crouch – whose studies of 'institutional entrepreneurs' (Crouch, 2005) will be at the centre of our attention in a later chapter – develops a series of modifications of the Polya urn that allow for such strategic judgements and the processes of reflection that they involve. He asks how, under conditions of uncertainty, actors expect their world to work: what judgements they form as to the contents of the Polya urn, based on the colours of the balls they have already drawn. He asks what search strategies actors may be able to follow in order to locate balls of a preferred colour, rather than simply taking whichever comes blindly to hand. He models actors as agile path creators, able to explore distant hills and valleys, rather than moving myopically along merely local contours. Our own aim is similarly to develop models of agile action on complex terrains that can inform a new policy analytics.

1.4   CONCEPTUAL AND METHODOLOGICAL BASE

How far is it possible to provide analytical tools for policy-makers in a world of non-linearity and path dependence? This is the central question of this book. Can we, in particular, equip policy-makers with the tools they need if they are to spot the feedback loops and 'tipping points' where new and dynamic trajectories of socio-economic change are set in motion, for better or worse, and illuminate the ways in which their own interventions can shape and steer these trajectories?

We must establish an appropriate conceptual and methodological basis. From a variety of different theoretical standpoints, a number of literatures have developed in recent decades that are concerned with such non-linearity and path dependency. This book focuses on two in particular. Both give pride of place to the self-reinforcing feedback loops which can drive socio-economic systems along distinctive but path dependent trajectories. One starts with agents and examines how, from their local interactions, larger and more complex patterns emerge. The other starts with institutions and examines how these delimit the scope for interaction by agents.

The first literature is complexity science, bringing to the social sciences insights and methods that have been developed largely in relation to physical and biological processes. Complexity science typically starts with particles, cells or organisms. It posits some simple rules of local interaction. It then demonstrates – often using computer simulations – that under certain environmental conditions ('control parameters') these local interactions will set up positive feedback loops from which complex patterns emerge at a global level, in processes of 'self-organisation'. For many of these phenomena – especially the biological – there has then been a further level of conceptualisation and analysis, involving mechanisms of evolution and adaptation to new niches, within an environment that is itself re-shaped in the process. These are 'complex adaptive systems' (Waldrop, 1992: Ch. 3; Kauffman, 1993: Ch. 7).

These perspectives have already been applied by a variety of social scientists, in two principal ways. As we shall see, some sociologists and social policy writers have used complexity as a fertile metaphor, generating new questions for social science at a general level (Urry, 2003). Sociologists and economists have also used complexity in the form of agent-based modelling, involving computer simulation: there has been an enormous expansion in such work during the past decade (Gilbert, 2008). Nevertheless, neither of these applications has generated a commensurate array of novel empirical enquiry, nor are corresponding instruments and indicators for use by policy-makers well developed. This gap is evident, not least, in social policy and related fields of study: but see Byrne (1998), Barnes et al. (2003), Blamey and Mackenzie (2007) and Sanderson (2006).

The second literature is institutionalism, especially 'historical institutionalism'. This starts with the choice of institutions by social, economic and political actors: it then examines how these institutions produce patterns of interests and normative commitments which constrain and shape the courses of action – and the types of institutional development – that are subsequently likely to take place. The legacy of institutions thus sets up positive feedback loops, locking actors into a particular range of likely institutional innovations and locking out others. As in complexity science, there is path dependency.

Aggregation of particles or cells: aggregation of interests and commitments. In both cases the aggregation creates a new and constraining world as far as the individual particle or social actor is concerned: a set of structures which constrain agency. However, that world also opens up new opportunities for agency and new niches that can be exploited by the 'first mover'. This latter aspect, a central feature of the complexity literature (especially with its interest in co-evolution and complex adaptive systems), has also become a central preoccupation of the institutionalist debate, as we shall see.

This book seeks to develop a conceptually coherent and methodologically novel synthesis of these two literatures, which serves then as the basis for a new policy analytics. It will not overlook adjacent strands of enquiry which resonate with the arguments developed here: these include the long-standing debates on agency and structure; the system dynamics literature; contemporary debates around rational action; social applications of Darwinism and evolutionary theory. Nevertheless, in any project, focus is everything and ours must be selective, if we are to develop a genuinely novel approach to policy analysis.

1.5   CONCLUSION

I began this chapter by referring to my own research and the dissatisfactions which have prompted this book. I have sought to explain in what sense the world of the policy-maker is complex and why our conventional methods of illuminating that world, as policy analysts, may have their limitations.

It is not just that the policy world is complex, however, it is also turbulent; and that turbulence has become only too apparent during the period that this book has been in the writing, with the international financial and economic crisis spilling over to affect central areas of social policy. The bouncy castle seems to have gone wild. Government leaders warn that conventional methods of policy intervention – the accumulated wisdom of our collective path dependent journeys – seem no longer to work. New models of a dynamically interconnected world are needed, so as to anticipate, steer and control this turbulence, but are as yet lacking. What therefore started out as an attempt to offer guidance to social policy-makers may perhaps have some wider interest, in the collective endeavour to understand and manage a complex and turbulent world.

We start in Part 1 with the problem of conceptualising social dynamics, weaving together perspectives taken from complexity and institutionalism. Chapter 2 offers an overview of recent writing in complexity; Chapter 3 is concerned with complex adaptive systems and with evolutionary models in particular; Chapter 4 with the application of these models to economic dynamics. Chapters 5, 6 and 7 are concerned with institutionalist writings. Chapter 8 integrates the two. In Part 2 we consider the methodological and modelling challenges that follow from this conceptual integration. Finally, Part 3 sets out new directions for policy analysis.

It may finally be worth offering some cautions as to what the book is *not* trying to do. It might have limited itself to reviewing the models of dynamic systems that are current in the natural sciences and exploring how these can be applied to the social world. It could have done the same in regards to agent-based modelling and simulation. These are, however, tasks already undertaken by others, with a rather impressive level of competence (Ball, 2004; Gilbert, 2008). I build on their work in Parts 2 and 3, and in a small way seek to extend it, but to tread in their footsteps is not my primary task.

Rather, the first concern of the book is conceptual and ontological, integrating complexity science and institutionalism. I argue that each is in need of the other, as far as social science is concerned. Complexity science is bereft of an adequate treatment of institutions; institutionalism needs the formal dynamic modelling of complexity science. More than this, however, I argue that there are remarkable – but so far I think largely unremarked – convergences between the two, which make plausible the project of integrating them. Part 1 builds the integrated conceptual vantage point from which Parts 2 and 3 then deal, respectively, with methods and policies.

The book is thus addressed to those who have a foot in both of these worlds or who wish to do so. It requires the reader to immerse him or herself in salient elements of each. This makes, no doubt, for what is at times a rather demanding journey. I have tried to make it as comfortable and simple as possible, but was unable to make it simpler.

PART 1

Concepts

2 The complexity paradigm

2.1 INTRODUCTION

Scientific enquiry is undertaken within communities using shared paradigms. These are, however, always provisional and are liable to be contested, transformed and replaced (Toulmin and Goodfield, 1967; Kuhn, 1970; Toulmin, 1972).

Paradigms can be shared across diverse fields of enquiry, albeit they must be adapted to the distinctive features of each scientific niche. Some of those dominant in the natural sciences have shaped social scientific approaches to the analysis of social dynamics. The triumph of Newtonian mechanics encouraged social scientists to look for the conditions of social equilibrium and inertia, even in face of pressures for change. Thermodynamics carried a message of ever-increasing entropy or disorder: much of social science has been an enquiry into hidden sources of order. Darwinian evolution has variously infused (and sometimes confused) social science and its attempts to address development rather than stasis. This sharing of paradigms was not, of course, the only influence on the direction and preoccupations of social scientists; nevertheless, their work required methodological justification and here these natural scientific paradigms were prominent.

These influences have not been entirely one-way. The ecology of scientific disciplines reveals them co-evolving, sometimes predatory upon each other but sometimes symbiotic. The last quarter century has seen a noteworthy coming together around a new paradigm of 'complexity'. One facilitating factor was the establishment of institutes specifically committed to the multi-disciplinary treatment of complex systems, notably that at Santa Fé (http://www.santafe.edu/). Another was the development and ready availability of computer power, with which complex processes could be simulated and explored in ways hitherto impossible.

As we shall see, however, the new complexity paradigm grows out of earlier currents of thought (as indeed is the case, Kuhn (1970) insists, with any new paradigm). Among the intellectual currents that it wove into a new synthesis were neo-Darwinian evolutionary biology (bringing together Darwin's interest in variation and selection with more recent molecular and genetic biology); thermodynamics and 'far from equilibrium' systems; information science and systems of distributed intelligence; economics and its treatment – reaching back to Alfred Marshall and even Adam Smith – of increasing returns and the growth of knowledge. Santa Fé did not invent complexity, even if it has played a key role in its development, consolidation and diffusion.

Complexity analysis has become popular in engineering and the natural sciences: it is now being taken up in economics and related disciplines. Ball in his study *Critical Mass* (2004) argues that it can be applied to a wide range of issues with which social scientists have long been concerned: markets, international relations, social networks, urban development, traffic management, racial zoning in cities. Most of his readers will agree that complexity analysis, as developed in the natural sciences, is a fertile source of metaphors on which social scientists can draw: but is it more than that? In particular, can it advance social science and policy analysis in terms of theorising, model-building and empirical testing? It is with this challenge that the present study is in part concerned.

We now introduce some of the key elements of the complexity paradigm and their potential significance for policy analysis.[1]

2.2   INCREASING RETURNS AND PATH DEPENDENCY

The previous chapter introduced the Polya urn. If the probability that a ball of a given colour is selected is unaffected by the balls already drawn, we can expect the final balance of withdrawals to approximate their initial distribution in the urn. In the contrary case, the balls initially drawn reshape the topography or probability distribution of subsequent moves, so that the final balance of withdrawals departs significantly and increasingly from that initial distribution: it is path dependent.

This seems typical of many technological innovations and their diffusion. Examples commonly cited include the introduction of the QWERTY keyboard and the triumph of the VHS over the Betamex video-system. One could, however, add a multitude of other technological and institutional examples, where early adoption by some significantly tips the scales, when others in that population are making their own choice as to which technology or institutional device to adopt. This means that markets may well select and entrench a technology that is not the most efficient. Only where a rival seems to offer a distinctive and differentiating niche of its own (Apple alongside PC, for example, in the case of computers), or when the 'majority choice' is becoming congested and a minority choice is for that reason attractive (in overcrowded public services for example) will this logic or inertia of the 'trodden trail' disappear. Even then, however, the minority choice, the differentiated niche, is defined by reference to the majority option and the path dependent logic of its development. (There is a whole literature on this so-called 'minority game', starting from Arthur (1994a).)

Such path dependency lay at the heart of Alfred Marshall's treatment of 'external increasing returns' (1920).[2] If a firm is wondering where to site its operations, there may well be benefits in locating close to other firms in the same industry, because of the pool of appropriately skilled labour that can be found there, specialist sub-contractors and know-how. Indeed, the more firms that co-locate, the greater these external increasing returns that each firm enjoys, including growth of the inter-firm pool of skill and knowledge (Loasby, 1999: 98). Notice that whatever the reason for the forerunners to locate there (maybe the pioneer just happened to like the local fishing or golf course), once they have established themselves the external increasing returns and the corresponding path dependencies start to operate and attract others.

External increasing returns of this sort are not peculiar to geographical agglomerations, they apply to networks more generally (Christakis and Fowler, 2009). Metcalfe's Law affirms that the value of a network to its members is proportional to the square of its nodes (Metcalfe, 1995). The new information technologies involve networks on a much grander and more rapid scale than before and may confer to an unprecedented extent the external increasing returns which Metcalfe promises. These returns may involve the definition of common standards, eliminating the costs of diversity; the creation of a 'captive market' for subsequent inventions, among those who have already bought into the network's standards; rules for the admission of non-members that put them at a growing disadvantage if they remain outside (Kelly, 1999). Networks thus have a very real power dimension: they offer hegemonic lock-in as much as technological advance, especially where this is underpinned by strong legal protection of intellectual property rights (Grewal, 2008). Indeed, this has led some to argue that the defence of networks – and of the standards and brands they embody – can become a more central objective of organisational behaviour than continuing innovation (European Commission, 2004b).

As already noted, congestion may in due course place a limit on these increasing returns. The previous chapter referred to Rogers's (2003) work on the diffusion of innovations. Rogers uses the logistic or S-curve to describe the diffusion of innovations, as a particular technology is adopted in turn by different population groups: innovators, early adaptors, late adaptors, late majority, laggards (see Figure 1.1) The early part of the S-curve depicts rapidly growing use, attracted by the external increasing returns; the later part manifests progressive satiation, whether due to growing congestion among users or the lesser appetites of the late arrivals. Krugman (1991, 1999) likewise develops economic models of urban-industrial concentration that combine increasing returns and congestion effects. It is in these terms – the neglect of eventual congestion and satiation – that Metcalfe's Law has been questioned (Krugman, 1999; Delong and Summers, 2001). In later chapters we return to these questions, with further attention, on the one hand, to the logistic curve, as a simple model of non-linear dynamics, on the other, to technological innovation: not in a single product, where satiation may indeed become a constraint, but across a successively expanding array of technologies.

Increasing returns of this sort are fundamentally at odds with the mainstream neoclassical economics that has dominated academic economic scholarship, in the Anglo-Saxon world at least, over the last century. They put in question the basic assumptions of neoclassical equilibrium: assumptions that look increasingly implausible as the pace of economic transformation accelerates. Instead, they require that we recognise economic activity as fatefully re-shaping its environment, producing self-reinforcing feedback effects. It is these dynamics that have been seized on by economists such as Arthur who, moving out from the neoclassical mainstream, have sought analytical tools grounded in the complexity paradigm to illuminate processes of change (Arthur et al., 1997).

Such insights have, however, long been central to a range of other economists outside the neoclassical mainstream, including Young (1928), Myrdal's account of 'cumulative causation' and Kaldor's critique of 'economics without equilibrium' (Kaldor, 1985; Toner, 1999).[3] They underpinned Keynes's dismissal of the long run ('in the long run we are all dead'): the short run mattered because fateful path dependencies kicked in and could lock the economy into a trajectory of under-employment (Skidelsky, 2009: 79ff.). They have also been central to development economics (Ramaswamy, 2000). Nevertheless, it has in general been left to other economists to articulate complexity science with these longer-standing alternatives to the neoclassical paradigm, as we shall see in Chapter 4; and even then, it has been with the tradition of Schumpeter and Hayek rather than Keynes and Kaldor that these connections have predominantly been made.

2.3   SELF-ORGANISATION IN 'FAR FROM EQUILIBRIUM' SYSTEMS

Classical mechanics involved the study of systems that could be expressed as a set of simple differential equations. Once the initial conditions were known, the equations provided a precise description of how the system and its constituent elements would behave. In particular, the stability and equilibrium conditions of the system could be identified. Moreover, the same equations could be run backwards: time was reversible.

Classical mechanics were concerned with the transmission of motion. In contrast, thermodynamics, as it developed in the nineteenth century, dealt with steam engines that transformed fuel into heat, mechanical energy and work; and, more generally, with physical, chemical and biological systems that were 'open', exchanging energy and matter with their environment and transforming it. Many of the processes of interest involved combustion and were irreversible, quite unlike those portrayed by classical mechanics.

In the course of transforming fuel into work, engines encounter friction and other heat losses, dissipating energy. This is a practical problem for engineers. It is also, however, of key theoretical interest, as the second law of thermodynamics. Thermodynamic systems are forever dissipating energy to their surroundings which cannot be retrieved; entropy or disorder across the system and its surroundings must progressively increase; there is an 'arrow of time'.

Thermodynamic systems that are subject to a continuous input of energy are pushed away from equilibrium. Nevertheless, they can 'self-organise', with order and structure emerging within them and entropy locally reducing, even as the entropy exported to their surroundings increases, and does so of course by at least the same amount, as the second law requires. This steers us away from the stability and equilibrium conditions of classical mechanics, to investigate what forms of structure and organisation may be possible in physical systems that are 'far from equilibrium'.

Onsager and Prigogine were among those who, working in the mid-twentieth century on the thermodynamics of physical and chemical processes, highlighted these properties of self-organisation in 'far from equilibrium' systems. This was the period when computing power was first becoming readily available. Prigogine developed simulations to explore processes of self-organisation in 'complex dissipative structures', something that in subsequent years has become commonplace (Prigogine, 1980; Prigogine and Stengers, 1984). His work remains a common point of reference for those from other disciplines who have sought to analyse biological and social systems in terms of 'far from equilibrium' dynamics, even if among scholars in the physical sciences the debate has moved on (see, for example, Martyushev and Seleznev, 2006).

One example of such self-organisation is the set of chemical reactions commonly described as 'reaction-diffusion systems'. These involve, on the one hand, the regular injection of a reagent at specific points and, on the other, differential rates of diffusion of the products of the reaction catalysed by this reagent. This exchange of matter and energy with the larger environment keeps such systems away from equilibrium. They are, however, capable of producing oscillations, standing and travelling waves and other spatio-temporal patterns (Prigogine, 1980: Ch. 5; Prigogine and Stengers, 1984: Ch. 5). One simple case – but of generic interest – is provided by the so-called Turing instabilities: we make use of this model in Chapter 10.

Such patterns of self-organisation involve differentiated but regular structure, whether in space (waves for example) or time (oscillations for example) or both. The structure depends, however, upon the system parameters: as these vary, its uniformities and symmetries may be broken and new and more complex patterns emerge. Even so, this self-organisation can happen only within a delimited range of parameter values: outside this range, the system may, on the one hand, subside into a more uniform state, close to equilibrium, or it may, alternatively, become chaotic. We elaborate some of these distinctions mathematically in Chapter 9.

One other approach to self-organisation merits more detailed discussion. For any far from equilibrium system, we start with a source of energy, on the one hand, the dissipation of that energy, on the other. Bak (1997) uses physical experiment, computer simulation and empirical data sets to observe and test what happens. He argues that the behaviour of such a system is discontinuous or 'punctuated': there is a succession of discrete events, as the energy input overwhelms the frictional inertia, and then builds up again, sufficiently to generate the next such event. Such systems therefore commonly get themselves into a delicately poised state of 'self-organised criticality'. This is a dynamic model which Bak applies across a wide range of physical, biological and economic phenomena, including earthquakes, sand piles and avalanches, river basins, speciation and extinction events, economic functioning and traffic jams (for popular discussions, see Ball (2004: 294–300) and Buchanan (2000)).

In the case of sand piles, with sand being poured from above, this seems intuitively obvious; the progressive build-up of material renders the slope ever steeper, with a landslide or avalanche the eventual consequence, but the pile forever hovering on the precarious brink of a further avalanche. With earthquakes, there is a gradual and progressive increase of subterranean pressure whose effect is initially arrested by the frictional resistance of existing geological formations, but which in due course proves overwhelming. In river basins, the flow of water erodes particular stress points on the river bank and, from time to time, produces smaller or larger reconfigurations of the whole network.

Something similar seems to characterise speciation and extinction events in the course of biological evolution. The fossil record reveals a pattern of 'punctuated equilibria': periods of stasis followed by sudden and widespread change, rather than a smooth and continuous process of adaptation and increasing fitness (Gould and Eldridge, 1977).[4] Here the source of 'energy' is the stream of genetic variation or novelty that each fresh generation throws up, and the superior fitness that these variations may confer on the organisms concerned. Against this, there may be frictional resistance from existing populations and species, able to modify their established niches without making any evolutionary adaptation; the same resilience or inertia may extend to the eco-systems they share with other species (Odling-Smee et al., 2003). It may be only when streams of genetic novelty remove a key species from the eco-system, undermining the survival prospects for all concerned, that a dissipating avalanche of extinction will occur.

In none of these cases are the scale and timing of successive events predictable, at least in terms of our current knowledge base. Nevertheless, viewed in the aggregate, it is found that they typically display a 'power law' distribution, according to the equation

$$y = x^a$$

where x distinguishes the events according to their scale and y indicates how many of the events there were of a given scale (for example, the number of earthquakes above a certain magnitude). The above equation can be re-written as

$$\log y = a \log x$$

If this is plotted on double log graph paper, we obtain a straight line graph whose gradient is 'a', the 'power' of the case in question. Such power laws, as we shall see, are the 'signature' of self-organisation in far from equilibrium systems: whether we watch the sand pile avalanches in the laboratory, re-visit the fossil record for mass speciation and extinction events, or conduct computer simulations of far from equilibrium systems and count the number and size of their 'punctuations' (Bak, 1997: Ch. 1). One test or requirement of explanations of self-organising processes is that they should explain why a power law operates and indeed the value of the power exponent (Bak, 1997: Ch. 1).

A power law means that earthquakes, avalanches, the branching of a river network and so on do not follow a normal or Gaussian distribution in their scale or timing (Figure 2.1). The 'tails' of the distribution are

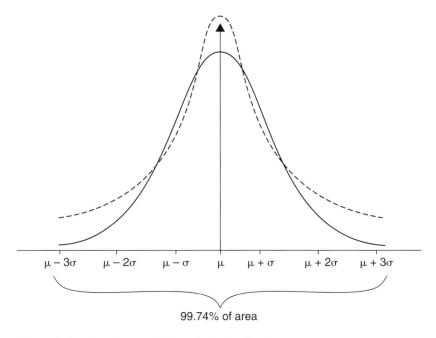

$$\mu - 3\sigma \quad \mu - 2\sigma \quad \mu - \sigma \quad \mu \quad \mu + \sigma \quad \mu + 2\sigma \quad \mu + 3\sigma$$

99.74% of area

Figure 2.1   Gaussian and 'fat-tailed' distributions

'fatter' than in a Gaussian: there are more very large and more very small earthquakes (dotted line in Figure 2.1). This is a characteristic feature of processes which are locally interconnected – the pressure exerted by one grain of sand on the next – but build into long-range system-wide processes. What also follows is that they are 'scale-free'. Scale-free means that large, intermediate and small-scale earthquakes and avalanches are forever at risk of taking place: there is no typical or average size to an event. In the case of ecological systems, scale-free means that as well as there being finely balanced food webs involving large predators and their prey, there will also, nested in the interstices of their habitats, be no less complex and finely balanced food webs involving micro-predators and their prey.

Nevertheless, it is also important to note that 'self-organised criticality' occurs only within a certain range of the system parameters. If the sand is too damp – or if rice grains of a certain size are substituted – the avalanche behaviour described above will not ensue (Bak, 1997: Ch. 4; Buchanan, 2000: Ch. 7). Likewise, if the rate of genetic mutation is too high, the evolutionary survival information that can be encoded in the genetic inheritance of each organism will be too rudimentary and no 'equilibrium' can form that can then be punctuated (Bak and Paczuski, 1996).

Even in this brief review of Bak's argument, we have seen that the 'energy' source and the abrasion or friction by which energy dissipates, which together make for a far from equilibrium system, and possibly for 'self-organised criticality', may take very different forms. In the case of earthquakes the energy source was the progressive increase of subterranean pressure; energy dissipated against the resistance of existing geological formations. In the case of biological evolution, the energy source was the stream of genetic novelty and the superior fitness thereby conferred; the friction was the inertia of resilient eco-systems and niche adaptation.

Bak himself does not have a well-articulated model of self-organised criticality in relation to human societies. However, various scholars have identified power laws and fat-tailed distributions in public affairs, notably in relation to government budgeting, and have offered corresponding explanatory accounts in terms of institutional 'friction' (Breunig, 2006; Jensen, 2009). We assess later the more general relevance of Bak's account for policy sciences.

2.4 LOCAL AGENTS AND EMERGENT ORDER

The 1980s and 1990s saw the dramatic expansion of easily usable computer power. This required software which was capable of handling large-scale and complex operations. Advances were achieved by disaggregating those operations into simple components – simple rules or algorithms – which could be left to interact over many cycles. In other words, simplification was achieved at the cost of multiple iterations: but with the computer power that was now available, this was a cost that could easily be paid.

These advances in software design immediately suggested a second line of application. Computer simulation could be used to model processes in the real world whereby simple local interactions, after many iterations, produce complex global patterns. Such simulation could also be used to explore under what conditions these patterns emerge: just as software needs to be tweaked, if it is to handle complex operations through simple algorithms, simple interactions in the real world produce organised patterns only under specific conditions. This has been the basis for an enormously fruitful interchange between software design and artificial intelligence, on the one hand, agent-based modelling and computer simulation of real world processes, on the other. Indeed, during the last few decades this has been the technology of choice in complexity science, across all the scientific disciplines which it has influenced.

It is not just that this offers a convenient and powerful tool for modelling complex natural and social processes. It also suggests a particular ontological and explanatory approach. The real world is in important respects composed of simple elements that interact with each other at a local level, according to some simple rules, but this in turn generates the complex and profound structures and patterns that we observe. This ontology seems well founded in many areas of empirical enquiry. There have, for example, been a series of studies of the behaviour of the humble slime mould (Prigogine and Stengers, 1984: 156–9; Ball, 2004: 148–52). In times of plenty, individual organisms live independently; in times of hardship, however, the whole colony coheres into a single mass. This can be explained by reference to the chemical signals that in times of stress act as attractants between immediate neighbours, and which then generate the global patterns of behaviour that colonies manifest to cope with environmental adversity. Such swarming behaviour is not of course peculiar to slime mould: it extends, for example, to flocks of birds and shoals of fish. In all these cases it seems that each individual navigates by reference only to the movements of its immediate neighbours – and their signals of dangers and opportunities – but this can suffice to produce the global patterns we observe.

These are all examples of simple local interactions that produce global patterns. In turn, global structures can be sustained through simple local interactions. An example is a colony of ants. Global order in such a colony does not result from any centralised system of command; instead, individual ants communicate with their immediate neighbours by chemical signals relating to food, danger and so on. Some of these signals – for example, the presence of food – may attract other ants to the quest; other signals – for example, the presence of ants already engaged in foraging – may divert other ants to other tasks in the colony. It is these reactions to local signals that sustain orderly functioning across the colony as a whole and have emerged as highly successful adaptations to evolutionary pressures (Johnson, 2001; Prete, 2004: Chs 1–2).

A similar analysis seems to apply to the development, organisation and functioning of cells in a multi-cellular organism. True, such an organism has a genetic blueprint, in the form of its DNA, and this is present in each cell nucleus (just as the individual ants in a colony share a common DNA, by reference to which each is hard-wired to respond to different local signals in the manner just discussed). Nevertheless, in the course of development each cell reads off from this DNA only those elements of relevance to its local situation, as triggered by communications from its immediate neighbours (Johnson, 2001: 83–6). In all these cases simple and myopic agents, reacting to signals from their immediate neighbours, produce and sustain complex global structures, albeit depending on the control parameters (in this case the DNA) of the system in question.

For modelling and simulation purposes, the aforesaid components or

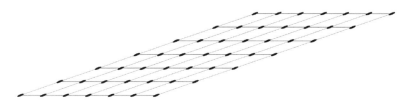

Figure 2.2   A grid or lattice

agents commonly take the form of 'cellular automata'. Each agent or automaton is located at a node of a grid or 'lattice' in multi-dimensional space; each then interacts with its immediate neighbours, according to specified rules, but not with any more distant agents (Figure 2.2). It is to this extent myopic. This, we should add, is not the only possible modelling strategy; in a later chapter we explore the properties of networks, where interactions are not limited to the purely local. Here again, computer simulation has been a powerful tool. In all these cases, however, the analytical goal remains the same: to understand how simple interactions among individual agents can produce dynamics and patterns at a global level.

Such models of cellular automata have been used to simulate social processes in the real world. Schelling (1978: Ch. 4) demonstrates how they can be used to illuminate the dynamics of racial zoning in cities. His cellular automata live at different addresses on a grid or lattice. Schelling then posits a 'tolerance schedule', a preference not to have within one's immediately adjacent neighbours more than a certain threshold proportion of another race; the general racial composition of the larger neighbourhood is however of no concern. Starting with an initial random distribution of households across the city, Schelling conducts repeated simulations, as households walk step-wise to an adjacent address, whenever their immediate neighbours exceed this racial threshold. He shows that even a rather mild level of racial antipathy – and concerned only with immediate neighbours – will quickly generate zones of racial segregation across the city.

In terms of the policy implications that one might draw, one seems clear: to rely on encouraging general multiracial tolerance may not be enough to secure racial mixing. This immediately, however, draws our attention to the institutional and policy context in which Schelling's racial segregation develops: the housing market in particular but also the labour market and city policies on zoning and development. These are left largely outside Schelling's discussion, as the taken for granted backcloth. What matters for Schelling is the critical value of the racial antipathy threshold: that is, the value which triggers or switches the city from one which is racially mixed to one where there is general racial segregation. 'Macro-behaviour' is the emergent result of 'micro-motives': how far both are susceptible to modification by policy interventions is, however, left unexamined. This is, however, of obvious and central concern and it will occupy much of our attention in ensuing chapters.

Models using cellular automata have appealed to economists in particular, who have seen them as approximating their own ontology of market interactions, while freeing them from the equilibrium assumptions of the neoclassical mainstream. Thus, for example, Scheinkman (2004) models volatile behaviour in financial markets. In conditions of heterogeneous beliefs as to future stock market behaviour, herding develops, as traders are attracted by particular opinion leaders: this produces growing agglomerations or 'bubbles' of trading activity, which are, however, highly unstable. As seen in the previous section, this behaviour exhibits the 'fat tails' of a non-Gaussian distribution: extreme events are far from unlikely. Soros (2008b) offers a similar account of the recent financial crisis.

Cassidy (2009) provides an elegant analogy of this financial instability. In June 2000 the Queen opened the Millennium Bridge, a narrow footbridge over the Thames. As pedestrians started walking across, the bridge began swaying and tilting alarmingly and it had to be closed. Why was this? Even though the pedestrians were not walking in step, their movements produced a slight sway in the bridge. Each of them now adjusted their gait to the sway; however, their now concerted strides served only to reinforce the sway. As in Schelling's example, local interactions produced global patterns: in this case, patterns which displayed increasing volatility. This was a positive feedback loop. Random local actions (the initial steps of the individual pedestrians) turned a stable environment (the footbridge) into one which moved globally, orchestrating their subsequent steps. This was a dynamic system moving away from equilibrium, volatile but with a trajectory which is hardly surprising or mysterious.

So far we have been concerned with agents that interact myopically with their immediate neighbours, according to simple rules, and the conditions under which this produces global patterns. This is, however, by no means the end of the matter. Holland (1975, 1995) has been one of the principal architects of agent-based modelling. He is concerned with the rules or algorithms which cellular automata follow. These typically take the form of simple 'if/then' statements: if the local situation is of type A, the cellular automaton responds with action x; if type B, then action y and so on (Waldrop, 1992: 181–3). Such algorithms can be varied, for purposes of computer simulation, so as to explore what – if any – patterns emerge.

Holland offers four further developments of central importance for our own discussion in subsequent chapters. First, he allows for chains or structures of such rules to develop, with the 'then' of one if/then rule triggering the 'if' of another. This means that complex systems and flows of information can be constructed out of simple if/then elements. Notwithstanding, therefore, the simplicity of these algorithms and the myopia of the agents, the system as a whole can embody rather a lot of organised and meaningful information. This is 'distributed intelligence'. Holland does not, of course, regard this as being of interest only to software engineers: he reckons it also characterises many phenomena of the real world, including the colony of ants and the complex multi-cellular organisms to which we have already referred.

Second, Holland allows the cellular automata to change the rules or algorithms, searching for and choosing those which work best. The simple agents we have discussed up to this point use if/then rules in their confrontations with each other: Holland's agents go one step further, confronting and assessing the rules to which they are subject and modifying them if this is beneficial. This search and assessment process involves them using rules or 'schematic preferences' that are initially broad brush but can then be progressively refined. In not dissimilar fashion, Arthur develops models in which heterogeneous agents continuously revise their market strategies, retaining those that are successful and discarding the rest (Arthur et al., 1997). This is a so-called 'adaptive walk'. The upshot is that the rules of agent interaction themselves evolve: the cellular automata progressively adapt to their environment and to the other agents with which that environment is populated. These are complex adaptive systems, which we consider at greater length in the next section.

Third, Holland endows agents with 'internal models' or representations of the world in which they move, allowing them in some degree to anticipate the consequences of their actions. This is a process of 'lookahead' (Holland, 1995: 31–4). How real world agents – human and non-human – develop these models, using them to navigate, will be central to much of our later discussion.

Finally, Holland sets about looking for 'lever points' where interventions, although local, can produce changes in global patterns and trajectories. This, he fully recognises, is no easy matter (Holland, 1995: 5, 40, 93–4). It is unlikely that the results of computational modelling will 'speak for themselves' in this regard: such modelling will need to be combined with improved theoretical understanding of non-linear dynamics and complex adaptive systems. Such lever points are of course of central interest to the present study, notably in the form of policy interventions. Consistent with Holland, however, we doubt that such points will simply emerge from the data; we first need to elaborate a conceptual understanding of social dynamics. Only then will we be in a position to bring theory and methodology together and, in some degree at least, to identify the lever points within particular policy areas.

2.5 COMPLEX ADAPTIVE SYSTEMS AND THEIR EVOLUTION

As we have seen, the behaviour of 'far from equilibrium' systems depends on exogenous control parameters. In physical and chemical systems, these may, for example, refer to the ambient temperature, acidity, atmospheric pressure and so on. In contrast, there is a strand of complexity science which treats the control parameters as themselves varying, as an endogenous element of the system. This might, for example, involve coupled sub-systems, with each re-shaping the control parameters of the other in a dynamic and evolving 'dance'. Such processes may never produce a stable equilibrium, since each reconfiguration of one sub-system only sets further processes of dynamic change in train (Waldrop, 1992: 146–7).

Similarly, as we saw in the previous section, concerned with agent-based modelling, Holland allows the algorithms that agents follow themselves to evolve, rather than being fixed. This enables cellular automata to investigate and adopt modifications to the algorithms which drive their behaviour. This sort of evolution allows us to speak of complex *adaptive* systems, which will be of central importance throughout this study.

Darwinian evolution provides the paradigm case. Genetic variation within a species produces organisms with novel characteristics, some of which may enjoy superior chances of surviving and reproducing; in the next generation these variants will be more numerous and after a number of generations may, indeed, constitute distinct sub-species.[5] This is not all. Genetic shifts in one species re-shape the biotic environment within which others struggle to survive: the 'control parameters' of their respective self-organisation. In some cases a mutually supportive process of 'co-evolution' may be set in train; in others the result may be a mutually antagonistic 'arms race'. Not that this process is ever complete or in equilibrium; the very process of adaptation creates new niches in which new waves of co-evolution can develop.

Modelling of these evolutionary processes and the dynamic couplings they involve has provided a powerful impetus to complexity science much more generally (see, for example, Maynard Smith, 2000). They are of central importance for our own analytical framework, as we shall demonstrate in the next two chapters. Further elaboration will accordingly be postponed to there. Nevertheless, we briefly re-visit the earlier discussion of thermodynamic systems.

Living organisms can of course be thought of as thermodynamic engines that extract nutrients and physical-chemical energy from their environment, so as to be able to engage in the 'struggle for existence' (O'Neill et al., 1986: Chs 2, 3, 6; Turner, 2000: Ch. 3; Odling-Smee et al.,

2003: paras 4.2, 4.5, 5.4.1). However, it is the selective effect of the natural environment and processes of co-evolution that determine which variants thrive and reproduce and the adaptations to which genotypes are therefore subject over successive generations. It is this process of selection and adaptation that takes species into particular evolutionary niches and shapes the terms on which the organisms of the next generation will extract resources and energy from their environment. When, therefore, we turn in the next chapter to this evolutionary process, the thermodynamics of the living organism are not forgotten, but it is the population dynamics of selection and adaptation that move centre-stage.

2.6   CONCLUSION

At the start of this chapter, we spoke of the new complexity paradigm that has developed in recent decades across diverse fields of scientific enquiry. We have traced several of its principal elements; we now underline some of their commonalities.

It will, first, be evident that complexity science takes us far from the classical focus on equilibrium and stability. It presents us instead with a 'far from equilibrium' world, where dynamic systems abrade against their environment, re-shape it and tilt its subsequent development. This is no longer the fixed *ceteris paribus* of a closed and reversible system, where external constraints ensure stability over time. Here are path dependent trajectories, with feedback, lock-in and ratchet effects.

Such trajectories need not, however, be disorderly; on the contrary, we have seen how order and global patterns – what are commonly referred to as the 'attractors' of the system – can emerge from simple local interactions. Thus, for example, each of Schelling's cellular automata is concerned only with its immediate neighbours; nevertheless, if it moves, because its tolerance threshold has been exceeded, this is liable to trigger a succession of more distant movements. These are then liable to re-shape the racial composition of the original neighbourhood, so that even those with more generous tolerance thresholds now find that these also are breached. Again, Bak's sand pile sees each individual grain of sand resting only against its immediate neighbours, but indirectly therefore lodged in a larger array of energy, mass and friction. It is this larger array – and not just the individual local neighbourhood – that is put in jeopardy, as further grains of sand descend onto the pile from above. Sooner or later this array must collapse, with the most fragile line of resistance bringing down an unpredictable number of others. Or, to take a further example, we have seen that individual affiliation to a network reinforces the attraction it exerts and the benefits that membership confers globally: thus does 'network power' emerge. In all these cases, local interactions tend to change the terms on which subsequent interactions will unfold globally. These are non-linear processes of emergence.

Depending on the algorithms and control parameters that regulate them, these dynamic systems commonly exhibit three zones of behaviour: order, chaos or an intermediate zone sometimes described as being 'on the edge of chaos'. It is this latter zone that attracts the attention of complexity scientists, offering as it does a combination of self-organisation and dynamic adaptability. As the system parameters are adjusted, we commonly find 'phase transitions' and 'tipping points', at which the behaviour of the system changes dramatically (Gladwell, 2001; Ball, 2004: Ch. 4; Scheffer et al., 2009). This is of interest to engineers and systems analysts; it is also of potential interest to policy-makers, seeking points of leverage that they may use for complex terrains.

Complex systems commonly display discontinuous or 'sticky' behaviour. In Schelling's model it is only when the proportion of another race among one's immediately adjacent neighbours reaches the critical threshold that the person in question moves. Bak's model of self-organised criticality is similarly sticky due to frictional resistance. In Gould and Eldridge's model of punctuated equilibria, established niches are sticky in face of selection pressures. The if/then algorithms of agent-based modelling also lend themselves to threshold-based interactions.

We have referred to power laws as the statistical 'signature' of self-organising systems. The size of the power gives an indication of the strength of the interactive effects that self-organisation involves. As we have also seen, a power law distribution is sometimes referred to as a scale-free distribution, because the extent to which it departs from a Gaussian distribution does not diminish as the scale of the system increases. Power laws are not a recent discovery in social science: in the late nineteenth century Pareto found that such a law applied to the national distribution of income and wealth within advanced countries; and in the late 1940s Zipf found such laws to apply to a variety of social regularities, including, for example, city size (Krugman, 1996: Ch. 3). To discover the generative mechanisms underlying such regularities is, however, quite another matter.

Such are some of the commonalities of complexity science. They reveal its potential relevance to the puzzles with which Chapter 1 wrestled: the non-linearities and path dependencies of the policy world, with its feedback loops and 'tipping points'. Indeed, already in the literature we have reviewed there are attempts to apply such complexity perspectives to the socio-economic realm. Nevertheless, some key limitations have also been evident. Most obviously, complexity science struggles to handle institutional contexts and structures.

Institutions matter because they articulate and enforce the rules of interaction among social agents. Indeed, we may take this as a generic definition of institutions. Of course, slime mould and ant colonies are also governed by rules of interaction, grounded in their DNA, while the rules for cellular automata are written into the computer software of their virtual world. However, for human interaction – even acknowledging some genetic component of behaviour – the situation is quite different, because social institutions – and the rules they articulate – are socially and politically constructed.

For many economists this does not appear as a particular problem. The methodological individualism they embrace is readily identified with that of cellular automata: individuals interact with their neighbours, according to whatever they offer in the competitive market place, seen as an open, level and unstructured playing field. Economists who recognise the institutional context and historical specificity of markets are very much a minority: see, for example, Polanyi (1944), Hodgson (2004), Loasby (1999), Nelson and Winter (1982) and North (1990). Thus, for example, in Section 2.2 we were concerned with increasing returns and the Marshallian benefits of co-location. However, as North (1990) notes, such benefits are available only to the extent that local agreements and standards are also developed, by means of which those local patterns of cooperation can operate. North here stands on the shoulders of writers such as Coase and Oliver Williamson, pointing to the crucial significance of shared institutions for reducing transaction costs among those involved.

If institutions matter in the economics of agglomeration, they also matter in the economics of racial segregation and polarisation. Nevertheless, as we saw, Schelling is content with 'micro-motives' and 'macro-behaviour', paying little attention to institutions or policy. He allows us to consider how different levels of racial antipathy may drive processes of polarisation; beyond this, however, he gives us little or no analytical leverage for exploring the consequences of alternative policies. Agent-based modelling of this sort may therefore be seriously incomplete as a tool for policy analysis on complex terrains.

Recall also our discussion of the complex forms of hierarchical organisation that are to be found among ants. Here, as we saw, chemical signals provided by the immediate neighbours of a particular ant serve to activate particular behaviours from among the wide range encoded within the DNA of the species as a whole. This has some at least superficial parallels with the bureaucracies of human societies, as captured most obviously by Weber. Order and predictability result from hierarchical coordination, the application of impersonal rules to sort and classify individuals, assigning them to one trajectory rather than another (Bowker and Star, 2002).

Such formal-rational procedures are applied on the basis of a common rulebook, just as the insect colony deploys genetically encoded information to maintain its own division of labour. Nevertheless, this is at best a useful parallel. Biological adaptation of this sort can hardly account for the variety of forms taken by human institutional hierarchies. Nor can it provide insights into the malleability and subversion of such organisational forms (see, for example, Lipsky, 1980). Here again we must recognise the overly limited treatment of institutions that complexity analysis has so far offered, given its roots in the physical and biological sciences.

Institutions are not entirely ignored. Agent-based modelling, while it involves a particular version of methodological individualism, need not preclude forms of action that are oriented to shared norms and understandings (see, for example, Cliffe et al., 2007). Nevertheless, even here the focus is on how norms may develop endogenously, as the emergent product of micro-interaction. There is little acknowledgement of the pre-existing normative and institutional structures that confront and indeed dominate our lives, lending or denying authority to the choices we make.

Institutions constrain and channel agent interactions; they can also, however, be subverted from below or reformed from above, as actors lift their gaze, reflect upon the overall socio-economic system in which they live and reinforce or re-shape the rules and architectures of those systems. In this, of course, they distinguish themselves from physical atoms, plants and animals. This is the stuff of politics and political choice. It suggests an agenda for complexity research in social science which builds upon, but is distinct from, that in the natural sciences. It accepts the potential value of modelling social dynamics as a self-organising system, analogous to those in the natural sciences. On the other hand, it insists that social science must also be centrally interested in the institutional 'control variables' and the socio-political processes by which these are re-shaped. This is the institutionally grounded complexity perspective that we seek to develop here.

3 Complex adaptive systems

3.1 INTRODUCTION

The previous chapter introduced complex adaptive systems. As we saw, Darwinian evolution provides the paradigm case. Each fresh generation of organisms throws up a stream of genetic novelty, driving the biological system away from equilibrium. Nevertheless, natural selection extinguishes the least fit; and from within these 'far from equilibrium' systems, order emerges.

This chapter explores these various forms of self-organisation, by reference to modern understanding of evolutionary mechanisms. As we shall see, depending on the values of their parameters, the behaviour of such systems can be seen as falling into the three zones – the orderly, the complex and the chaotic – that we have already encountered. In subsequent chapters we examine how far this provides us with a model of potentially wider applicability, including to human societies.

3.2 ADAPTIVE WALKS ON FITNESS LANDSCAPES

3.2.1 Genetic Novelties and Adaptive Walks

The genetic make-up of an organism (its 'genotype') consists of ordered strings of genes which carry information in the form of DNA. These strings can mutate or recombine to produce genetic novelties in the offspring.

Each gene can be represented as a dimension of genotypic space. The gene in question can then take a variety of values or 'alleles'. We can then model the genotype as searching for novelty by varying one gene at a time ('point mutation'), switching it to one of the other permitted values (for purposes of modelling, it is often assumed that there are just two possible values). This search process thus involves movement to an immediately adjacent point in genotypic space. More ambitious searches involve sexual recombination ('cross-over'), with whole strips of genes being swapped and recombined in the offspring.[1]

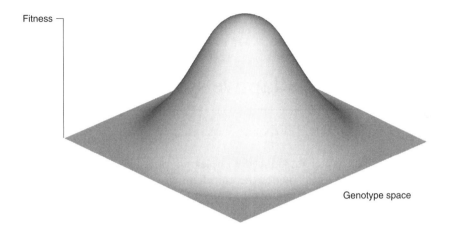

Fitness

Genotype space

Figure 3.1   Single peak fitness landscape

Thus, for example, a string of four genes might take the form <0011>. Depending on which of the four genes is varied (switched to the other permitted value), four novel strings could be produced by point mutation, each a single 'step' from the original. Alternatively, sexual recombination with <1100> could produce a variety of offspring, such as <1111> and <0000> that span the parents' genetic space but could not be produced from either of them alone by variation of a single gene.

Genetic novelty may produce offspring whose fitness as 'phenotypes' exceeds that of the species more generally and which thus enjoys greater reproductive success. Equivalently, we might say that the population of which they are for the moment outliers will over a number of generations 'migrate' towards the genotype they have pioneered. But how shall we model this migration?

One of the iconic metaphors is of an 'adaptive walk' across a 'fitness landscape' (Figures 3.1 and 3.2).[2] This is a landscape whose 'footprint' or horizontal coordinates span genotypic space (visually represented perforce as two dimensions, but in principle referring to as many dimensions as there are genes). Meanwhile the vertical coordinate – the height of the landscape – captures the level of 'fitness' that the corresponding phenotype will enjoy, deriving from the contributions of the various genes.

The landscape provides a visual representation of fitness. But what is the topography of this landscape; what scope does it provide for a species to explore beyond its own evolutionary 'pocket'; and how does this affect

Fitness

Genotype space

Figure 3.2   Rugged fitness landscape

shifts in the genotype? How, moreover, are the landscapes of different species interlinked in processes of co-evolution? It is these questions that go to the heart of contemporary studies in complex adaptive systems and that will be of particular interest for the present work. We explore them by reference to Kauffman's work (1993, 1995a); his account of fitness landscapes will then serve as one of the central expository devices of this book.[3]

3.2.2   Kauffman's NK Model

Kauffman first investigates the topography of fitness landscapes and the scope they offer for adaptive walks and shifts in the genotype of a given species. At this stage he ignores the interactions between the fitness landscapes of different species. Much of his analysis involves theoretically informed conjecture coupled with computer-based simulation, using alternative values of the key parameters.

Kauffman is particularly interested in the contrast between landscapes which are smooth – like Mount Fuji – and those that are 'rugged'. The scope for adaptive walks is very different on these two landscapes. On very smooth terrains, if an adaptive walk in a given direction produces enhanced fitness, further moves in the same direction are likely to do the same and will allow a continuing ascent. On rugged landscapes, in contrast, walks that permit continuous ascent are unlikely. The genetic population has, so to speak, wagered its chances on a particular set of phenotypic characteristics and there are limitations in the extent to which these can be modified on a step-wise basis, without prejudice to overall fitness.[4] Here, therefore, the genetic population may find itself locked into immobility on its local peak (Kauffman, 1993: 39–40).

The ruggedness of the landscape depends on the degree to which different genes interact in determining the fitness of the phenotype, rather than contributing independently of one another: the extent, that is, to which they are 'epistatically' connected. Where these interactions are minimal, the fitness landscape is smooth or 'correlated'; where they are stronger, the landscape is rugged or uncorrelated. This is Kauffman's so-called NK model: N is the number of genes on the string, K is the average number of epistatic interactions between them. Kauffman shows that $K = 0$ yields a Mount Fuji, with a steady monotonic rise from any point towards a central fitness peak. With $K = 2$ or 3, local peaks develop. As K increases further, towards a maximum value of $N - 1$, these peaks multiply and the landscape becomes much more rugged. This is of course reminiscent of our discussion in Chapter 2 of the three zones in which dynamic systems may typically find themselves, depending on the values taken by the system parameters.

Up to this point, Kauffman has concentrated on random mutation of individual genes ('point mutation'), producing movement to immediately adjacent positions in genotypic space. He also, however, examines the scope for 'long jumps', by means of which more distant positions can be evaluated, in terms of the level of enhanced fitness that they offer. In general, the costs of such searches do not justify the likely benefits; they may enable escape to a more distant and higher peak, but they are also costly, in terms of the descents into low fitness valleys that they risk.[5] This conclusion does, however, depend critically upon the assumption that such long jumps are performed 'blind' (Kauffman, 1993: Ch. 3); in human societies things may be different.

Sexual reproduction is a form of 'middle range' jump, where genetic material is combined between two organisms of a given species. This is no 'long jump' to a distant part of the fitness landscape; it does, however, involve more than a purely local or myopic search. Kauffman sees it as a means of spanning or surveying a whole region (Kauffman, 1993: 112–120). It is particularly apposite when the fitness landscape resembles a *Massif Central*: a cluster of peaks within a larger plain. If a species inhabits such a landscape, its offspring – sexual recombinations of the parents' genetic material – are well placed to explore other positions within the same hilly region and to discover peaks that may be superior to those of the parents.[6]

Kauffman draws two further inferences, based upon his simulations. First, a Mount Fuji landscape, with its gentle slopes, imposes only a mild selective discipline on phenotypes; there is plenty of scope for new genetic variants to appear and to survive, even those with somewhat inferior levels of fitness. More rugged terrains, being steeper, impose a stronger discipline and ensure that less fit variants quickly become extinct. On the other hand, Kauffman demonstrates that very rugged terrains see the average level of fitness offered by their local peaks substantially reduced. As a result, while the less fit variants are quickly eliminated, those that survive – even the best – have only mediocre levels of fitness. Here are what Kauffman describes as two 'evolutionary catastrophes'. On the gentle slopes of low interaction landscapes ($K = 0$), selective pressures to eliminate the least fit operate only feebly; on their high interaction counterparts, in contrast, variants become entrapped on local peaks with a generally low level of fitness. In both cases processes of natural selection fail to drive the species towards greater fitness: complexity overwhelms selection. Kauffman argues that intermediate landscapes ($K = 2, 3$) offer some of the selective disciplines of ruggedness, but without suffering the loss of fitness that higher values of K typically entail. It is they, therefore, that have the highest evolutionary value.

3.2.3 Co-evolution: Kauffman's NK(C) Model

Kauffman now develops the second stage to his argument (Kauffman, 1993: Ch. 6, 1995a: Ch. 10). Consider two distinct species, co-existing within the same eco-system. The phenotypes may be living side by side – the bird and the berries, the bee and the flowers – but in genetic terms they are of course at vast distances from each other. Nevertheless, the interactions between the phenotypes create mutually favourable environments; these enhance the fitness of the phenotypes in question and their dominance within the ecological niche they inhabit, as well as the replication of their respective genotypes.

This is co-evolution. It helps to explain the remarkable patterns of mutual adjustment among different species that are so prominent in the living world (Darwin, 1859: Chs 3–4). Such processes can arise not only among different species of organism but also among simpler entities such as proteins and amino acids, reacting with each other in processes of collective auto-catalysis. This seems, indeed, to have been key to the development of early life forms (Waldrop, 1992: Ch. 3; Kauffman, 1993: Ch. 7). It can also involve a species in 'borrowing' genetic material from some quite unrelated species and re-deploying this for its own purposes, in a process of lateral gene transfer.[7] Co-evolution can also, however, take antagonistic forms, where predators and prey are locked in an 'arms race' of capacities for pursuit and defence, albeit total victory for the predators may well prove pyrrhic.

Co-evolution is unlikely to be even-handed in its benefits. Some genetic variations in the species concerned will be favoured more than others; others may be adversely affected, with their replication discouraged and their numbers progressively depleted, to the point of extinction. In short, although fitness landscapes are raised in some places, in others they may be lowered. Phenotypic interactions couple these genetically far separated landscapes. Through co-evolution, each warps and deforms the other, encouraging new patterns of genetic adaptation.

Such dynamic linkages are more difficult to represent pictorially than the fitness landscapes presented earlier: their formal tractability is also problematic. One possibility, following Pimm, is to construct a 'community landscape' for the shared eco-system (by analogy with fitness landscapes for individual species) and examine how different combinations of species lead the community to climb different 'local peaks' (Kauffman, 1995a: Ch. 10). Nevertheless, as Kauffman argues, this use of the landscape metaphor in relation to an ecological community is 'worrisome', because it assumes that it is meaningful to speak of the fitness of the community as a whole. It may be less of a problem when, in later chapters, we turn to human societies, where the notion of a shared welfare – or fitness – landscape may be more appropriate.

Co-evolution involves dynamic linkages between phenotypes (for simplicity we assume just two). Nevertheless Kauffman models them as interactions between their genotypes.[8] This is his NK(C) model, with C denoting the number of interactions between the genes of the co-evolving species. Each species is assumed to take turns in exploring new points on its own landscape for their fitness, just as happened in the NK model. In this case, however, this adaptive walk warps the fitness landscape of the other species, and it is on this reconfigured landscape that the other species must now take its turn.

We again summarise Kauffman's results in broad terms. In his NK model we saw that fitness landscapes vary between two extremes: Mount Fuji, with a single global peak ($K = 0$), and highly rugged landscapes, with lots of local peaks (K large). Each, as we saw, was confronted with a particular evolutionary catastrophe, in terms of the rigour of fitness selection or the general level of fitness across the various peaks. An intermediate landscape ($K = 2, 3$) avoided both dangers.

In the NK(C) model there are likewise two polar cases: referring now, however, not to the fitness terrain of each individual species, but rather to the dynamics of their interactions. On the one hand, each species may find that successive moves made by its counterpart transform its own fitness landscape to such an extent that the fitness peaks it seeks to ascend forever recede. This is a chaotic 'Red Queen' dynamic, an unceasing arms race which re-shapes the very landscape on which the race is pursued, and obliges each species to run in order to stay in the same place, so to speak.[9] At the opposite pole is an 'evolutionarily stable state' (ESS).[10] Here each species is already at a fitness peak and therefore has no incentive to move; each therefore leaves its eco-system neighbours with their fitness landscapes undisturbed and co-evolution ceases.

These two polar cases derive from particular values of the K and C variables. When K is high, the fitness landscapes of the species concerned are rugged; if in addition C is low, the disturbance arising from movements made by other species across their own landscapes will be only limited. The net result is the stability of the ESS, where even the modest disturbances that are generated are insufficient to move the species affected from their imprisonment on specific and steep-sided local peaks. In contrast, when K is low, there are few peaks on the fitness landscapes of the species concerned. If in addition C is high, the disturbances arising from adaptive walks on other landscapes are great. The net result is the 'Red Queen' regime; disturbances arising from movements on co-evolving landscapes are considerable, and the gentle slopes of Mount Fuji are insufficient to confine the species thus affected to its present location.

Kauffman argues – in a manner analogous to the NK model – that an intermediate dynamic, between these two polar cases, delivers an optimum mix of adaptability and fitness, as far as the speed of likely evolutionary development is concerned.

3.2.4   Tuning the System Parameters

Having analysed the polar cases between which NK and NK(C) landscapes are arrayed, and the 'evolutionary catastrophes' that they tend to produce, Kauffman argues finally that evolutionary pressures of selection and self-organisation tend to 'tune' the landscape parameters, moving biological systems towards intermediate landscapes. Kauffman refers to this as 'the edge of chaos'.[11] He seeks, for example, to demonstrate that through the normal dynamics of genotype variation and adaptive walks, a species can adjust the values of K and C, so as to maximise the benefits it takes from co-evolutionary dynamics (Kauffman, 1993: Chs 5–6; Kauffman, 1995a: 187–9). Be that as it may, such tuning of system parameters will certainly be of significance when, in subsequent chapters, we apply these perspectives to human societies.

3.3   EXTENSIONS TO KAUFFMAN

We have seen how Kauffman handles genotypic variation and population migration across fitness landscapes (the NK model) and the co-evolution of species with dynamically coupled fitness landscapes in a shared eco-system (the NK(C) model). Nevertheless, his models entail certain stylised or simplifying assumptions, appropriate to his own purposes but not nec-essarily to our own. We now make some of these simplifications explicit: in particular, those that are significant for our efforts in subsequent chapters to move from the biological to the social. It is, however, important to note that these simplifications are evident just in the NK and NK(C) models, not in Kauffman's larger treatment of evolutionary processes.

3.3.1   Variation and Deepening

In his NK model, Kauffman posits a genotypic space of N dimensions and a corresponding fitness landscape. It allows us, so to speak, to see a human and a chimp and a gorilla on peaks close to each other and, more distant, a pig and a horse. It also allows us to see their common ancestors, and thus to look back in time. It can, indeed, be thought of as extending to include all species that have ever lived.

   The model allows step-wise mutations from today's genotype, with the new phenotype then enjoying a level of fitness assigned by its new position on the fitness landscape. It appears to allow the chimp to undertake an adaptive walk by which its genotype and phenotype would become that of a gorilla or even, after more of a journey, that of the pig or even that of a common ancestor now extinct. (After all, the extent to which organisms share a common genetic inheritance – and thus a shared landscape – must not be under-estimated; even if step-wise searches are only short-range, they may over the course of millennia enable substantial journeys across the fitness landscape.) Such a journey would of course require a sufficient number of mutations, and the chimp would continue the journey only if at each stage this did not require any major and costly descent into low fitness valleys.

   This implication of the simple NK model is, however, unhelpful. Evolution is no simple Markov process, with history merely setting the point of immediate departure for each step-wise modification; instead there is strong path dependency. The chimp's evolutionary journey pro-gressively registers itself in the chimp's genetic structure; the very process of moving from the chimp's current peak involves a journey – and thus further genetic changes – that no other species has ever made (see similarly Darwin, 1859: 238–9).

Different species make their own evolutionary journeys, even though these are all offshoots of the journey begun by common ancestors. Each species differentiates itself by constructing – not just occupying – a region of genotypic space distinct and as yet unexplored: an M-dimensional niche or add-on to the N-dimensional space which it has hitherto shared with other closely related species. Genotypic space is thus relativistic: it is constructed by reference to each individual species. Kauffman works with a fixed number of dimensions, where adaptive walks and genetic novelty consist in switching the allele values of individual genes; we, however, will construe such novelty as the progressive 'deepening' of the fitness landscape, as the species builds successive dimensions of its distinctive genotypic space.[12] To see agents as constructing the space that they occupy will also be appropriate when we turn from the biological to the social realm.

Every time a new dimension is added in the search for fitness, there is an orthogonal move from $N + i$ dimensional space into $N + i + 1$ dimensional space (where i is part of the M-dimensional add-on). The $N + i$ dimensional peak may now turn into a saddle point. This is the starting point for further ascent, a new front in the adaptive struggle, conducted within the higher-dimension genotypic space that has now opened up. The extent to which the array of peaks and valleys in this new space is correlated with the array in i-dimensional space depends, of course, on the system parameters and the consequent ruggedness of the landscape. This will constrain the scope for walking from peaks in $N + i$ dimensional space through saddles in $N + i + 1$ dimensional space to higher peaks and, beyond that, to yet further saddles and peaks in $N + i + 2$ dimensional space.[13]

Such a walk through a rugged landscape, involving a sequence of orthogonal turns into new dimensions of genotypic space, in search of monotonic ascent, I henceforth describe as a 'perilous path'. This is a sequence-dependent succession, a string or necklace of linked saddle points. In many cases, of course, instead of leading to some new saddle or pass, from which further orthogonal ascents can then be made, the path peters out in some lonely spur.

The perilous path is itself an emergent phenomenon, a search for new ascents but constrained at each orthogonal turn by the need to avoid valleys of reduced fitness. Even if a monotonically ascending route exists, the more rugged the landscape, the more narrowly defined this route may be, and the less the scope for ascending over a wider swathe of hillside. Only in the case of a Mount Fuji, the antithesis of ruggedness, will this higher vantage point be accessible from any direction and along any path: here the order in which successive dimensions of space are opened up and their terrain ascended is irrelevant. This is, indeed, an alternative way of describing the condition that K should take the value of zero: in rugged spaces, sequence matters.

There is one further simplification that limits Kauffman's treatment of variation and novelty. As we have seen, his models allow the allele values of the genes to change, at each step in the adaptive walk, and produce novel phenotypic characteristics. However, what also matters is how the genes are connected to each other. Phenotypic novelty can result from changes in these connections and the re-deployment of genetic endowments. This may indeed include the wholesale duplication of sub-systems of the genotype, applying their proven capacities to new tasks. Kauffman's models, however, limit themselves to the K parameter, a simple measure of the average connectivity among genes. This is much too crude.

Here again, in such re-deployment there is strong path dependency. The aforementioned chimp cannot but drag with it, so to speak, its whole genetic endowment, re-deploying this as best it can to produce its new phenotypic characteristics. Mutation of ancient and deep-seated genetic structures is rare; it is by re-deployment and reconnection that their contribution to phenotypic fitness is optimised. Shubin (2008: 201) expresses this with particular elegance: 'Looking back through billions of years of change, everything innovative or apparently unique in the history of life is really just old stuff that has been recycled, recombined, repurposed or otherwise modified for new uses . . . . [Our body is] 'a time capsule that . . . tells of critical moments in the history of our planet and of a distant past in ancient oceans, streams and forests' (see likewise Darwin, 1859: Ch. 6 and Ch. 13 ('morphology')).[14]

3.3.2   Selection and Widening

The walk across a fitness landscape starts with a mutation in a particular organism, but progressively 'widens' to the larger population, if that mutation proves itself by superior fitness and reproductive success. Nevertheless, with multiple genetic mutations taking place, any population is always somewhat heterogeneous, a smear rather than a single point in genotypic space, even though it is a single reproductive community or species (Kauffman, 1993: 34, 95ff.). This heterogeneity means that some elements of the population are more able than others to migrate across the fitness landscape: those others – that we may refer to as 'second movers' – may be more suited to following some rival genetic mutation that has also met with success. Or, alternatively, they may, having begun the journey, discover some secondary route of fitness ascent that for them at least is more easily travelled.[15] From a single population or species there may therefore emerge several sub-species, each constructing its own adaptive niche, its own distinctive region of genotypic space.

As already noted, the narrower the 'perilous path', the more precisely the 'well-trodden path' that the larger population must beat, in the wake of the first mover. This depends on the ruggedness of the landscape. Where it is smooth, any route will do and there are no valleys that would require a costly descent; the perilous path can be 'widened' across a broad swathe of the hillside and migration is unconstrained. However, such landscapes fail to hone the genotype. Of greater evolutionary value, therefore, are landscapes of intermediate ruggedness, where there are valleys to deter some from following, but where those who do move can capture a novel niche and may indeed differentiate themselves as a new sub-species. On the other hand, if the landscape is too rugged, it may prove difficult to find any monotonically ascending path. Thus evolution 'towards the edge of chaos' here reappears in the following form: there are evolutionary benefits if the fitness landscape is of intermediate ruggedness, because this makes it more probable that there exist monotonically ascending perilous paths through successive dimensions of genotypic space, while also imposing costs to movement and thus privileging those within the larger population best adapted to such a move.[16]

Any population subject to the pressures of natural selection will benefit in evolutionary terms if it can survey the broader swathes of hillside that each of its higher fitness mutations reveals. Kauffman, we recall, offered some discussion of sexual reproduction as a means of surveying larger expanses of the fitness landscape. Terrains involving a *Massif Central* were particularly suitable. Gavrilets (2004) provides an account of the population dynamics involved in speciation which likewise makes reference to sexual selection and reproduction (see especially Ch. 1 and Part III). On the one hand, he is interested in the consequences of 'disruptive natural selection': a sudden change in the biotic environment (for example, the intrusion of a new predator) or the abiotic (for example, the disappearance of some land bridge and the consequent separation of two communities), which will have a differential impact on the various elements of the population concerned. On the other hand, he explores the role of sexual selection and reproduction in accelerating speciation in face of the aforementioned disruptions. Thus for both Kauffman and Gavrilets, sexual selection is a device for rapidly surveying fitness landscapes where some advantaged points (the genotypes of the parents) have already been identified. Later chapters will consider the social analogues of these surveying methods.

We may note one final corollary. The fitness landscape is the terrain across which species move, in their search for higher peaks. However, it is also a record of their various and respective genetic endowments; of the genotypic mutations by which their landscape journeys have been made; and of the phenotypic fitness improvements that these journeys have achieved. Thus, while the fitness landscape displays the new and future journeys that are available, it is also the product and record of past evolutionary journeys, driven at each stage by mutation, selection and self-organisation.

3.3.3   Co-evolution and Warping

Kauffman's NK(C) model deals with co-evolutionary dynamics among species in shared eco-systems, driven by relations of competition, symbiosis, parasitism and predator-prey. In the real world, of course, such dynamics are never absent. Nevertheless, in abstracting from such dynamics the NK model serves Kauffman as a useful expository device, allowing him to examine fitness search in abstraction from co-evolution, before making this the centre of attention in the NK(C) model.

Kauffman's NK(C) model explores co-evolution between populations – at the macro-level, so to speak. Nevertheless, when a genetic mutation explores the fitness landscape for hitherto unsuspected possibilities of further ascent – a 'perilous path' – it does so in part by testing what novel co-evolutionary dynamics can thereby be set in train. It is after all misleading ever to speak of fitness per se: fitness is always by reference to a particular ecological niche, and the relationships this involves with other species. The contours of the perilous path are contingent upon the co-evolutionary dynamics that emerge: continuing the geographical analogies, we might refer to it as a 'Surtsey'.[17] Only where co-evolutionary dynamics twist or warp the fitness landscape so that the perilous path leads upwards, will the larger population ascend in the wake of their mutant pathfinder.

Eco-systems can be very complex, as also therefore can their co-evolutionary dynamics. Just as adaptive walks through genotypic space exhibit strong path dependencies, so also the eco-system that emerges depends on the sequence in which species are introduced (Kauffman, 1995a: Ch. 10; Solé and Bascompte, 2006: 183–5). There is a further parallel: just as we saw with genotypes, eco-systems and food webs may contain ancient structures developed early in the evolutionary process. Modification of the connections within an eco-system – for example, the loss of one species from such a food web – can produce dramatic cascades of far-reaching change (Bornholdt and Schuster, 2003: Ch. 10).

The NK(C) model offers, however, only a limited account of these dynamics. As we have seen, Kauffman models the relationship between phenotypes sharing a common eco-system as a set of epistatic connections between their genotypes. This allows him to retain a close resemblance with the NK model; as in that model, he explores the consequences for system dynamics of variations in the relevant (in this case the C and K) parameters. However, what matters in an eco-system are the numbers and the characteristics of the various species involved. These 'characteristics' refer most obviously to fleetness of foot, sharpness of teeth and nutritional content (these characteristics are thus in part in the eye – or the stomach – of the beholder). If one species moves across its NK landscape to a higher fitness peak, its numbers will increase and its characteristics will change: as predator or prey it can now move quicker or see better; as prey it tastes better or worse; as partner in symbiosis it becomes more congenial to some neighbours, less to others. It is to these changes that the co-habiting species will now respond, producing a reciprocal impact on the fitness landscape of the first species.

This is the co-evolutionary 'arms race', with an ever-changing supper menu and guest list. Here each species explores the turbulent world of Surtsey, in a race for monotonic ascent across its own particular fitness landscape.[18] These co-evolutionary dynamics involve linkages that are clearly quite different from the epistatic connections within the genotype with which the NK model was concerned. The fitness of a given phenotype is shaped not by the individual genes of the other, co-evolving species, nor even by the overall fitness of that other phenotype, but by the interaction of the two phenotypes in their shared eco-system. This is missed by Kauffman's model.

Elsewhere in his study Kauffman explores these dynamics by reference to large-scale random Boolean networks, using computer simulation (Kauffman, 1993: 181–209). These are networks of elements which, like the alleles of the NK model, can be switched off or on; but which do so in obedience to simple rules of network interdependence, defined in terms of necessary and sufficient conditions (and/or). Kauffman explores what happens across the network when different elements are switched on/off. He shows first, that when individual connections are switched along the lines indicated, various chain reactions are set in motion, but that typically there are specific domains of the network that remain invariant or 'frozen'. This invariance involves 'forcing structures': strong mechanisms of path dependence which ensure that 'upstream' elements lock others into behaviour which is unaffected by wider turbulence (Kauffman, 1993: 203–4). He further shows that the extent of these frozen sections becomes rather small as K increases, but rather large as it falls towards zero; K set at 2 or 3 generates frozen sections of intermediate extent.

With particular reference to co-evolution on NK(C) landscapes, Kauffman then demonstrates that frozen components can percolate through particular regions of an ecosystem, in the form of the 'evolutionarily stable state' we discussed above, even while other regions continue to evolve, maybe even experiencing Red Queen chaos (Kauffman, 1993: 256ff.). Then, however, as biological evolution 'tunes' the landscape parameters, the 'frozen' components of these co-evolutionary dynamics start to 'melt' and the 'forcing structures' they embody are unlocked. This in turn unleashes new avalanches of change, with high levels of extinction of particular species and sub-species; it also, however, allows new species to emerge and a new array of frozen components eventually to be established (Kauffman, 1993: 259ff., 1995a: 224ff.). This can of course be related to the larger discussion in complexity science, concerned with invariant structures, avalanches and punctuated equilibria, introduced in the previous chapter.

3.4   AGENTS OF CHANGE

The metaphor of the adaptive walk across fitness landscapes risks ascribing agency to the genotype. Genetic variation produces a range of organisms with subtly different characteristics, by reference to which selective pressures will favour one genotype over another and drive the evolutionary journey. It is in the genotype that successive generations of organisms record their heroic struggles for existence; and it is from the encoded information that new variations are then produced. However, genotypes themselves are not active. By the same token, it is unhelpful – except perhaps as metaphor – to describe the gene as 'selfish' or to see such selfishness as the driver of biological and even social change.

As we have seen, the agents in Kauffman's models are rather simple. The characteristics of the phenotype are directly determined by the information encoded in the DNA of the genotype. However, the capacities that these characteristics represent – and which progressively develop as the evolutionary journey proceeds – are left largely unexamined. What Kauffman lacks – although it is arguable that for his purposes this hardly matters – is an adequate account of the living organism. It is after all organisms that are more or less fit and that reproduce the next generation with more or less success. The organism is the living agent which carries genes, feeds, reproduces and dies. It is far more than a mere vehicle for the genotype.

For a moment, therefore, we pause and consider the organism in relation to its genotype and its larger environment. Noble (2006) presents the development and functioning of the organism and the growth of its capacities as complex and multi-level processes that draw on its genetic endowment but also its larger environment. He eschews reductionist accounts that treat genetic endowment as determining these processes; it is, rather, a database on which the organism draws as it develops, with cells and proteins selecting and combining elements from the database for given functions (Ch. 1). How they do this depends not on instructions from the genes, but on the chemistry of the organism as a self-organising complex system and on its larger environment, including, for example, the egg cell inherited from the mother (pp. 35, 41, 48–9). It is these multi-level processes that produce the phenotypic characteristics whose fitness is selectively tested. Nevertheless, the evolutionary outcome of that test is of course the selective modification of the genotype, as Noble fully acknowledges. He likewise echoes Shubin's account, discussed earlier, of how the modular components of the genetic endowment are regularly re-deployed and switched to produce phenotypic characteristics of sufficient fitness; albeit this leaves our bodies as the untidy museum of those shifts, a 'complicated series of bodges' (Noble, 2006: pp. 103–4).

For Odling-Smee also, the organism is much more than a mere ancillary to the genotype (Odling-Smee et al., 2003: 240, 243). It struggles with rivals and predators, its biotic environment; it also actively re-shapes or 'engineers' its abiotic physical environment. As well, therefore, as being subject to the selective pressures of that environment, as a result of which some organisms are able to reproduce with more success than others, the organism also in some degree adapts that environment to itself. It is to this that Odling-Smee refers as 'niche construction' by organisms (Odling-Smee et al., 2003). By adapting the local environment to the organism, this can buffer and moderate the selective pressures of that environment and its evolutionary consequences. It may, indeed, warp the fitness landscape no less effectively than co-evolutionary dynamics and enable populations to ascend the 'perilous path' (Odling-Smee et al., 2003: 302). It follows that, alongside the genetic and ecological legacies with which we have hitherto been concerned, a legacy in terms of the engineered environment is also a significant modifying factor in phenotypic development.[19]

As Noble and Odling-Smee argue, it is important for evolutionary biologists to appreciate the organism as an active agent engaged in the struggle for existence. The adaptive walks with which much of this chapter has been concerned go on behind the backs, so to speak, of these organisms: the process is blind. When, however, we move to the study of human societies we find organisms endowed with the capacity to understand those processes and bring them into the daylight.

3.5 CONCLUSION

This chapter has been concerned with the dynamics of complex adaptive systems. These were introduced in Chapter 2, in our presentation of the complexity paradigm. We have now seen how such systems can self-organise and their dependence on the values taken by the system parameters. We have seen how dynamically coupled sub-systems can shape the parameters to which each of them moves, in an endless evolving 'dance'.

Darwinian evolution has provided, as it did Kauffman, our paradigm case of such complex adaptive systems. Kauffman's account of biological evolution is simplified and stylised but it serves his purposes. If we have modified his account it is because ours are different. In particular, we seek a model of the evolution of complex adaptive systems that can be applied to human societies.

In the chapters that follow, we move therefore from a world of biological evolution to one of human societies. Of course, the development of human societies has a major impact on the habitat of other species and is generating widespread cascades of extinction. Human activity also modifies the selective pressures which impinge upon the human species itself, with potential consequences for our own evolutionary development. When, therefore, we move from biological evolution to human societies, this does not imply that the former is of no relevance to the latter.

We again take inspiration from Odling-Smee et al. (2003) and his account of niche construction. There are two lines of his discussion that are of particular interest. First, Odling-Smee is interested in how organisms adapt their biotic and abiotic habitats to their needs. Population-community ecologists have much to say on the first of these, the biotic, and the ways in which organisms and species develop particular niches in relation to other species. As we have seen, Odling-Smee focuses his attention more particularly on the abiotic: more precisely, he seeks a perspective which embraces both and locates them by reference to evolutionary processes of genotypic mutation and natural selection. He thus brings together the organism as engineer, shaping the physical environment, and the organism as neighbour, interacting with other organisms and species. In the ensuing chapters we pursue this same dual focus: human beings in relation to technology and in relation to the institutions of social interaction.

Second, Odling-Smee (2003: Ch. 6) compares the various channels by which an organism can acquire information beyond its own immediate experience (see also Maynard Smith and Szathmáry, 1995). There is, first, the genetically encoded information inherited by each new generation, as to how organisms can successfully operate within different selective environments (Maynard Smith and Szathmáry, 2000; Odling-Smee et al., 2003: paras 4.4, 5.4.1, 5.4.3).[20] This information is tested and revised in each generation, as new mutations are exposed to contemporary selective pressures, before transmitting the legacy to their own descendants.[21] In some species, however, organisms are also able to obtain information from other individuals. This is the case with humans in particular, where cultural products and processes allow shared learning. Here, instead of the random variations of genetic mutation, we have 'smart' learning, allowing the ready transfer of lessons from the older generation, but also the 're-blending' of that cultural inheritance by the young (Odling-Smee et al., 2003: 258–9).

As we have already noted, niche construction – by adapting the local environment to the organism – tends to buffer it against the selective pressures of the environment. Nowhere is this more the case than with cultural niche construction: indeed, 'cultural transmission can overwhelm selection'[22] (Odling-Smee et al., 2003: 278–9). In turning to human societies and examining the relationships that humans establish with technology and the institutions of their social interactions, we may be able to deploy models of evolutionary adaptation, but these will be grounded not in the molecular biology of the genotype but the dynamics of cultural niche construction. Here we come full circle. Charles Darwin (1859) started from his observation of husbandry practices and artificial selection and from this he made the mental leap to posit natural selection. In adapting his model of evolution and natural selection to human societies, we move back into the world of civilisation and active husbandry from which Darwin began.

4 The economy as a complex adaptive system

4.1 INTRODUCTION

Darwin began with the world of civilisation and active husbandry (Darwin, 1859: Ch. 1). The breeder or horticulturalist looked out for any novel characteristics manifested by offspring in each new generation and in particular those that better met the demands of the breeder or horticulturalist concerned. These superior varieties were then selected for breeding, so as to combine and progressively accentuate such advantageous characteristics. Of course, this was not the end of the story. The breeder might produce new varieties of pigeon or tulip but how these would fare in the wider world was a separate matter – whether we refer to the interest shown by purchasers or how they would thrive when exposed to natural predators and competitors. The source of variation and selection was artificial not natural; nevertheless, the ultimate fate of the variants was outside the hands of the breeder. We of course are concerned not with pigeons and tulips but with the husbandry of technologies and institutions, so that they better meet the purposes of those concerned. Again, however, the selection of apparently superior varieties is only the first step, not least because what counts as superior – and superior for whom – may itself be fiercely contested.

The present chapter continues our consideration of complex adaptive systems, now by reference to economic rather than biological dynamics. Evolutionary economics has benefitted greatly from the new thinking on complexity and the new computational tools for simulating dynamic processes. At the same time, modern evolutionary economics remains grounded in earlier economic thought, including Schumpeter in particular. For him, 'swarms of innovation' and technological progress provided the engine of capitalism, with profits going to those enterprises whose innovations secured widespread adoption (Wagener and Drukker, 1986: Chs 7,11). Without enterprises producing novelty the world would be static and predictable; with innovation it was forever turbulent. Nevertheless Schumpeter had enough confidence in the market to believe that this turbulence would – to use the language of complexity – be self-organising.

Our first task is to understand this struggle and to relate it to the account of evolutionary dynamics offered in the previous chapter.

Of course, there are always pitfalls in using our understanding of processes in one field as the source of explanatory models in another: whether it is Darwin taking insights from artificial selection and positing processes of natural selection, or our own extension of models of evolution developed in biology to processes of socio-economic evolution. Any such extension must therefore be accompanied by appropriate caveats. Human beings are living organisms and as such subject to processes of biological evolution; nevertheless, as agents of change they are unique. Our second task will be to understand and elaborate the implications of this.

The centrepiece of our discussion will be the work of Potts: his study *The New Evolutionary Microeconomics* (2000) and his collaborative work with Dopfer (Dopfer and Potts, 2008), *The General Theory of Economic Evolution*. We venture into related studies as appropriate.[1]

4.2 THE DYNAMICS OF ECONOMIC EVOLUTION

Potts (2000) offers a strong model of the enterprise, in terms of the knowledge it develops, the competence with which it designs and selects technologies and its expectations as to how these technologies will perform. This is the enterprise engaged in expert 'husbandry', seeking to discover technologies more fit for purpose. The enterprise is the source of technological novelty and variation: it is the population of technologies that then evolves. Which varieties become predominant in the larger economy will determine which enterprises make profits and which fail.

In Chapter 2 we spoke of Darwinian evolution as a system pushed 'far from equilibrium' by the continuous appearance of genetic novelties and the harsh demand for fitness imposed by the natural 'struggle for existence'. Here in Potts, the economic system is similarly driven 'far from equilibrium' by the continuous stream of technological novelties, with 'fitness' now the expression of a particular political economy. This stands in sharp contrast to the Walrasian mainstream of neoclassical economics, still in thrall to the equilibrium assumptions of Newtonian mechanics (Robinson, 1964: Chs 3–4; Beinhocker, 2007: Chs 2–3).[2]

4.2.1 The Combinatorial Ontology

Walrasian economics is concerned with the various resources or elements – factors of production, goods and services – that economic agents exchange. It assumes that these are infinitely divisible; as prices change, one element is progressively substituted for another. Rates of substitution can be explored through well-established methods of simultaneous differential equations. In contrast, it is production not exchange that Potts makes central. Now the different resources or elements are complements not substitutes; they are therefore needed in combination, if production is to take place (Potts, 2000: 71–4). Most fundamentally, production involves combining new elements with the heritage of the past (see similarly Kaldor, 1985: 61–2; Toner, 1999: para 1.3.3). Even consumption is now conceived as a process of production and reproduction, rather than the mere exchange of money for goods and services, with consumers searching for the combination of characteristics that particular commodities offer and that will better meet their preferences.

Potts is centrally interested, therefore, in the connections that economic agents construct among these various elements. These include technologies, organisational structures, distribution networks: all part of the 'connective geometry of the economic system' (Potts, 2000: 3). As we move outside the domain of economic life narrowly conceived, the range of such connections widens even further, to include institutions, language and concepts. It is primarily through changes in these connections, rather than just increases or improvements in individual elements, that economic actors advance.[3]

Walrasian economics assumes a topographically uniform terrain; there are, therefore, no locally distinctive interactions (Potts, 2000: Ch. 2). Against this, Potts argues that social and economic space is 'non-integral'; it is constructed by human actors, who build new connections among particular locations, but leave others unconnected. These connections are built at multiple nested levels, with systems of elements being connected in higher level systems or hyperstructures (Potts, 2000: Ch. 4 and para. 5.2.3). It is then the connections within these hyperstructures that dictate the dynamic properties of the economic system (Potts, 2000: para. 3.4). Drawing on Simon's work on the 'decomposibility' of modular systems, Potts argues that the path taken by an economic system typically involves 'increasing decomposition in some areas and . . . increasing interconnectedness in others'. It is by re-tuning these connections – thus connecting and decomposing the system along different lines – that the decision-maker or policy-maker can seek to steer and manage it (Simon, 1996: Ch. 8. Earl and Potts, 2004; Egidi and Marengo, 2004).[4]

This combinatorial ontology can be summarised diagrammatically. Potts starts with 'elements' (resources) organised for production. The economic agent may then introduce two sorts of modification. First, individual elements can be added, including by exchange with other agents. Second, the connections among them can be modified. In general, of course, both

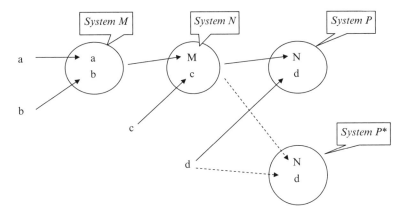

Figure 4.1   The combinatorial ontology

processes are underway, with systems of elements being connected with other elements and systems of elements into larger 'hyperstructures'.

Figure 4.1 depicts this process. Each lower case letter denotes an element, each upper case a system of connections. As successive elements are added, they are combined with the existing system into a new and higher level hyperstructure of greater complexity. Thus System M combines elements a and b; it is then itself combined with element c into the larger system N; the latter is in turn combined with element d into System P.

In general, of course, Potts's micro-economic agent has a variety of choices as to which elements to add and how to combine them. In the diagram, System P might not be the only way in which System N can be combined with element d; System P* might do so very differently. And of course, the economic agent might have chosen to combine System N not with element d at all, but with some other element altogether.

It will be immediately evident that this also closely matches the ontology of variation that we developed in the previous chapter. There also, agents were depicted as engaged in the construction of space – in that case genotypic space. This involved, on the one hand, changes in individual elements (alleles), on the other, changes in the hyperstructures by which these elements were connected. Moreover, just as Figure 4.1 depicts a variety of trajectories of development, as new elements and combinations are introduced, the evolutionary journeys depicted in Chapter 3 developed in a variety of different directions, depending on which allele values were changed, which new connections and re-deployments of the genetic legacy were made. Indeed, although Darwin himself did not of course appreciate the role of genetic change in producing variations, Figure 4.1 captures the basic dynamic of his evolutionary 'tree of life' (Darwin, 1859: Ch. 4). We will appeal to this diagrammatic representation of the combinatorial ontology throughout this study.

Although technologies are being continually re-deployed, they cannot all be held perpetually plastic. Potts posits that it is the oldest that become fixed as part of the capital stock of the larger economic order (Potts, 2000: para. 5.2.3). This is a plausible simplifying assumption, which serves to underline, albeit crudely, that timing and sequencing matter. It also resonates well with our account in Chapter 3 of connections within the genotype and the immutability of ancient and deep-seated genetic structures (Shubin, 2008).

4.2.2   Micro-Meso-Macro

Such is Potts's account of the micro-economic actor and the generation of novelty or variation. We turn now to the larger evolutionary dynamic, as treated in Dopfer and Potts (2008). Dopfer and Potts analyse the generic dynamics of interacting technologies – and indeed institutions – seen as systems of rules. The exposition is rather abstract and formal, appropriate to their purposes but less so to ours. The presentation can, however, be facilitated, without undue distortion, by referring to the conceptual framework of Kauffman deployed in the previous chapter.[5]

Kauffman's NK model started with the appearance of new combinations at the micro-level, in the form of genetic mutations; this we discussed in terms of 'deepening'. Dopfer and Potts (2008: Ch. 3) invite us to start with the micro-economic agent, as depicted in Potts's original study, who as we have seen is engaged in an analogous process of 'deepening', involving new technologies and organisational structures. Individual entrepreneurs invest in such novelties, hoping for extra profit not only from the higher productivity they bring but also, and crucially, from the new markets they create. They wager that this will propel them along a virtuous path of first mover advantage (Potts, 2000: 155–6).[6]

Kauffman next examined how genetic novelties are variously taken up within the larger population, in what we referred to as processes of 'widening'. This is what Dopfer and Potts characterise as 'meso': the process by which an invention is diffused, progressively replacing existing technologies and other rules of connection. Notice that it is these technologies and rules that evolve. This may involve new or reorganised markets, new flows of profit and finance, a changed distribution of labour and of incomes. At the same time, Dopfer and Potts recognise that rules do not exist in abstraction from human actors; they are 'carried' by populations of micro-economic agents and the organisations they form. The evolutionary dynamics therefore involve structural changes – differentiation, diffusion, disconnection, destruction – in these populations of carriers as well as in the rules themselves (Dopfer and Potts, 2008: paras 1.4.2, 4.1).

Dopfer and Potts analyse 'meso' as a trajectory of 'origination, adoption and retention' by carriers of the novelty in question (Dopfer and Potts, 2008: para. 4.2). This trajectory is, however, far from certain: most novelties fail. For the first mover, to invest in novelty is therefore potentially lucrative but it also costly and risky. Albeit in their own language, Dopfer and Potts make the same argument that we developed in the previous chapter. The first mover must peer beyond the local peak for a 'perilous pathway' which can be offered to others; this will bring profit, which can be used to sustain the search for further advantage and continued ascent. However, this applies only on terrains which are of intermediate ruggedness. On a smooth landscape – a Mount Fuji – the whole population of potential carriers can drift towards the ascending pathway the first mover has discovered, with little cost or risk involved, leaving little first mover profit (see Figure 3.1). On very rugged landscapes, in contrast, there are so many local peaks that last movers will be reluctant to pay the first mover who beckons from a somewhat higher peak, because they can have little confidence that it will be really worth it, or will grant them a sustained advantage over others. Only on intermediate landscapes is there scope for profitable novelty.

It is in any case uncertain whether the creation of any particular novelty will produce a new point on the fitness landscape higher than its surroundings. The novelty may eventually produce a Fuji or a *Massif Central*; for the moment, however, it is just one of many Surtseys, each offering the possibility of profit precisely because of this uncertainty, but also the risk of ruin. This is a period of turbulence, in which alternative novelties are being appraised and variously picked up across the larger population of potential carriers (Dopfer and Potts, 2008: para. 4.3.2). The latter find themselves therefore in a 'fog of uncertainty' (Dopfer and Potts, 2008: 47). Nevertheless, by the 'retention' stage, much of this uncertainty has been removed and the shape of the landscape, including the new extensions, the Surtseys, has stabilised. However, the scope for first movers to earn profits is by now much reduced, not least because 'second movers' have found alternative bye-ways of their own (Dopfer and Potts, 2008: para. 4.2.3).

In his NK(C) model, Kauffman turned finally to the adaptive interaction of diverse phenotypes within a shared ecosystem, modifying and warping their respective fitness landscapes. For Dopfer and Potts, this shared ecosystem is the macro-terrain of the economy as a whole (Dopfer and Potts, 2008: Ch. 5). This is where multiple meso-trajectories of origination, adoption and retention interact, abrade and co-evolve. At this macro-level, co-evolutionary dynamics 'warp' the fitness landscapes, not least for the first mover. The stakes for the first mover – the micro-originator of a given invention – are therefore even greater than at the meso-level. Even so, with an initial advantage, and some skill in anticipating the larger consequences of these dynamics, the first mover may be able to keep ahead of the crowd and, even while they are still adjusting, develop further waves of innovation. Nevertheless, there is forever the haunting fear that others will steal an innovative march; and it is this, even more than the hope of riches, that keeps first movers on their mettle (Dopfer and Potts, 2008: para. 4.2.1).

4.2.3   The Overall Dynamics of Economic Systems

Kauffman was interested in how the parameters of his models produced significantly different evolutionary trajectories in terms of fitness and adaptability. In the NK(C) model the polar cases were the chaotic 'Red Queen' regime and the 'evolutionarily stable state'. Each of these extremes in some degree constituted an 'evolutionary catastrophe'; nevertheless, an intermediate dynamic delivered an optimum mix of adaptability and fitness.

Dopfer and Potts are similarly concerned to identify polar cases of the dynamic trajectories at work within their 'micro-meso-macro'. They refer in particular to 'macro coordination', defined in terms that correspond to Kaufmann's 'evolutionarily stable state' (Dopfer and Potts, 2008: para. 5.2). Here, as with Kaufmann, there is no further evolution: 'no structural change, technological change or institutional change'. Nevertheless, this is no more than an ideal type; creative human actors – new first movers – are perennially generating new combinations, new points on the technological landscape, which in turn stimulate new meso-trajectories and new waves of co-evolution within the macro-economy (Dopfer and Potts, 2008: paras 5.2.1–2). At the opposite pole is 'endogeneric coordination failure' of varying degrees, including some that are akin to Red Queen chaos (Dopfer and Potts, 2008: para. 5.4).

As we have seen, the basic unit of analysis is the dynamic trajectory of 'micro-meso-macro'. Where such a trajectory pervades the entire economy, Dopfer and Potts refer to it as a 'regime'. Regimes perennially generate novelty that will eventually lead to their being superseded: nevertheless, such regime change is path dependent and any regime will be coloured by its antecedents (Dopfer and Potts, 2008: para. 6.2.1). This Dopfer and Potts see as the basis for an analysis of regime sequence.[7] The analysis of regime transitions is the subject matter of economic development; the tuning of such transitions is the stuff of economic policy (Dopfer and Potts, 2008: para. 6.2.3).

4.3   AGENTS OF CHANGE

Just as it was necessary in Chapter 3 to take stock of the organism as an agent of change, we consider now the corresponding capacities of human entrepreneurs. They search for new hybrids; and while, like Kauffman's adaptive agents, they may give priority to local searches, they are also able to span multiple niches and draw lessons from afar. They can also tap into their shared cultural and organisational memories, the residues of the past, which even if fallen into disuse are available always for recycling. They have the capacity to anticipate, if only imperfectly in the form of conjectures, the larger consequences that their innovations will set in motion. It is on the basis of these conjectures that they wager and invest against each other. Finally, while processes of biological evolution may, as Kauffman argues, tune the parameters of co-evolving fitness landscapes, so that they evolve towards 'the edge of chaos', they do so only in the course of millennia. In contrast, human beings can – albeit imperfectly – tune the parameters of social and economic change deliberately.

Human beings reflect upon their world, developing their knowledge of the combinatorial possibilities that are available and the changes in connective geometry that will bring first mover advantage.[8] Such knowledge is scarce and is therefore a valued, if intangible asset. It is also essentially dynamic, incomplete and being forever revised. This is quite different from a Walrasian world: 'In a world of omniscience there can be no such concept as knowledge' (Potts, 2000: 17).

Potts therefore develops his general theory of production systems in terms of the organisation of scarce knowledge and competence. He draws on a wide literature, ranging from Penrose's resource-based theories of the enterprise (Penrose, 1959) to the evolutionary economics of Nelson and Winter (1982) and Loasby (1999: Ch. 4). Enterprises are not just collections of factors of production, they are also 'repositories of competence' that create, coordinate and deploy knowledge: knowledge of the 'specific connections that seem to work in a particular environment' (Potts, 2000: 58–9, 138–9). The micro-agent is therefore in pursuit not only of new technological combinations, but also of those organisational and governance structures that will most effectively generate knowledge assets (Potts, 2000: paras 4.4.3, 5.3). However, it is only as these deliver added value and profits that the organisational structures in question and the composite agents they involve are able to stabilise (Potts, 2000: 130).[9]

Knowledge is scarce in relation not only to the present, but also to future possibilities. Nevertheless, Potts presents his micro-economic actors as bringing with them more or less well-articulated 'mental models', which embody conjectures and expectations as to how this world will unfold.

They preview the various combinatorial dynamics in which they might invest their energies and the dynamic processes of competence acquisition these are likely to involve (Potts, 2000: para. 4.4.1). It is by reference to these future possibilities – as interpreted through their mental models and expectations – that micro-economic actors make their combinatorial choices. This leaves plenty of scope for disagreement, heterogeneous strategies and failures; contrast this with the neoclassical world of timeless certainty, in which there is neither disagreement nor disappointment. There is also plenty of scope for learning; but learning as articulation, negotiation, advocacy, contestation and the eventual triumph of one conjecture over another.

Knowledge may be scarce and valuable when first developed, but it slowly leaks away and diffuses, losing its local specificity and scarcity value (even if it is protected by intellectual property rights (IPR) legislation and is in part tacit, bound up in specialist teams within an organisation). Hence the strategic importance for the first mover, of continuously developing this knowledge in new directions, thereby retaining and reinforcing positional advantage. For Potts it is, after all, not so much factor endowment and choice of technologies as such that bring profits, but the positional advantage they confer.

It is to the dynamic relations between the formation of composite agents, the deployment of technologies and the appropriation of their fruits, under conditions of uncertainty and competing conjectures as to how these dynamics will unfold, that much of this book is devoted.

4.4   IMPLICATIONS FOR PUBLIC POLICY

Dopfer and Potts turn finally to the implications for public policy. Again, there are clear resonances with Kauffman; but whereas he looks to evolutionary pressures to tune the landscape parameters, Dopfer and Potts look to public policy-makers and their re-shaping of the 'connective geometry' within which economic agents interact.

What then are public policy-makers to do; and in what degree can their actions be enlightened by policy analysts? Dopfer and Potts distinguish 'first order rules', defining how resources and social interactions are organised; 'second order rules', by means of which entrepreneurial agents creatively explore possible new connections; and, finally, the 'zero order' constitutional rules in which all others are embedded (Dopfer and Potts, 2008: Ch. 1). They classify public policies similarly. Zero order policy involves intervention 'to change the underlying structure of property rights, competition law, legal trade agreements, environmental regulation, labour laws, monetary and financial institutions, public infrastructure and generally all social, political and cultural institutions that affect the economic order' (Dopfer and Potts, 2008: para. 7.3). First order policy involves direct intervention in the provision of goods and services. Second order policy involves intervention in society's capacity to generate novelty and to develop knowledge; it focuses on education and the institutions that have come to be bracketed under the general heading of 'national innovation systems' (Nelson, 1993).

Social and economic development can face 'evolutionary catastrophes' where, on the one hand, there is too little variation and novelty or where, on the other, there is so much turbulence that no settled regimes can emerge. Dopfer and Potts are well aware of this; their final chapters can be read as an application to the economic order of Kauffman's conclusion, that complex and dynamic co-evolving systems must develop close to the 'edge of chaos' if their promise, in terms of fitness and adaptability, is to be optimised. In particular, they recognise that sufficient variety must be maintained to stimulate new waves of creativity (Dopfer and Potts, 2008: para. 6.2.3). For Dopfer and Potts, it is therefore second order policy that is key, supporting the creative capacity and dynamic evolution of the economy. Where this entails some reordering of constitutional rules, zero order policy also has a place; first order policy, however, has none.

Of course, public policy-makers are hardly omniscient; like any other actors, they live in a complex and opaque world. They search and experiment, as they seek to shape this connective geometry, using appropriate 'technologies' of policy intervention. They build alliances and develop their capacity and knowledge, in relation to such interventions. It is with these challenges that Part 3 of this book is concerned.

4.5   OPEN QUESTIONS

Potts provides a powerful critique of neoclassical economics. His work also contributes to the task we set in the opening chapter of this book: to develop conceptual and analytical tools for understanding processes of dynamic change and the scope for policy intervention. His contribution is rooted in complexity analysis in general, evolutionary theory in particular, albeit 'without the biology' (Potts, 2000: xi). As in neo-Darwinism, there is a mechanism for generating novelty and variety, albeit not through the random mutation of genes, rather through creative and imaginative selection and recombination of technologies by human agents. There is also a mechanism of selection, involving the differential adoption of these novelties and differential population dynamics. Finally, as in the neo-Darwinian account of evolution offered by Kauffman and others, there are processes of self-organisation and co-evolutionary dynamics, within constraints and along pathways shaped by previous transitions, albeit the tuning of these processes is itself in some degree subject to human agency and choice (Dopfer and Potts, 2008: para. 6.3).

The account which Potts provides has limitations as well as strengths. Even so, these are better seen as lines of potential further conceptual and analytical development, which invite treatment using his intellectual tools, maybe in combination with those of other scholars. In reviewing these limitations, we are therefore also seeking to identify the additional tools that are needed, if we are to complete the tasks set out in Chapter 1.

4.5.1   Power and Politics

Biological evolution may tune biological systems; however, the direction of human development is a matter of politics. What new connections are to be made within the 'connective geometry' of the economy and which sub-systems decomposed? Whose self-organisation is to be favoured? What are the trade-offs and in what degree of uncertainty are they shrouded (Potts, 2000: para. 4.4.1)?

However, although Dopfer and Potts from time to time refer to the importance of politics and power differentials, nowhere do these come to the centre of attention. They defend their approach in terms of an intellectual division of labour: evolutionary economics focuses upon choice, whereas an evolutionary approach to sociology or politics would emphasise power and lack of choice (Dopfer and Potts, 2008: 40). However, this hardly serves our own purpose.

Thus, for example, Dopfer and Potts recognise that zero order 'constitutional' rules 'are significantly political, social, legal and cultural and therefore evolve at the speed of consensus (*or domination*)' (Dopfer and Potts, 2008: 9, emphasis added). In securing the wider adoption of a novel rule, power is also implicitly acknowledged, as entrepreneurs engage in 'campaigns of persuasion' to win the adhesion of the wider population of agents (p. 47) and secure a dominant position (p. 52). Political resistance to change is also recognised (pp. 57, 68), whether it comes from those fearful of redundancy, or from yesterday's first movers, now a special interest group seeking to hang onto their rents in face of further change (pp. 57, 96). Dopfer and Potts do not, however, consider what political conditions are needed to ensure that there is sufficient variety in terms of carriers of novelty; or whether, for example, the economic rewards accruing to yesterday's successful entrepreneurs may provide them with the institutional means to stifle innovation today and consolidate their own position into tomorrow.

Dopfer and Potts recognise also that evolutionary dynamics may produce 'exclusion, extinction, domination or enslavement' (p. 75, fn. 43). However, with their attention on the first mover, little is said about those who experience the downward dynamics of the last mover, with their scope for manoeuvre being progressively narrowed, their competence rendered obsolete, their chances of survival eked out within precarious niches. Firms that do not attain even local peaks are likely to go out of business. As Potts recognises (2000: para. 3.3), households – and presumably local communities – can also be regarded as economic micro-agents, albeit they lack the option of going 'out of business' and may find themselves the wards of public welfare.

Public welfare interventions can be construed as the effort by the public authorities to build or restore competence where these do not exist, at levels sufficient to ensure survival. This means, however, that whereas Potts focuses on micro-change-makers, the households and communities who benefit from this restorative social policy are largely change-*takers*. They pursue their livelihoods by adapting to – and surviving within – a world that is being re-shaped by much larger powers. Potts hardly gives these the significance that they merit within any analysis of needs, capacities and prospects for survival.

To this extent, the analysis that Dopfer and Potts offer of public policy is unduly limited. Notwithstanding their protestations to the contrary (Dopfer and Potts, 2008: 96, para. 1.3), they have not entirely escaped from the intellectual attractors from within which their own journey began: Hayekian laissez-faire economics and post-Darwinian evolutionary theory. This leaves them with a view of history – and of public policy – that is at risk of relying on the benevolence of the free market or of evolutionary selection and that underplays fundamental political choices.

4.5.2 Actors and Institutions

As we noticed earlier, the 'connections' in which Potts is interested are defined rather broadly, to include new technologies, designs, organisational structures, distribution networks: all elements of the 'connective geometry of the economic system' (Potts, 2000: 3). Potts takes some interest in institutions and organisations. They are means of effecting connections; they also serve to create locally specific structure and thus to construct non-integral space (Potts, 2000: 45). Far from being 'imperfections' in the market, as Walrasian economics insists, they are essential to the functioning of a dynamic and creative economy (Potts, 2000: 97–8). Potts is also interested in structures of institutional governance: in particular those that will facilitate the generation of knowledge assets (Potts,

2000: 100, 137 and para. 4.4.3). However, while he refers to a substantial array of literature concerned with economic institutions, Potts does not offer any detailed treatment. In his subsequent work with Dopfer, institutions appear in the form of generic rules, but again only at a rather high level of abstraction.

Potts recognises that as a result of interactions around processes of 'micro-meso-macro', new actors may emerge. He and Dopfer discuss how economic agents often take action to coordinate and organise trajectories of innovation into 'clusters', of producers and consumers, for example, 'tuning' their dynamics so as to exploit their benefits. However, the specific institutional conditions within which new composite actors can readily negotiate a consistency of purpose and expectations are again left largely unexamined. Nor does Potts offer any systematic review of the diversity of institutional settings within which economic interactions take place and the likely consequences for group formation.

In short, Potts has left us with an evolutionary perspective not only 'without the biology' but also in considerable measure without the institutions.

4.6   CONCLUSION

This chapter has been concerned with the economy as a complex adaptive system and, more particularly, the application of an evolutionary model. We now set this in a somewhat broader context of economic analysis.

In Chapter 2 we noticed the significance of increasing returns and their corollary, that markets may well not produce efficient solutions. Later in that same chapter we referred to economists such as Schelling and Scheinkman, who model the emergence of macro-level manifestations of flocking behaviour and social polarisation from local neighbourly interactions. On both fronts, the equilibrium assumptions of neoclassical mainstream economics are put in question. On the other hand, accounts of economies as complex systems have provided a plausible new basis for the political creed of economic liberalism. Claims abound that 'free markets are clearly creative self-organising systems' (Parker and Stacey, 1994: 16), albeit the status of such claims – and their empirical basis – is often left obscure. Evolutionary models in the tradition of Schumpeter – including that of Potts – to some extent echo such claims; see also Beinhocker (2007: Ch. 13), asserting that markets – in contrast to governments – gear such evolution towards the needs of the population generally. Schumpeter was hostile to state intervention, as a threat to the dynamics of innovation (Wagener and Drukker, 1986); Potts offers similar strictures against 'first order' public policy. In this respect at least, Schumpeter and Potts share somewhat the neoclassical confidence in the market.

It can, however, be questioned whether markets if left to self-organise will effectively exploit the external economies which, as we saw in Chapter 2, are central to the process of economic growth. Scholars such as Myrdal, Hirschman and Kaldor instead look to public policy to nurture and steer these co-evolutionary dynamics of capitalist industrial societies (Toner, 1999: para. 7.1). It can also be argued that leaving markets to self-organise may produce social consequences – in terms of social inequality and polarisation, for example – that undermine social consent and threaten a backlash against the very market institutions on which prosperity is said to depend. Keynes in particular doubted whether – to use the language of complex systems – a modern economy could self-organise at full employ-ment of national resources and economic capacity without the active intervention of the state. Only the state could provide the stability within which capitalist entrepreneurs and their 'animal spirits' could flourish. The returns that entrepreneurs could expect on their investments and on the inventions they brought to market depended on the general level of activ-ity in the economy and this was itself dependent on public policies; indeed, the very value of assets and investments could not be assessed independ-ently of the level of aggregate effective demand and hence of state activity (Wagener and Drukker, 1986: 38–9). Keynes thus saw the state as continu-ally tuning the system parameters: not just from the outside, as it were, by appropriate tuning of the interest rate, but also by direct intervention: most obviously in terms of expenditure, but also income maintenance and investment (Wagener and Drukker, 1986: Ch. 4).

This Keynesian perspective is given added salience by the turbulence unleashed by the recent economic crisis. In the financial markets at least, Schumpeter's 'swarms of innovation' seem to have been over-stimulated and 'light touch' regulation has proved inadequate. Soros (2008b) cap-tures well the dynamics of the international economy as a 'far from equi-librium system', where animal spirits generate self-destructive volatility through flocking behaviour. His ideas have been taken up by Arthur and others at the Santa Fé Institute (Arthur et al., 1997: 16, 37). His account is couched in part in terms of a race between financiers inventing new products to escape regulation, but generating volatility that undermines system stability, and policy-makers who establish new regulatory instru-ments, only to find that the ground again shifts and the race starts afresh. This 'arms race' is a dynamic of micro-meso-macro, played out initially within the financial system, but spilling over through macro-couplings into the wider economy and society. Or we might couch it in terms of Bak's 'self-organised criticality', with the new products that financiers invent providing a continuing source of energy and novelty, but from time to time sending poorly anticipated cascades of change sweeping through the system. The race is then to offload the costs of the avalanche – with potentially major socially deleterious consequences. To this we return at greater length in Chapter 17.

Public policy is thus of central interest, not only because this is a study written for policy analysts, but also because it arguably has a fundamental role to play in the steering and the management of society and economy as a far from equilibrium system. However, if public policy-makers are to 'tune' the parameters of social and economic co-evolution, they will need to be appropriately equipped.

5 Institutional settings and architectures

5.1 INTRODUCTION

Institutions have until now been somewhat peripheral to our discussion. As Chapter 2 demonstrated, complexity science struggles to handle institutional contexts and structures. There is in particular little acknowledgement of the pre-existing normative and institutional structures that dominate our lives, enforcing the rules of our interactions and giving or denying authority to the choices we make. Chapter 3, concerned with biological evolution, concluded by pointing to the importance for humans of cultural and institutional niche construction but offered little or no further discussion. Chapter 4, concerned with the economy as an evolving system, made reference to institutions as part of the 'connective geometry' of the economic system, but only at a rather high level of abstraction.

We now develop a treatment of institutions which recognises their central place in social dynamics. We do so by demonstrating the remarkable – but so far insufficiently remarked – convergence between theories of institutionalism and of complex adaptive systems. It is this convergence that renders plausible the project of integrating them conceptually and ontologically.

Chapter 3 adopted an ontology of mutation and recombination and applied it to genotypes. Chapter 4 did the same in relation to technologies. Each chapter used this as the basis for an evolutionary account of change. We now do the same in relation to institutions. The present chapter considers the diversity of institutional forms. Chapter 6 considers how 'institutional entrepreneurs' weave them into novel combinations and how these then evolve. This is the 'deepen-widen-warp' of institutional change. Chapter 7 is concerned with the larger positional dynamics thereby set in motion and the scope for tuning and husbandry. We draw from the extensive literature on institutions particular elements appropriate to our purposes; we combine and organise them in what is, to some extent, a novel way, but without doing violence to the authors concerned. This is itself, therefore, a combinatorial approach – now however applied to their arguments and our own analytical goals.

We dealt with biological evolution in a single chapter, as also economic evolution. In assessing the relevance of these models to institutional change, our discussion is spread across three chapters. This is in part because, although theories of institutionalism are variously converging on this ontology, as we hope to demonstrate, it remains to bring them together, as a counterpart to Potts's treatment of technologies and the connective geometry of the economic system. It is also because while the biological and economic are important points of reference throughout this book, and we will indeed need to elaborate upon various aspects in subsequent chapters, it is institutions and social dynamics that have even greater salience and that demand a correspondingly more detailed treatment.

As Streek and Thelen observe, 'definitions of institutions abound . . . [but] . . . none of them has yet become firmly institutionalised in the social and political sciences' (Streek and Thelen, 2005: 9–16). A preliminary note on terminology may therefore be helpful. We will, first, refer to the various 'terrains' on which life chances, power and advantage are distributed and contested: the education system, the labour market, the healthcare system, social security. Other writers use a variety of terms to cover similar ground, albeit with their own nuances: Fligstein, for example, sees social action as taking place in 'arenas, what may be called fields, domains, sectors or organised social spaces . . .' (Fligstein, 2001: 15, 28ff., 67ff.). It will also be necessary to distinguish the different systems of rules that may govern social interactions; we will refer to them as the alternative 'institutional settings' that can prevail on a given terrain. This is consistent with writers such as North (1990: Ch. 1), identifying institutions with the rules of social interaction they embody, but distinguishing them from the social actors – including the organisations – to whom such rules are applied.

5.2   INSTITUTIONAL DIVERSITY

There is a large sociological and political science literature concerned with institutional diversity. These variations matter because, as we have seen, institutions articulate and enforce rules of interaction among social agents. They shape the patterns of action and group formation that typically emerge; and, as Potts argues, the organisation of competence and knowledge that can then be deployed.

The literature is itself rather diverse in how it maps this institutional diversity. We start with Scharpf's analysis of actor-centred institutionalism (Scharpf, 1997). He distinguishes several ideal types. First, there is the institutional minimalism (or even anarchy) presupposed by such writers as Hobbes and Hayek. This need not mean the war of each against all;

however, the most that can be expected in terms of cooperation is mutual adjustment (Scharpf, 1997: Ch. 5). Market relations provide the most obvious example, albeit just how 'minimal' are the institutional underpinnings they require is much debated, with mainstream economists heavily criticised by institutional economists, political scientists and sociologists, for under-estimating this. Second, there is hierarchical coordination or direction 'in the shadow of the State', the ultimate repository of compulsion and force. Here individuals are subject to formal-rational processes operated by managers and officials, but with their own preferences and the information of which they dispose in greater or lesser degree ignored. Finally, there are various forms of network and association governed by negotiated agreement, majority vote, deliberative democracy.

Scharpf adduces the implications of each of these institutional settings for actor strategies, interactions and patterns of cooperation. He also shows how different settings create positive or negative conditions for the emergence of cooperation (pp. 39–40). Such emergence takes us from a world where a myriad of individuals adjust to their immediate neighbours, to a world of composite actors, pursuing their goals collectively (pp. 5, 80). Scharpf also examines the stability of the outcomes that result and the conditions under which they degenerate into non-cooperation (Chs 5–8).

Common across the literature more generally are models that correspond to Scharpf's institutional minimalism, on the one hand, hierarchical coordination on the other. There is less agreement as to what other settings should be distinguished. Thompson, for example, chooses networks (Thompson et al., 1991), while Ouchi (1980) focuses on clans. These efforts have a longer pedigree. Durkheim (1964) was concerned to understand the social division of labour and the solidarity of complex societies, not by reference to the market, the centre of attention for liberal political economy, nor by reference to the state and its enforcement of the law, as advocated by Comte. For Durkheim, organic solidarity within the division of labour depended on the emergence of cooperative frameworks and institutions that were congruent with local conditions and thus 'spontaneous', rather than being imposed by some distant legislator; they would also express common interests, rather than just private acquisitiveness. A similar threefold distinction is evident in Etzioni's analysis of modes of organisational compliance: instrumental, coercive and moral (Etzioni, 1961).

Notwithstanding this variety, it seems generally agreed that what is problematic – both analytically and practically – is the moral basis of institutional settings where neither mutual adjustment nor hierarchical direction suffices. Here, as Scharpf argues, there is a need to negotiate a normative basis for cooperation and trust: both 'weak trust' (confidence that agreements will be honoured and basic standards of honesty respected) and 'strong trust' (confidence that each party will avoid harm to the other and will, indeed, promote the other's well-being) (Etzioni, 1961: 137–8). It is these negotiated moral communities that present the more obvious conceptual challenge and that we therefore consider at somewhat greater length in the next section. We may then be better placed to understand mutual adjustment and hierarchical direction also.

5.3   NEGOTIATED MORAL COMMUNITIES

We explore the defining elements of negotiated moral communities by reference to Ostrom's (1990) discussion of 'institutions for collective action'. As with Durkheim, Ostrom develops her analysis of cooperative institutions by distinguishing them from market institutions of mutual adjustment, on the one hand, hierarchical direction by Leviathan, on the other. Her interest is in the 'commons': natural resources such as water or fish stocks which are fixed in supply but easy to access, and whose progressive depletion by self-interested individual actors has ultimately tragic consequences for society as a whole. She starts with the two policy prescriptions that are commonly held forth: the privatisation of the resource in question, to enable its efficient exploitation within the normal disciplines of commercial behaviour; and state regulation, to protect against the depredations of unbridled individual greed. As an alternative to these, however, and on the basis of an extensive review of empirical case studies, she examines the dynamics of 'self-organising and self-governing common pool resources'.

Ostrom surveys cooperative arrangements in farming communities in Switzerland, Japan, Spain and elsewhere that have endured for many hundreds of years with only minor adjustments. She also investigates the governance of water resources in various parts of the USA and fishing communities in Canada. From this she adduces a set of common design features: four in particular. Those who are entitled to draw from the common pool should be clearly identifiable. Those affected by the operational rules should also be able to participate in modifying them, customising them to local circumstances. Monitoring and enforcement procedures should be embedded within the community of participants. Finally, these normative regimes should enjoy support from wider institutional arrangements and external governmental authorities (Ostrom, 1990: Ch. 3, 2005: Ch. 8).

Ostrom's argument is that if cooperative arrangements having these design features can be negotiated, they can in important respects operate more effectively than their rivals: privatisation and state direction. To enforce the directives of Leviathan can be very costly in terms of the monitoring and enforcement of compliance; the costs of establishing market institutions and supervising their operation are similarly high. Against this, cooperative regimes can displace the enforcement costs onto those actually involved in the production and distribution of the natural resource in question and, by enlisting their active involvement, minimise those costs.

5.3.1 Institutional Settings and Rules of Interaction

The various institutional settings in which we are interested involve distinctive rules of interaction and produce quite different outcomes. Institutionally minimalist settings involve simple rules of one-to-one 'mutual adjustment' similar to those presupposed in much of complexity analysis. Simple rules of myopic administration can similarly characterise systems of hierarchical coordination, with formal-rational procedures for classifying and processing clients, whether individuals or communities. What rules, however, should characterise the negotiated moral communities with which we have been concerned here, the third of our institutional settings?

Ostrom herself offers an approach to this question. She distinguishes institutional rules that forbid, require or permit – the so-called 'deontic operators' – and argues that these comprehensively span the range of possible institutional rules (Ostrom, 1990: 139–40, 2005: Ch. 5). We can utilise these distinctions in order to clarify the contrasts among our three institutional settings.

Mutual adjustment within institutionally minimalist settings requires operational rules to classify the various individuals who may be encountered and to prescribe what action is then to be taken. These are rules that require and forbid (even if in practice they are couched in softer terms). If an actor is encountered of type A, then the obligatory response is action x; responses y and z are forbidden. Institutional rules of permission have no place here. The same goes for hierarchical direction. The difference is that here the rules are applied just by the myopic administrator; the other actors are just 'cases', and the classification and treatment they receive are in principle no different from the sorting of inanimate objects.

What deontic operators apply in negotiated moral communities? And to whom do they apply?

Ostrom's design principles, to which we have already referred, provide a first step towards answering this question. They involve, first, a series of permissions, extended to all those individuals who are clearly identified as members, but forbidden to all others: entitlements to draw on the common pool, to hold to account those charged with monitoring and enforcement, and to participate in any modification of the rules of interaction. They involve, second, a series of responsibilities – requirements and prohibitions – placed upon these same individuals: to subject themselves to the disciplines and obligations of community membership and to accede to such sanctions as monitoring and enforcement may bring, in the course of protecting the rights of others within the community. Notice that to permit may also entail enabling particular capacities and powers: what Ostrom refers to as the 'constituting' of the actions permitted (Ostrom, 2005: 144–5). In subsequent chapters we shall have much to say in regards to such capacities and enabling.

Institutional minimalism and hierarchical direction presuppose myopia. For the myopic individuals within these settings, the rules of entitlement and obligation are determined exogenously, as are any procedures for monitoring and sanctions. For negotiated moral communities the matter is quite different. Here instead of routinely following a set of rules for their interactions, individuals apply a normative regime. They make judgements of what is appropriate on their part – and that of others – by reference to the nested layers of rules which make up the regime. They frame their own courses of action – and they interpret and monitor the actions of others – by reference to that framework and the goals and values which it embodies. All this is, however, open to regular re-negotiation through a process of community dialogue. This does not mean that the rules of interaction are here any looser or less effective than in the other institutional settings; it does, however, mean that compliance is secured by mobilising individual commitment to the overall purposes of the regime, rather than through instrumental or coercive compliance with whatever operational rules have been laid down for individual interactions.

5.3.2 Negotiating a Moral Community

Consider finally how this works out, not among the long-established hill farmers of Switzerland, the water extraction authorities of California, or the fishermen of Nova Scotia, but rather within the virtual communities of the internet.

Johnson describes the development of the world-wide web (Johnson, 2001: Ch. 4). Its interconnections develop according to a power law: they are 'scale-free'. Instead of these interconnections being random, with the number of connections a given site has following a normal distribution, particular sites emerge as key nodes, with many more connections than expected. This is a simple logic of increasing returns: the more sites a site is connected to, the more attractive it is as a link for new pages, which thereby obtain for themselves a short cut to a wide range of other sites. As Johnson points out, there is no process of adaptation here by reference to any external criterion of evolutionary fitness, nor by reference to any purposeful governance. It is myopic mutual adjustment.

Johnson proceeds, however, to tell the story of Slashdot, a small virtual community which started life as a modest bulletin board but which attracted users from far and wide, unwittingly becoming a hub of their interactions, but with no form of community management. This was a public space but one which was threatened with over-exploitation. In Ostrom's terms, it faced the tragedy of the commons. Johnson describes (Johnson, 2001: 154–62) how, in response to this crisis, a normative regime emerged.

Anyone who has used Slashdot a few times is appointed a monitor and required to rate contributions by other users, using a stock of credit points ('karma') that are progressively disbursed, at which point the period as monitor comes to an end. The peer reviews are appended to the contributions, enabling other readers to ignore the low quality postings. Those users whose contributions are highly rated by monitors earn credit: they are henceforth more likely to be made moderators themselves, and their subsequent contributions begin life with a higher rating than usual (hence the term 'karma'). Those who provide contributions of poor quality are rarely appointed monitors. Quality contributions are thus encouraged and those who provide quality rise to become monitors and leaders. Moreover, what counts as 'quality' can itself be made a matter of deliberation within the community. For example, contributions that attract the greatest variation in peer reviews – and thus give evidence of being controversial – can be privileged over those which receive the highest average grading. That is a matter of collective choice within the community.

This Slashdot community involves many of Ostrom's design principles for a negotiated moral community. Although the community remains open, and there are no clearly defined boundaries to those who may enter Slashdot, the system of peer review using scarce karma has the effect of relegating low quality contributors to the margins, so that they have little scope for over-exploiting the scarce public space. Indeed, as the numbers of contributors increases, and the dangers of over-exploitation become more intense, the quality standards become higher, karma scarcer, and the relegation of poor quality contributions to the periphery more intense. High quality contributors self-organise on the high fitness peaks. Participation in the modification of the operational rules is open to all, but again in proportion to the karma they earn, this karma granting them more substantial moderation roles, and thus the opportunity to ensure that their notions of quality prevail. Finally, while the introduction of the system of karma lifted the burden of regulation from the shoulders of Slashdot's originators, making Slashdot self-policing, they retained the ultimate power to modify the quality algorithms and to oversee the leadership emerging from within the Slashdot community. Thus the moral community of Slashdot was constructed in the shadow of the 'state', the originators.

The deontic operators that Slashdot employs are thus similar to those which we adduced earlier for Ostrom: permissions, entitlements or rights, extended to all those individuals who are clearly identified as members of the normative regime in question, but forbidden to all others; permissions to make use of the public space that Slashdot provides and to share in quality monitoring; and a series of requirements (responsibilities) to respect the quality standards of community membership, and to take a turn in applying such standards. The most obvious variation is that whereas for Ostrom the boundaries of membership must be clearly defined, for Slashdot membership is a matter of degree, calibrated by the amount of karma that a contributor earns.

Finally, let us note that for Slashdot, as for Ostrom, rules of cooperation do not emerge in a vacuum; they involve negotiation with people who have practical interests embedded within existing arrangements and, to be effective, they must be congruent with the specific pattern of threats that are endangering the commons. The explosion in the numbers of users was contemporaneous with 'the rising tsunami of Linus and the Open Source movement' (Johnson, 2001: 153); the first efforts to manage the explosion involved hierarchical direction, until the costs became too great, and the originators of Slashdot were forced to institute a new self-governing regime. The Slashdot regime has in turn become part of the institutional legacy on which subsequent web communities have drawn, in their own practical efforts to govern interaction on the virtual commons (Johnson, 2001: Ch. 4).

5.4   INSTITUTIONAL ARCHITECTURES

This chapter is concerned with the combinatorial ontology, as applied to institutions. That ontology, as first encountered in Chapter 3, involved genes combined in hyperstructures and shaping the fitness characteristics of the phenotype in question. In Chapter 4 it involved technologies combined in hyperstructures for purposes of production.

In the present chapter we have so far considered how to characterise the diversity of institutions, as a series of ideal types. We now consider how empirically they are connected and combined in larger institutional architectures. These architectures involve multiple terrains, multiple institutional processes and multiple tiers, across which social interactions and strategic games may develop, as actors pursue their various purposes (Ostrom, 2005: 56–64).

5.4.1 Multiple Terrains

Modern societies display a multiplicity of institutional terrains, with most actors involved in many of them simultaneously. There are commonly trade-offs between the goals pursued on one terrain and those pursued on another; and there may be scope for cooperation or conflict, not just within individual terrains but across them. Just as important, the outcome of interactions on one terrain may affect the resources which each actor can then bring to the struggle on another; or indeed, whether they can even get access to that other terrain.

These terrains are connected in various fateful ways. As Fligstein (2001: 109) emphasises, 'every society comprises a huge number of fields [what we are calling 'terrains'] connected in a great many ways. A given field may be both dependent on some fields and, at the same time, dominant over others.' How these linkages develop and are sustained, as a coherent and enduring set of relationships – in short, how they are constituted – 'needs to be a constant arena of focus'.

5.4.2 Multiple Processes

On some terrains a variety of institutional settings may be in play and can be variously invoked by the social actors concerned. As Jones and Sergot (1996) point out, this is most obvious in quasi-legal situations, where a given case may potentially fall under a variety of different legal provisions, and where the choice of the appropriate legal basis for dealing with it – what they term the 'state of affairs' – will have fateful consequences, not only for how it is handled, but also very often for the likely outcome, the winners and the losers. This has, for example, been the main battleground on which struggles between the European Union (EU) institutions and national governments have been fought. This has, for example, been the case with the length of the working week, and whether this falls under health and safety legislation and is therefore, under the EU treaties, a matter for majority decision-making rather than unanimity. The choice of the appropriate legal basis can then of course itself be contested.

This sort of ambiguity as to institutional procedure, or the presence of several competing jurisdictions, may also permit so-called venue or forum 'shopping', as actors choose where and how to pursue a given set of goals. Here again, actors differ in their power to make use of such opportunities and the skill and creativity with which they do so. Such forum shopping has been given considerable attention in the international relations literature, where overlapping but fragmented mandates among the various international organisations of the modern era offer plenty of scope for such creativity (Davis, 2006). This work on venue shopping is part of a larger international relations literature concerned with two-level games (Evans et al., 1993). This focuses primarily on the strategies employed by national negotiators in pursuit of international agreements, which then require ratification by domestic constituencies; here we will be just as concerned with the strategies of sub-national and even local actors.

5.4.3   Multiple Tiers

As we saw in our discussion of Ostrom's work, institutions are typically nested within the more fundamental institutions of social, legal and governmental order or governance. These embody higher-order rules, setting the terms on which actors can engage in strategic games across multiple institutional terrains. Ostrom (1990) distinguishes constitutional choice rules, concerned with the overall legal-political architecture of institutions; collective choice rules, defining the institutional setting that is to prevail in the case, for example, of water management; and operational choice rules, governing micro-level interactions (p. 52).

Thus, for example, she examines efforts in various parts of California, during the 1960s and 1970s, to address the over-exploitation of water resources, by negotiating cooperative agreements, aimed at securing sustainable levels of production and some equity in distribution. She draws attention to the role of particular legal and constitutional rules that set the context in which a water agreement could be negotiated and within which that agreement, once reached, could be nested; she points, for example, to the creative use of litigation and the readiness of the courts to endorse the agreements reached by the participants, making them legally enforceable. Some types of legal and constitutional rules may facilitate the process of negotiation, others may impede it: but all will leave their mark on the sort of negotiated framework that emerges. In Scharpf's terms, the negotiation of institutions for collective action here took place 'in the shadow of the State'.

One further element of Ostrom's analysis is particularly relevant here. It may be possible to devise rules of cooperation that are congruent with the specificities of a given local common pool tragedy. However, for these rules to be practically instituted, in place of those already existing, requires negotiation with people who have practical interests within these existing arrangements. This may involve mobilising the support of the higher level institutional powers; it may also involve providing a justificatory narrative by reference to a shared ideological heritage. In short, institutional creativity does not take place on a *tabula rasa*: it involves practical negotiation with actors who have real world interests, embedded within historically specific settings. Any exercise in institutional creativity or transformation – and any analysis of such endeavours – must start from the practical interests of the present.

5.5   CONCLUSION

We seek an account of institutional dynamics that will complement Potts's treatment of economic and technological dynamics. As a first step, this chapter has considered the diversity of institutions and their connection into complex architectures.

As we have seen, Scharpf explores the various institutional settings in which actors may find themselves, the types of composite actors likely to emerge and the various types of games, cooperative and uncooperative, which then play out. Ostrom is likewise interested in the interaction rules and deontics embedded in institutions, but also in the forms of community that these involve. What both of these authors recognise is that institutional rules of interaction have to be understood by reference to the populations of micro-agents that 'carry' them. This was also a central tenet of Dopfer and Potts, in their treatment of the evolutionary dynamics of the economy. This will remain at the centre of our attention when, in the next chapter, we consider the evolution of social institutions.

Scharpf provided us with our starting point in exploring institutional diversity. His concluding chapter examines the implications for the various types of polity that dominate our contemporary world. This is Scharpf's ultimate interest: to research and inform policy, providing policy-makers with better-grounded beliefs about the world in which they operate, enabling them to act more rationally. In many ways, therefore, Scharpf's project is consistent with our own. There are, however, at least three respects in which we go beyond his work.

First, already in his opening chapter Scharpf introduces the notion of connected or two-level games. His example is of governments negotiating, on the one hand, with the trade unions, on the other, with the electorate, over the balance to be struck between unemployment and inflation. Nevertheless, in general he limits himself to the analysis of unconnected games, played on a variety of discrete institutional terrains. In subsequent chapters we consider actors pursuing strategies across several terrains and using their advantage on one to create positional leverage on others.

Second, Scharpf considers how far institutional settings are themselves susceptible to political action and policy intervention. He is particularly interested in the task of leadership which, for him, is to define trade-offs between efficiency and equity and make corresponding policy interventions. He also examines the conditions under which policy interventions are made accountable to lay actors. This is, however, limited to discussion of the various constitutional mechanisms that are in place to secure public scrutiny. In contrast, we are interested in the circumstances under which institutional architectures are shaped by other than the formal political process: whether by social movements from below or powerful private interests from outside. We are interested in the new composite actors that typically emerge within different institutional settings and their interest in maintaining or contesting the institutional status quo. We consider the conditions under which such contestation can be managed and 'civilised', or alternatively may threaten to tear the polity apart.

Third, Scharpf's principal focus is on game-theoretic approaches. Actors are interdependent in the strategies they pursue. This presupposes a world where the actors have already shrunk to a number which can negotiate with each other and the issues for negotiation can be reduced to a manageable agenda. This is why Scharpf is so interested, as we have seen, in identifying the consequences of different institutional settings for the development of composite actors. However, this is not the only sort of analysis of interdependent strategies that is possible. Scharpf himself refers briefly to 'autodynamic coordination', involving positive and negative feedback mechanisms, arising from 'interdependent utility functions' within a mass of individuals (Scharpf, 1997: 53–4). This is, of course, what we are in this study discussing in terms of self-organising systems.[1] What for Scharpf was little more than a footnote, to his own main interest in game-theoretic situations, for us moves centre-stage.

6 Institutional dynamics

6.1 INTRODUCTION

The previous chapter examined the alternative institutional settings that operate on the various social terrains through which life chances, power and advantage are distributed. It considered how these are connected into complex institutional architectures, across which social actors pursue their purposes. These were the elements and connections in our combinatorial ontology of institutions.

The present chapter is concerned with how these combinations evolve: the 'micro-meso-macro' or 'deepen-widen-warp' of institutional change. We draw heavily on the work of Thelen, Pierson and Fligstein. We start, however, with Crouch, who in his study *Capitalist Diversity and Change* (2005) develops an account of entrepreneurs that nicely complements that of Potts, but applied now to institutions.

6.2 INSTITUTIONAL ENTREPRENEURS

In the previous chapter we saw that theorists have tried to make sense of the wide diversity of institutions to be found in human societies. We highlighted in particular the 'mutual adjustment' of markets, 'hierarchical direction' and 'negotiated moral communities'. These are of course ideal types, abstracting from the messiness of the real world by reference to the theoretical debates that are underway. There is, however, always the danger that such ideal types will be too easily equated to empirical reality. If such an equation is made, suggesting that no intermediate cases exist and that there are strong pressures for societies to move towards one or other of these 'poles', this must be demonstrated and not merely assumed.

Crouch challenges any such assumption. His principal target is the 'varieties of capitalism' literature and its contention that advanced Western societies tend to be either 'liberal market economies' or 'coordinated market economies' (Hall and Soskice, 2001). Crouch fully accepts that capitalism exists in different forms, notwithstanding the pressures of globalisation. However, he is critical of those who seek to reduce these forms to just a few and to argue that in any given country, capitalism will 'lock in' to one or other of these types, pulling a wide range of national institutions into a common *Gestalt* (Crouch, 2005: 46, 48–9). Thelen is similarly concerned to incorporate into the 'varieties of capitalism' debate a more dynamic analysis of transformative processes (Streek and Thelen, 2005: Ch. 1; Hall and Thelen, 2008).

Instead of allocating countries to one or other of these theoretical types, Crouch argues that they should be studied in order to establish which theoretical types are to be found empirically combined within them, in what proportions and with what modifications over time (Crouch, 2005: 26). This, he insists, is truer to the use of ideal types by such writers as Weber. It also avoids assuming that each empirical case is bound to converge on one or other of these types. Moreover, instead of taking these types as fixed, they can be used as flexible tools, adapted and applied to new situations, as capitalism in its empirical manifestations changes and develops (p. 31). What Crouch says about the ideal types employed in the 'varieties of capitalism' literature could equally be said about the ideal types employed in the previous chapter.

Crouch goes on to argue that, even within the constraints of social, economic and political institutions, there is scope for institutional innovation. Enterprises and other micro-level actors are by no means reduced to passivity (pp. 19, 32). They are active agents; indeed, such agency transcends national boundaries, as they create cross-national linkages and 'have access to knowledge, links and practices existing outside the national borders' (pp. 42–3).[1] Crouch points to the 'clash and conflict' and 'irritants' that result as institutions abrade against each other, creating openings for such innovation (pp. 4, 58). He similarly cites approvingly Sewell's account of institutional transformations that arise from 'the multiplicity . . . and intersection of structures' (pp. 18–19). He adds, however, that institutional innovation never takes place on a *tabula rasa*. Institutional legacies matter, as does the timing and sequencing involved in the construction of that legacy.

How should this quest for institutional innovation be characterised? Crouch (p. 37) highlights the role of institutional entrepreneurs: 'creative political schemers, looking for chances to change and innovate'. They may conform to the rules of the institutions within which they live their lives; but they may also bend the rules, challenge them, escape or seek to transform them (pp. 19–20), so as the better to achieve their particular aims. They therefore 'cast around for elements of institutions that they could *recombine* in unusual ways at opportune moments in order to produce change' (p. 3, emphasis in original). More specifically, they 'work at the manipulation of governance' – that is, at the meta-processes through which institutional settings are enforced, legitimated, coordinated and steered (p. 22). They create novel combinations which, viewed from the standpoint of the foregoing ideal types are bound to appear as 'hybrids', but which may eventually themselves become the principal theoretical reference points.[2]

As different social actors contest each others' power, and as abrasion takes its toll on institutional arrangements, these arrangements may lose their significance and, for the moment at least, be left just 'lying around' (p. 64). Nevertheless, from this *bricolage* or recycling, future institutional entrepreneurs may be able to assemble new institutional forms, to weave new designs (pp. 87–8). The waste and redundancy left by past institutional changes provide the potential raw material of future transformations. Under conditions of uncertainty and exogenous shock, this can also serve to increase the resilience of socio-economic systems, by providing a rich and diverse range of institutional materials from which responses to those shocks may be built. Also of potential interest are the institutions and modes of governance that are being used by neighbours – or that these same actors are using in other sectors – and which might be borrowed and adapted (pp. 91–3). This is a far cry from the neat function-alist world, where the logic of isomorphism or complementarity squeezes out any institutional form that is not consistent with that logic.

Crouch thus embraces an ontology of combination and recombin-ation similar to that which appeared in the evolutionary economics of Potts (refer back to Figure 4.1) and indeed in Kauffman's evolutionary biology. This is what makes Crouch's approach of particular interest, as we develop a conceptual and methodological approach that combines and integrates the institutionalist and complexity paradigms.[3] He and Potts place at the centre of attention creative actors who, armed with mental models of how the world works, scan the array of available materials with a view to combining them in new ways.[4] In the case of Potts, the 'available materials' are resources for production; the ways of combining them are technologies, selected by reference to the characteristics they enable the entrepreneur to produce. In the case of Crouch, the available materials are institutions; they are combined using systems of governance, selected by reference to the composite actors they bring together and the capacities and knowledge assets they enable them to deploy.

Both Potts and Crouch insist that actors find themselves on terrains that are 'complex'. Modelling the environment in which actors finds themselves must therefore be in sufficiently 'fine detail' to respect this complexity and must not treat actors as though they were located in a topographically uniform 'abstract space' (Crouch, 2005: 101). In the case of Crouch, this involves, first, opposing the argument of the 'varieties of capitalism' writers that there are unavoidable pressures towards institutional congruence; instead, actors may be able to discover a substantial variety of institutional logics readily available, whether in the form of the 'redundant' residues of past institutional configurations, or those operating on adjacent terrains. Second, Crouch points to the complex connections (architectures) which link different institutions and across which actors may pursue multi-level strategies, including the building and dismantling of such connections.

Potts and Crouch recognise that on such complex terrains rationality is bounded, knowledge is incomplete, mental models leave much uncertainty and the search for more desirable combinations involves costly investment. Actors will need some simple algorithms to inform this search, so that they can design new technologies and modes of governance. Both think of the entrepreneur as searching for new institutional or technological combinations using simplified templates. Crouch depicts the institutional entrepreneur as using some simple models of different types of institution, expressed as strings of ones and zeros, and using these as search tools in the task of weaving a new institutional hyperstructure (Box 6.1). Following Holland, Potts portrays the search process in terms of 'schematic preferences', by which the actor conducts an initial 'broad brush' search which is then progressively refined (Box 6.2). There are differences between Potts and Crouch but the similarities are more important.[5]

Potts and Crouch focus their attention on agile entrepreneurs whose novelties are liable to have potential consequences for society at large. They present entrepreneurs as variously seeking to mobilise knowledge assets and systems of governance. More generally, however, we are all in some degree entrepreneurs, albeit the scope for this is itself socially structured. Agile entrepreneurship, we might say, is itself 'scale-free'. We might then also deploy the language and literature of emancipation, liberation and empowerment, to capture entrepreneurship by those in more constricted circumstances, as they seek to re-weave the *bricolage* amidst which they live and to create thereby new opportunities, for themselves and their communities.[6]

6.3   HOW INSTITUTIONS EVOLVE

In Chapter 4 we started with Potts's entrepreneur, combining resources for purposes of production. We then placed this in his larger account, with Dopfer, of the evolutionary dynamics of 'micro-meso-macro'. We have started the present chapter with Crouch's very similar institutional entrepreneurs, combining institutional forms in new structures of governance.

BOX 6.1   CROUCH'S MICRO-ONTOLOGY OF
INSTITUTIONAL DESIGN

Crouch (2005: Ch. 5) starts by recognising that actors deploy their energies across a number of institutional terrains. On a given terrain F the possession and development of particular capacities C will enable actors to pursue their aims; but which of these capacities become available depends on the particular institutional setting I that is in place in that terrain. Crouch's institutional entrepreneurs strive to modify the institutional setting I, so that it delivers the capacities C which will enable them to achieve their particular aims.

In formal terms, therefore, Crouch envisages a system composed of the following elements:

- A variety of terrains (or in his language 'fields of action') $<F>$.
- A set of capacities activated by particular institutional settings $<C:I>$.

For a given terrain or field, Crouch proceeds to summarise the various institutional settings $I_1. \ldots I_i$ in terms of the string of capacities $C_1. \ldots C_j$ that each makes available. Each institutional setting is presented in terms of a string of ones and zeros, which defines the patterns of capacities that are activated or not activated on the terrain F in question. These are of course simplified or abstracted accounts of such institutional settings.

Modes of governance are the mechanisms through which institutions are coordinated and steered. Different modes of governance combine institutions in different ways. It is therefore by acting on these modes of governance that institutional entrepreneurs can re-shape the institutional setting $<I>$ and the capacities $<C:I>$ that are available to them on terrain F.

Crouch now proposes a set of 'elemental choices' or basic dimensions of governance modes, each in the form of a polar alternative: for example, is it concerned with procedural or substantive matters; is communication horizontal or vertical; is it geared to provide benefits for the public or for a private association. These provide him with the dimensions by reference to which different modes of governance can be distinguished. Each mode can be represented as a string of zeros and ones, according to the 'elemental choices' which it embodies.

The institutional entrepreneur aims at modes of governance that will mobilise the capacities he or she requires. For this process of search and design, Crouch assumes that the institutional entrepreneur uses ideal typical simplifications of the sort just described, in order to make sense of the governance practices which lie immediately to hand, but then transforms and recombines these, to produce distinctive and innovative hybrids. The modalities of transformation and re-combination that Crouch identifies (Crouch, 2005: 126–7) are very similar to the modes of institutional innovation that we identify and elaborate in Section 6.3 of this chapter (layering, diffusion, incorporation, and so on).

We now therefore add to Crouch's system as set out above:

- A set of governance arrangements $<G>$, each of which involves a particular combination and organisation of institutional settings I and of the associated combination of capacities $<C:I>$.
- Modes of mutation $<X>$ of the governance arrangements $<G>$.

We now draw on the analysis of institutional change that is offered by the champions of historical institutionalism, and consider in particular how far this also provides us with an evolutionary account.

Historical institutionalism starts with the choice of institutions by political actors (Pierson, 2004). It then examines how these institutions produce concerted patterns of interests, which constrain and shape courses of action and the directions of subsequent institutional development. Institutions typically set up positive feedback loops, locking actors into a limited range of possible institutional innovations and locking out others. This does not necessarily reify institutions and processes of institutional path dependency; on the contrary, it is only to the extent that institutions re-shape and engage the interests of actors that they lead to institutional lock-in. As in complexity science, this path dependency means that context and initial conditions matter. Hence, for example, the difficulties involved in trying to transplant one set of political institutions – liberal democracy is the obvious case – from one setting to another, without regard to the specificity of local conditions.

BOX 6.2   POTTS'S MICRO-ONTOLOGY OF TECHNOLOGY DESIGN

Potts (2000: Ch. 5) models 'the logic of a technology-using and knowledge-creating agent' and the rules of search and experimentation that such agents employ.

The agent uses technologies to combine resources and produce what he or she wants (recall Chapter 4). The agent develops a hyperstructure of such technologies and proceeds to modify this, varying its individual components but also swapping sub-sections of the string with other agents. At each stage the agent assesses the resulting hyperstructure against the ideal technology set which he or she is seeking to set in place.

In formal terms, therefore, Potts envisages a system composed of the following elements:

- A set of resources $<V>$ that are accessible to the agent (drawn from the larger universe of resources $<V^*>$ that are available to the society more generally).
- A set of technologies $<E>$ that are accessible to the agent (drawn from the larger universe of potential technologies that could be constructed through successive re-combinations).

This allows for additional resources $(V^* - V)$ to be drawn by exchange from other agents; and additional technologies to be adopted by combining with them.

The search question is this: given the existing technology set T at the actor's disposal, and the technology set T^* that the actor wants to set in place, what additional technologies T^1 could be combined with T so as to yield an adequate approximation to T^*?

Because the search process is undertaken in a multi-level, hyperstructured space, it is both difficult and costly for the agent to identify and rank all the available technologies. The agent therefore uses 'schematic preferences' to classify and sort technologies on a satisficing basis. Following Holland (1995), these 'schematic preferences' are simplified strings P which, initially at least, contain many elements that are # ('don't care'). By means of this iterative process, the agent can progressively identify those technologies that will, in combination with the existing technologies, enable the agent to create the preferred T^* – or at least a sufficiently good approximation.

Potts then allows the search rules – schematic preferences – themselves to evolve, as the human agent envisages new possible combinations of existing and potential technologies. He allows them to mutate in ways very similar (albeit not identical) to those that we encountered in Chapter 3, in reference to genetic variation (point mutation, inversion and so on – see Mitchell (1996, Ch. 1)).

We now therefore add to Potts's system as set out above:

- A set of schematic preferences $<P>$.
- Modes of mutation $<X>$ of the schematic preferences.

Pierson emphasises, by reference to a wide range of scholarly literature, the simple but important point that the sequence, according to which institutional changes occur, matters. Small events can send political systems onto quite distinct tracks, which are then reinforced through time, and which produce distinct menus of opportunities for later institutional development and innovation (Pierson, 2004: 44–6). This is of course reminiscent of our discussion of the Polya urn in Chapter 1 and of increasing returns in Chapter 2. Institutional developments can also over time produce a changed array of social capacities that are at the disposal of a society (in terms of human capital and skills, for example); this in turn shifts the menu of possibilities that the society can contemplate at subsequent moments of political choice (Pierson, 2004: 74–7).

Along with Pierson, Thelen has been among the most prominent scholars to have offered an account of how institutions evolve. She distinguishes several common modes of institutional change: 'layering' and 'conversion', 'displacement', 'drift' and 'exhaustion' (Thelen, 2003; Streek and Thelen, 2005). Her concern is to transcend the gulf between theories of institutional stasis due to path dependency and lock-in and institutional transformation due to exogenous shocks. She does not entirely demonstrate that these modalities of change amount to a comprehensive lexicon, nor that they are mutually exclusive; nor does she explore systematically their empirical interrelations. Nevertheless, the fruitfulness of her approach is well attested by a variety of empirical applications (Thelen, 2004; Palier and Martin, 2008: Ch. 1; Palier, 2010: 366–71). On this we now seek to build (Table 6.1).[7]

Table 6.1   Institutional evolution

Potts	Room in relation to Potts	Thelen	Pierson	Room in relation to Thelen and Pierson	
New combi-nations	New combi-nations	Displaceent			
Micro	Deepening	Layering	Layering		
Meso	Widening	Conversion	Conversion		
Macro	Warping	Drift	Diffusion	Incorp-	Horizontal
		Exhaustion	Abrasion	oration:	Top-down
					Bottom-up

In her discussion of 'displacement', Thelen is concerned with the way in which institutional actors recombine the various institutional elements that they find in their vicinity, perhaps transposing a particular institutional setting from one terrain to another, or reviving an institutional form half-forgotten in their past, or borrowing (willingly or otherwise) an institutional form from elsewhere. This is of course closely reminiscent of Crouch and his combinatorial ontology. It may well involve extensive re-deployment of institutional legacies: a re-deployment as significant here as was the re-deployment of genetic legacies that we traced in Chapter 3 (Shubin, 2008) and the re-deployment of technological legacies in Chapter 4 (Potts, 2000).

'Layering' involves building some novel institutional arrangement alongside the entrenched and dominant institutional regime: 'parallel or potentially subversive institutional tracks'.[8] Displacement and layering thus involve institutional entrepreneurship, opening up new dimensions of institutional space, albeit just local, initially at least.[9] This is what we have previously referred to as 'micro' creativity and 'deepening'.[10]

As Thelen argues, such creativity establishes a vantage point from which leverage may develop in relation to existing institutions. If these innovations win wider credibility – and develop a sufficient constituency of support – they may be given greater prominence, with those dominant institutions being dismantled or at least marginalised (Pierson, 2004: 137). (This is of course by no means inevitable; the novelty of layering may remain no more than a peripheral add-on; and indeed, with many such novelties forever bubbling up, most will remain merely local or simply die away.) Traditional arrangements are pushed aside; actors defect and switch; old institutions are crowded out and lose their grip, as their domain progressively shrinks (Streek and Thelen, 2005: 19–24). This is the language of 'meso' and 'widening', as an institutional novelty that was initially just local expands its sway and is adopted more generally. It is also the language of population reorganisation and migration, as institutional clienteles and stakeholders move across to new institutional affiliations, which are better suited to their preferences. (See also Pierson (2004: 90–2) on such processes of demographic shift, for example, in regards to the beneficiaries of contributory pension schemes, where the time lags involved may involve several decades.) These are what Potts referred to as the 'carriers' of the institutional rules in question: structural changes in these populations are the concomitant of evolution of those rules (Dopfer and Potts, 2008: Ch. 4).

Such shifts are a common impetus to what Thelen refers to as 'conversion', where institutions are redirected to new goals, functions or purposes. They are not the only possible impetus; as Thelen notes, conversion can also result from exogenous shifts in public policy priorities, for example, or in power relations. Nevertheless, Thelen is most interested in the endogenous shifts that produce conversion (Streek and Thelen, 2005: 16–24). These will often arise as the consequence – intended or otherwise – of the layering and the tensions and ambiguities these novelties generate in relation to mainstream institutions.

How far, finally, do 'macro', 'warp' and the dynamics of co-evolution resonate with these accounts of institutional change? Such resonance is evident, first, in Thelen's account of institutional 'drift' and 'exhaustion' (Streek and Thelen, 2005: 24–6, 29–30). She points out, for example, that wider social change may reduce the range of risks that welfare programmes cover and hence their reach. Even if they suffer no major retrenchment, the landscape on which they operate is progressively warped and, if they merely drift, instead of being actively re-shaped, they become less fit for purpose. Institutions may thus become progressively exhausted and 'worked out'; their path of development may, as we suggested in Chapter 3, 'peter out on a lonely spur'.

Thelen also addresses another of the lines of 'macro' or 'warp' that was central to our earlier discussions. Following Trampusch, she traces the 'perverse dynamic' that characterised German early retirement policies in the aftermath of German unification. On the one hand, early retirement was used extensively to soften the impact of mass redundancies; on the other hand, the costs of this pushed up non-wage labour costs and thus exacerbated unemployment further (Streek and Thelen, 2005: 29–30, 203–228). This is reminiscent of the Red Queen co-evolutionary dynamic we met in Chapter 3.

Pierson, meanwhile, also builds upon Thelen's initial distinction between layering and conversion. What he, however, adds is 'diffusion'. He cites the particular example of professional and organisational standards being disseminated, both nationally and internationally, by epistemic communities which straddle the boundaries between different polities. This can produce 'institutional isomorphism' and convergence in the institutional logic of different polities (Pierson, 2004: 138–9), although as Crouch argues, it is also possible for institutional entrepreneurs in a given country to weave the elements thus diffused into quite distinctive domestic patterns.

This is, however, just a specific (if important) example of a more general process: particular institutions being incorporated into the institutional logic of more powerful actors and institutional systems, so that they become detached from the more immediate concerns and struggles which led to their establishment. Just as common as the 'horizontal' diffusion that Pierson discusses is the 'vertical' incorporation of one institution and its particular provisions into the logic of a superordinate and over-arching institutional regime: as, for example, when central government imposes new and common national standards on regional and local authorities. Institutions can also be captured from below and bent to more local purposes, as, for example, with 'uploading', when actors who have developed new institutional arrangements at the micro-level seek to have them generalised across the society as a whole, as part of the macro-level institutional settlement. This is the 'bottom-up' counterpart to 'top-down' incorporation.[11]

Diffusion, incorporation and uploading involve the sideways, top-down and bottom-up transformation and 'warping' of institutions, through their capture by corresponding groups of actors and institutional logics. They involve new forms of macro-coupling to other institutional orders. More generally, Pierson emphasises like Crouch the abrasion between institutional arenas, disrupting some and re-coupling others (Pierson, 2004: 136). No less than the interconnected species in a Kauffman NK(C) landscape, these institutional terrains form dynamically coupled systems, albeit how the couplings are to be conceptualised and modelled is no mean challenge, as indeed it was in Kauffman's case.

Finally, both Pierson and Thelen are concerned to counter some of the conventional accounts of 'punctuated equilibria' in policy studies, insofar as these rely on exogenous shocks to do the puncturing (Thelen, 2003). Both point to situations where, notwithstanding apparent stasis, long-term and often slow changes in background social and economic conditions (technology, demography, climate, the spread of literacy) in due course meet thresholds or 'tipping points' and trigger bursts of change (Pierson, 2004: Chs 2–3; Streek and Thelen, 2005: Ch. 1). This is consistent with the discussion of endogenously generated punctuated equilibria offered by Bak, as well as with Kauffman's treatment of frozen and melted structures and cascades of novel reconfiguration.

This acknowledges nevertheless that stasis can occur. Countries can get 'locked in' to a particular set of socio-economic institutions, with little or no scope for agile institutional entrepreneurship (Petmesidou and Mossialos, 2006). As we saw in Chapter 4, Potts likewise recognised the 'evolutionary catastrophe' of an 'evolutionarily stable state', where there is 'no structural change, technological change or institutional change'. Here as there, however, this is no more than an ideal type; no society is so closed, so de-coupled from the larger world, that it is immune to its stresses and abrasions; and there are always creative entrepreneurs on the lookout for the new opportunities that may eventually emerge.

6.4   CONCLUSION

Chapter 4 demonstrated the appropriateness of an evolutionary model for understanding the dynamics of economic change. We used the model of 'micro-meso-macro' put forward by Dopfer and Potts but we also showed how this could be seen, more fundamentally, in terms of the processes of 'deepen-widen-warp' that emerged from our treatment of Kauffman and biological evolution. We have now demonstrated, by reference to some of the principal scholarly literature in historical institutionalism, that it is by reference to those same processes that we can understand institutional evolution.[12]

As Potts insists, it is technological and institutional rules that evolve – the rules of the 'connective geometry' of the socio-economic system. To repeat, however, these rules do not exist in abstraction from human actors; they are 'carried' by populations of micro-economic agents and the organisations they form. That is why we are also centrally interested in the structural changes that take place in these populations of carriers and the forms of differentiation and domination, for example, to which they are subjected.

In extending our general evolutionary model to institutional dynamics, there are, however, certain dangers. Potts's account of 'micro-meso-macro' can be read in the tradition of Schumpeter, celebrating the 'swarms of innovation' and technological progress that drive capitalism. Entrepreneurs create novelties and take them to market and, if these are taken up by the wider population, they will be rewarded with profits and the satisfaction of seeing that larger population having their preferences more adequately met. Of course, some elements of this population may embrace the novelty in question sooner than others; the very heterogeneity of any population means that they will be variously willing to pay the asking price. As we saw in Chapter 4, therefore, it is typical for these evolutionary dynamics to create new lines of structural differentiation within populations. Nevertheless, as the asking price falls, any given technological novelty can be expected beyond a certain 'tipping point' to extend in due course to most of the population in question, if only because, as seen in Chapter 2, the benefits of adopting the 'majority choice' become overwhelming.

The situation can be rather different in the case of institutional dynamics. First movers may construct new layers not so much in order to 'take them to market', in the hope that they will be adopted by the wider population, but rather to construct new lines of structural differentiation within that population. Instead of thinking in terms of early and late adoption of some new technology, we must now think of layering and conversion as processes by which first movers re-fashion institutions, so as to incorporate those sub-populations on new and possibly adverse terms. These sub-groups are not so much late adopters as stand-by passengers; they are at the back of the queue in the struggle for positional advantage. It is with this that the next chapter is concerned.

7 The struggle for positional advantage

7.1 INTRODUCTION

This chapter will complete our treatment of institutions, evolving as part of the 'connective geometry' of human societies.

We have used a combinatorial ontology. Complex adaptive systems combine heterogeneous elements into hyperstructures; but a continuous stream of novel re-combinations endlessly reconfigures them. This process of reconfiguration we have conceptualised in terms of 'deepen-widen-warp'. This was the ontological and conceptual framework which we drew from Kauffman's work in Chapter 3; that we applied through Potts to economic dynamics in Chapter 4; and that we have now applied in Chapters 5 and 6 to institutions, in an account that resonates with some of the leading scholarship on institutionalism. It enables us to bring together the economic analysis of Potts and the institutionalist analysis of Ostrom and Scharpf, Crouch and Thelen, Pierson and Fligstein. It also, as promised in Chapter 1, allows us to demonstrate the convergence between institutionalist and complexity perspectives.

The present chapter considers the larger positional dynamics that are thus set in motion and the extent to which they can be 'tuned' by those involved. It both completes and moves beyond the evolutionary model of socio-economic dynamics with which our discussion has so far been concerned.

7.2 THE DRIVE FOR CO-EVOLUTIONARY DYNAMICS

The previous chapter demonstrated the similarity between the accounts of entrepreneurs offered by Potts and by Crouch. Both provide combinatorial ontologies of human creativity: Potts in relation to technological innovation, Crouch in relation to institutional.

The economic agents depicted by Potts deploy their new technologies within specific institutional settings. These include the ways in which enterprises can be organised and the forms of regulation to which they are subject. They also include the relations between enterprises and their customers, suppliers and workforce, which as we have seen may involve adverse – even predatory – incorporation. Crucially they also include the construction of new markets: markets whose standards and regulations are fateful for which technologies gain precedence and whose extent shapes the scope for specialisation and for benefitting from increasing external returns (see also Young, 1928; Kaldor, 1985: Ch. 3). Economic agents are thus likely to be involved in institutional struggles, with a view to enhancing the opportunities for profit that their innovations bring. In short, economic entrepreneurs are typically also institutional entrepreneurs.

Potts here builds on the work of institutional economists. Thus, for example, Coase (1937), Williamson (1975) and North (1990) point out how shared institutions – for example, across the enterprises in a particular industry – can reduce transactions costs among those involved. Nevertheless, Potts argues that in modern economies what is even more important are institutions that build knowledge and competence, enabling enterprises to marshal human capital, scan the best practices of their rivals and build new supply chains (Dopfer and Potts, 2008: para. 3.2.2): institutions that have come to be bracketed under the general heading of 'national innovation systems' (Nelson and Winter, 1982).

Meanwhile, the institutional entrepreneurs depicted by Crouch engage in institutional innovation not as an end in itself, but because different institutional settings activate different sets of capacities. This includes those capacities which they reckon are crucial to the pursuit of their various aims, including not least the mobilising of economic interests and power. Thus, if new institutional configurations deliver a different array of capacities, it is typically because they enable people who lack positional leverage to be incorporated on often adverse terms.[1] If Potts's economic agents are typically also institutional entrepreneurs, Crouch's institutional entrepreneurs are commonly in pursuit of economic interests and power.

This suggests one further conceptual and methodological step. In order to gain and multiply their advantage, agile first movers may often seek to transform and re-tune both technologies and institutions *in a single self-reinforcing process*, so as to capture and exploit a 'first mover' position that confers power and advantage. Such technologies and institutions can be conceived as modifying each other in a process of co-evolution – and one which is directed and nurtured by agile human agents in light of their mental models. This is not blind co-evolution of two species within a common eco-system (something that we examined in Chapter 3), but *co-evolution of two modes of human activity concerted by an agile first mover*.

(Beinhocker (2007: Chs 11–12) offers a similar account of the co-evolution of 'physical' and 'social' technologies, in a 'reciprocal dance' (p. 16).)

To suggest that such co-evolution is possible is not to imply that it will inevitably be set in motion. It is perhaps better to think in terms of a succession of 'abrasions' between the design of technology and of institutional governance: abrasion that opens up opportunities for co-evolution that agile actors may seize, but with no guarantee that any will actually do so, nor that if they do so this will necessarily be the most efficient or the socially optimum path. Moreover, while 'co-evolution' is commonly discussed by reference to the accelerated processes of adaptation and enhanced fitness that it generates, it can also produce defensive adaptation and buffering against change, as those involved reinforce their chosen niches (Odling-Smee et al., 2003). Finally, while our principal focus has been upon the co-evolution of technologies and institutions, even within these two realms further cycles of co-evolution may also of course be set in train: between economic and state institutions, for example, and between firms and their various interlocutors, including labour unions, suppliers and customers.[2]

To repeat, however, this drive for co-evolutionary dynamics is the business of those who seek to be agile first movers, purposeful opportunists wanting to capture and exploit opportunities for positional advantage. Instead of the blind evolutionary dynamics of Darwinian natural selection, we have human agents capable of understanding the dynamics of technological and institutional change and in some degree steering and managing them. The information available may be imperfect and their turbulent world full of uncertainty; nevertheless, they are ready to apply their 'mental models' of that world and to wager their ventures. However, this struggle for positional advantage involves competing interests and competing models of how that world should be shaped. Power and politics thus move centre-stage.

We now flesh this out through the work of Pierson and Fligstein, Kristensen and Zeitlin.

7.3   FIRST MOVER POSITIONAL DYNAMICS

Pierson (2004) gives considerable importance to 'first mover advantage': in other words, to whichever actor first occupies a particular institutional terrain and can thereby set the contours of engagement for competitors. Such occupancy tends to set positive feedback processes in motion, which reinforce the position of the first occupier and define the setting within which losers find themselves. This is not, however, inevitable; to move first can be risky and costly and the occupation of a particular institutional terrain may discourage the first mover from further exploration, opening opportunities for yesterday's losers to recapture the initiative.

Those who have lost out in previous rounds of political and institutional struggle are more likely to be a catalyst for change if, over time, their circumstances have changed and they are now in a stronger position to mount a challenge. Having a strong motive is, however, not enough; what is also needed, if a challenge is to be effective, is that these agents should have the skills, the social networks and the authority necessary to build coalitions for reform. These factors loom large in Ostrom's study also. She seeks to identify the participants involved in institutional innovation; their internal group structure; who initiated action; who paid the costs of entrepreneurial activities; what kind of information they had; what were the risks to which they were exposed; and what broader institutions they used in establishing new rules (Ostrom, 1990: 103). As this last element underlines, however, for Ostrom as for Pierson, this institutional creativity takes place in an institutionally and historically specific context, with new rules being defined by reference to those already in operation, and existing institutional powers being bent to the strategies of the institutional reformers.

Although Pierson attends to yesterday's losers, it may be the victors who undertake institutional innovation and can do so rather effectively, from their position of strength. But why should first movers continue to pursue institutional innovation, if existing arrangements serve their interests well? First, processes of social, economic and technological change can change the context within which institutions operate, even if only over the long term; they can eventually put in question the extent to which yesterday's winners find that their interests are well served (Pierson, 2004: Ch. 3). Second, as institutional realms 'abrade' against each other, they may provide openings for already dominant actors to revitalise and extend their dominance to new terrains and niches. Moreover, as Potts observes, there is forever the haunting fear that others will steal an innovative march; it is this above all that keeps first movers on their mettle.

What is also worth stressing is that the very process of interaction on institutional terrains can lead to the development of new actors, distinct from yesterday's winners or losers, but ready to join the fray. This is, as we have seen, central to the perspectives both of complexity theory, stressing the emergence through self-organisation of new actor agglomerations, and the institutional analysis of such writers as Scharpf, exploring how different institutional settings can create positive or negative conditions for the emergence of various composite and collective actors, including, for example, labour unions and pressure groups (Scharpf, 1997: Ch. 3).

Institutional change can lock in some actors and lock out others but it can also unleash new actors.

Fligstein's analysis of the social architecture – the 'connective geometry' – of markets has many parallels with Pierson's of political institutions (Fligstein, 2001). Thus, for example, he too insists that timing and sequence in institutional development are crucial; we live amid the residues left by historical innovations. With different sectors of the economy having emerged at different historical junctures, the institutional arrangements that prevail in these different sectors attest in part to the relative power of different stakeholders when those industries were being formed (pp. 108, 110). The architecture of markets is also the archaeology of markets.

For Fligstein, the institutional challenge that faces firms, as they seek to take advantage of new technologies, is to establish and maintain stable patterns of social organisation, both internally and externally. However, the distinction between the internal and external institutional environments of the enterprise is not unproblematic. The boundary is regularly re-negotiated, for example, through processes of vertical integration and merger. How to coordinate and manage competing subsidiaries – and their efforts to re-order the institutional architecture of the corporation – may well become the central dilemma of enterprise governance (pp. 70ff.). We add, however, that while an enterprise enjoying incumbent dominance in a given market may seek a stable environment, this is likely to be stability on its own terms; and indeed, it may use a period of turbulence to ensure prolonged instability for its rivals.

The general stability of the larger social and economic environment may, as Fligstein argues, be a common good – in Ostrom's terms, part of the 'commons' – preserved through some implicit or explicit negotiated moral community. As with Ostrom, however, Fligstein insists that such communities need some wider underpinning from the statutory authorities; they are sustained 'in the shadow of the State'. Efforts to invoke and shape the authority of state institutions are therefore integral to the strategies that enterprises pursue. State action is, however, no merely passive reflection or residue of such efforts. Market and state institutions will 'abrade' against each other in unanticipated ways, creating new turbulence and offering opportunities not only for yesterday's winners and losers, but also for new actors and alliances that have meanwhile emerged. One major form of such abrasion can occur under conditions of regionalisation (such as that associated with European integration) and globalisation, with national markets, on the one hand, national political institutions, on the other, incorporated into the logics of superordinate institutional regimes (pp. 94–7, Ch. 9). These will be among the policy concerns that Part 3 of this study addresses.[3]

Finally, Fligstein casts the larger task of the enterprise and indeed the state as the negotiation of shared understandings and commitments, conferring legitimacy on the institutions they establish. Their task is to this extent a cultural project, and one that involves a fundamental struggle for dominance. This framework of shared understandings – what Fligstein refers to as a 'conception of control' – is a legitimating narrative, an expression of unequal power (pp. 35, 68–9). For example, he contrasts the financial conceptions of control that dominated US business in the1980s and the new forms of control based on open standards that have emerged in relation to the new information technologies. Pierson likewise recognises that those pursuing institutional change need not only skills and social networks but also the cultural authority necessary to build a coalition for reform, the ability to articulate a wider political vision for hitherto myopic actors.

More generally, we need to recognise that individual preferences and needs are socially constructed; institutions are always more or less fragile in terms of the legitimacy they command; institutional lock-in is therefore always contingent upon the maintenance of these symbolic universes (Berger and Luckmann, 1967). Challenges to these meaning systems – for example, by Weber's charismatic break-outs from conventional ways of living – put all sorts of path dependency in question. In short, we admit the essentially contested and political nature of these basic parameters of social life. The positive feedback and path dependency, which both complexity analysis and neo-institutionalism depict, presuppose a certain degree of stability of individual perceptions, interests and the institutional architectures of societies. These are, however, the products of social interaction and nothing is incontestable.

7.4   LOCAL PLAYERS IN GLOBAL GAMES

Much of the foregoing discussion has been pitched at a rather abstract and formal level. We now therefore make it more concrete and give it more substance by reference to a specific empirical case: Kristensen and Zeitlin's *Local Players in Global Games* (2005). This is concerned with the development and functioning of APV, a UK-based multinational corporation (MNC) engaged in the manufacture of pumps, valves and related equipment for processing liquid foodstuffs: ice cream and the like. It is a study of technological innovation and institutional entrepreneurship in struggles over the future prosperity – indeed, the survival – of the corporation in question.

The last quarter of the twentieth century saw the international business environment dramatically transformed through mergers and acquisitions, which allowed mega-corporations to emerge and to dominate global commerce. The strategic environment in which these mega-corporations do business has been the subject of an enormous management literature (see, for example, Pettigrew et al., 2003). Among the common themes have been the focus on core competencies and the outsourcing of non-core activities; the building of global value chains, with corporations through their subsidiaries exploiting the comparative advantage offered by different national milieux; and the subordination of the enterprise as a whole to the imperative of building shareholder value: an imperative imposed enterprise-wide by the chief executive and the corporation's headquarters, albeit with subsidiaries having some limited local discretion.

Kristensen and Zeitlin challenge this perspective. Their MNC had been built up through mergers and acquisitions, but the latter were as much the outcome of strategic choices by the subsidiaries as of predatory action by the corporation headquarters. While headquarters may have been interested in acquiring a particular subsidiary, as offering a specific set of local resources and opportunities, the subsidiary was generally no less interested in the access to global opportunities which affiliation to this multinational would afford. Once inside the corporation, these subsidiaries commonly set about bending the corporation as a whole to their local strategic agendas, pursuing these on the new global terrain that incorporation affords and seeking to widen their 'mandate' in relation to other parts of the business (Kristensen and Zeitlin, 2005: Ch. 2).

These local strategic agendas were embedded in the local communities where subsidiaries are based: the local labour markets, skills reservoirs, training facilities, networks of industrial cooperation. Here Kristensen and Zeitlin draw on the 'varieties of capitalism' tradition (Hall and Soskice, 2001). As with Crouch, however, Kristensen and Zeitlin are interested in the way that local actors weave novel institutional patterns. Some subsidiaries found that these local resources were well geared to supporting them, enabling them to exploit the new opportunities that the MNC afforded; they could then bring benefit to those local communities, reinforcing their own dominance. Others discovered the opposite.

The corporation was the terrain on which these different local players pursued their positional struggle. These strategies involved the mobilisation of both local resources and cross-corporation alliances and posited quite different futures and survival strategies for the corporation as a whole. They brought together technological and institutional innovation in what we earlier described as a drive for co-evolutionary dynamics; rival subsidiaries championed different engineering innovations, but these were also struggles over organisational mandates (Kristensen and Zeitlin, 2005: Chs 3–6). They were also struggles over different quality standards: standards which carried consequences for the reputations for quality and reliability which different subsidiaries would enjoy and therefore also for their claims to pole position in the development plans of the corporation as a whole. Some subsidiaries, indeed, were veterans of battles within international standardisation bodies, seeking to ensure that their own technical standards would be adopted over those of others (pp. 49–50). The struggle between different technologies, quality standards and institutional reputations can hardly be disentangled.

As the corporation expanded, the unintended consequence was 'an increasing diversity of evolutionary logics', pushing the corporation 'far from equilibrium' and confronting it with diverse possible futures (p. 17). The corporation might strive, as Fligstein argues, to maintain stability; however, competing 'evolutionary logics' brought turbulence and instability, as different knowledge entrepreneurs within the corporation struggled for dominance. The challenge was how to encourage, manage and channel these entrepreneurial spirits: allowing some to diffuse across the corporation, re-defining its core strategy and competencies and the terms on which its different activities were valued, while avoiding the danger that the corporation would tear itself apart. As stewards of the business, the challenge for headquarters was to combine inventiveness and adaptability with civility, while maintaining a diversity of strengths.

Ice cream manufacturing is not, perhaps, of most obvious interest for the policy sciences. Nevertheless, Kristensen and Zeitlin set this particular case in the larger context of corporate and public governance in the modern world. Thus, for example, they draw attention to new modes of policy-making in the EU, including the Open Method of Coordination (OMC), as a parallel case of local players engaged in global games across a multinational organisation and regularly contesting its governance. Indeed, Zeitlin in a contemporaneous study with Pochet documents those OMC players and games (Zeitlin and Pochet, 2005): on the one hand, national governments and civil society organisations and the communities in which they are embedded; on the other, the 'corporate headquarters' of the OMC in the EU institutions. Here are institutional strategies of credit-claiming and blame avoidance; the struggle for involvement in governance of the OMC process; the encouragement of policy learning and performance improvement but also the recourse to bureaucratic routines in the hope of limiting turbulence.

These then are some of the dilemmas of corporate and public governance in a complex and turbulent world, where agile first movers pursuing positional advantage bring innovation and change but threaten chaotic and destructive macro-dynamics. It is in part with such dilemmas that Part 3 of this study will be concerned.

7.5 CONCLUSION

In the opening section of this chapter, we undertook both to complete and to move beyond the evolutionary model of socio-economic dynamics with which much of our discussion has so far been concerned.

We began our discussion of complex adaptive systems with the work of Kauffman and, more particularly, his model of evolutionary dynamics. This is solidly in the neo-Darwinian tradition, involving micro-novelty, population selection and wider co-evolutionary shifts. We elaborated Kauffman's account into one couched in terms of the deepening, widening and warping of these landscapes. This is what Potts refers to as 'micro-meso-macro': his terminology is more appropriate to his own readership of economists. From the Darwinian legacy Potts removed the biology; we have now added an institutional grounding. *Mutatis mutandis*, this will remain the underlying perspective throughout this study. It is in this sense that our evolutionary model of socio-economic dynamics is now complete. As with any model, of course, there will be a trade-off between simplicity and tractability on the one hand, realism on the other.

Darwinian evolution is blind and without intent. Speciation and co-evolution, involving the ascent of 'perilous paths' to ever-greater fitness, unfold 'behind the backs', so to speak, of the organisms and populations involved. It is not immediately obvious that the evolutionary dynamics of socio-economic change, as captured in 'deepen-widen-warp', are any different. True, the novelties emerge from the creativity of the micro-economic and institutional entrepreneurs to whom Potts and Crouch have introduced us, not from random mutations of the genotype; but once sent forth, along with a myriad of other novelties, the selective disciplines of 'meso' and the abrasions and co-evolution of 'macro' may well appear no less blind, with outcomes that social scientists find it difficult to predict, save in the most stable of times.

Nevertheless, we have also pointed to the scope for agile human agents to reflect and to offer conjectures and anticipations – informed by 'mental models' of the world – as to how these dynamics will play out; and not only to anticipate, indeed, but also to steer and nurture their co-evolution, in a self-reinforcing process of technological and institutional innovation. This is a deliberate effort to reach beyond the myopic and ascend the 'perilous path' of greater fitness in the struggle for socio-economic existence. This is no longer a wholly blind process, albeit there are now a multitude of actors with sight, and the capacity to implement their vision, or at least to make the attempt. It is in this sense that we have moved beyond the evolutionary model of socio-economic dynamics.

As agents extend their monotonic ascents, the perilous paths across their own landscapes, other agents may find that theirs are curtailed or even turned into descents. These are interlocking Surtseys. In this race, positional advantage is always provisional and the agile re-deployment of capacities, competencies and knowledge all-important, as the study by Kristensen and Zeitlin amply illustrates. As they also argue, the competing 'evolutionary logics' which these various agents pursue pose challenges for the civility and governance of the society as a whole. This takes us from evolution to politics and to the questions of public policy with which this book is ultimately concerned.

Nevertheless, we must not under-estimate the variety of ways in which deepen-widen-warp may play out politically and the hard public choices they may involve. Consider, for example, the role of scandals and committees of enquiry in the development of British public policy (Butler and Drakeford, 2005). Here it is not the merit of some novel practice but the demerit of some malpractice that drives larger change. Butler emphasises that the identification of good practice and the design of new policies involves deliberate, tortuous and above all political processes: processes moreover that invoke a particular moral narrative. The entrepreneurs with whom Potts is concerned may produce their inventions and watch to see with what eagerness they are taken up by consumers; they may even engage in 'campaigns of persuasion' to encourage this uptake; in general, however, there is no public process of anguished moral deliberation. With Butler in contrast, more fundamental legitimating values are put in question and re-worked.[4]

For a public policy scandal to develop, it is necessary but far from sufficient that here are administrative failings, carelessness or institutional brutality. Only under specific circumstances does this trigger more general public alarm, sufficient to produce a public enquiry. Thus, for example, a scandal can hardly develop unless it captures the sympathy and imagination of the wider public and the media, evoking alarm at the 'assault . . . upon the collective sense of security . . . [and] danger to collective identity' (p. 227). Equally, a scandal can hardly develop where there is a consensus; there must be 'claim makers', institutional entrepreneurs who already contest the status quo and can develop an alliance for reform. The challenge is to explain – even if we cannot predict – these tectonics of policy change: the pressures, the lines of resistance, the earthquakes that can suddenly and dramatically change the welfare landscape.

Butler offers an essentially dynamic perspective, an ongoing interaction between professional practice, public debate and policy reform. Time and sequencing matter, as a succession of events progressively raises public concern, to a level which can be addressed only by a public enquiry. At

the same time Butler acknowledges periods of stasis and punctuated equilibrium; he asks under what conditions traditional practices persist unques-
tioned or change becomes possible, with 'the development of a momentum
to escape the gravitational pull of the *status quo*, vested interests or the
indifference of the wider public' (p. 2). It is a perspective of welfare tectonics, abrasions and avalanches, with 'landmark scandals' the cairns that
mark these topological shifts.

Butler is concerned with top-down policy change. This defines new
shared understandings; it distributes and withdraws legitimacy; it builds
a coalition for reform; it re-negotiates the moral community. This is institutional re-tuning and wholesale conversion, the adoption of a new moral
and political vantage point by reference to which professional practice will
henceforth evolve. This is not a micro-agent engaged in a step-wise search
for a higher peak on a fitness landscape, in the hope that others may then
follow, making this a 'well-trodden path'. It is, rather, the re-definition of
professional and organisational fitness, moving the whole range of micro-
agents onto a new landscape. Even so, the reformer does not bring change
on a *tabula rasa*; it is existing institutions and the *bricolage* of the past that
must be re-woven, even if scandal and public alarm enlarge the canvas on
which this re-weaving is politically possible.

8 Conceptualising social dynamics

8.1 INTRODUCTION

In this chapter we complete the conceptual discussion of Part 1. As we have seen, this brings together institutionalism and complexity: two literatures whose intellectual antecedents are quite distinct but whose conceptual convergence is rather striking.

There have been three major sources of inspiration on which we have drawn: in physics, evolutionary biology and the social sciences. We began with Newtonian mechanics and its concern with equilibrium and stability. This provided a paradigm of scientific rigour which continues to dominate our thinking: not only in the natural sciences but also, for example, in the mainstream of economics, from where, for better or worse, it casts a wider spell over the social sciences more generally. However, we noticed in Chapter 2 that, from the nineteenth century onwards, engineers and scientists became increasingly aware of systems pushed 'far from equilibrium' by flows of energy and matter, but even so capable of producing distinctive structures and patterns of 'self-organisation'.

Self-organisation in 'far from equilibrium' systems is by no means confined to the domain of physics and chemistry. It pervades the biological world also. This is in part because each living organism is of course subject to the laws of thermodynamics, as it extracts nutrients and physical-chemical energy from its environment, so as to survive and reproduce. However, as we saw in Chapter 3, the Malthusian 'struggle for existence' that Darwin described, while it does not forget the thermodynamics of the living organism, brings centre-stage the population dynamics of selection and adaptation. Within a given population, organisms are likely to have slightly different characteristics; those whose characteristics are best fitted for the particular environment in which they are deployed will reproduce with greatest success. Over successive generations, a population dynamic is thus set in motion, which makes the organisms bearing these characteristics most numerous. Whatever population equilibrium may appear thereby to have been established is, however, always provisional; it may be put in question by the new variations and characteristics that appear in the next generation, especially if the fitness demands imposed by the abiotic and biotic environment have shifted. Thus the system perennially reorganises itself, by reference to the relative fitness of the different variants that successive generations of the population produce, albeit this process may be somewhat 'sticky', with periods of stasis followed by periods of reconfiguration.

Human societies are societies of living organisms. All that has just been said therefore applies to them also. In addition, however, human beings are able to reflect upon the processes of self-organisation that they observe in the natural and social worlds and in some degree to steer and manage them, depending on the technologies and institutional means of cooperation that they are able to deploy. The struggle for existence now therefore centres on this deployment, as we saw in Chapters 4–7. It starts with the hunter and gatherer imitating nature by conjuring with fire; it encompasses Darwin's horticulturalist and pigeon breeder, selecting from among the variants that each new generation produces those that are most suitable for human purposes, including being commercially profitable; it continues with entrepreneurs selecting those technologies and institutional forms which seem likely to bring them social, economic and political advantage.

It is not just that human creativity breeds technological and institutional novelty. More than this, humans nurture these variations and their co-evolutions and reach out to re-shape the terrain on which they will variously prosper. However, with whole swarms of innovation to hand, and a multitude of agile entrepreneurs, there is an endless struggle for positional advantage. It is this struggle that drives change and self-organisation in social systems, just as the struggle for fitness does in evolutionary biological systems.[1] This may push the socio-economic system 'far from equilibrium' and into a war among these agents; or it may end with the policy-maker seeking to civilise this struggle among competing evolutionary logics and choosing which form of self-organisation should prevail. Institutions, power and politics move centre-stage, even if the thermodynamics and evolutionary biology of human beings as living organisms are not forgotten.

This is the conceptual framework for social dynamics that we propose, the paradigm that will guide our methodological and empirical strategy. Part 2 will be concerned with identifying appropriate methods and models. As we shall see, however, the level of complexity implied by our overall account of human societies, in terms of a struggle for positional advantage, in general defies formal modelling. Even processes of biological evolution can be captured by formal models only if we are ready to limit our viewpoint to one aspect of the dynamic, while holding the others fixed. Only in relation to physical processes is the scope for formal modelling well established, although even here there are limitations. Accordingly, we will need to be rather eclectic in our approach, drawing insights from biological and physical model-making wherever this can be done appropriately, but always aware of the perils of applying such insights to human societies and their dynamics.

Before however proceeding to consideration of models and methods, we conclude Part 1 by taking stock of our conceptual framework and its relationship to wider theoretical debates.

8.2 AGILE AGENTS IN 'FAR FROM EQUILIBRIUM' SYSTEMS

We have developed an account of agile entrepreneurs: first movers who strive for positional advantage, pushing social systems 'far from equilibrium' and attempting to shape their 'self-organisation'. They struggle to survive in a world rendered turbulent by these strivings; but a turbulence which also brings new openings for their enterprise. This enterprise involves searching for new combinations of technologies and institutions: a search that can span multiple niches, drawing lessons from afar and tapping into the residues of the past. It also involves re-tuning the dynamics of social and economic change, so as to secure self-reinforcing positional advantage.[2]

This is a far cry from the simple cellular automaton that figured in the introduction to complexity science we offered in Chapter 2. First, our agile agents have more highly developed cognitive capacities and search strategies. Nevertheless, like those simple automata they rely heavily on the application of 'if/then' algorithms, allowing most situations to be assessed by reference to standard templates and routine responses. Loasby (1999: Chs 3, 8) locates this within the exigencies of human evolution. Survival required that the brain should be able quickly to recognise predators and prey, not that it should make careful comparisons of the costs and benefits of different strategies. Such cognitive 'short cuts' may not be entirely sufficient, save in times of stability, but in times of turbulence their use is imperative, precisely so as to allow maximum attention to be brought to the challenge of the new.

Second, these agents draw on shared knowledge of the specific connections that seem to have worked in particular environments and that can be given expression in the 'if/then' algorithms just mentioned. Loasby emphasises that this knowledge is dispersed or 'distributed', being applied within particular local environments. Just as Kauffman gives us an account of a species spreading itself across a landscape and, through its various mutations, exploring the landscape's nooks and crannies, Loasby pictures an economy as a dispersed population of enterprises, applying a shared stock of knowledge to local niches, but then enriching the stock and their capacity to exploit it (Loasby, 1999: 141–2). It is institutions and culture that carry this knowledge (Douglas, 1986; Bowker and Star, 2002). There is, therefore, no need for each actor to assess each situation by reference to the full range of possible behaviours (an immensely costly activity in terms of the energy and time involved); instead, they can draw selectively from a shared inventory of templates and apply them to specific local niches. This is a second cognitive short cut. Nevertheless, only in highly routinised situations do social interactions proceed in entirely 'taken for granted' ways. More generally, there are a variety of rules available, a variety of definitions of the social situation. In some degree at least, there is scope for negotiation or contest over the rules that should apply or 'count' in the local here and now.[3]

Third, these agents deal with a turbulent world where knowledge is limited, particularly in regards to future possibilities. Nevertheless, they have the capacity to anticipate the larger consequences that their innovations may set in motion. They bring with them more or less well-articulated mental models, embodying conjectures as to how this world will unfold under conditions of uncertainty. This is a third cognitive short cut. It is on the basis of these mental models that agile actors make their combinatorial choices and invest, hoping for virtuous spirals of first mover advantage. These choices are, however, quite different from those at the centre of orthodox economics: 'The neoclassical framework is geared to study choices in terms of exchange relations in a timeless environment. The evolutionary framework is geared to study choices in terms of combinatorial relations in a turbulent environment' (Potts, 2000: 145).

We pause to consider how this relates to larger debates about social action. There are plenty of theoretical perspectives in social science which leave socially meaningful individual action merely epiphenomenal. Individuals are seen as simply adjusting, in some theoretically rather uninteresting way, to the changing social structures and circumstances in which they find themselves. In contrast, an action frame of reference brings individual definitions of the situation centre-stage; as also therefore the contestation of such definitions, the strategies of action they inform and the social interactions – cooperative, competitive, conflictual – which ensue. Social systems here appear as the emergent outcome – to some extent unanticipated – of social interactions among a myriad individuals (Dawe, 1970).

We take an action frame of reference as indispensable to social scientific enquiry and explanation; it is within this that we situate our account of agile actors. Nevertheless, we also seek to understand the social systems that emerge from their interactions. These provide the 'connective geometry' within which subsequent interactions are then possible; and indeed, it is with the strategic re-weaving of that geometry that those interactions will be centrally concerned. Nevertheless, this geometry is not wholly plastic. Sub-systems are dynamically coupled, producing dynamics that range from stable states to Red Queens. It is these dynamics that we seek to understand, even while retaining an action frame of reference.

Much has been written in recent years about the merits and limitations of rational choice and rational action theory in sociology, political science and economics (Coleman, 1990; Goldthorpe, 2000: Ch. 3; Hedström, 2005). Our own approach is more nuanced. Following what has been said above, we see much social action as involving pattern recognition and responses that Weber (1949) would have described not so much as rational but as 'habitual', made by reference to an inventory of templates and 'rules of thumb'. We further recognise that such templates are encoded within social institutions, as much as within the cognition of individual actors. Here, therefore, are two economies in the cognitive load placed upon individual social actors. On the one hand, much of the interaction in which they are involved requires no more than simple if/then pattern matching; on the other, the patterns in question can be readily 'downloaded' from the stock of semantic information that social institutions carry and make available.

It does not follow that all action and interaction is habitual. Faced with novel situations, uncertainty and turbulence, human actors must deploy mental models as to how the world will unfold; the more so, when they are faced with fellow actors who are also trying to 're-tune' that world. This goes beyond rational action theory as normally articulated. There the social actor is confronted with a given menu of options carrying particular costs, benefits and consequences; in Potts's words, this confronts the actor with 'choices in terms of exchange relations in a timeless environment'. We, however, have highlighted the agile first mover, who rather than taking that menu as given, actively re-shapes the rules of the institutional – and indeed the technological – landscape on which social interactions play out, precisely so as to re-shape the options it offers (Dopfer and Potts, 2008: para. 3.2.1). This is what Potts, again, referred to as 'choices in terms of combinatorial relations in a turbulent environment'.[4]

Habitual action involves the actor recognising a pattern and making a standard response. Agile action involves the actor re-working the pattern, according to the combinatorial logic we summarised in Figure 4.1, and having regard to conjectures as to how the world is likely to unfold. Between these two forms of action there is a dual connection. First, as we have seen, the cognitive economy in the former leaves maximum energy for the latter. Second, however, we must recognise that empirically, which matters are handled in which way is itself fluid. It is when actors detect anomalous patterns, including, for example, those that fall outside certain critical thresholds, that this alerts them to the need to make an agile response. These are typically situations that offer opportunities or present threats of major strategic significance (including for example the public scandals discussed by Butler and Drakeford (2005)). In short, what the if/then rules in this case prescribe is that the matter be removed from the if/then realm of the habitual. This is therefore a fluid agenda and one which will vary greatly between actors, depending on their interests and the agility, resources and positional leverage of which they dispose (for a somewhat parallel discussion, see Nelson and Winter, 1982: Ch. 5).

Of course, we might decide to re-define rational action, so as to encompass this wider range of subjectively meaningful actions (Hedström, 2005: 62). It is after all 'rational' to be agile and to re-shape the menu whenever possible, so as to make it more attractive (and irrational to ignore such possibilities, merely adjusting to whatever menu results from the contests of others). It is also 'rational' to adopt wherever possible simple if/then rules of habit, so as to reduce the energy required by careful calculation and to benefit from the ease of the 'well-trodden path'. Goldthorpe, for example, offers a discussion of the evolution of human cognitive architecture similar to that which we have discussed in relation to Loasby, with its 'simple, fast and frugal heuristics'; this, however, he continues to regard as being on a continuum with other forms of rationality (Goldthorpe, 2007a: 180–1). Gilbert goes even further, seeing rational action as action according to any 'reasonable set of rules', as distinct from 'acting randomly or irrationally' (Gilbert, 2008: para. 1.3.5). Nevertheless, whatever terms are used, we must recognise this connected logic of habitual and agile action in an uncertain and turbulent world, rather than just the rational assessment of the benefits and costs offered in a static world.[5]

Finally, it is evident that our understanding and ontology of social actors must go hand in hand with our understanding of the social world they inhabit. We may, on the one hand, view that world as entirely 'emergent' from the individual actions of those involved. This is the perspective on the social world with which the mainstream of complexity science has so far endowed us, as we saw in Chapter 2: unable to acknowledge the pre-existing normative and institutional structures that confront and dominate our lives, lending authority to the choices we make. We may, alternatively, see the social world as a fixed context and menu of choices to which the individual actor must simply respond, making his or her calculations of individual benefit, however defined. Against both of these, however, we understand 'agile actors' by reference to a complex, turbulent and uncertain world, but a world which they also and unavoidably shape, through the processes of deepen-widen-warp traced in the preceding chapters. Here the world is no fixed context of *ceteris paribus*; instead, agile actors and their world form a dynamically coupled system, with path dependencies of mutual interdependence. This perspective is consistent with longer-standing analytical traditions that use an action frame of reference, including Weber's *Verstehendesoziologie* (Weber, 1949), Berger and Luckmann's social constructionism (Berger and Luckmann, 1967) and even indeed Marx's account of *Homo faber* (Avineri, 1968: Ch. 3).

8.3 EVOLUTIONARY MODELS OF SOCIAL DYNAMICS

8.3.1 From Biology to Social Dynamics

In developing our conceptual framework for social dynamics, we have rested heavily on evolutionary models. The starting point was Kauffman's NK and NK(C) models of adaptive walks on fitness landscapes. From there we began to consider how a model of evolution might be applied to the dynamics of human societies. Drawing on Odling-Smee et al. (2003), we argued for seeing the organism and the species both as engineer, shaping the physical environment, and as neighbour, interacting with other species in shared eco-systems. We set about pursuing this same dual focus in the case of human societies: human beings in relation to technology and in relation to the institutions of social interaction.

It was with Potts (2000) that we took the first step in our own 'adaptive walk' through conceptual and methodological space, by abandoning the biology. Instead of genetic mutation we have human creativity, generating novelty in the 'connective geometry' of the economic system and assessing its potential by reference to mental models and expectations as to how those novelties will play out. Potts's subsequent work with Dopfer (Dopfer and Potts, 2008) completed the evolutionary picture in terms of 'micro-meso-macro'. This will remain a regular point of reference in our discussion, as will our own preferred language of 'deepen-widen-warp'.

If, however, Potts left us with an evolutionary perspective 'without the biology', it was also in large measure without the institutions either.[6] To include institutions in our account of evolutionary dynamics has therefore been the second step in our 'adaptive walk'. We have drawn extensively on the sociological and political science literature, where we have found a remarkable convergence with the combinatorial ontology with which Potts and Kauffman endowed us. Here moreover we find pertinent and insightful application of an evolutionary metaphor, not only by Thelen but also by Pierson, for example, who notices how actors may 'establish new ecological niches' and in doing so 'activate previously dormant possibilities' (Pierson, 2004: 56, 73, 136; see also North, 1990: 73–4). We have, however, noted that rather than any fitness criteria for institutional evolution being defined by the biotic and abiotic environment, they are instead constructed through the governance systems that are in place, and thus through the political process. We thus ended up with an account of institutional dynamics which centres on recombination and novelty; path dependent walks on co-evolving and mutually abrading landscapes; and governance struggles over the boundaries and content of the political.

As the third step in our adaptive walk, instead of seeing institutional and technological evolution as merely having close parallels, we have argued for seeing them as brought together in a single self-reinforcing process: a sort of co-evolution through which agile entrepreneurs re-tune both, so as to capture and exploit first mover advantage. Not that this will necessarily prove fruitful: entrepreneurship may lead merely to defensive adaptation or to a cul-de-sac, a lonely spur on the evolutionary landscape. It may alternatively be overtaken by more successful entrepreneurship on the part of rivals. Even where entrepreneurship does bear fruit, this is contingent and temporary, for this is an adaptive walk along a perilous path.

Finally, we recognise policy-makers also as aiming to shape the institutional and technological landscape, modifying the 'system parameters' and the 'connective geometry'. Like other actors, public policy-makers live in a complex and opaque world; they search and experiment using 'schematic preferences' and 'world models'; they develop conjectures as to how social dynamics will unfold under conditions of uncertainty. Dopfer and Potts, Scharpf and Ostrom, Pierson and Fligstein help us in understanding their situation; in the course of this study we build on their insights.

8.3.2   The Struggle for Existence

We now summarise this evolutionary framework in more formal and abstract terms.

We started with the combinatorial ontology of neo-Darwinian evolution. Populations of organisms, as they reproduced, generated a variety of new combinations in genotypic space. These involved, on the one hand, changes in individual genes (alleles), on the other, changes in their connections: what in Chapter 3 we referred to as 'deepening'. Potts adopted the same ontology, applied to 'elements' organised as technologies for purposes of production. These could be modified by varying the elements or by connecting them into larger hyperstructures. A similar ontology was also evident in Crouch (2005), albeit in his case the elements are institutions, while the hyperstructures are systems of governance.

We sought in Figure 4.1 to capture diagrammatically the essential and generic elements of this combinatorial ontology. Figure 8.1 provides an extended version of the story. System N can be developed into System P or System Q, depending on the additional new element d or e with which it is combined. System Q can similarly develop into System R or System S. These elaborations allow us to depict three additional themes of our evolutionary framework.

First, whereas a multitude of variations may appear, only a small number are adopted and retained by the larger population. This is Darwin's process of natural selection; Dopfer and Potts's account of 'meso'; what in Chapter 3 we referred to as 'widening'. The corollary is extinction of some of the combinations dominant in the existing population. In our diagram, System N produces two lines of descendants, but that associated with P fails to survive to a further generation of descendants, alongside R and S.

Second, Darwin and his successors speak of the mutual adaptation of species and their co-evolution. In Chapter 3 we referred to the consequent 'warping' of landscapes. Dopfer and Potts point to processes of 'macro', as mesos abrade against the wider world and co-evolve with each other. Pierson, Fligstein and Thelen offer complementary accounts of institutional evolution. Here we find Red Queen dynamics, evolutionarily stable states and punctuated equilibria.

We may think of each species as developing within its own version of Figure 8.1. These different landscapes interlock and warp each other, with consequences for the selective disciplines that operate on each. The same goes for sets of technologies and institutions. We may not be able to depict these interactions without making the diagram hopelessly complicated; nevertheless, we must bear in mind that the selective disciplines which extinguished the descendants of System P will themselves have been defined in part by these warping or buckling effects of other evolutions. These effects can in principle take place on any scale, on the one hand depressing a wide swathe of the landscape, on the other being more 'fine grained', twisting adjacent sub-regions in quite different directions.

There is a third elaboration of our diagram that captures these co-evolutionary dynamics in a different but complementary manner. Eco-systems evolve as well as species. As we saw in Chapter 3, eco-systems and food webs can be very complex, incorporating ancient structures developed early in the evolutionary process. Modification of the connections within an eco-system – for example, the loss of one species from such a food web – can produce dramatic cascades of far-reaching change.

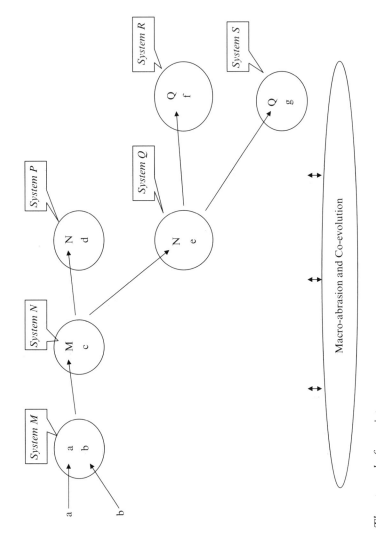

Figure 8.1   The struggle for existence

Here again therefore we have a combinatorial ontology with strong path dependencies, dependent on the order in which species are introduced. Figure 8.1 can be applied here also.

Indeed, we may then think of a species as moving at the interface between these two landscapes or surfaces: genotypic endowment on the one hand, eco-environment on the other. It rearranges ('deepens' and 'widens') each landscape in turn, so as to secure on one landscape a new vantage point from which to rearrange the other. It is by this alternation of adaptive walks across the two landscapes that the species in question engages in the struggle for existence, braiding these two legacies into a 'perilous path' of fitness ascent. The same goes for socio-economic evolution across the interlocking surfaces of technology and institutions, as analysed by Potts and Crouch, Pierson and Thelen and others.[7]

There is of course contingency in all of this: which elements are added in which order; what sorts of new connection are made when, as yesterday's systems are incorporated as sub-systems into today's more complex hyperstructures; what co-evolutions are set in motion by the succession of abrasions against the larger eco-system and how these in turn modify and constrain the terms on which the race for positional advantage is henceforth waged. The hyperstructures of Figure 8.1 that exist at any particular moment encode this contingency and path dependency. To disentangle and understand this messy history of successive reconnections and contingencies is the central task of dynamic analysis.

What further elaborations we allow to our diagram and its representation of evolutionary combinatorial processes will depend on whether we are applying it to socio-economics, to biology or to some other field. Thus, for example, in the case of socio-economic dynamics, there would seem in general much more scope for re-combining elements and systems hitherto remote from each other than in the case of biological evolution. In Chapter 3 we noted the role of lateral gene transfer, when in remote times genetic material was 'borrowed' from bacteria and incorporated into the make-up of our own distant ancestors. This sort of borrowing in social systems is emphasised by Crouch, for example, with national policy-makers adopting institutional models from elsewhere. Depending on the context, there may likewise be more or less scope for internal 're-wiring' of existing sub-systems, not just their incorporation into new and larger hyperstructures; and the replication of sub-systems across a range of other functions. Sub-systems may have back-ups and inbuilt redundancy, to provide resilience in case of attack or enable ready adaptation if new opportunities arise. Such extensions will appear in subsequent discussion, depending on the context, but for the moment we leave them unexplored.

This is the model of complex adaptive systems with which we are now endowed and that we shall variously seek to deploy in subsequent chapters.

8.3.3   The Evolution of Ideas

For Darwin, the evolutionary dynamic unfolds behind the backs, so to speak, of the organisms involved. Nevertheless, even for Darwin, this is only in part the case, because one group of organisms – human beings – are able to reflect and learn, with a view to undertaking artificial selection. They not only select from among the variations of pigeons or plants that occur in each new generation; they also encourage such variations by appropriate hybridisation and then protect the offspring from the predations of their natural enemies.[8]

As we have seen, Potts and Crouch depict the entrepreneur in similar terms, in relation to technological and institutional variations. Indeed, the entrepreneur is commonly concerned to cultivate both, in a single self-reinforcing process. Nor are these efforts limited to the workplace, so to speak; as North and Fligstein argue, the entrepreneur seeks to construct an external environment, in terms of markets, regulatory systems and the communities in which these particular variations are likely to thrive. Beyond this, the entrepreneur is on the lookout for further opportunities for beneficial macro-abrasion between these 'mesos' and others.

In looking for these opportunities, the entrepreneur will have to make conjectures as to the larger but uncertain world in which the viability of these variations will be tested. For Potts and for Crouch, this involves applying various mental models for envisaging how particular new combinations of technologies and institutions are likely to fare. These mental models are themselves not fixed however: Potts at least allows them to mutate and evolve, at the cognitive level.[9] Beinhocker (2007: Ch. 15) offers a similar account of the evolution of business plans; Kingdon (1984: Ch. 6) of the evolution of public policy proposals.

This we might describe as a process of ideational evolution within the epistemic community of entrepreneurs. Like any evolutionary process it involves struggle and destruction; indeed, involving as it does human interaction, the struggle is for positional advantage. This is creativity as a collective cultural process. This reinforces Potts's commitment to evolutionary theory 'without the biology' and with human creativity central. In his most recent work, he goes further, exploring the interactions between the economic and cultural systems: 'Schumpeter meets [Raymond] Williams' (Potts, 2008b: 5). Nevertheless, ideational evolution, leading to the growth of knowledge, has been the concern of a wider scholarship. As well as the cultural evolution of Williams (1961), this includes the hermeneutics of Gadamer (Bleicher, 1980: see especially Ch. 5; Gadamer, 1980); the philosophy of history of Collingwood (1939, 1942); and the accounts of the development of scientific knowledge offered by Kuhn (1970) and Toulmin (1972: especially Ch. 5).[10] It is by reference to this humanistic tradition that ideational evolution is best understood, rather than, for example, the reifications of 'memes' (Dawkins, 1976) and other applications of evolutionary theory to human affairs that remain subservient to the biological legacy.

8.4   FIRST MOVER DYNAMICS

Alongside 'far from equilibrium' systems and evolutionary models, a further conceptual focus of preceding chapters has been first mover dynamics. Before going any further, several different elements in this notion can be distinguished. There is, first, the idea we encountered in Chapter 2, that the 'early bird catches the worm'; once a particular technology or set of institutional rules is established, and attracts a certain proportion of the relevant population, it is likely to prove irresistible to the rest of that population. We noted that where there are several early birds – VHS and Betamex, for example – there can be no presumption that the most efficient will win. We saw that sub-populations may sometimes find it expedient to adopt a different technology precisely in order to differentiate themselves. We also recognised that to move first may involve risks; the bird that is risk-averse may prefer to move second, even if by that stage the best worms have gone.

There is then the second idea that the advantage gained yesterday translates into better chances today, on this or on other terrains. The bird that caught the juiciest worm yesterday is strongest in the battle today, for worms but also for mates. When we move from the world of birds to that of socio-economic relations, this advantage takes two forms. First, the outcome of yesterday's struggle leaves the spoils with the victor, resources which may well tip the balance today. This is the so-called 'Matthew effect': to him that has, more is given, while from him that has not, even what he has is taken away. Second, however, yesterday's victory may not only confer extra resources for today's struggle, it may also confer power to choose the weapons, to shape the terrain on which the struggle unfolds and the rules that must be followed. In short it may confer positional leverage.

On terrains which are fixed and where the weapons and rules are given, this may be of little significance. On complex and turbulent terrains where the agile have every opportunity to re-make the weapons and rules, positional leverage may be everything. It allows actors to block developments they oppose; to keep others guessing as to what they will do next; to build resilience and maintain freedom of manoeuvre; to offload uncertainty onto others and to destabilise them so that they cannot mount a challenge (Marris, 1996). In short, the struggle for positional leverage seeks to occupy the future: come what may, tomorrow is likely to turn out well for the protagonists in question, allowing them to weave their own perilous paths, rather than being obliged to move to the rhythms of others. This is why, as Keynes for example observes, the accumulation of wealth is often not so much for eventual consumption, it is for some indefinitely distant date, to ensure a place in the sun, whatever the future disposition of the world (Tily, 2007: 142).[11]

It is turbulent situations such as these that have been prominent in the preceding chapters. First mover dynamics involve positional competition and this commonly spills across multiple terrains, certainly when we are dealing with human societies. It is not just that protagonists extend their positional struggle across the institutional terrains that their society makes available; they commonly go further, seeking to modify the rules of interaction within and between terrains, revising the institutional architecture and the larger socio-political 'settlement' within the society as a whole.

This does not preclude long-term institutional arrangements for cooperation. We recall Potts's discussion of the emergence of composite economic actors and the building of appropriate organisational and governance structures; also Ostrom's concern with negotiated moral communities and Kristensen and Zeitlin's hopes for corporate civility. Cooperation and shared endeavour are however always contingent, in the ever-renewed struggle for positional advantage. They mobilise capacities and build obligations but on terms that themselves express that struggle. Cooperation, domination and adverse incorporation are hardly distinguishable empirically.

Various other literatures reinforce this account of positional struggle and will be points of reference in later chapters. Hirsch (1977) provides a simple but influential account of positional goods and the 'positional economy'. The distribution of its fruits – unlike those of the 'material economy' – is a zero-sum game; in some degree at least, educational credentials may have this character. Hirsch sought clear principles – not just in theoretical terms but as a matter of practical politics – as the distributional basis for such positional goods and to avoid an ever-intensifying but self-defeating competition.[12]

Consistent with Hirsch's approach, Goldthorpe published a series of papers from the mid-1970s, concerned with the international political economy of western industrial societies, after the post-war decades of economic expansion. This was a period in which faltering growth confronted policy-makers with a zero-sum distributional game, to an extent which until then had been avoidable (Goldthorpe, 1974, 1978, 1984, 1985). These papers set social politics in the context of the welfare 'settlements' of the post-war period: settlements which now came under renewed strain, as organised labour and capital each sought to escape the zero-sum game by revising the settlement. These strategies of institutional contestation did not remain within the realm of welfare policy narrowly conceived; they were liable to range across a variety of socio-economic terrains: from education to the labour market, to the social security system and the housing market. Advantage gained on one terrain shifted the balance of forces available to contest another, outflanking established institutional arrangements and forging new opportunities for leverage.

Positional struggle and advantage are also recognised in a third literature, albeit in a rather different vein, that of game theory. There are a variety of sequential games, with multiple rounds, and correspondingly complex possibilities. A Stackelberg game is, however, heuristically helpful because of its simplicity, being limited to a single round; one player goes first and others have then to accommodate themselves as best they can, on the terrain that the first mover has already occupied (Stackelberg, 1952; Tirole, 1988: para. 8.2). Stackelberg himself applied this to industries with a dominant firm; subsidiary players undertake 'satisficing' behaviour by reference to whatever the first mover has done. Stackelberg depicts a nested structure of positional advantage within the resulting market: 'The oligopolists of the first category rule the roost and they fight for the most favourable positions in the market. The oligopolists of the second category must adjust their position to that of the stronger competitors, but they compete with one another for the crumbs left by the latter. [Similarly], those of the third category take their cue from the first and second categories and help to dominate the next categories below them . . .' (Stackelberg, 1952: 221). As Stackelberg notes, such a market enjoys greater stability than simple oligopoly because there are clear distinctions in terms of size and therefore power. Similar pecking orders are common among communities of predators.[13]

We may thus see first movers as striving for positional advantage; and, to this end, pursuing strategies of deepen-widen-warp, as far as the fitness landscapes they inhabit are concerned. There are, however, many would-be first movers in play, all engaged in the co-evolutionary 'arms race' to which Kauffman and Maynard Smith draw attention; all tending to modify the parameters of the fitness landscapes which their neighbours inhabit, for better or worse; all contesting the positional advantage and leverage that others seek to exercise. What each must at all costs avoid – in face of the countervailing efforts of other first movers – is that their 'perilous path', instead of offering ascent through a succession of new saddles, instead subsides, becomes fragmented by deep intervening valleys, or loses itself in a *cul-de-sac*. The moment of opportunity is however only brief. Thus as Bak points out, while co-evolutionary avalanches can enable a whole succession of mutations 'to take place at a rapid pace, [so that] . . . big jumps between . . . highly fit states are effectuated by cumulative small jumps', this can 'exist only in the temporary environment of a burst' (Bak and Paczuski, 1996: 8).

What Darwin (1859: 136) described as a 'race for life' is therefore also a race against time; a race to take advantage of a brief window of opportunity, and if possible to hold it open a little longer, before succumbing to the rhythms of others. It is this that reinforces the intensity and fatefulness of the race in which first movers are thus engaged. Yet, of course, such races are neither ubiquitous nor inevitable. Protagonists may get locked in a stable state, an ESS, which none has the incentive and capacity to leave, whether this is more a matter of collusive stasis or enforced order. Nevertheless, as new opportunities appear, one protagonist or another is liable to wager some fresh adventure and the race will be renewed.

8.5   CONCLUSION

As Darwin observes, 'we behold the face of nature bright with gladness' and its 'superabundance of food'; but we too easily overlook the concomitant destruction of life entailed by the incessant 'struggle for existence' (Darwin, 1859: 50). The same goes for the forms of self-organisation that emerge in human affairs, variously accommodating the interests of different social groups and structuring the race for positional advantage. If below the surface of nature's superabundance it is necessary to discern the struggle and destruction this entails, it is also necessary, below the order and regularities of social life, to discern the exercise of power and positional advantage by which these regularities are reproduced. If this is order, it is so because some social actors have succeeded in negotiating or imposing that order on others, shaping the terms on which, for example, the economy 'self-organises', or different communities are empowered. This is, however, always provisional and contingent, in face of the ever-renewed struggle for positional advantage and control (Dawe, 1970).

Darwin's gardener or pigeon breeder brought human purpose to the savagery and pointlessness of the 'struggle for existence': influencing the variations that appear, selecting among them, protecting them, shaping the ensemble of flora and fauna which will make up the garden as a whole.[14] In human affairs no less, fundamental choices of public policy and purpose are posed, as to which forms and directions of self-organisation we wish to cultivate, which intertwined perilous paths to favour. Kristensen and Zeitlin look for a system of governance that can reconcile these animal spirits and build a virtuous circle of trust, respect and mutual commitment. Ostrom looks for what we termed a negotiated moral community, capable of nurturing the terrains of our collective life and protecting them from predatory despoliation. This does not, however, emerge of itself: leadership and public policy are involved. This is husbandry of the social fabric, the arts of civilisation rather than those of hunter-gatherer and predator.

Nevertheless, it would be wrong to think of public policy exclusively in terms of responding to swarms of innovation and civilising the struggle for positional advantage. Public policy can involve the wholesale 'conversion' of institutions, without waiting for these to emerge 'spontaneously' from experiments in 'layering'. Political leaders may engage in 'slash and burn' rather than husbandry, so as to clear the ground for new growth; they may reject existing policies and practices and seek to re-define the most fundamental legitimating values of their society. Even so, their efforts are never wholly on a *tabula rasa*; the remains of the existing connective geometry will still shape the obstacles and opportunities they face; their efforts will set new waves of change in motion, but always on a landscape not entirely of their choosing; and it is by reference to the scandals and *culs-de-sac* of the past that they will champion the legitimacy of the new.

It is with these questions of public policy that Part 3 of this study will be concerned. First, however, we must consider by what methods the conceptualisation of social dynamics we have developed may most appropriately be made the object of empirical enquiry.

PART 2

Methods

9 Attractors and orbits in dynamic systems

9.1 INTRODUCTION

The foregoing chapters have elaborated a conceptual model of social dynamics which combines insights from complexity science and institutionalism. As we have seen, these two paradigms, although of very different provenance, share certain key tenets. Initial conditions are fateful. Mechanisms of change are endogenous. There is path dependency, positive feedback and lock-in.

In Part 2 we consider how this conceptualisation of social dynamics can be handled analytically, in terms of formal models and measuring instruments. We seek to build an analytical toolkit which can be used empirically. It may of course prove overly ambitious to hope for a single such methodology, powerful enough to guide research into all areas and aspects of social and economic change. It may instead be necessary to make do with a number of methods, all inspired by and consistent with our conceptual approach, but serving a variety of substantive purposes.

We have drawn on a wide range of conceptual perspectives, much wider than the social sciences; we now draw on a similarly broad range of methodological approaches, considering how they can be re-deployed for studies of social dynamics. At the same time, we consider how far social scientists are already if unwittingly 'speaking prose': making use of dynamic perspectives which match those of complexity science. This should help us to establish what added value the latter offer and how their inappropriate use can be avoided.

The goal of scientific enquiry is to understand the generative processes that underlie natural – and indeed social – phenomena. This typically starts by selecting the key elements of the phenomenon in question – the 'stylised facts' – so as to be able to model them in more abstract form, analyse their implications and compare these with empirical observation (Harré, 1972: 57, 90ff.; Kaldor, 1985: Ch. 1).[1] It was therefore first necessary to undertake some conceptual elaboration: to consider the ontology of the phenomena of interest. Having made this the task of Part 1, we are now ready to proceed to more or less formal modelling. Nevertheless, to

---

BOX 9.1   DEFINITIONS: DYNAMIC SYSTEMS

A *system* is an ensemble or combination of interacting elements.

A *dynamic system* is one that changes over time, in terms of its state relative to the external world and/or the relationships – the forms of combination – among its constituent elements. These changes constitute its *trajectory* (otherwise known as an *orbit*) through *state space* (otherwise known as *phase space*): the n-dimensional world of the system in question.

Dynamically coupled systems are systems that interact with each other and shape each other's trajectories.

A *forced system* is one that is constrained by some external force. Where that force varies over time, this is said to be a *non-autonomous forced system*.

---

be clear: these are not necessarily models that can be turned into statistical regressions, they are models used to tease out dynamics and structure step by step.

Formal mathematics can often help in elaborating the implications of such models; it is with the mathematical representation of dynamic systems that the present chapter is therefore concerned. Nevertheless, the processes thus modelled must forever be left open to empirical checking (Gilbert, 1993: Ch. 1). We add that mathematics, because of its very abstraction, also has utility as a common language of dynamic systems, suggesting homologous dynamics across very diverse fields and setting up hypotheses for empirical exploration. It can also help us in visualising dynamic systems and the changes that result when we change their parameters. Nevertheless, models need not have mathematics as their source. It was after all on the husbandry practices of artificial selection rather than the mechanics of Newton that Darwin drew for his model of natural selection; the value of that model did not depend on its being expressed in mathematical terms.

Those who are reluctant to plunge into the mathematics of dynamic systems may wish at first reading to omit Sections 9.2, 9.3 and 9.4 of this chapter. Nevertheless, these are less demanding than may appear at first glance.

The mathematical modelling of dynamic systems was developed originally in relation to physics: more specifically, classical mechanics as established by Newton (Toulmin, 2001: Ch. 4). This used linear differential equations, which express rates of change and allow the stability or otherwise of dynamic systems to be assessed. Over the course of the subsequent centuries, this approach was extended in the form of the general field equations of Maxwell, concerned with electromagnetic radiation, and Einstein, in relation to gravity and general relativity. This gave physics the appearance, at least, of being the most systematic and rational of enquiries, which other branches of investigation should therefore seek to emulate. Formally rigorous and empirically powerful, it seemed to embody *par excellence* the principles of rational thought that were emblematic of scientific research; rooted in Euclidean geometry, it provided an ultimate Platonic vision of the timeless and law-like functioning of the cosmos (Toulmin and Goodfield, 1967: 49–52). It was through imitation of mathematical physics that neoclassical economics – through Walras, for example – established its intellectual hegemony (Beinhocker, 2007: Chs 2–3). Mechanical metaphors similarly influenced the endeavours of political theorists such as Hobbes (Ball, 2004: Ch. 1) and early sociologists such as Comte, Durkheim and Pareto, as well as some subsequent approaches to social 'system dynamics'.

This was not of course the only attempt to apply consistent approaches to the natural and social worlds, nor was the direction of imitation always from the natural to the social realm. The nineteenth century saw the development of statistical theory initially by reference to human populations: a field where the task of identifying significant variables in imitation of mathematical physics was clearly challenging, and some way had to be found of identifying patterns within large masses of what might at first glance appear to be random behaviour. Such statistical methods were subsequently transferred into the physical sciences, to deal in probabilistic terms with physical systems which appeared similarly intractable to traditional approaches in terms of simple mechanistic explanation (Stewart, 1997: Ch. 3; Ball, 2004: Ch. 3).

This recognition of statistical indeterminism in the physical sciences challenged the widespread confidence in classical mechanics. Another challenge came in the form of quantum mechanics and quantum uncertainty. Again, what was in question was the expectation that deterministic equations of motion could be identified, which would yield well-defined solutions, depending on the parameters of the system in question. A third challenge, as we saw in Chapter 2, came from thermodynamics and its concern with 'far from equilibrium' systems. This rejected the reductionism of classical mechanics – the attempt to explain systems by reference to the behaviour of the individual parts; it stressed instead the interrelationships among these parts and the emergent properties of such systems (Bertuglia and Vaio, 2005: Chs 3, 27).

Meanwhile, within mathematics itself the simplicities of linear systems were being put in question by such scholars as Poincaré. It is with these complexities that Sections 9.3 and 9.4 of this chapter are concerned, before we return in Section 9.5 to the use of such models in empirical science. We start, however, with the mathematics of linear and non-linear dynamic systems. Our treatment is no more than preliminary and non-technical, referring readers who want a deeper treatment to appropriate texts.

9.2   LINEAR AND NON-LINEAR SYSTEMS

As we have seen, classical mechanics supposed that the dynamic development of physical systems could be captured in an appropriate set of linear differential equations.[2] Given the initial state of the system in question, these could then be used to predict its ensuing trajectory and stability. This involved two assumptions: first, that an appropriate set of such equations could be formulated and solved, not just in the simplest cases (for example, a single planet revolving around the Sun); and second, that the initial state of such a system could be measured with a sufficient degree of accuracy.

The first of these assumptions does not always hold. Even if the equations describing the dynamic development of a system can be formulated, sometimes they can be solved only computationally (that is, by computer approximation). Formal solutions remain beyond reach: as, for example, with multiple planets, the so-called 'many-body problem', addressed by Poincaré in particular (Stewart, 1997: Ch. 4). Likewise, while the second assumption may hold in many cases, natural scientists and mathematicians have been obliged to recognise a wide range of cases where it does not, so that even slight differences in the measurement of the initial state can produce quite different predictions for the system's subsequent trajectory.

Nevertheless, we start with linear systems, their properties and the assumptions on which they depend, before proceeding to non-linear cases and the more complex challenges to which we have alluded. From these we will draw for our analysis of social dynamics.

9.2.1   Linearity and its Limitations

A linear model is one which combines variables through addition alone. It may therefore be expressed in the form:

$$y = c_1x_1 + c_2x_2 + c_3x_3 + \ldots + c_nx_n \qquad (9.1)$$

where y is the dependent variable; x_1, x_2, etc. are the independent variables; and c_1, c_2, etc. are constants as far as x_i are concerned.

Notice that there are no interactive terms on the right hand side of the equation, that is terms in which the various x_i terms are combined non-additively. This allows the equations to be readily and straightforwardly solved: hence their popularity.

A simple pendulum without friction and suffering only small perturbations provides a paradigm case. Under larger perturbations, interactive and non-additive terms have to be included in the equations, which in general cannot then be solved, even if they can be approximated by computational methods. How 'small' a perturbation has to be, in order for the linear approximation to hold, can however be answered only by examination of each specific case.

Although the simple pendulum provides a useful illustration, it should not be supposed that linear models are confined to those involving small oscillations. For example, a geometric growth model involves a simple linear relationship between the growth rate and the current size of the entity in question. This simple linear model can, for example, be applied to population growth in the absence of environmental constraints:

$$dn/dt = r\, n(t) \qquad (9.2)$$

where $n(t)$ is the number of the population at a given time t, dn/dt is the first derivative, the rate of change, and r is the growth rate.

It is also possible to construct linear models of the interaction of two such populations. All that is required is that the growth rate of each population should depend on a strictly linear (that is, additive) combination of the numbers in each of the two populations, avoiding any higher order interaction effects. Bertuglia and Vaio (2005: Ch. 11) explore the following model:

$$dn_1/dt = r_{11}\, n_1(t) + r_{12}\, n_2(t) \qquad (9.3)$$
$$dn_2/dt = r_{21}\, n_1(t) + r_{22}\, n_2(t) \qquad (9.4)$$

where $n_i(t)$ and dn_i/dt are defined as in equation (9.2), while the coefficients r_{ij} represent interdependence of growth rates. The relationship between the two populations might then be one of cooperation (r_{12} and r_{21} both positive), competition (both negative) or parasitism (r_{12} and r_{21} have opposite signs).

Such a system of interrelated linear equations is somewhat more complicated than its predecessor. Nevertheless, as well as solving the equations that describe the system, we can also analyse its stability and evolution. In order to do this, we first have to express the system of equations in simpler and more parsimonious terms. This involves moving the coefficients r_{ij} to a new set of axes, chosen so that the equations can, as it were, be viewed by reference to their major avenues and intersections rather than from side-streets. In mathematical terms, the equations are rotated by reference to the eigenvectors of the system and 'shrunk' or 'stretched' by reference to the corresponding eigenvalues. The stability and evolution of the equations above can be summarised with elegant simplicity by reference to these eigenvalues (positive or negative, real or imaginary).

Throughout the foregoing discussion, for a linear model to be appropriate it has, to repeat, been essential that perturbations should be of only modest amplitude. Two further considerations also affect whether a linear model is applicable. One concerns the effects of 'friction', as in the case of a pendulum with damped oscillations. As we shall see, friction is a key factor in the analysis of dynamic systems. The other consideration is whether the system we are dealing with is 'autonomous' or non-autonomous. In the latter case, the dynamics of the system depend not only upon the configuration of elements within that system (for example, the position and length of a pendulum) but also upon the state of the external force, as this varies over time. In such cases, even if all the forces in play are known, the dynamics may be entirely unstable and unpredictable.

9.2.2   Non-Linearity

Non-linear systems are in general less straightforward to solve than linear systems. They fall into a number of different types, each requiring its own particular treatment.

Both of the linear models of population growth discussed above – for a single population and for interacting populations – has a (more realistic) non-linear counterpart (and both indeed have been influential in the social sciences). It is with these that we commence our discussion.

Logistic function of population growth
Population growth rates are limited by the availability of environmental resources. This is the 'carrying capacity' of the environment. Here, in contrast to equation (9.2) above, the relationship can be expressed in terms of the so-called 'logistic function' as:

$$dn/dt = r\, n(t) - r/c\, n^2(t) \tag{9.5}$$
or,
$$dn/dt = r\, n(t)\, (1 - n(t)/c) \tag{9.6}$$

Here c refers to the carrying capacity. This exerts an influence on the growth rate that becomes larger, as the population grows. It thus represents environmental 'drag' upon population growth. This is a 'dissipative'

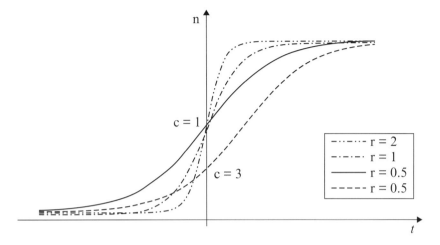

Figure 9.1   The logistic function

system, so-called because this drag or friction dissipates its energy. The squared term means moreover that the equation is non-linear, with the dissipation growing rapidly as the population grows, so that the growth rate dn/dt tends to zero and the size of the population reaches a plateau (upper right hand side of Figure 9.1). In contrast, in the early stages, when the value of n is very small, it approximates to a linear equation, because the second term becomes vanishingly small (lower left hand side of Figure 9.1).

This model of logistic growth has found widespread application in the social sciences. For example, it underlies Rogers's account of the diffusion of innovations, discussed in Chapter 1 (Rogers, 2003). Nevertheless, it assumes that carrying capacity is fixed. In the case of human societies, this will need to be relaxed, not least as a result of the diffusion of the very innovations with which Rogers in his own application of the logistic curve was concerned. Even in the case of biological processes, the pressures of limited carrying capacity will increase the scope for new variants of a species to develop within alternative niches, in some degree at least bypassing these constraints.

Volterra-Lotka model of predator-prey
For the interaction between two populations, in particular for a predator and prey, a more elaborate model is that due to Volterra and Lotka. Here, in contrast to equations (9.3)–(9.4), we have:

$$dn_1/dt = r_{11} n_1(t) - r_{12} n_1(t) n_2(t) \qquad (9.7)$$

$$dn_2/dt = r_{21} n_1(t) n_2(t) - r_{22} n_2(t) \qquad (9.8)$$

where r_{11} is the reproduction rate of the prey, r_{12} is the mortality rate of the prey due to predation; r_{21} is the reproduction rate of the predators (how many are born for each prey consumed); and r_{22} is the mortality rate of predators.

This system of equations is of course non-linear, because of the interactive terms in both (9.7) and (9.8). These express the rate of encounters between predator and prey. For low initial numbers of prey, the numbers of predators are also small, as therefore are the losses from predation, so that the prey are able to grow rapidly in numbers. As they do so, however, their encounters with the predator population increase, limiting the growth of the prey population. Meanwhile, although the growth in the number of prey encourages the growth of predators, it also intensifies the competition among them, thereby threatening their numbers. Under this basic Volterra-Lotka model, predators and prey each evolve according to endless cycles of growth and decay, never tending towards any stability.

There are a number of variants on this basic model. In particular, it is perfectly possible to incorporate the 'carrying capacity' of the environment in which the prey live, by borrowing appropriately from equation (9.6) above, rather than unrealistically assuming that the food source for the prey is limitless. Our equations now take the form:

$$dn_1/dt = r_{11} n_1(t) (1 - n_1(t)/c) - r_{12} n_1(t) n_2(t) \qquad (9.9)$$
$$dn_2/dt = r_{21} n_1(t) n_2(t) - r_{22} n_2(t) \qquad (9.10)$$

This is a dynamically coupled dissipative system. Predators and prey have reciprocal bursts of growth and decline. These oscillatory dynamics can under some values of the coefficient c, the carrying capacity for prey, form a closed orbit, an endless 'limit cycle'; under others, however, they can demonstrate unpredictable or chaotic evolution. We return to this shortly.

Forced and non-autonomous systems
As we have already noted, some non-linear systems may be forced and non-autonomous. This is the case when one system, driven by exogenous factors, imposes its own dynamics on those of another. This is to be contrasted with dynamically coupled systems whose influence is reciprocal and where there are no exogenous factors. The dynamics of forced and non-autonomous systems may involve a limit cycle or be completely chaotic, depending on the system parameters.

The textbooks commonly illustrate such a forced system by reference to a pendulum whose pivot itself moves according to an externally imposed rhythm. The equations that describe such systems explicitly include time: in particular, the rhythm that is imposed exogenously. Time was of course present in the foregoing equations dealing with the dynamically coupled systems of the Volterra-Lotka model; however, this referred only to their internal dynamics. If we had added an additional element in equation (9.9), to represent seasonal variation in the food source available to prey, this would have rendered the system forced and non-autonomous.

Forced systems have figured in our earlier discussion. In Chapter 3, for example, we saw that Kauffman explored the dynamics of large-scale random Boolean networks. He showed that when individual connections were changed, specific domains of the network would remain invariant or 'frozen', even while the remainder proceeded through a succession of transformations, as the initial changes wrought their effects. This invariance, we saw, involved 'forcing structures' which enable 'upstream' elements to lock others into place, unaffected by wider turbulence. This Kauffman then related *inter alia* to an analysis of punctuated equilibria and associated cascades of change. These will remain key elements in our discussion of social dynamics, whether or not we present them in mathematical form.

9.3   CHAOTIC AND COMPLEX SYSTEMS

When dynamic systems can be expressed in terms of linear models, it is possible to say with precision what state the system and its various elements will attain, once we know their starting point. In other circumstances, modelling is more challenging; nevertheless, all is not lost. Even if we cannot solve the equations of the system and predict exactly how its individual elements will move, we may be able to describe the general trajectory along which the system travels and to pronounce, for example, on the extent to which this is confined to a certain neighbourhood of state space and remains dependent on the initial conditions (Kauffman, 1993: 175–80; Bertuglia and Vaio, 2005: Ch. 8). It is with the analysis of trajectories in these terms that the mathematics of chaotic and complex systems is centrally concerned.

In examining these trajectories, mathematicians have often found it convenient to use the heuristic language of 'landscapes', with a topological approach to state space (Figure 9.2). This coincides with our own preferred metaphor in earlier chapters of this book, notably in relation to Kauffman and Potts. There is one caveat: whereas Kauffman provided us

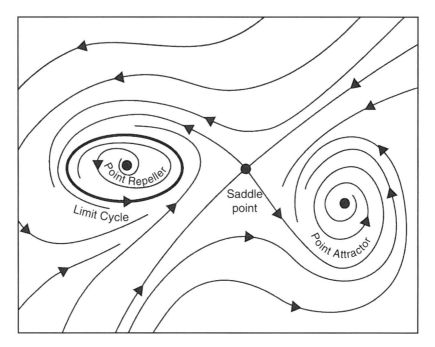

Figure 9.2   The topology of state or phase space

with a model of fitness landscapes in which hills are ascended by search agents, we will for present purposes (since this is the normal practice among the writers with whom we are concerned in this chapter) think of trajectories as behaving like fluids, flowing downhill within basins and away from peaks.

The topology here is described in terms of 'attractors' (valley bottoms) and 'repellers' (mountain tops). The larger area or watershed which drains towards a given attractor is its 'basin of attraction'. Some attractors and repellers are single points; others are closed loops ('limit cycles'). Saddle points (mountain passes) are stable in one plane, unstable in another. All are approached or left asymptotically. The diagram illustrates these various topological features, using appropriate directional 'contours'.

9.3.1   Dynamics in State (or Phase) Space

Again, we start with simple linear systems, even if these are of interest mainly as a point of reference, before we proceed to more challenging cases.

Earlier in this chapter we dealt with simple pendulums, oscillating at

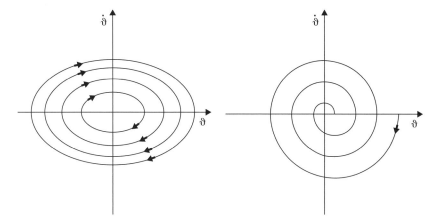

Figure 9.3   Oscillating systems in state space

small amplitude with and without friction. Figure 9.3 represents their movement in state space: a space in which the pendulum is continuously varying the balance it strikes between kinetic energy (vertical axis) and potential energy (horizontal axis). In the frictionless case on the left hand side, when the pendulum is at one or the other end of its swing, its kinetic energy (acceleration) is zero and its potential energy makes up the entire energy of the system; when the pendulum is at its lowest point of swing, its potential energy is zero and its total mechanical energy is kinetic. This mechanical energy is in turn determined by the amplitude of swing to which the pendulum is initially lifted. Different radii in the diagram, with various concentric ellipses, correspond to different overall energy levels of the system, which in each case is conserved: there are no attractors. In the dissipative case on the right, with friction damping the movement of the pendulum, the initial energy is progressively lost, as the system moves asymptotically towards a point attractor.

   Non-linear cases are more interesting. In general, what matter for the orbits and attractors generated by non-linear functions are the particular values taken by the system parameters. Bertuglia and Vaio (2005: Chs 21–22) explore this by reference to the logistic map (the discrete time counterpart to the continuous time logistic function which we discussed earlier). The corresponding equation (compare equation (9.6) above) is:

$$n_{k+1} - n_k = r\, n_k\, (1 - n_k/c) \qquad (9.11)$$

where k refers to successive time intervals and iterations. If we choose appropriate units in which to measure the carrying capacity c, and if we define a new growth parameter λ = (1+r), we can express this equation in simpler terms as:

$$n_{k+1} = \lambda\, n_k\, (1 - n_k) \tag{9.12}$$

Consider now the behaviour of such systems for different values of the parameter λ.

For modest values, non-linear systems such as this will generate point attractors and repellers of the sort already discussed.

For intermediate values, non-linear systems commonly generate an ensemble of attractors about which the system then orbits, in a periodic orbit analogous to the limit cycle we discussed above, in the case of the Volterra-Lotka model. The size and period of the orbit can, however, vary greatly. Thus, in the case of the logistic map, as the growth rate and thus the parameter λ increase, the size and period of the limit cycle also increases, with successive bifurcations – doubling and redoubling – of its constituent attractors.

For still larger values of the system parameters, we move into the realm of chaotic behaviour. Here successive bifurcations have produced a periodicity that tends to infinity; the trajectory of the system therefore never repeats itself and each trajectory remains sensitive to the particular conditions from which it started. This contrasts with all the foregoing cases, where as the system approaches the attractors in question, the influence (or 'memory') of the initial conditions is lost. There the future was wholly predictable by reference to the attractors in question; here, in the case of chaotic behaviour, future trajectories remain indeterminate, being forever sensitive to even the smallest of variations in their initial conditions. Nevertheless, the boundaries between these three zones are not entirely well defined: for example, elements of the fixed orbits associated with the intermediate zone appear faintly even within the chaotic zone.

Having thus introduced the notion of chaotic development, it is necessary to give this greater precision.

9.3.2 The Curious Case of the Strange Attractor

Attractors confine orbits to a particular neighbourhood of state space. Ordinary attractors – whether point attractors or limit cycles – 'capture' these trajectories, so that all details of their future state can be predicted by reference to the attractor. Modest – or even not so modest – variations in the initial conditions, or errors in their definition or measurement, are of little significance; the attractor in question exerts its pull upon any given trajectory, which is compelled to approach it, albeit asymptotically.

In contrast, some attractors are said to be 'chaotic', inasmuch as orbits remain sensitive to initial conditions, as we have just seen; they never 'lose their memory'. In these circumstances trajectories also remain sensitive to even slight errors in measurement of these initial conditions, or of their subsequent states. With such attractors, it is impossible to predict with entire precision how trajectories will develop.[3]

We now introduce the notion of a 'strange' or chaotic attractor. Chaotic attractors are always strange: strange attractors are generally – although not always – chaotic. While 'chaotic' refers to an orbit's sensitivity to initial conditions and the unpredictability of its future evolution, 'strange' refers to its geometry: in particular, the fact that although trajectories or orbits remain forever within a delimited neighbourhood, they never repeat those previously traversed. It is this geometry that now requires clarification.

A strange attractor is a 'fractal': in mathematical terms its dimensionality is non-integral (not a whole number). However, what this signifies may not be immediately obvious to the non-mathematician, who has been taught to think of spatial dimensions as integral and mutually orthogonal. Nor, indeed, is it immediately clear how the mathematical account of fractals relates to those of the natural scientist.

For the natural scientist, a fractal is a natural phenomenon with organised structure at all levels. One class of fractal is those that are 'scale-free': as we increase the level of magnification the structure does not change; instead it recurs and recurs again on a smaller and smaller scale. Commonly cited examples include a coral reef, the indentations of a coastline, a snowflake. This is not just a matter of scale, it also says something about the pattern of growth or 'aggregation' involved (Stewart, 1997: 209–11). A coral reef 'emerges' as each branch and twig becomes the source of new growths, themselves shaped by the locally specific topological features already established. This is sometimes referred to as 'self-similarity' (Stewart, 1997: Ch. 11) or 'preferential attachment' (Barabási, 2003).

Stewart (1997: 205) reconciles these two views of fractals – that of the natural scientist and that of the mathematician – by pointing out that the snowflake or the coral reef, with their endlessly sprouting arms at all scales, occupies only a portion of the space defined by its extremities. Thus even the most elaborate snowflake, considered as an object in two dimensions, leaves a lot of 'blank space' amidst its various protuberances. To this extent, it can be thought of as occupying just a portion of the two available dimensions: in the case of the snowflake, for example, the typical fractal dimension is 1.26. This is consistent with the strict mathematical definition of dimensionality, even if it jars with the conventional

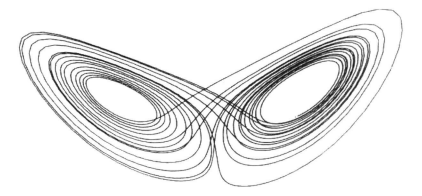

Figure 9.4   The Lorenz attractor

understanding of dimensions among non-mathematicians (for a fuller treatment, see Solé and Boscompte, 2006: 132–4). It is also consistent with Potts's account of 'non-integral' space in his micro-economics (recall Chapter 4).

A metaphor for thinking about fractal dimensions is the solenoid (Stewart, 1997: Ch. 6). Wire is wrapped turn by turn around a spindle; from time to time the windings then recommence, as the wire is wrapped back on itself. This is an infinite line, confined to the surface of the spindle but never repeating earlier paths. Bertuglia and Vaio (2005) offer another metaphor. As we have already seen, what is distinctive about strange attractors is that, although trajectories remain within a delimited neighbourhood (this is after all what is meant by an 'attractor'), they move along a path which is forever distinct from all those previously traversed. In a two-dimensional state space this is possible, Bertuglia and Vaio point out, only if the trajectory can move fleetingly into a third dimension, in order to 'step over' earlier paths with which it would otherwise intersect. It is in this sense that strange attractors have a non-integral dimension: there is an extra dimension, but this is confined to that local neighbourhood where 'stepping over' is required.

The Lorenz attractor, shaped like a butterfly's wings, is the best known strange attractor (Figure 9.4) (Stewart, 1997: 126). Each 'wing' involves a trajectory that spirals outwards in the plane of the wing, but then moves through a third dimension across to the other wing, where the spiralling recommences. The new 'wing', into which each such shift moves the trajectory, is however never identical to a wing previously traversed: in effect, an infinite stack of wings is revealed as the trajectory continues.

Notice that, as well as the 'stretching' involved in the progressive spiral of each wing of the Lorenz butterfly, there is also the 'folding' as the trajectory moves briefly through an additional dimension and shifts from the outside of one spiral to the inside of the other. The same brief movement occurs with the solenoid, as one winding is completed and the wire begins to fold back upon itself. It is the 'folding' motion – as distinct from the 'stretching' – that moves the trajectory through the additional fractal dimension, both with the solenoid and the Lorenz 'wing', and allows the trajectory, although infinite and non-repeating, to be contained within a delimited neighbourhood.

In summary, then, fractals and strange attractors involve partial and local manifestations of additional dimensions of state space. Topologically speaking, the connectedness of this dimension of space is incomplete. It is, as we have seen, this additional if partial dimensionality that allows trajectories to 'fold' and thereby avoid repeating themselves, so retaining their dependence on initial conditions. This is why, to repeat, it is in general the case that chaotic attractors are strange and strange attractors are chaotic.

9.3.3   The Topology of Strange Attractors

The various fractals we have discussed each offers an ensemble of basins of attraction. For example, each 'wing' of the Lorenz butterfly and each 'layer' of winding in Stewart's solenoid is such a basin. As a trajectory moves between these wings or layers, 'folding' itself through the local and partial extra dimension that the fractal offers, it moves between adjacent basins; it then proceeds to explore its new – if also temporary – home, as it 'stretches' itself.

Adjacent basins are separated by saddle points, which thus constitute points of bifurcation in the landscape (see Figure 9.2). However, in the main an ordinary saddle repels, no less than a peak; an orbit cannot cross it because all the contours divert the orbit back into the basin from which it has come. Even at the limit, where the trajectory coincides with one of the lines leading to the point attractor at the 'head of the pass', it is to this point and no further that the orbit leads. The saddle is a 'separatrix'. If the orbit is to pass through the saddle into the adjacent basin of attraction, the geometry of the saddle itself will need to be locally distinctive, so as to allow the orbit to traverse it. In topological terms, the centre of a strange attractor constitutes an exceptional sub-region, a 'chaotic saddle', with precisely these properties. It provides an exit from a basin of attraction that would otherwise not only confine the trajectory but also force it to repeat itself.

Depending on the angle from which it is viewed and approached, a saddle is both a valley bottom (an attractor) and a peak (a repeller). More generally, every saddle has a multi-dimensional surface (or 'manifold') which is valley-like and by reference to which it is stable and another surface, orthogonal to this and hill-like, by reference to which it is unstable. Together these span the n-dimensional space within which the saddle sits. An ascending – or a descending – path need not therefore end when it arrives at a saddle: an orthogonal turn allows it to continue. In this perspective, we may think of strange attractors as being the narrow gateways that offer orthogonal turns in such paths.

The local geometry of a strange attractor is thus distinctive, offering orthogonal twists that 'fold' orbits into new basins. Here stretching can begin anew, beyond the local neighbourhood of the chaotic saddles.

9.4   IMPLICATIONS AND APPLICATIONS

We now turn from the mathematical treatment of dynamic systems to their empirical relevance. We thus re-visit a question posed at the start of this chapter: how, on the one hand, to explore the properties of mathematical models, while at the same time establishing the appropriateness of these models for illuminating empirical phenomena of interest. This will also allow us to connect the mathematics of non-linear systems to the conceptualisation of social dynamics that we offered in Part 1 of this book.

We consider these issues from three standpoints.

9.4.1   Closed and Open Systems

In Chapter 2 – and again early in the present chapter – we noted the reliance of classical mechanics on closed mathematical systems. This was an abstraction from an empirical world whose turbulence could not be encompassed within an analysis of the stability and equilibrium conditions of closed systems. We also, however, saw that thermodynamics, developed in the nineteenth century, dealt instead with open systems: systems, that is, that exchange energy and matter with their environment and as a result are driven 'far from equilibrium'. However, such systems could exhibit order and structure, they could self-organise.

In the preceding pages we have dealt with closed mathematical systems, linear and non-linear. It might therefore seem that the discussion so far offered in this chapter can have little relevance to the open, 'far from equilibrium' systems with which Part 1 was concerned. Any open system can, however, taken in conjunction with its larger environment, be considered as a closed system. Recall the Volterra-Lotka predator-prey model, as in equations (9.9)–(9.10) above. There is, on the one hand, a source of

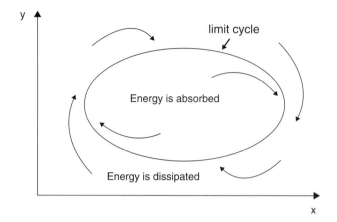

Figure 9.5   The limit cycle in state or phase space

energy constantly renewed, on the other, a dissipative force, forever drain-ing energy from the system (Bertuglia and Vaio, 2005: 98–100). For the prey, feeding supplies the source of 'external' energy; growth is limited by the carrying capacity of the environment, the dissipative force. For the predators, the 'external' energy source is the prey; the dissipative force is their own mortality rate. This is an open system enclosed within its larger environment.

As we have seen, the Volterra-Lotka model may give rise (depending on the values of the parameters) to a limit cycle (Figure 9.5). This is an attrac-tor: if the system starts off in the interior of the limit cycle, it tends to move 'outwards'; while if it starts off at some point outside, it moves inwards. Whatever energy it starts with, the system ends up captured in this single orbit, determined by the parameters of the energy source and the dissip-ative force, so that they are in balance (Stewart, 1997: 87). It is in this sense that the predator-prey system self-organises.

The logistic function and map are likewise closed systems, but ones that relate the open system of population growth to its wider environ-ment: recall equations (9.6) and (9.12). As we saw in discussion of the logistic map, the system parameter λ dictates the ensemble of attractors by reference to which the system behaves: how, in other words, it self-organises, and at what value of λ this self-organisation turns into chaos. Here also, therefore, the mathematics of closed non-linear systems serves to illuminate the dynamics of the open 'far from equilibrium' systems that we find in the physical, biological and social worlds and the forms of self-organisation that they seem to display.

9.4.2   Order, Chaos and Complexity

In Chapter 2 we distinguished zones of order, chaos or complexity. This distinction has recurred subsequently, not least in the present chapter. We have seen that the dynamics of non-linear systems depend on the values taken by the system parameters. Typically some values of these parameters produce point attractors within a realm of 'order'; here trajectories move towards the attractors, lose their 'memory' and have a predictable future. Others produce chaotic evolution; here trajectories remain within the neighbourhood of the strange attractor, but their orbits are chaotic and cannot be predicted by reference to that attractor. Within an intermediate zone the system self-organises among a number of states, albeit the pattern of such self-organisation depends on the particular values of the system parameters.

Nevertheless, the boundaries between zones are not watertight. Elements of the fixed orbits associated with the intermediate zone also appear faintly within the chaotic zone; meanwhile, strange attractors lurk on the boundary between the zone of chaos and the intermediate zone of complexity, offering to enlarge enormously the variety of orbits that the system can take, compared with the depths of the intermediate zone. This is hardly surprising: as Stewart (1997: 208) notes, 'Surfaces are the boundaries between competing regimes, the places where alien worlds make contact with each other. The topography of surfaces is significant throughout science.' In any case, within the intermediate zone, even small variations in system parameters can produce major changes to the limit cycles. The overall result is that within this intermediate zone, a system will tend to 'wobble' between different limit cycles, and may even be captured by strange attractors, thereby accessing novel basins of attraction.

Moreover, in the turbulence of real world dynamics – as distinct from mathematical models – system parameters are hardly ever fixed. On the contrary, any real world system continually encounters exogenous shocks to its system parameters and its structural stability. Such shocks could be due to some change in the physical or biotic environment; Stewart, for example, discusses the local turbulence set in train by abrading surfaces and interfaces (Stewart, 1997: Ch. 5). In the socio-economic realm, shocks may result from an intervention by a policy-maker or a Schumpeterian entrepreneur or from the abrasions among institutions that Pierson describes. These perturbations can create a new array of attractors towards which the system then begins a new journey. We thus move from the world of closed mathematical systems – closed in the sense that once their parameters and initial values are specified, we do no more than study the system's subsequent development – to that of real world systems, exposed to endless abrasions and perturbations.

9.4.3 Time in Dynamic Analysis

Earlier chapters, concerned with biological evolution and socio-economic development, stressed the significance of path dependency for complex dynamics. Initial conditions mattered, as did the subsequent sequence of adaptations. Thus, for example, in our elaboration of Kauffman, we saw that the genetic legacy of a species provides it with both capacities and constraints in the process of progressive speciation. We also saw that for political scientists such as Pierson, institutional inertia is pervasive, the past casts a long shadow and politics are unavoidably conducted 'in time'.

Time has also pervaded the present chapter, in our discussion of a system's 'memory'. We have contrasted the zone of 'order', where memory of initial conditions is lost, and the zone of 'chaos', where that memory forever remains. The zone of complexity has an intermediate character. This, however, leaves complexity as something of a mathematical no man's land between order and chaos; the relationship with our earlier chapters on biological and socio-economic change is somewhat unclear. Again, therefore, we face the somewhat problematic relationship between mathematical models and our understanding of real world phenomena.

Novelty perturbs the existing order, whether it results from Darwin's mutations or is produced by Crouch and Potts's entrepreneurs. That order has been created by a succession of past perturbations of this sort and the dynamics they have set in motion ('micro-meso-macro' or 'deepen-widen-warp'); it bears their imprint. Its inertia now however limits the effects that the new perturbations can have. These limitations may even absorb and entirely overwhelm the new perturbation and bring it to nought. It is also however possible that the new perturbation will set in motion a dynamic of change, even on rather a large scale, and in some cases producing a chaotic avalanche. If we are speaking of Darwin's mutations, these effects and their consequences develop blindfold. If we are speaking of human actors and socio-economic change, those involved may actively seek to anticipate and nurture particular processes and directions of change.

It follows that instead of thinking of complexity as a mathematical intermediate zone, it may be better to think of evolutionary processes or agile agents as weaving a complex path between order and chaos, the zones of no memory and total recall. These are both realms where there is a coherent mathematics on which we can draw. Whether the complex path woven between them is itself susceptible to mathematical modelling is a rather separate question. Be that as it may, to think in these terms allows us to maintain consistency with the discussion of Part 1. In particular, it allows us, on the one hand, to acknowledge the constraint and inertia imposed by the social and economic structures woven by yesterday's actors (and also indeed the capacities with which they equip us); but at the same time to recognise the novel dynamics that agile agents may be able to introduce, in some cases sending the system in question along a new trajectory, one whose effects will thereafter be etched in the 'memory' of the system.

9.5   MATHS, MODELS AND METAPHORS

What then is the promise of mathematics, as far as the analysis of complex social dynamics is concerned?

Bertuglia and Vaio (2005: 315) conclude that from a mathematical perspective the study of complexity is 'substantively vague in terms of definition, ineffective in terms of methods and lacking in terms of results'. They blame the – until recent – tendency of mathematicians to prefer linear models. They anticipate that progress will come, on the one hand, from developments in mathematical techniques, on the other, from a reconsideration of the very foundations and scope of mathematics.

This may be both too damning and too over-ambitious. The mathematics of non-linear systems are by no means under-developed and further technical developments can be expected. The challenge now, however, is to investigate complexity not so much as a mathematical zone intermediate between order and chaos, but rather as an empirical arena for the clash, abrasion and turbulence of real world systems. Such turbulence arises not only from exogenous stochastic shocks, but also from the endogenous generation of novelty, most obviously in biological and social processes: novelty that sets new pivots and couplings in place, changing not only the system parameters but the very architecture of the system. It is these dynamics that we seek to capture, using the mathematics surveyed in this chapter. From their *bricolage* we re-deploy and apply such tools as may in combination provide this illumination. This is a pragmatic task and one whose proof will be in the empirical pudding.

Cohen and Stewart (1995: Chs 1, 6) argue for a differentiated view of modelling and the place of mathematics within it. In relation to the physical world, mathematical analysis can indeed be asked to yield laws. This it cannot do, for the moment at least, in relation to biological and social processes; nevertheless, here it provides powerful models and metaphors involving both verbal and mathematical elements (pp. 184–6). Even in relation to the physical world, however, the boundaries between metaphor, model and law are blurred (Harré, 2004).

As far as our present discussion is concerned, what sorts of mathematical model and metaphor can be applied to the analysis of social dynamics as conceptualised in Part 1 of this book?

This chapter has, first, dealt with models of logistic growth and of species interactions in shared eco-systems. Both are relevant to our interest in evolutionary dynamics and will serve as regular points of reference in subsequent chapters.

We have, second, seen that mathematics examines the properties and evolution of dynamic systems by reference to their parameters: the eigenvalues and eigenvectors, for example. The logistic map displays quite different behaviour as the growth parameter λ increases, moving the system from the orderly to the intermediate and then to the chaotic zone. It may be illuminating to take such changes in the quantitative parameters of a closed mathematical system as a metaphor for the qualitative changes in open biological and social systems that result from the perennial flow of novelties that transform their architectures and hence their dynamics.

This approach has good pedigree. Thus, we have seen that parameter changes in non-linear systems can lead to progressive bifurcations in the attractors of the system: recall again our discussion of the logistic map. Prigogine draws attention to these progressive bifurcations as a central feature of self-organisation in far from equilibrium systems and the building of 'complex dissipative structures' (Prigogine, 1980: 106). As we shall see in the next chapter, Kauffman and others use such progressively more complex bifurcations to model the 'ontogeny' of the embryo, as it develops from a few cells, to build a progressively more complex structure. We will even consider whether this can usefully model the development of social structures and the political choices posed at such critical junctures. Prigogine is ready to refer to physical and chemical systems making 'choices' at such junctures. This may in the natural sciences be a metaphor too far; in the case of social dynamics, however, system 'choice' at such junctures is no mere metaphor: it is the stuff of politics.

The mathematics of this chapter therefore leaves us with an invitation to model the emergence of social and institutional structure by reference to these analogies. To repeat, this is to use mathematics as a metaphor for the structures that define the critical junctures and choices of social and political life. It is in part to the social and political science of social structure that the next chapter will be devoted, as we move from mathematical metaphor to empirical enquiry. Maybe our earlier critique of complexity science, that it endowed us with no tools for coping with the institutions of human societies, was too harsh, in overlooking the potential value of such metaphor.

Third, it may be possible to represent in terms of strange attractors the biological and social processes by which novelties are introduced, changing the system parameters and indeed the very architecture of the system. Whether this can be more than metaphor – whether, for example, it is possible to demonstrate that strange attractors are real properties of dynamic social systems and that those properties can be measured – is less easy to say. In one case at least, however, this is what we now seek to argue.

While we have the Volterra-Lotka models of species interactions in shared eco-systems and Kauffman's simulations of NK and NK(C) landscapes, we lack any overall integrated mathematical model of evolution, encompassing variation, selection and co-evolution. Nor do we have a mathematical model for our account of social dynamics, summarised in Chapter 8, in terms of 'deepen-widen-warp', or Potts's 'micro-meso-macro'. Nevertheless, an analogical use of the mathematics of this chapter may be possible.

The central feature of 'deepen-widen-warp' was the 'perilous path'. Each species, through the genotypic mutations it produced, opened new and orthogonal dimensions of genotypic space and tested whether, with appropriate re-deployment of its genetic legacy, its fitness peak would now be revealed as a mere saddle, allowing it to ascend to new levels of fitness. Equally, however, from these new heights, it explored the potential for new co-evolutionary dynamics within its eco-system, so as to raise the height of the local fitness landscape. At each stage these efforts 'stretched' the species into new trajectories of development, albeit never without limit, as the additional fitness potential of any given niche was tested and eventually exhausted.

The resonance with our earlier account of strange attractors and their geometry should be evident. The species confronts in turn the constraints imposed on its fitness by, on the one hand, its genetic legacy and, on the other, its eco-system; it searches across each surface or 'manifold' in turn for an exit from those constraints, a new basin in which further fitness ascents may be available. We may think of the evolutionary 'struggle for existence' as a race across these two surfaces. Not that this will necessarily continue indefinitely: it may be truncated or, using our previous language, it may peter out on a lonely spur. Throughout, however, the journey is path dependent (except on a smooth Mount Fuji), as it is for any trajectory with respect to a strange attractor: memory is never lost.

This is reminiscent of the 'Devil's Staircase' developed by Cantor (the French mathematician whose writings on number theory anticipated some of the theory of fractals): a monotonically ascending mathematical function involving a succession of plateaux and ascents. The Cantor staircase

– more precisely, the ensemble of ascents nested among the plateaux – embodies features of a strange attractor. Bak (1997: Ch. 8) has already related this function to the evolutionary process. He asks us to view the Cantor staircase as a succession of punctuated equilibria, with speciation and extinction events: periods of stasis (the plateaux) interspersed with periods of novelty and reconfiguration (the ascents). He points out the correlation empirically of mutation and extinction events, as between different species, and thus the entwining of their respective staircases: evolutions 'march to the same drummer' (p. 148).[4]

Notwithstanding the metaphorical power offered by this race up the staircase, the analytical value of this matching of mathematical models and empirical phenomena is of course a matter for practical investigation. To do so is difficult enough, even in the most mathematically congenial of the physical sciences. Nevertheless, at the very least we now have a mathematical narrative to accompany Figure 8.1, the diagrammatic summary of 'deepen-widen-warp', and one that helps us in visualising the evolutionary dynamics involved. We recall again, however, that whereas biological evolution takes place 'blind', in human affairs it is driven by enterprising first movers, racing against time to turn rugged local peaks into monotonically ascending perilous paths or, at the very least, to ensure that they do not become isolated on a lonely spur. Now the struggle is among competing evolutionary logics – alternative but intertwined Cantor staircases – jostling for position and exposing alternative political choices and scenarios for the society as a whole.

There is a fourth and final metaphor which we may draw from this chapter for our analysis of social dynamics. The fractal is one of the emblematic concepts of complexity science. If complexity science is to have any relevance for social analysis, it is incumbent on us to demonstrate this relevance in relation to fractals. In one sense this is already established. The combinatorial ontology which formed the basis for Part 1 started from Potts's account of social and economic space as non-integral. Growth by preferential attachment or aggregation – the basis of fractal development in nature – has recurred as a theme of the preceding chapters, whether as the flocking of cellular automata (Chapter 2), the triumph of co-evolutionary dynamics in the process of speciation or the struggle for positional advantage in human societies. Nevertheless, we take the metaphor one step further.

As empirical phenomena, fractals reveal patterns and organised structure recurring at multiple but interrelated levels. They are widespread features of ecological systems, with micro-ecologies nested within larger-scale structures (Solé and Bascompte, 2006: Ch. 4). Indeed, we might also cast in these terms Darwin's account of variations, sub-species, species and genera, unfolding through evolutionary processes as 'the great Tree of Life . . . with its ever branching and beautiful ramifications' (Darwin, 1859: 101).[5] However, dynamic systems do not necessarily generate fractals. Depending on the system parameters, they may, on the one hand, dissipate and degrade into a stable equilibrium at a point attractor; on the other hand, they can be energised into chaotic dynamics whose behaviour cannot be precisely predicted.

The agile actor stands at the heart of our ontology of social dynamics: the author of new combinations, the builder of connections in non-integral space, the creative source of deepen-widen-warp. For Potts and for Crouch, the focus is on the entrepreneur, the first mover. Only a few of us, however, run large corporations or lead governments or bring new patents to markets: the most typical first movers of whom we might instinctively think. Most of us in our everyday lives are change takers not change makers, constrained by external forces. Nevertheless, in our own micro-worlds, we confront critical junctures and responsible choices that re-shape the lives of those around us. Albeit on this more limited canvas, each of us is an agile first mover, re-weaving this canvas within a turbulent environment. Here we construct new dynamics, we open gateways to new basins of attraction. This is our own particular fractal adventure, the niche for which we are, in some degree at least, responsible.

We may of course claim otherwise, refusing to accept that responsibility. In some societies this may be a not unreasonable position to take. An autocratic government, with its systems of citizen surveillance and privilege for party members, may freeze the mass of its people into sullen compliance. A breakdown of government, on the other hand, may allow widespread lawlessness and social chaos, wherein niche construction is again barely possible. Even in liberal democratic societies, the scale of the canvas varies enormously: not only between the CEO and the ordinary employee, but also across social classes and other national and international divisions. The structure of a society sets the unequal terms of these canvasses and the scope for social actors to re-shape them in the struggle for positional leverage. It may leave some with so constrained a canvas that fatalistic acceptance of their lot – and of the uncertainty to which they are exposed – alone makes sense (Marris, 1996).

This can then indeed provide a normative vantage point, from which to view the outcomes of processes of social and economic self-organisation: the scope for agile action and fractal adventure that those in different social positions are afforded. In Part 3, where we turn to specific areas of policy, this is the normative position of which we make key use.

9.6 CONCLUSION

In earlier chapters, in particular our discussion of Kauffman, we considered how evolution 'tunes' the parameters of a biological system, so that it evolves 'towards the edge of chaos' and maintains a high level of adaptability. We went on, for example in our discussion of Crouch and Potts, to consider whether it may be possible to 'tune' the socio-economic system through policy interventions, so as to steer the co-evolutionary dynamics of technology and social institutions, thereby exploiting their synergies.

How far can our discussion here illuminate the policy task of 'tuning' the parameters of the socio-economic system?

We may distinguish two sorts of stability in a dynamic system. First, dynamic stability: how far does a particular trajectory change if the initial conditions vary (variations that may be 'real' or simply the result of measurement errors)? Second, structural stability: how do trajectories and orbits change in consequence of changes in system parameters?

In regards to the first of these, dynamic stability, there are a number of stability criteria that have been applied to the trajectories of non-linear systems, notably those due to Poincaré and Lyapunov. Both define stability by reference to the distance which emerges between the trajectory before and after the variation in the initial conditions, and whether this reveals convergence or divergence between the two. Poincaré's approach is to measure the distance between the two trajectories or orbits; Lyapunov prefers to measure the distance between corresponding points on the two orbits (that is, points that are at corresponding moments in time). Lyapunov exponents are negative for ordinary attractors (orbits move closer as they approach the attractor). However, attractors in two or more dimensions always have several such exponents. In the case of strange attractors there is always one that is positive, capturing the dependency of orbits on initial conditions and the progressive magnification of initial differences, and providing, indeed, a quantitative measurement of the degree of chaos that the system affords (Peitgen et al., 1992: 709).

Bertuglia and Vaio (2005: Ch. 19) suggest how these criteria might be applied to real world systems, including socio-economic systems. They express the hope that by appropriate historical studies, it may be possible to identify comparable periods of development whose specific trajectories are sufficiently close – as judged by the Poincaré or Lyapunov stability criteria – to allow one to identify the corresponding attractors (and even whether they are 'ordinary' or 'strange'), by reference to which the two trajectories were shaped. This would be a formidable undertaking. Nevertheless, as Bertuglia and Vaio also recognise, even if such attractors could be identified, this would, if they were to become generally known, itself tend to influence market behaviour, thereby modifying the very attractors thus revealed.[6] Economic actors – including policy-makers – make judgements as to how others are likely to behave and how they will learn from any conjectures advanced as to the dynamics of the market system. Here therefore Bertuglia and Vaio move to a position close to that of Keynes and Potts, as we saw in Chapter 4, stressing the role of uncertainty, expectations and mental models of socio-economic processes in the decisions that economic actors take.

Stewart (1997: 96–7) is concerned with structural stability, even if he does not discuss socio-economic systems as such. He considers (Ch. 15) how – on the basis of an understanding of attractors (including strange attractors) and trajectories – it may be possible to design control systems to control chaotic development. (This is a dynamic counterpart to, for example, a thermostat in a central heating system.) As we have seen, a strange attractor may be thought of as a localised saddle point, with a stable manifold and an unstable manifold. Stewart shows how orbits can, in principle at least, be controlled by continually adjusting the system parameters so that the orbit moves continually towards the stable manifold (pp. 314–16). This is the manifold which, in the language of fitness landscapes, allows further ascents.

Stewart (pp. 317ff.) provides a range of empirical examples of design problems in engineering and medicine that have been usefully addressed in this way. The adjustments they involve may, of course, themselves be a lumpy, discontinuous and path dependent activity, the seizing of certain critical moments, the throwing of particular switches, rather than a continuous and smooth process. In Part 3 we consider whether this approach might also be applied to policy-making.

10 Patterns in time and space

10.1 INTRODUCTION

The concern of this study is with social dynamics. Time therefore matters.

In our opening chapter we took stock of several common approaches to the dynamic analysis of social change. The first was the tracking of household circumstances through panel and cohort studies. Panel studies are commonly used in the analysis of changing patterns and risks of poverty. They allow researchers and policy-makers to assess whether households remain in poverty for long or short periods or experience recurrent episodes, never entirely escaping. Such panel studies commonly involve annual updates. Time therefore enters such analyses in a simple sense: how do the circumstances of a given household compare with last year and the year before? In addition, however, the flows of income and expenditure that such enquiries seek to capture – and that then serve to illuminate the dynamics of poverty – are themselves nested in diverse calendars: the weekly expenditure on food, the monthly pay cheque, the fuel bills varying over the different seasons of the year, the capital expenditure on cars and houses.

As well as panel studies of this sort, there are analyses of household circumstances based on administrative data relating to the receipt of social benefits. Here again, time enters in a simple sense: are households dependent on benefits short or long term and how do changes in benefit rules change this time profile? However, in making use of such administrative data sets, what also matters is the very way that an 'episode' of receipt has been defined by the administrative rules in question. As Buhr and Leibfried (1995), for example, demonstrates, these rules carry an implicit definition of discrete intervals of time; it is through these definitions that the administrative diary of benefit receipt is then mediated, rather than the timescale which may make sense to the households themselves, as they juggle their income and expenditure.

Cohort studies are more variable in the timescales by reference to which they operate. However, not uncommonly they may return to the cohort for further rounds of data collection at certain key stages in the cohort's development: entry to schooling and the labour market, mid-career, retirement. Here it is, in other words, the larger calendar of the life course – and the individual's weaving of his of her biography through the institutional transitions of the wider society – that provides the cohort study with its rhythms. It follows that these are in turn by no means fixed, as the typical ages of such transitions change (school leaving age, retirement age) or become more or less variable, as a result of changes in social attitudes, government legislation, economic and demographic shifts.

A second approach to the dynamic analysis of social change that we considered in our opening chapter was concerned with the diffusion of new technologies and institutional practices across a population. Following Rogers, the timescale is here commonly defined in terms of early and late adopters and is modelled by reference to the logistic curve, capturing the early stages of struggle for acceptance, the middle stages of rapid spread and the later stages of progressive satiation. Less clear is what happens – and the challenges in terms of conceptualisation and measurement – when we move beyond a single innovation and its life cycle, to consider interlocking streams of innovation and the larger socio-economic changes that 'general purpose technologies' may produce.

Time mattered in our account of physical and biological systems, including, for example, the 'arrow of time' in thermodynamics and the path dependency of evolutionary dynamics. In our treatment of institutionalism, time and sequencing were again centre-stage. Institutional lock-in and inertia may for some time limit opportunities for change; nevertheless, continuous 'abrasion' between different institutional arrangements, coupled with long-term changes in 'background' conditions (technology, demography, climate), will sooner or later punctuate the stasis.

Finally, in our survey of the mathematics of dynamic systems, we noticed the importance of time for coupled systems that are forced and non-autonomous. Here the dynamics of one system impose an external discipline or calendar on another, so that it is 'obliged to march to the same drummer' (Bak, 1997: 148); we are denied the possibility of describing its evolution simply in terms of its internal rhythms.

Events and processes are distributed in time but they are also and necessarily distributed in space. Already in Chapter 2 we saw how global patterns can emerge from simple local interactions: recall, for example, the models of Schelling and Bak. The combinatorial ontology which we adopted from Chapter 3 onwards involved the reconstruction of space, whether genotypic, technological or institutional: first of all locally, then potentially widening to reconfigure space more generally. Our discussion of first mover dynamics referred to sequence and timing but also the occupancy of space. A Stackelberg game involves the oligopolistic dividing up of market shares. Fligstein has corporations constructing new institutional arrangements and forms of control, but predominantly in new and more fluid parts of the economy (Fligstein, 2001: 103). Similarly, it has been in novel areas of policy left unoccupied by member states that the European Commission has most easily been able to build new EU competences (Leibfried and Pierson, 1995: 22, 32, 434).

The shared knowledge that we highlighted in our account in Chapter 8 of agile agents was *distributed* knowledge: knowledge, that is, of what works in the particular local niches across which the community in question is spread. Similarly, one of the lessons we may draw from the study of ecosystems is that space matters. Many of the models of such systems that have traditionally been used deal with 'well-stirred pots', which do not take locally specific developments into account (see, for example, the Volterra-Lotka model discussed in the previous chapter). Where they do, they find that the dynamics of ecological systems and evolutionary change are significantly modified, with the speed of such change much greater, for example, in locally isolated populations (Corfield, 2001; Solé and Bascompte, 2006: especially Ch. 3).

We must expect, therefore, that spatial and temporal patterns will be closely interrelated: what Prigogine (Prigogine and Stengers, 1984: 17) describes as the 'timing of space'. This chapter considers what analytical tools may help us map the patterns in time and space that social systems describe.

10.2   SEQUENCE AND TIMING IN SOCIAL SCIENCE

Two writers in political science and sociology have in recent years highlighted sequencing and timing as crucial to social scientific analysis. Among the historical institutionalists, it is Pierson (2004: Chs 2–3) who most explicitly and deliberately considers their importance. Among sociologists, Abbott (2001b) has been prominent in seeking to demonstrate that 'time matters'.

10.2.1   Pierson

In his study *Politics in Time*, Pierson (2004) argues for sensitivity to a variety of timescales and to the importance of timing and sequence. He questions the general focus in social science upon the immediate, where both causes and effects are manifest in the short term. Equally, he challenges the tendency to attempt explanation by reference to 'variables' that 'are ripped from their temporal context' (p. 1); he questions whether 'the social significance of historical processes can be easily incorporated into the "values" of particular "variables" at a moment in time' (p. 78).[1] He proceeds by offering an appreciative but critical review of a wide variety of political science studies.

Pierson deals first (pp. 55–8) with situations where two separate events or social processes occur at the same historical moment, producing a distinctive train of consequences. This conjunction may, of course, be purely accidental. If, however, the conjunction results from continuing abrasion between different social processes, the scope for analysis and theorisation will be much better, even if empirically such linkages and continuing abrasions may be difficult to demonstrate. This sort of sustained interaction is what we have hitherto spoken of in terms of dynamically coupled systems and co-evolution. It is however important to add that such couplings and abrasions, if they are to be effective, must become meaningful at the level of social action, not at some macro-level that is dissociated from social actors.

Pierson deals next (pp. 58–63) with the treatment of sequence in rational choice analysis. This highlights, in particular, the significance and fatefulness of first mover advantage, not least in controlling the agenda of decision-making and determining turn-taking. Such first mover advantage has of course been a pervasive theme of this study.

Pierson now considers (pp. 63–7) sequencing in relation to path dependency. The latter embraces at least three distinct processes or arguments. First, the decision to establish certain institutional arrangements and procedures may be difficult to reverse because of the procedural time and trouble involved. Second, the institutional arrangements and procedures in question may generate increasing returns for a significant constituency: not just vested interests in a narrow sense (pension rights, opportunities for rent-taking) but streamlined arrangements within which a wide variety of actors can build added value. Third, in establishing particular institutional arrangements, the array of institutional and administrative capacities is modified in specific directions; the direction and timing of these modifications will shape how the society can then respond to particular new challenges. In each of these three cases, the timing and direction of institutional reforms will shape and constrain the subsequent possible trajectories of social change; and 'forsaken alternatives become increasingly unreachable with the passage of time' (p. 64).

Such path dependency has of course figured strongly throughout the present study, albeit not always operating as rigidly as suggested by some of the political science literatures reviewed by Pierson. Thus, for example, in our treatment of Kauffman, we noticed that in walking across fitness landscapes, genetic endowments were regularly re-deployed to secure phenotypic benefit; or in Shubin's words, 'everything innovative or apparently unique . . . is really just old stuff that has been recycled, recombined, repurposed or otherwise modified for new uses' (Shubin, 2008: 201). Crouch, writing like Pierson from the institutionalist camp, is similarly eager to stress the plasticity of institutional arrangements and the scope for reworking the *bricolage* of the past to new ends. In contrast, many of the studies which Pierson reviews – concerned, for instance, with the administrative and fiscal capacities of the state – seem to stress the fixedness of institutional legacies: clay rather than putty, swords that can hardly ever be turned into ploughshares.[2]

Pierson turns next (pp. 67–71) to situations in which, notwithstanding path dependency, there may be occasional bursts of change, set in motion – but maybe at some remove – by earlier critical events. Sequencing need not produce self-reinforcement and stasis; it may instead trigger new trajectories and chains of events, which lead to some new and far-removed destination. He also considers (pp. 74–7) the consequences of long-term and often slow changes in background social and economic conditions. The effects of this cumulative shift need not be gradual; there may, rather, be thresholds or 'tipping points' at which sudden avalanches (p. 83) of consequences follow. Pierson refers to Granovetter's work on thresholds and Schelling's exploration of the level of racial antipathy beyond which communities will self-organise along racially segregated lines.

This is consistent with our discussion at various points of punctuated equilibria and the cascades of novel configuration these can produce (Kauffman and Bak). It also recalls the discussion of non-linear systems in Chapter 9, where at critical values of the system parameters the behaviour of the system changes dramatically. Pierson is, however, careful not to fall into an overly deterministic account of such threshold effects: they present critical junctures for choice and agency and history remains 'open'.

Pierson now turns (pp. 90–92) to processes through which new subpopulations emerge, so that gradually the larger population of which they form part undergoes a significant shift in its dominant characteristics – or alternatively splits into two quite distinct populations. The living age and die; existing entitlements are superseded, albeit only after lagged periods; the weak are ousted by those who frame and capture a more productive niche. We discussed these population shifts in Chapter 6, in relation to Thelen's work, and Potts's discussion of the 'carriers' of the institutional rules.

Finally, at times Pierson adopts the same language of attractors and trajectories that we have employed. Thus he refers to structural accounts that relate outcomes to earlier structural changes but give little value to the immediate triggers of change; the latter are held to be of only superficial interest for changes which, given the structural factors cited, were in any case highly likely to occur, sooner or later. These are appropriately conceptualised as 'attractors' (pp. 93–5). Second, Pierson notes (pp. 95–6) that what happens at critical junctures can send social development along 'strikingly divergent' trajectories: trajectories which can be self-reinforcing as feedback loops kick in, even if the full effects then emerge only at some considerable temporal distance from the critical juncture.

Pierson may not offer a toolkit of formal models for investigating sequence and timing in institutional change. Nevertheless, on the basis of his review of the political science literature, he lays out the methodological precepts which such investigations must respect, including those which, even without formal models and relying on qualitative methods, contribute massively to institutional scholarship. His review also reveals that the convergence between such scholarship and complexity science is, if anything, even stronger than our discussion in Part 1 has already demonstrated and that the case for forging a shared analytic approach to social dynamics is correspondingly reinforced.

10.2.2 Abbott

As the foregoing discussion makes clear, there are a number of senses in which it can be said that 'time matters'. It can refer to the timescale – long term or more immediate – within which particular processes unfold, whether as effects or as the causes of other processes. It can refer to the 'timing' of a particular event or process, relative to other events, whether these latter are stochastic shocks or arise from the regular abrasions between social sub-systems. It can refer to triggers and switches: events and processes which create thresholds or tipping points, critical junctures and bifurcations. It can also refer to the whole sequence of developments, by virtue of which an agent moves through 'state space', re-deploying but never escaping the endowments of the past.

Through his various writings, Abbott offers a sociological perspective on the importance of temporality that has some similarities with that of Pierson and, indeed, the larger perspectives that we have sought to develop through preceding chapters. Thus, for example, by reference to the sociology of the Chicago school, Abbott (1997) considers how social 'facts' and social dynamics must be analysed by reference to both time and space. For the Chicago school, some social dynamics played out in neighbourhoods whose connections with the larger socio-economic system were stable and rather limited. In consequence it was possible to study the sequence of stages through which such neighbourhoods typically developed with only limited reference to these larger contexts. These were their 'natural histories' (Abbott, 2001b: 147–51; see also Faris, 1967: Ch. VII). Other neighbourhoods – and other social spaces such as organisations and professions, for example – involved regular abrasion against environing factors; time mattered and they variously pursued 'careers' in relation to that larger context, or had careers thrust upon them. Finally, the level of such abrasion might be so great that the research focus would necessarily be on the interactional processes themselves – their 'macro' co-evolution – and the cascades of change that such interactions could – not always predictably – unleash across the city. It is these contingent and reciprocal interrelationships of time and social space that Abbott underlines.[3]

Abbotts's *Time Matters* (2001b) is concerned *inter alia* with trajectories and attractors, turning points and fateful choices. It also offers (p. 40ff.) a useful and critical review of the way that time is handled in conventional causal models. In particular, Abbott insists that such models generally overlook the way that the different variables which they deploy may operate within quite different timescales, reflecting the variety of abrasions and dynamic couplings to whose tempo they play. In addition, however, Abbott goes beyond Pierson, in suggesting how sequences may be identified and their significance empirically investigated.

He offers two principal approaches (for his overviews of alternative methodologies, see also Abbott, 1990, 1995). The first is concerned with sequence and temporality as mediated through narrative: the past 'encoded into the present', with successive 'presents' the 'beads on a narrative string' (Abbott, 2001b: 212). This has some resonance with Kuhn, Collingwood and Toulmin, as discussed in Chapter 8. It is of potential importance for the concerns of the present book; nevertheless, in Abbott it remains under-developed. The related narrative of evolving intellectual paradigms in sociology that Abbott offers in *Chaos of Disciplines* (2001a) also has affinities with Kuhn and may indeed, with its attempted deployment of the language of 'fractals', appear close to our own concerns; this promise is, however, hardly realised, at least in terms of delivering clear methodological and analytical approaches for empirical research.

The second approach that Abbott deploys, that of optimal matching, is rather different. Drawing on the work of Sankoff and Kruskal (1983), this uses dynamic programming to compare two or more sequences: identifying their similarities and measuring the extent to which they differ. These dynamic programming methods map the 'walks' which would be necessary to bring discrepant elements of the sequences under comparison into alignment: if not complete alignment, then sufficiently close to serve the purposes and research questions of the investigator. This is of course somewhat reminiscent of the matching procedures posited by Potts for the exchange and combination of technology strings (Chapter 6, Box 6.2). Potts, it will be recalled, adapted Holland's search algorithms.

These involved plenty of # ('don't care') symbols, but searches could then be refined and honed to secure a more exact match. Not that dynamic programming can cope only with strings of the sort we assumed in our exposition of Kauffman and Potts; it can also be used to explore and compare sequencing which involves multiple loops and cycles (Sankoff and Kruskal, 1983: Ch. 3).

Such techniques are of obvious and major importance in molecular biology and genome analysis, but also in a wide variety of other practical applications and areas of scientific enquiry, ranging from machine-based speech recognition to dendrochronology to our understanding of both human language and bird songs (Sankoff and Kruskal, 1983: Ch. 1). Notice immediately, however, that it is never a matter of simply identifying those sequences that are similar: of noticing, as it were, that two strings of beads display the same alternation of different colours. The strings are of interest only if they have a larger significance. In some cases – genome, dendrochronology – the sequences under study illuminate the process of historical development by means of which these sequences of information came into being. Sequence matching may thus, in appropriate cases, illuminate the evolutionary steps that have produced two sequences and their common ancestry (Sankoff and Kruskal, 1983: Ch. 2). In other cases – genome, speech – a sequence we observe is of interest in illuminating corresponding processes of ontogeny (the stages by which an organism develops) or speech generation. When this sequence can be matched against another and novel sequence, in genetics, for example, researchers are entitled, if only on a provisional basis, to infer similarities also in the functions that the novel structure performs. Nevertheless, we must not forget that genetic endowments are regularly re-deployed and modified for new uses (Shubin, 2008); and that, indeed, it is these successive re-adaptations that are of particular significance for the system in question. What all this underlines, therefore, is that to identify and match sequences, while often suggestive, is not the end of the matter, only the start.

Abbott himself uses such techniques for identifying typical sequences that are of interest sociologically. Thus, for example, he investigates the extent to which different professions follows the same pattern of development, in terms, for example, of regulating access, fees and training and securing state licensing (see, for example, Abbott, 1990, 1991). He points out that these developments are multi-tiered and that professions may therefore exhibit distinct – if interrelated - sequences at local, regional and national levels. Whether the sequences he reveals are of theoretical interest is less clear; they do indeed reveal that professionalisation is a 'complex dynamic process' (Abbott, 1991: 380) but offer only a start in understanding and modelling those dynamics.

Second, in collaboration with DeViney, Abbott traces the sequence in which major welfare programmes were established in different industrial countries during the late nineteenth and twentieth centuries (Abbott and DeViney, 1992). Using the optimal matching techniques discussed above, the 'distances' between the adoption sequences of different countries can be mapped. The question that then arises, however, is how this information should be used. For example, are distinctive sequences to be taken as explaining other differences that then unfold in the countries concerned; or are common sequences of interest because they reveal common processes of development? Abbott and DeViney adopt the latter approach. Sequence is thus the dependent variable, to be explained by reference to shared processes of socio-political evolution, rather than an independent variable, serving to explain how other societal developments unfold.

Abbott now makes the same three-fold distinction we saw in his account of the Chicago school. Sequences may be explained by reference to the characteristics of individual countries, seen as having their own independent histories: their levels of economic and state development, the degree of working-class mobilisation and so on. Or, second, it may be that within particular clusters of countries, contagion and diffusion in regards to welfare programmes (and, we might add, abrasion against similar socio-economic environing factors) produce a distinctive sequence of programme development across the cluster. Finally, it may be that such contagion and diffusion are generalised to such an extent world-wide that adoption sequences within individual countries are merely random variations around a common dominant theme.

Nevertheless, despite the variety of explanatory models that Abbott and DeViney apply, in terms of country level differences, diffusion effects and global processes, the results are paltry. Whether this is because of the quality of the data employed or the structure of the explanatory models adopted is unclear. The exercise underlines that to identify and compare sequences is arguably the easy bit; in itself, however, it reveals little if anything of interest. What is more fundamental is to deploy a theoretical framework which identifies sequence as being of central theoretical interest and data whose quality is sufficient to the task.

Optimal matching techniques of the sort Abbott uses have not of course stood still, since Sankoff and Kruskal's aforementioned contribution. Mount (2004) provides an accessible overview in relation to genome sequence matching in particular (see especially Chs 1, 3, 5–6). Two features are particularly noteworthy. First, Mount surveys methods of profile and block analysis that allow matching of sequences within particular regions as well as globally (Ch. 5); as we shall see in succeeding chapters, such differentiation – in terms of zones offering different degrees of association

– is of more general interest. Second, he considers how these sequence matching techniques can be deployed for the mapping of shared evolutionary histories (phylogeny), while remaining alert to multiple timescales of evolutionary change even for similar sequences, and the co-locating within the genome of sequences of quite diverse origins (Ch. 6). The cautions as far as social analysis is concerned are again rather obvious. The identification of similar sequences of historical development – for example, the development of welfare programmes – may suggest similar social, political and economic processes at work; they may also suggest similar patterns of social interaction and interests in the here and now and a similar range of available futures. Nevertheless, in themselves they do not suffice to demonstrate and explain those latter similarities.

10.3   COMPLEXITY SCIENCE AND THE TIMING OF SPACE

Various strands of literature within complexity science provide perspectives and models of spatial and temporal patterns and their interrelations. We review some of these literatures and their potential relevance for the analysis of social dynamics.

10.3.1   Turing Instabilities

Turing (1952) provides an early and path-breaking model of spatial organisation, which has been widely influential across many areas of science. He poses the question: can spatial patterning emerge from spatial homogeneity?

We follow Kauffman's exposition of the Turing model (Kauffman, 1993: Ch. 14). Two agents – for example, two chemicals – are involved; their local interactions influence each other in two quite different ways. One is an activator, which catalyses both itself and the second agent. The other is an inhibitor of both agents. Both diffuse across the medium in question, but the inhibitor diffuses the more rapidly.

Introduction of an additional quantity of the activator at a particular point leads to both agents increasing in that locality; however, the additional inhibitor now diffuses more rapidly, depressing the levels of activator more generally within a flanking region, and producing thereby an alternating pattern of concentrations of the two agents. This pattern has a 'wavelength' determined by the respective diffusion coefficients.

This is a dissipative structure of the sort we discussed in Chapters 2 and 9. On the one hand, we have a source of energy, the additional quantities of activator that are being continually introduced, while, on the other, there is a process of dissipation, as the inhibitor diffuses.

A linearised – and thus simplified – version of the Turing model can be presented in terms of a set of equations similar in form to some of those whose dynamics we explored in Chapter 9:

$$dn_1/dt = r_{11} n_1(t) + r_{12} n_2(t) + D_x \nabla^2 x \qquad (10.1)$$
$$dn_2/dt = r_{21} n_1(t) + r_{22} n_2(t) + D_y \nabla^2 y \qquad (10.2)$$

Here $n_1(t)$ and $n_2(t)$ refer to the concentrations of the two chemicals at a given point in space, while dn_1/dt and dn_2/dt refer to the rates of change in these concentrations over time. The last term in each equation represents the diffusion process: it consists of the D_x or D_y diffusion coefficients for the chemical concerned – thus the speed at which diffusion occurs – coupled with the Laplacian operator ∇^2, which expresses the second order derivative, the rate at which the concentration of a given chemical changes through space. This final term, normally a negative quantity, can thus be considered as loosely parallel to the final 'drag' element in the logistic function we discussed in Chapter 9.

Kauffman follows what has by now become a familiar procedure. He examines how the behaviour of this system of equations varies as its key parameters, its eigenvalues and eigenvectors, are 'tuned'. In particular, he shows that, depending on the ratio of the diffusion coefficients r_{ij}, the above system of equations can produce a sustained macroscopic alternating pattern of concentrations of the two agents.

Kauffman now builds on Turing to analyse morphogenesis: the formation of structure within organisms as the embryo develops (see also Prigogine and Stengers, 1984: 171ff.). The different elements of this structure are built according to a particular developmental sequence (another example of the 'timing of space'). He demonstrates – most extensively in the case of the fruit fly *Drosophila* – that Turing's model (applied to the chemical and mechanical properties of such a system) can account remarkably well for the sequence and symmetries of the compartmental boundaries that develop within the different structures of the embryo.

When Kauffman examines the above equations, he shows that some simple mathematical functions of the Laplacian operator make for system stability: they are so-called 'eigen functions' (Kauffman, 1993: 568–71). On circular and elliptical two-dimensional surfaces these eigen functions take the form of lines, saddles, parabolas and other simple shapes. It is precisely these basic shapes that structure the emerging architecture of *Drosophila* as the embryo develops (pp. 584–91).

This is not all. In his examination of the Turing equations, Kauffman also shows that the pattern of alternating concentrations that can emerge depends upon the boundary conditions or, put more simply, the size of the expanse in question: only those wavelengths will be included that are of a size allowing an integral number (that is, of whole waves) to 'fit' (otherwise they will be 'damped out' by the dynamical system). As size increases, 'a succession of patterns of increasingly complex waveform will amplify and die in succession'. Kauffman proceeds to demonstrate how, as the *Drosophila* organism grows in size, these boundary conditions change, and hence also the succession of geometries that *Drosophila* manifests as it develops (pp. 587–90).

Finally, Kauffman notes that some of the patterns that the Turing model predicted to emerge at certain stages in the morphogenesis of *Drosophila* do not. This seems to be the result of earlier structural developments selecting out those that are permitted to develop subsequently (pp. 590ff.). In other words, successive phases of structural differentiation within a given organism seem able to edit the parameters of the Turing model as the next phase of bifurcations gets underway, thereby tuning the 'symmetry breaking' – the further structural refinement – that will subsequently emerge.[4]

Whereas Kauffman applies Turing's model primarily to morphogenesis (as indeed had Turing himself), Solé and Bascompte apply the model to ecological systems (Solé and Bascompte, 2006: 68–84). Here we find the populations of different species distributed in varied spatial patterns which can, as before, be analysed as far from equilibrium dissipative structures, using the simple Turing model. Again, we have local interactions among the individual members of species on the one hand, diffusion of species on the other, but at different rates: the two key elements of the Turing model. Solé and Bascompte develop their analysis with particular reference to the predator-prey systems we discussed in Chapter 9: the prey is the activator while the predator is the inhibitor. The Turing effects emerge in predator-prey systems where three conditions are met: local predator populations grow in response to a local growth in prey; as predator numbers increase, this causes congestion and tends to reduce their individual consumption of prey; predators diffuse away from this local growth at a faster rate than prey. The result is the formation of patches of high prey density interspersed with areas of low density.

It is thus apparent that a rather simple – if clever – model seems able to account for remarkably complex patterns and structures in space and time (Kauffman, 1993: 637ff.). Indeed, given this generic significance, we might even expect it could also be of importance for our account of social dynamics. It will of course be necessary to detach ourselves from the biology and the chemistry; and in place of the sequential bifurcations and symmetry breaking that Kauffman traces, to recognise the role in human affairs of political choices at critical junctures. It is to this that we now turn.[5]

The conceptual framework we developed in Part 1 gave pride of place to the agile first mover, the entrepreneur who forged novel technological and institutional combinations in expectation of winning enhanced leverage over a wider terrain – whether in the form of profit taking or in terms of institutional governance. In Potts's language this is 'micro': it involves the reconstruction locally of social and economic space, even if there is also an eye to the eventual larger-scale 'macro' dynamics that this may set in motion.

This can rather readily be expressed in terms of Turing. First movers are activators; their rivals are inhibitors (as indeed is the wider population of sluggish change takers whose inertia binds them to the status quo). Their interactions take place around the local technological-institutional spaces which first movers are attempting to construct. First movers seek to recoup their investment in technological-institutional change within that local arena and the pathways of further innovation which they build directly from this point of departure. Their rivals, diffused across a broader variety of technological-institutional niches, may have been caught off balance by the micro-innovation in question; nevertheless, as 'second movers' they are now well placed to weave a wider range of secondary adaptations, albeit in doing so they also, in some degree, lock themselves into the first mover's chosen innovation.

In one sense, all that this does is to re-state the obvious: socio-economic evolution like biological evolution tends to promote the development of distinct niches, which display the patterning of which Turing speaks. Nevertheless, the Turing model is of interest in offering a simple but generic mechanism underlying such patterning, in terms of activator and inhibitor and differential rates of diffusion across the space in question. For us it is of particular interest, in displaying the connections between our conceptual framework, of first movers and evolutionary dynamics, and the possibility of modelling social structural patterning. However, just as the morphogenesis of *Drosophila* involves at each stage the selection of those structural developments that will be permitted to develop subsequently, in the social world there is scope for political contest over such selection. Only if we bring power and politics centre-stage are we entitled to draw analytical insights from the Turing model.

10.3.2   Percolation Thresholds and Criticality

We have made much of the dynamic relationship between local innovation and the emergence of global patterns. This gives us an obvious interest in the conditions under which local neighbourhoods abut against each other, to an extent that produces global connectivity.

Consider an expanse, within which particular neighbourhoods are either occupied or unoccupied. Ask then whether it is possible to traverse the entire space by walking only across occupied neighbourhoods. We start with just a few sites randomly occupied, the rest vacant. We then allow further sites chosen at random to be occupied. We eventually reach a stage where there is a cluster or network of sites spanning or percolating the entire space.

This process of percolation can be modelled (Solé and Bascompte, 2006: Ch. 4). What is noteworthy is that there is a clear threshold or phase change. Below this, there are plenty of local clusters but neighbour to neighbour propagation across the entire space is not possible; above this threshold such propagation is readily achieved. The threshold is a switch or 'tipping point' (Gladwell, 2001 and Chapter 2 of this book): it is the point at which local interactions (occupied neighbourhoods abutting each other) generate long-range or global connectivity. As well as the 'giant component' that actually provides the long-range pathway, there are of course lots of smaller clusters; at the threshold, their size distribution displays a power law.

Percolation thresholds of this sort have important practical and policy implications for the management of eco-systems. Thus, for example, ecologists have studied how such connectivity and accessibility of habitats affect the distribution of species and are therefore fateful for eco-diversity (Solé and Bascompte, 2006: Ch. 5). Species vary of course in their typical range of dispersal and thus in what counts as a neighbouring patch; a species which diffuses on a broad basis will 'see' the landscape as more connected than would otherwise be the case and it will have greater scope to colonise (Solé and Bascompte, 2006: 157–8). The loss of habitats can mean that for some species at least the landscape moves below the percolation threshold and they become locally isolated. This may not matter if the species in question is of only peripheral importance to the food web; if, however, it is a so-called 'keystone species', this may disrupt the food web and produce far-reaching re-balances, with avalanches of extinction and major loss of bio-diversity (Solé and Bascompte, 2006: 171, 231ff.).

So far we have considered how, as local neighbourhoods are occupied, a critical percolation threshold is eventually reached, where local adjacency suffices to enable global connectivity. We have also noticed the implications for bio-diversity of the fragmentation of such connectivity. However, it is also possible to argue – as indeed with many other far from equilibrium dissipative systems – that the dynamic processes at work actually drive the system towards this percolation threshold. This is a specific case of the more general argument for 'self-organised criticality' advanced by Bak (1997), as seen in Chapter 2. It also offers a model of punctuated equilibrium, of the sort we saw were of interest to Pierson, with occasional bursts of change, set in motion – but maybe at some remove – by earlier critical events or slow changes in background conditions.

In such models, threshold effects are again of key importance. One example is the case of forests and forest fires (Solé and Bascompte, 2006: 165–6). On the one hand, we have the slow development of local connectivity (abutting local neighbourhoods of forest): on the other, a recurrent source of instability (spontaneous ignition caused by lightning strikes or barbecues) which causes general disconnection. However, the latter can produce its effect only when the density or extent of the former across the space as a whole reaches a certain threshold. We can therefore find that the landscape in question manifests 'self-organised criticality'. There is a steady build-up of afforested neighbourhoods over an extended period, but as this approaches the percolation threshold, it becomes increasingly probable that random sparks will produce, not just a local blaze of the sort that are regularly encountered during the summer months, but a forest fire that causes more general devastation. Even so, the scale of these fires can even then not be predicted; the percolation threshold leaves many clusters of forest only feebly connected; depending on where the fire starts, many clusters of varying sizes will be left standing. Moreover, self-organised criticality can obtain only for a certain range of the underlying parameters. In the case of the forest fire, spontaneous ignition must not be so frequent and widespread that neighbourhoods of trees rarely survive to abut; on the other hand, they must not be so rare that forestation becomes so dense as to cover every square metre of land, so that when a fire does eventually start, nothing is left standing from which new growths can begin afresh.

This discussion of percolation thresholds and criticality focuses attention on the connectivity or segregation of landscapes and eco-systems; and, by extension, that of different social milieux. It may, for example, have relevance to public health policies, and our understanding of how diseases percolate through populations. It may also be relevant to the design of national innovation policies, seen as building linkages among different 'knowledge institutions' in the innovation eco-system and thus facilitating the propagation or percolation of inventions. Finally, as we have suggested, it may also help us – notably by reference to notions of self-organised criticality – to model and to understand processes of punctuated equilibria, as discussed by Pierson. To this we return in subsequent chapters.

10.3.3   Diffusion and Domination

The preceding discussion focused attention on the percolation of species. However, species vary in their patterns of dispersal and their colonisation of habitats. These variations are fateful for the ecological communities that develop; these are built up over long periods and are heavily path dependent in relation to the sequence in which different species enter them (Kauffman, 1995a: Ch. 10; Solé and Bascompte, 2006: 251–4). Time therefore matters for the configuration of these ecological spaces.

Solé and his colleagues offer a variety of models of differential dispersal and competitive colonisation, where weaker species survive only as 'fugitives' on the periphery of the dominant. Nevertheless, it need not follow that it is the top predators that are the most abundantly dispersed, nor that they are most protected against extinction, such may be their dependence on humbler prey. The fragmentation of habitats or the extinction of particular species can have major reverberations for bio-diversity; these consequences depend, however, on the complexities of the food web and the effects are often counter-intuitive. Nor of course need they pervade the entire eco-system; some sections may remain robust or 'frozen', locked in place by persistent remnants of the hierarchical architecture that a food web entails (Solé and Bascompte, 2006: Chs 5–6).

The development of eco-systems involves colonisation, competition, niche differentiation, hierarchy and extinction. These are also of course the ingredients of human civilisation. We may therefore expect to deploy some of the literatures that have figured in the foregoing discussion. How far do human societies abut on each others as neighbours: whether we are talking about spatially separated societies – most obviously, organised in different nations – or different social classes and other groups, sharing a single geographical space but in other respects connected only weakly? What scope do their local interactions offer for 'global propagation'? How far do societies vary in their capacity to disperse or to colonise? How useful by reference to human societies is the notion of the keystone species? How far do the analytical methods employed in relation to complex adaptive eco-systems provide us with time-sensitive methods for analysing domination and dependence in social space? We address some of these questions in the next section.

We remark finally on the obvious fact that these ecologically inspired models are set in the wild: in the world of predators and prey, hosts and parasites, symbiosis and specialised niches. This is an environment beyond deliberate manipulation by the creatures within it. These models have been widely utilised in the social sciences: the predator-prey model in particular. This is appropriate where human actors live in a world beyond deliberate manipulation: a world of hunters and gatherers. It is not so appropriate in a world of husbandry, where we shape and manage our environment: in short, a world of civilisation. To use predator-prey and similar models in these circumstances risks missing precisely what is distinctive and fundamental about human societies.

10.4 APPLICATIONS OF COMPLEXITY TO SOCIAL SYSTEMS

We began this chapter by recalling the importance of timing. We noted also, however, that timing unfolds in space: temporal and spatial patterns are woven together. We reviewed in more detail the account by Pierson of just how it is that 'time matters'; we went on to consider Abbott's worthy – if incomplete – efforts to develop empirical methods for studying sequences and patterns in time and space.

In the preceding section, we took several strands of research into complex adaptive systems where temporal and spatial patterns are at the centre of attention. We considered some of the models and analytical approaches that have proved useful there and we made some modest suggestions as to how these might be applied in the social realm. We now reinforce those efforts, in relation to some of the 'careers' or trajectories in space and time with which Abbott was particularly concerned.

10.4.1 Neighbourhoods and Professions

As we saw earlier, Abbott considers how neighbourhoods and professions abrade variously against the larger socio-economic system. Those communities whose external connections are minimal enjoy a way of life which develops according to its own internal logic or 'natural history'. Where the abrasions are more intense, the rhythms of the wider society intrude. Finally, where abrasions are even more intense, it is upon the abrasive interactions themselves that analysis must focus, along with the cascades of change that from time to time they unleash. Here 'one cannot study the individual case directly . . . [or] . . . make predictions of any but the most general sort' (Abbott, 1997: 1157).

Abbott's work on professions in the USA reveals that the levels of such abrasion and interaction are rather high. Professions are involved in 'turf wars' and the researcher must study the rules, strategies and tricks of their interactions. It is also necessary to take into account the larger technological and organisational changes – and the long-term and often slow changes in background social and economic conditions to which Pierson pointed – which can 'induce yet further cascading changes in the interactional field' (Abbott, 1997: 1157).

Abbott thus sets his work in an explicitly ecological context. Central to his interest are the boundaries between professions and how these are constructed and reconstructed as the division of professional labour develops (for example, in the case of social work: Abbott, 2001b: 267–73). Just as his study of *Chaos of Disciplines* (2001a) is concerned with evolving intellectual paradigms and their boundaries, his *The System of Professions* (1988) deals with the corresponding development of professional boundaries and jurisdictions. This involves professions 'growing, splitting, joining, adapting, dying' as they compete for domination (Abbott, 1988: viii, 2). Abbott examines their continually changing boundaries, and the boundaries within each profession between heartland and periphery (p. 71), as they move into virgin territory or jostle with other professional groups on landscapes already well colonised (pp. 91ff.). These boundaries matter because they are associated with claims to jurisdiction and to wider advantages and privileges; they define stakes and pecking order and power in a positional competition (pp. 71–2).[6]

Abbott is not the only scholar to address professional boundaries and organisational dynamics. Enders (2009) is interested in the consequences for national higher education institutions (HEIs) as international influences intensify: in particular, the growth of the international student market; the increasing readiness of publics and policy-makers to judge their universities by reference to international, not just national peers; and the growing visibility of international league tables (including in particular the Shanghai Jiao Tong). HEIs that were once protected, as closed national preserves, are now 'open' systems exposed to these cascades of change sweeping across the global landscape. All are getting caught up in the global reputational competition.

Enders highlights the way that in countries such as Germany, where universities have traditionally enjoyed broad parity of status, there is now a marked shift to engage with those global league tables. To this end, government is privileging a core of research-intensive universities best placed to represent Germany in that race. This is a process of deliberate stratification of the German higher education system, constructing new boundaries, and defining a heartland and a periphery.

These boundaries are being constructed by reference to the international reputational hierarchies that already prevail, centred on research output. Germany is a late mover and must compete on a terrain not of its own making. Nevertheless, Enders uncovers the deeper positional dynamics involved. Academic elites in Germany were quick to welcome the plans for designation of research-intensive universities; however, social networking among these elites then played as much of a part in the selection of Germany's privileged core as any more objective indicators of academic outputs. Although, therefore, international pressures push national higher education systems 'far from equilibrium', they have also allowed agile institutional entrepreneurs within the German national system to seize and consolidate positions of domestic advantage, incorporating potential rivals on adverse terms.

In these elite decisions, concern for the wider purposes of higher education had few effective champions. What seems likely to happen in Germany is what has happened elsewhere: the loss of reputation attaching to these other purposes, as academic research outputs are privileged, and the consequent reduction in the diversity of institutional mission; or, at least, the subordination of those other missions to research (King, 2009: Ch. 7). This risks reducing the diversity, adaptability and resilience of the higher education system as a whole: something of central concern for public policy and the governance of higher education. This is institutional 'layering' as adverse incorporation; 'self-organisation' as positional competition and the exercise of differential power.

Neither Abbott nor Enders offers any formal modelling or quantitative analysis. How useful, therefore, are the analytical approaches reviewed in the preceding pages? First, inasmuch as both Abbott and Enders offer accounts in terms of organisational boundaries and eco-systems, the models of colonisation, competition, hierarchy and niche differentiation that we discussed earlier could be of value. In general, we did not spell out the formal models which we reviewed: the sources we cited do so.

Recall also, however, our discussion of Turing instabilities. In Kauffman's hands, this became an account of the emergence of spatial structure, in a sequence of bifurcations and 'symmetry breaking' accompanying the growth of *Drosophila*. It is tempting to suggest that – albeit with many caveats – this could provide the inspiration for modelling the 'morphogenesis' of Abbott's professions: a process which involves the progressive development and refinement of boundaries and one whose sequencing might then, in turn, be captured through some of the sequence analysis methods that Abbott elsewhere propounds. We have already argued that a social application of Turing could be made in terms of agile first movers ('activators') and their rivals ('inhibitors'): we now set that in the context of inter-professional competition.

Finally, Enders's account of HEI dynamics captures well the ontology of positional dynamics we made central to Chapter 8. This sees the advantaged seizing on the new opportunities opened up by the internationalisation of the institutional terrain of higher education; then extending and ascending their 'perilous path', nimbly tuning these new structural opportunities to the specific capacities and resources they are most readily able to deploy.

10.4.2 Nations and Trajectories of Development

Nations also move along trajectories or 'careers'. As with Chicago's neighbourhoods, we must expect that these will depend on the pattern and intensity of abrasions with the larger socio-economic system. Too little, and the country concerned may remain frozen in time: see, for example, Petmesidou's account of Greek socio-economic development (Petmesidou and Mossialos, 2006). Too much, and it becomes difficult to speak of well-defined trajectories at all, because of the cascades of change that sweep unpredictably across the international arena. As we saw earlier, Abbott attempts to identify similar sequences and careers in the development of welfare programmes, as between different countries, and to explain these similarities in terms of country level differences, diffusion effects and global processes. However, his indicators are rather crude and he insufficiently identifies the theoretical questions at stake.

Again, Abbott is not of course the only scholar to address interlocking national trajectories or careers. John Darwin (2007) provides an erudite and compelling account of imperial power in Eurasia and interdependent patterns of development over recent centuries. First, he considers how, across the Eurasian landmass, waves of predatory colonisation wove webs of production and organisation in novel dynamics of economic, techno-logical and institutional co-evolution: albeit often at the cost of bringing local ways of life to the point of extinction. He gives central attention to communication, connectedness and percolation and to processes of col-onisation, competition, niche differentation, hierarchy and domination. The ecological models which we have discussed – drawing in particular on such authors as Solé – would seem fertile sources for more formal treatment of these dynamics.

Thus, for example, Darwin points to the role of diaspora in establish-ing new webs of trade relations, building long-distance connections and opening new markets: most obviously in relation to the West's expansion after 1830. The latter constituted a 'new form of commercial imperium that fell well short of colonial rule' (p. 247). Nevertheless, state power was heavily implicated; what mattered was which parts of Eurasia were able 'to control the new flows of wealth to reinforce the power of the state against external attack' (p. 213). Resistance to European encroachment was possible only if an indigenous network of communications and con-nections could be maintained: a 'security zone' or hinterland (pp. 259–60). India was uniquely vulnerable. On the one hand, its erstwhile rulers the

Mughals had only recently been ousted; on the other, the financial and commercial infrastructures were so sophisticated that they were readily appropriated by the British (pp. 262ff.). In such a situation, the power of indigenous elites crumbled; new webs of production and exchange took their place, with new niches of specialisation and new patterns of hierarchy and dependence (p. 239).

Second, Darwin's study demonstrates the relevance of the model of socio-economic evolution that we developed in Part 1 of this study and that has continued to inform our discussion, concerned with adaptive change in complex systems. Thus, for example, he notices how different societies within Eurasia avoided or succumbed to the risk of being trapped on a fitness peak of only modest height: a fate that befell Ming and Manchu China in particular (pp. 45, 201). He also assesses the exposure of different Eurasian societies to European empire-building, commercial expansion and cultural influence, and their interest in borrowing Crouch-like from those neighbours, so as to attempt adaptive walks of political and economic reform (pp. 202–3).

First mover advantage – expressed in political-military as much as economic terms – was key to European dominance (p. 162). This had two aspects: on the one hand, the power of initiative, with institutional rules restricting the scope for any political opposition to develop (p. 413); on the other, occupancy of the 'central place' in the division of labour and cultural resources (pp. 211–12). As we have stressed throughout this chapter the dynamics of time and spatial organisation are thus closely interrelated.

Forced entries and overthrows, as much as commercial success, yielded the resources which built the power of the 'fiscal-military state' (p. 165). No less than Fligstein, therefore (see Chapter 7), Darwin reveals commercial expansion and the development of state capacity as co-evolving processes. First mover advantage also gave leverage. Once India – and in particular Bengal – had been drawn into the British orbit, the wealth arising from this trade could be used to support commercial entry to south China (pp. 179–80). Not that this precluded others from benefitting: from within the larger population of rivals and 'change takers', others could frame secondary explorations of their own, building on the new terrain established by European advance (recall our discussion of Turing's activators and inhibitors). Nevertheless, such ancillary projects tended to be led by other Europeans (p. 257); and their rapid advance 'constantly outflanked indigenous peoples' and kept them off balance (pp. 253–6).

Finally, Darwin's account underlines the significance of timing, sequence and contingency. He gives examples of historical contingency: the setbacks suffered by France in the Seven Years War allowed the progressive expansion of Britain's maritime interests, at precisely the time that

India was seeing the aftermath of Mughal decline, creating major opportunities for British commercial appetites (pp. 170–6). Soon however, with the British and Indian economies now more closely coupled, the imports of Indian textiles would provide the impetus to defensive mechanisation of Lancashire's own textile industry. This would in due course not only expand to penetrate India's captive markets, but also provide the spur to Britain's industrial revolution (pp. 197–8).

Just as important is Darwin's account of the 'race against time'. This is, first and foremost, concerned with the race to which we have just referred, between the European first movers and the peoples whose socio-economic sphere they invaded: peoples who then sought to frame secondary adaptations of their own, but on a technological-institutional terrain not of their making, and always therefore at risk of being outflanked. In the 'temperate lands of settlement' such as the North American plains, the Europeans 'had decisively won the race against time by the 1870s' (p. 256); elsewhere the race had more varied outcomes, with European dominance never complete.

John Darwin's account is extended into the present century by Arrighi (2007).[7] At one level Arrighi is concerned with the contrasting histories of socio-economic development in Europe and East Asia, by reference to scarce and plentiful factors of production and rates of productivity growth (Part 1). More fundamentally, however, he is concerned, like Darwin, with the international struggle for positional advantage (Parts 3–4) and therefore with the linkages of economic, technological, military and political competition and the forms of imperium and international hegemony which different superpowers seek to impose. However, in addition to the various instruments of statecraft which Darwin highlights, Arrighi is also concerned with exchange controls and currency devaluations, trade deficits and surpluses, foreign direct investment and the US extortion of fiduciary tribute from its East Asian 'vassal' states in the post-World War II period. His account is to this extent the richer.[8]

Two of Arrighi's arguments (Ch. 11) are of particular relevance. First, he contrasts the European and East Asian inter-state systems and their contrasting dynamics during the eighteenth to the twentieth centuries. The European system involved a high level of competition among powers of not dissimilar weight, a competition that found expression as much in external wars of conquest aimed at extracting resources world-wide as in direct inter-state conflict. The East Asian system was by and large centred on China, overwhelmingly the largest power, and concerned to consolidate and maintain its hegemony through well-entrenched systems of tribute and protection, with war and conquest rare. Once the European powers were able to subordinate China, the rest of East Asia soon followed.

Second, however, US support to its East Asian vassals during the post-World War II period and their economic take-off soon percolated through the Chinese diaspora into China itself, allowing it – from within what John Darwin might call its re-established hinterland or security zone – to rekindle old inter-state economic relations. The Western-dominated international system has not collapsed but it has, Arrighi argues, set in motion novel dynamics that are allowing China to re-weave the *bricolage* of those former relations into the global architecture of the twenty-first century.

In these studies of national development trajectories, it is again the case that none of the principal authors we have used offers any formal modelling or quantitative analysis. Other students of the international order offer models that hold some promise. Thus, for example, Snyder and Kick (1979) use 'world systems theory' to map the structural positions of countries within the global 'eco-system', by reference to their involvement in networks of trade, military interventions, diplomatic relations and treaty memberships. They blockmodel these network data (a technique we will consider in Chapter 11) to distinguish core, semi-peripheral and peripheral nations. They also use regression analysis to assess the implications of structural position for economic growth. There is, however, little on policies to break out of structurally disadvantaged positions: least of all by reference to the re-connecting of sub-systems of inter-state economic relations, as discussed by Arrighi in relation to China. Nor is there anything on building national resilience and resistance to foreign intrusion, as discussed by Darwin.

Held et al. (1999) in his well-known treatment of globalisation offers indicators of national enmeshment in the global environment, in terms of trade and finance, military power, migration and so on, and the patterns of stratification among nations that each dimension reveals. There is, however, little on the path dependent Stackelberg games, by which those nations that occupy the most advantaged positions in the world system shape the terms on which others then become incorporated. Nor does Held consider how these nations progressively re-shape the rules of globalisation within which the race for positional advantage subsequently plays out.

For explanatory accounts and analytical methods it may therefore be more fruitful to look to our earlier discussion of eco-systems and the processes of diffusion, colonisation, competition, hierarchy, domination and extinction that they typically involve. These focus our attention on the abrasive interactions themselves and the cascades of change they unleash, as much as the timing of particular social, economic and policy reforms in individual countries. We take some preliminary steps in this regard in Part 3 of this book.

10.5 CONCLUSION

Part 1 developed an institutionally grounded complexity perspective, as the basis for our conceptualisation of social dynamics. The present chapter, concerned with patterns in space and time, has drawn its formal models largely from complexity science. The social scientists who have figured have, on the one hand, laid out the methodological precepts that analysis of such patterns must respect; on the other, they offer careful and rigorous historical and qualitative accounts of specific cases. Where they venture more formalised approaches to modelling and measurement – Abbott on sequences, Snyder and Kick and Held on globalisation – the results have been at best incomplete.

It is not, however, a simple matter of deploying a better set of models, even if these are supplied by our complexity writers, including, for example, Turing and Kauffman, Solé and Bascompte. As we saw in Chapter 9, scientific enquiry involves a subtle exploration of empirical patterns, captured in terms of their 'stylised facts' and modelled in more abstract terms. In many ways to apply such models involves the use of metaphor; it therefore requires careful attention to the senses in which a given model must be adapted and modified, lest it be applied inappropriately. Models themselves are complex adaptive systems, which must dance in concert with our understanding and stylisation of the facts in question.

As we have seen, it is when the dynamics of one system impose an external discipline or calendar on the dynamics of another, that it becomes impossible to describe the dynamic evolution of the latter simply in terms of its own internal rhythms. Thus if time matters, it matters because – and insofar as – the sequence of development within one system determines what configuration of elements it then exposes to abrasion against other systems. The task is to identify these external couplings, from whose abrasions at critical junctures new co-evolutionary processes may be set in motion, old equilibria punctuated and cascades of wider change unlocked. In approaching this task we will need formal dynamic models but also the skill in applying them to institutionally complex terrains.

We started with time. Nevertheless, events and processes are distributed in space. We have suggested how the morphogenesis and ecological dynamics of social space might be approached in new ways, using the models that complexity science supplies. We must also recognise that countervailing projects of space construction may be in progress, as social actors jostle to drive change in new directions. Thus are socio-political settlements constructed and reconstructed; they involve the – always provisional – negotiation of each side's scope for activation and the inhibitions to which this must be subjected.

11 Connections and networks

11.1 INTRODUCTION

We are interested in combinations and connections among the elements of systems and how, as these change, they generate novel dynamics. Thus, for example, in our treatment of Potts we were concerned with new combinations of technologies and the dynamic processes of 'micro-meso-macro' through which these percolate through the connective geometry of the economic system. We saw that Crouch was concerned with institutional entrepreneurs who recombine institutions and weave new governance forms. For both writers, social and economic space does not come fully connected: it is, in Potts's phrase, non-integral. Social and economic actors are perennially reconnecting this space, driving it in new directions that take it 'far from equilibrium', but never escaping the path dependencies of earlier transformations.

We have also made much of the way that sub-systems are coupled and, again, the implications for their dynamics. Thus, for example, in Chapters 9 and 10 we explored the coupling of predators and prey and the larger dynamics of food webs in which species are connected in hierarchies of interdependence. It is evident, therefore, that our methodological toolkit must equip us to analyse selective connections across a multi-dimensional space, how these connections change and the dynamic processes these changes set in motion.

One standpoint from which to study connections is the analysis of networks. Networks connect elements into systems: they are therefore prima facie of interest (for a popular treatment, see Christakis and Fowler, 2009). So far we have, admittedly, used the language of networks to only a limited degree. Thus, for example, in Chapter 2, our treatment of increasing returns referred to the work of Marshall, Arthur and Krugman on local networks, clusters and agglomerations. In Chapter 3 we saw that Kauffman was centrally concerned with the connections among genes that determine the shape of fitness landscapes and that he explores the generic dynamics of such connections using Boolean networks. Nevertheless, beyond these limited references, there is an extensive literature on networks, both in social science and in complex systems research, that we have so far ignored. It is with these literatures – and the analytical and empirical tools that they yield – that the present chapter is concerned.[1]

First, there is a literature which is concerned with the analytical and computational modelling of networks; that is, with exploring the properties of networks through mathematical equations or computer simulation. Such models are in general highly formalised; the goal is to see how network properties vary with different values of the system parameters. Articulation with empirical data is in general only fleeting.

Second, there is a literature that starts from the opposite end, so to speak, seeking to discern the underlying patterns within empirical data sets of networks. Among the key approaches are blockmodelling and the search for 'structural equivalence'. There is in general only a limited concern with formal models, although the search for underlying patterns may well be informed by theory development in the relevant disciplines (including social science).

A third literature is also concerned with empirical data sets: however, it aims not so much to identify underlying patterns and structures as to use summary metrics to compare networks and to track their properties over time. This might, for example, mean identifying particular percolation thresholds and tipping points, of the sort discussed in previous chapters.

These literatures did not emerge in this order historically: the opposite in fact. Nevertheless, it is convenient to treat them in this order, given their respective interest for the present study. The first literature is heavily indebted to the complexity literature and continues the discussion of dynamic modelling begun in Part 1. The second takes us from formal models to empirical analysis, the central aim of Part 2. The third is of interest for Part 3, concerned with summary indicators that are, not least, suitable for tracking and tuning processes of social change by reference to policy interventions.

11.2   MODELLING OF NETWORKS

Recent decades have seen a dramatic growth in the modelling of network dynamics, both mathematical and computational. Much of this literature is heavily influenced by complex system dynamics. As in Chapters 9 and 10, we review these models for their potential application to our interest in social dynamics.

11.2.1   Random Graphs

Early studies of random graphs, by Erdős and Rényi, modelled the links between nodes as being randomly distributed: hence the name

---

BOX 11.1   DEFINITIONS: NETWORKS AND GRAPHS

A network can be thought of as a set of *points* or *vertices* or *nodes*, connected by *lines, links* or *edges*. In mathematical terminology this is a *graph*.

A *lattice* or *grid* is a graph whose nodes are organised in rows and columns: immediate neighbours are connected to each other but beyond this, connections are absent. Schelling's city dwellers inhabit a two-dimensional lattice (see Chapter 2, Figure 2.2). So do the species interacting on adjacent patches of a complex ecosystem, as analysed by Solé and Bascompte (see Chapter 10).

In contrast, *random graphs* allow connections to any of the elements in the system. The *diameter* of a random graph – the largest distance to be traversed between any two nodes – is accordingly much smaller than with a lattice, where it is only via all the intervening neighbours that any two nodes are connected and there are no 'short cuts'.

In a *directed graph* the direction of the links matters: otherwise the graph is said to be *undirected*. A *signed graph* is one whose links are labelled as being either positive or negative.

A network can most obviously be presented as a diagram displaying nodes and links. However, any network also has a corresponding *adjacency matrix*. This shows which nodes are connected to which other nodes: thus cell (i, j) displays the connection between node i and node j, giving it the value one or zero. Cell (j, i) will then refer to a connection in the opposite direction. A connection within an undirected graph can be represented by a pair of connections in opposite directions; the adjacency matrix of an undirected graph is therefore symmetrical above and below the leading diagonal.

(Newman et al., 2006: Ch. 2). While this is rare in the real world, their analysis defined questions and produced results, by reference to which non-random graphs have subsequently been investigated. Thus, for example, Erdős and Rényi examined how, as connections increase within a network having a fixed number of nodes, giant components suddenly emerge, to which smaller clusters then rapidly attach themselves, in a sudden phase transition. This recalls our discussion in Chapter 10 of percolation through eco-systems.

Work of this sort, for random and other types of graph, is relevant to the analysis of the spatial ecology of different species and the habitats they occupy, as we again saw in Chapter 10. It has also led to studies of the robustness or vulnerability of different sorts of networks, for example, in the face of biological or computer viruses and the speed with which these can percolate through a system (Bornholdt and Schuster, 2003: 76–9, Chs 2–5; Ball, 2004: Ch. 16). These studies examine the consequences for networks if links are attacked and removed: and how resilient they are, in the face of an attack which is directed at random or, alternatively, at highly connected nodes.

11.2.2   Non-random Graphs[2]

To repeat, however, random graphs are rare in the real world. One alternative to which empirical studies have drawn attention is 'small world' networks. Like random graphs, small worlds have a small diameter, but there is also lots of local clustering of links (Watts, 2003: Ch. 3; Ball, 2004: Chs 15–16). Commonly cited empirical examples include neural networks, power grids and actor collaboration in the film industry.

Small worlds typically involve some nodes, connected through long-range links, each of which is then connected to a large number of local nodes. Granovetter (1973) famously argued that it is these long-range links ('weak ties'), connecting people to those who are in dissimilar social positions to themselves, that are crucial to social cohesion and information exchange. Perri 6 (1996) has applied this argument to social policy, evaluating policies in terms of how far they extend the weak ties of disadvantaged groups, rather than isolating them within the local environment of 'strong ties'. Vidgen et al. (2007) investigate 'small worlds' in communities of research scientists: not just investigating the diameters of such networks, but also the subjective meanings of these connections for the participants, the positional struggles involved and the geopolitical priorities pursued by the community leaders.

For our present study, however, 'scale-free' graphs are of greater interest, because they express 'increasing returns' and positive feedback. Figure 11.1 displays a random graph on the left hand side, a scale-free on the right. The world-wide web is a commonly cited example; academic citations are a second (Ball, 2004: Ch. 16). As we have seen, in their study of random graphs Erdös and Rényi held the number of nodes constant and explored the phase transitions evident as the general level of connectivity varies. In contrast, studies of scale-free networks start from the recognition that networks typically grow by the addition of new nodes, which then attach themselves to existing nodes; and do so, not on

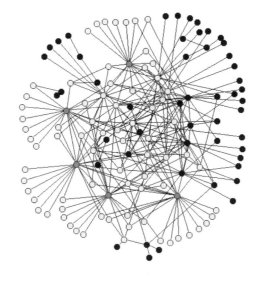

Figure 11.1 Random and scale-free graphs

a random basis, but preferentially in relation to those that are already popular (recall our discussion in Chapter 5 of the Slashdot experience). The latter thus constitute attractors, 'well trodden paths' (Barabási, 2003: para. 3.2.3). This is, therefore, a dynamic model which views networks as self-assembling. With each new node connecting to the already popular nodes, the resulting global distribution of connections reveals a power law; hence the label 'scale-free' graphs.

This basic model of scale-free growth has some limitations, however, of particular significance for our own analytical perspective. First, it is likely to be the older nodes that are best connected; in this gerontocracy, new nodes cannot acquire a level of popularity sufficient to displace their elders. Bianconi and Barabási (2001) have therefore modified the basic model, so that it allows attachment by reference not just to the connectivity of existing nodes, but also their varying degrees of fitness, however defined. This allows nodes to compete for the attention of newcomers by reference to their own fitness as well as their connectedness; those newcomers can themselves also then compete for subsequent cohorts of arrivals. This is of course a feature of socio-economic and institutional change to which we have drawn particular attention; micro-creativity can draw populations to newly discovered attractors or fitness peaks and can indeed generate larger macro-dynamics that transform the whole landscape.

A second limitation is that the basic model of scale-free growth treats any connection, once made, as enduring. However, various elaborations allow for nodes and links to be removed, not just added, and for nodes to 'age', with their scope for acquiring new links decaying (Newman et al., 2006: section 4.3). Nevertheless, empirical studies of scale-free networks often persist in assuming that once connected, always connected, with little interest in the atrophy of stale connections.[3] Such studies then say little about the related processes of disconnection and reconnection, for example, as consumers withdraw their loyalty from one product or brand and preferentially attach themselves to another. What is needed is a metric which captures this dual process. Other modifications to the basic model include an allowance for saturation effects, limiting the number of links a node can acquire. The effect of all these modifications is a departure from a strict power law, or at least modifications to the power law exponent (Fenner et al., 2007).

Third, there is also sometimes insufficient recognition that as networks grow quantitatively they can also change qualitatively. In the case of the internet – one of the most popular examples on which researchers have focused – service providers typically attract users by offering new technologies and services, on top of those already available. Simple agglomeration may of course be one driver of user growth, with new customers attracted by the realisation that, with everyone else now on-line, the advantages of being connected – and the disadvantages of not being – are growing. Nevertheless, it may be not just this quantitative factor that draws people in, but also the addition of further dimensions of service; and indeed, this may be the factor which, as well as connecting the previously unconnected, also induces those who are already connected to switch to a new provider. The offer of these additional dimensions may, in short, be a key element of the 'fitness' that attracts preferential attachment.

This is of obvious relevance to our larger conceptualisation of innovation dynamics, as summarised in Chapter 8. Micro-innovation involves opening up new dimensions of genotypic, technological or institutional space, in search of higher levels of fitness, however construed. It thus involves 'deepening' the connections within this space, as distinct from merely 'widening' them, so as to extend their existing benefits to a larger swathe of the population. This is how profits are earned, power is reinforced and leverage is secured in relation to that larger population; this secures a return on the costs which the innovation required.

It is in light of this that we can reconsider 'Metcalfe's Law', which, as we saw in Chapter 2, asserts that the value of a network to any user grows in proportion to the square of the number of members. In this simple form, the law has been strongly criticised. Not least, beyond a certain point additional users are likely only to produce congestion, detracting from the value of the network, as far as existing members are concerned. For them, the value of the network may resemble a logistic curve, rather than offering continuing explosive growth (Windrum and Swann, 1999; Delong and Summers, 2001).

Once, however, we recognise processes of network 'deepening' as well as 'widening', the picture dramatically changes. Continuing growth in the value of the network is indeed possible, but always at a price which users will differ in their readiness to pay. Deepening involves up-front investment by creative first movers; it permits these first movers to recuperate their investment from the prices they charge to their first customers, those for whom early entry to new levels of the network represents good value. As other customers follow, there is progressive widening of the new dimensions. It is only in this more dynamic perspective that Metcalfe's Law remains compelling.

11.2.3 Directed Graphs

In the foregoing discussion, the direction of the links between nodes has in general been of little significance. We turn now to the discussion of directed graphs, where this directionality is of central importance. It is important empirically because many real world networks are indeed directed; and analytically because directed networks or graphs enable us to incorporate elements of hierarchy and multi-level organisation.

In general, the directed link indicates the dependence of one node upon one other (albeit the form of that dependence varies). It is, however, also possible to define more elaborate chains of dependency, where one node is dependent on the joint or several effects of two or more nodes. This is, for example, the case with Boolean networks, where the dependencies are defined in terms of the operators AND/OR. In the latter case (OR), if any one of the 'upstream' nodes is active, this is sufficient to trigger the dependent node. In the former case (AND), all the upstream nodes must be activated jointly in order to reach the triggering threshold. It is these more elaborate chains of dependency that are typical of the real world; most modelling, however, deals only in simple directed links.

Commonly discussed real world examples of directed graphs include the world-wide web (where hypertext organises other pages) and predator-prey food webs (thought of as directed from prey to predator), something we discussed in Chapter 10 (Bornholdt and Schuster, 2003: Ch. 10; Solé and Bascompte, 2006: Ch. 6). It is in terms of directed graphs that Sommer (2003) and Solé and Pasotor-Satorras (2003) treat the molecular biology of genetic structure: in particular, the role of genes which serve as switches, triggers and suppressors, regulating other genes in complex 'cross-talk' between cells, modules and sub-nets. This is of potential relevance for us: we are interested not only in connections, but also in hierarchy and regulation; in systems of control which sort 'downstream' elements, enabling or disabling their potentialities; and in patterns of 'adverse incorporation' which reinforce dependency. The analysis of directed graphs seems a promising basis.

Within the Bornholdt collection, it is the final chapter, by Jain and Krishna (2003), that is particularly significant, in terms of modelling directed graphs and the associated system dynamics. The authors are interested in autocatalytic sets (ACSs) and the key role that they appear to have played in the origins of life. An ACS comprises a set of simple molecular organisms, none able individually to self-replicate, but each providing a catalyst for each of its fellows: a process of symbiotic and co-evolutionary boot-strapping for collective self-replication (see also Kauffman, 1993: Ch. 7). Jain and Krishna use graph theory to explore the properties and dynamics of such ACSs, but with the aim of illuminating the dynamics of co-evolution more generally.

They proceed in two stages. First, they model population dynamics on a fixed graph. They take a set of coupled ordinary differential equations, which can be thought of as a generalisation of the Volterra-Lotka equations discussed in Chapter 9, so as to include multiple species and to allow not only predator-prey dynamics but also hosts and parasites and symbiosis. The populations of the different species grow and decline within the shared eco-system, depending on the coefficients of species interconnectedness. Jain and Krishna show, in particular, that it is those species that are connected through ACSs that tend to grow most rapidly, outperforming other non-ACS structures (para. 16.3.1).

Second, they allow the network or graph itself to evolve (paras 16.4–16.5). At each stage, they remove the node (species) that is performing least well, as measured by its population size, along with its links. A new node is then introduced and randomly connected to the existing nodes. The population interactions are then re-run. This alternation between population dynamics on a fixed graph and the evolution of that graph by reference to population success is the core of the model. The model thus incorporates both novelty and selection (through the addition and removal of nodes, respectively) and co-evolution (the ACSs).

Jain and Krishna (para. 16.5) demonstrate that population growth dynamics are strongly associated with the discovery and expansion – through novelty and selection – of ACSs, through which mutually associated species can accelerate their growth. This is self-organisation through co-evolution; it reveals how an ACS is able to bootstrap collective self-replication and to do so with such evident evolutionary success. Nevertheless, subsequent removals could lead to a key node within an ACS disappearing (compare our discussion of keystone species in Chapter 10). Equally, the introduction of a new node may engender a new ACS which competes with the first, even exposing the latter to catastrophic collapse (paras 16.5.3–16.6). Also interesting here is the case of a dormant structure, which the arrival of a new node serves to kick into life as part of a newly dominant ACS, at the same time as the erstwhile dominant ACS is weakened. There are obvious links to our earlier discussions of punctuated equilibria and cascades of change.

In all of this, Jain and Krishna employ a variety of means to display the dynamics they uncover. These include 'snapshots' of the graph at different stages of its evolution and print-outs of the simulation runs, displaying crashes and recoveries. What they also demonstrate is the close relationship between the eigenvalues and eigenvectors of a directed graph and the ACSs embedded within it (and thus between the algebra and the topology) and also, therefore, the differing system dynamics (something we have encountered at various points in previous chapters).[4]

11.2.4   Signed Graphs

A signed graph is one whose links are labelled as being either positive or negative. This may, for example, be relevant for the modelling of friendships or international alliances.

Within a graph, a cycle is a series of nodes and links that starts and ends on the same node. In a signed graph, a cycle is said to be balanced if it shows, so to speak, that the enemy of my enemy is my friend. This requires that the number of negative links in the cycle be an even number (or zero); or, equivalently, that the product of the signs across the cycle be positive. An overall census across all cycles gives a measure of overall balance or imbalance in the graph or network (Wasserman and Faust, 1994: Chs 4, 6).

From here some researchers have built models of social dynamics, based on the assumption that structural imbalance will create pressures for change. 'Each actor strives to minimise imbalance and continues to do so until balance is reached or no further change towards balance is possible' (Doreian, 2002: para. 7.3; Doreian et al., 2005: Ch. 10). Nevertheless, these models in general do not allow for persisting sources of novel instability; nor do they allow for evolution of the larger system parameters (for example, the general level of connection). The focus is on movement from a situation of instability to one of stability and equilibrium.

Ludwig and Abell (2007) go somewhat further (again using computational modelling). Here, for a given set of nodes, additional positive and negative links are introduced and connected at random. Any node that exceeds a certain threshold level of imbalance has one of its links removed, albeit there are of course then consequences for the balance enjoyed by other nodes. This is much closer to a properly evolutionary model; there is a source of perennial novelty, a criterion of fitness and a process of selection. As the unfit are removed, this generates a cascade of dynamic consequences. The evolution of the system depends on the system parameters: on the one hand, the threshold level of imbalance, on the other, the parameter defining the probability of new links being positive rather than negative.

Cascades of structural re-balancing sweep across the system, but with a scale and frequency that depend on the system parameters. For intermediate values of those parameters, the system evolves towards a state of 'self-organised criticality' (recall our earlier discussion of Bak). Outside this intermediate zone, either there is such a preponderance of stable cycles that instabilities fail to undermine them, or so little stability that cascades quickly dissipate. The parallel with our earlier discussions of the intermediate zone between order and chaos will be obvious.

The signed graphs we have discussed so far are undirected. There are, however, approaches which deal in directed signed graphs, albeit not

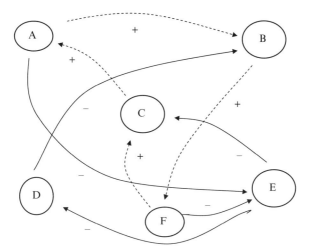

Figure 11.2   Runaway loops

necessarily under that label. Building on the earlier work of such writers as Checkland and Coyle, Powell has developed qualitative system dynamics as an approach to the analysis of organisational strategies (Checkland and Scholes, 1990; Coyle, 1996; Powell and Bradford, 1998, 2000). He first maps the various processes within the organisation and its environment and their network of interdependence. He then labels each line of interdependence, to indicate its direction but also whether the relationship is direct or inverse: whether, in other words, an increase in the 'upstream' variable causes a change in the 'downstream' variable that is positive or negative.

Within this map, Powell proceeds to identify cycles all of whose links are positive. These are cycles which loop back on themselves in self-reinforcing circles (rather like the ACSs investigated by Jain and Krishna). When any one element starts increasing, the whole sub-system experiences explosive growth; when any starts decreasing, it experiences implosive collapse. Powell refers to them as 'runaway loops': in Figure 11.2 the runaway loop is marked as a dotted line. What is then left is to assess first, how positive is positive – this will determine the speed at which the cycle 'runs away'; and second, how well connected the sub-system in question is to the system as a whole, so that its runaway loops have wider influence.

11.2.5   Affiliation Networks

In all the modelling of graphs that we have discussed, new nodes and links – directed or undirected, signed or otherwise – emerge from nowhere, so to

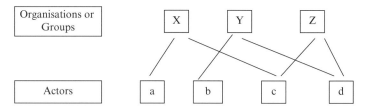

Figure 11.3   Two-mode networks

speak, and attach themselves – on a random or non-random basis – to those that already exist. We then observe how the graph develops and how this depends on the various parameters we have set in place. These models thus incorporate structure and structural development. Nevertheless, it is structure that emerges only as the graph itself develops; it has no prior history.

Within the network literature there is, however, a further distinction that can be deployed to good effect (Doreian et al., 2005: 9–11, Ch. 8). The networks to which we have so far referred are 'one-mode' networks. Links connect nodes to each other. Rather different are two-mode networks – otherwise known as membership or affiliation networks – where, for example, individuals come together in particular organisations or groups or meeting points. It is these latter that link individuals together, but that are themselves then linked through the said individuals, in reciprocal fashion. Figure 11.3 illustrates a simple case.

Among the classic studies are Doreian's study of voting behaviour across different legal cases, by US Supreme Court judges, and Davis's 1941 study of women participating in social events (for discussion of both, see Doreian et al., 2005: Ch. 8; see also Wasserman and Faust, 1994: Ch. 8; Carrington et al., 2005: Ch. 7). Each organisation enjoys participation from multiple individuals and each individual connects to multiple organisations.

This is still an essentially static analysis. Watts, however, adds a dynamic element, and offers what is for us a potentially more interesting perspective (Watts, 2003: 118–21). The affiliations that individuals have to organisations or groups may be seen as constituting their positions within a pre-existing social structure. It is then possible to investigate how, as any new organisation or meeting point is established, or some new legal case arises, the new affiliations to these that individuals establish are related to those prior structural affiliations.

Figure 11.4 presents the previous diagram in terms of Watts's approach. The three existing Groups X, Y and Z are now thought of as defining the pre-existing social structure in which the social actors are variously

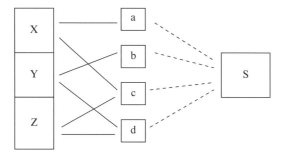

Figure 11.4   Structural development and history

embedded. Watts will then investigate which of them affiliate to new organisation S and how far these affiliations are related to the prior structural locations. This is structural development and history: we exploit this approach later in this chapter.

11.3   EMPIRICAL ANALYSIS OF NETWORKS

Earlier in this chapter we identified three principal approaches to the analysis of networks. So far we have been concerned with analytical and computational modelling; we now turn to the elucidation of underlying patterns to be found within empirical data sets and the development of summary metrics: always with the aim of developing analytical and empirical tools for our interest in social dynamics.

11.3.1   Empirical Patterns

It is in the sociological study of networks that the analysis of empirical data sets has most obviously developed specific procedures. The challenge, of course, is to simplify such data sets into more parsimonious terms, so that their 'underlying' features can be distinguished from those that are more ephemeral.

The traditional approach has been to take the adjacency matrix of a network and simplify it through a process of 'blockmodelling': pioneered by Homans in the 1950s (Scott, 2000: Ch. 2) but substantially developed only from the 1970s (Wasserman and Faust, 1994: Chs 9–10). This was seen as identifying patterns of 'structural equivalence': that is, those individuals in a social network who were connected in similar ways (although 'similar' was a not unproblematic notion). This was then taken as revealing structurally located social roles which all the individuals in question shared – for example, that of 'nurse' or 'manager'. Identification of these 'structural equivalences' would lay bare the array of social roles in that society and indeed their interrelations. Blockmodelling was therefore seen by many of its practitioners as a data-driven tool of sociological enquiry, enabling the empirical data to 'speak for themselves'. Initially it was a rather laborious matter of pencil and paper; computational algorithms are, however, now available (Butts, 2001).

In their critical review of blockmodelling, however, Doreian et al. (2005) reject the notion that the empirical data can 'speak for themselves' and that they can, indeed, without prior theoretical commitments on the part of the investigator, lay bare wider and more fundamental features of social structure. Blockmodelling employs a variety of 'models' in order to simplify the adjacency matrix; these express particular ideal types of social relations. As Doreian argues (section 7.4), the selection of these ideal types requires justification by reference to prior theoretical and substantive understanding of the networks in question. This is a deductive approach, in place of the traditional inductive methodology.

Doreian is also critical of the narrow range of models and ideal types that blockmodellers have typically employed. The range should be extended to encompass directed and undirected graphs, signed graphs and networks where links have values other than zero and one (Chs 9–10). This will, however, require corresponding creativity in the range of models and ideal types deployed, tapping into the profuse analytical and theoretical insights which even our own short review in the previous section of this chapter revealed. Finally, Doreian points out that more than one blockmodel may 'fit' a given empirical data set. He therefore highlights the need for a 'goodness of fit' criterion, by which to discriminate among such contenders, and used in conjunction with an assessment of their theoretical plausibility in any given case (pp. 192ff., 228, 231–3).

As yet, however, there seems to be some considerable disjunction between the modelling literatures discussed in the previous section and the empirically oriented approaches which Doreian champions. True, his closing pages make reference to those modelling literatures, citing, for example, Barabási and Watts; and he evidently anticipates that they could enrich the blockmodelling toolkit. Meanwhile the Newman et al. (2006) collection, which reproduces many of the dynamic models we reviewed in the previous section, for its part makes no reference in its index to blockmodelling at all. The overwhelming focus is on the algebra of graphs and networks and their computational simulation. To bridge this gulf seems as yet to be unfinished business – indeed, barely begun.

11.3.2 Summary Metrics

Within sociology, there is a long-standing tradition of using summary metrics to compare networks and track their properties over time. Much of this older literature was concerned with the 'statics' of networks. Nevertheless, in principle summary metrics might also serve to identify particular critical thresholds and tipping points; and, indeed, to illuminate thereby particular junctures for policy intervention.

For the moment we take note of some of the principal metrics that have been in common use (for general discussions, see Wassermann and Faust, 1994: Ch. 5; Scott, 2000: Ch. 5; Croft et al., 2008: Ch. 4). The 'density' of a network is the proportion of possible connections that actually exist. The 'centrality' of a node refers to its connectedness. 'Prestige' is the counterpart of centrality in a directed graph, referring to the connectedness of a given node as far as incoming links are concerned; in some contexts 'dominance' may be a more appropriate way of denoting this. Each of these metrics can then be elaborated in a number of refinements (see, for example, Everett and Borgatti, 2005). In recent years, a variety of software tools have become available that allow networks to be analysed and visualised and these metrics calculated and compared (for example, UCINET[5] and NetDraw[6]).

Nevertheless, as already suggested, these are essentially static metrics of network structure. As such they ignore the dynamic processes which all of the preceding discussion has highlighted. Thus, for example, as Watts aptly points out, while much effort has been devoted to measuring the 'centrality' of different nodes, in itself this may tell us little about the dynamic behaviour of the network in question (Watts, 2003: Ch. 2). In contrast, Gladwell (2001) invites us to identify 'tipping points' in the dynamic evolution of networks and other systems; Solé and Bascompte and other ecologists point to percolation thresholds; Bak similarly argues that 'self-organised criticality' involves critical thresholds which are widespread in natural and social dynamics.

It is against this background – and in the specific context of policy interventions – that we will in Part 3 consider what dynamic indicators may be appropriate.

11.4   THE EMPIRICAL INVESTIGATION OF CONNECTIONS

It is no mean task to give the various models we have reviewed empirical substance. Within the empirical networks to which this chapter has referred, for purposes of illustration, network links or edges have corresponded to a wide variety of relationships between the nodes concerned, including communication, diffusion, domination and dependence. Each of these, when considered as a social relationship, is theoretically problematic and contested. To capture such a relationship in a simple link (whether directed or undirected, signed or unsigned) is hazardous, even if it allows for some interesting modelling opportunities. The same goes for network nodes, whether we take these as referring to technologies, institutions, social actors or organisations. It is no less problematic to operationalise empirically the algorithms that drive the evolutionary models of Jain and Krishna, Ludwig and Abell, or the various rules employed by Barabási for describing how nodes become connected to their fellows.

Institutional and technological connections, the heartland of this study, provide no less a challenge for modelling. It was through the work of Dopfer and Potts (2008: para. 1.4) that we approached these connections, seen as comprising systems of rules and their carriers.[7] Our institutionalist writers were similarly concerned with the rules of social interaction articulated by different institutional settings. Ostrom in particular, through her deontic operators, reached towards a treatment of rules as generic and abstract as Dopfer and Potts. Her more recent work turns this into a methodology and programme for systematic empirical enquiry, wider than her earlier interest in common pool resources (Ostrom, 2005). This shows how, in principle, qualitative accounts in the institutionalist tradition can be combined with formal modelling, for purposes of empirical investigation. We attempt something more modest, but not without parallels.

The models we choose for the present study must embody the principal elements of our ontology. First, social actors have multiple affiliations within a social structure. This is a legacy which has both shaped and limited their capacities: a legacy which they drag with them but which also empowers them, even as they modify and develop it. This requires that we select models which can in some degree incorporate history. One-mode networks – of the sort that figured prominently in our discussion of network dynamics – can do this to some extent: we can watch the network as it develops, and the extent to which later phases grow out of earlier ones. Nevertheless, as already suggested, models of two-mode affiliation networks may offer more. We have seen, in particular, that Watts treats the affiliations that individuals have to organisations or groups as constituting their positions within a social structure; he then investigates how far their affiliation to new groups depends on those prior positions (recall Figure 11.4). This well captures our interest in the legacy of connections that social actors drag with them.

Second, social actors make new connections and combinations and discard old ones, by reference to their fitness for purpose. This is evolutionary development, but driven by human creativity rather than random variation, husbanding rather than natural selection. Evolutionary models that involve random variation in nodes and links may nevertheless offer some useful insights; recall, for example, those of Jain and Krishna, Ludwig and Abell, both of which had new nodes appearing and the less fit then removed from the system. These models can be used to display processes of co-evolution and bootstrapping through auto-catalysis, punctuated equilibria, cascades of structural reconfiguration, crashes and recoveries, system resilience.

Nevertheless, these models hardly capture the central place we accord to human purposes. One approach may be to capture actors' perceptions of 'fitness for purpose' in terms of 'signed graphs', within which these actors then seek consistency or 'structural balance'. This is intuitively attractive for social science because it can be applied, in an action frame of reference, to the subjective logic of the situation in which individual actors find themselves and the coherence they seek to impose on the disparate systems of rules in which they are embroiled (Dawe, 1970). This means of course that we cannot expect to label each link 'positive' or 'negative' by external observation; this must be ascertained by enquiry of the actors themselves.

Third, social actors are engaged in a positional struggle. In re-weaving their connections, they may seek not 'structural balance' but new fronts that can be opened, with a view to establishing new points of leverage and co-evolutionary advantage. This is the co-evolutionary 'arms race' described by Maynard Smith and Kauffman, the 'race against time' which John Darwin compellingly recounts, the process of 'deepen-widen-warp' on which our ontology in Part 1 centred. In the language of those earlier chapters, each social actor seeks to progress upwards along a 'perilous path', an ever-continuing effort to re-weave and re-deploy connections, in order to secure monotonic ascent of the fitness landscape, even if this means relegating others to some lonely spur.

Here it is Powell's use of signed directed networks, in his qualitative system dynamics, that seems to offer modelling promise. Powell asks analysts and actors to identify 'runaway loops' available within an organisation's hinterland: either to take advantage of their autocatalytic dynamics, or to avoid and stifle them, depending on the positional interests of the actor in question. It is their 'mental models' of how these loops are liable to unfold in an uncertain world that inform their strategies for building positional advantage.

We illustrate now how an approach in terms of multiple affiliations, signed networks and the runaway loops of positional advantage might be fruitfully developed.

Jervis (1997, Ch. 6) uses structural balance theory by reference to international relations. The simplest case – the enemy of my enemy is my friend – would here seem readily applicable. As each nation seeks structural balance or consistency in its relations, the system tends to drive those involved into polarised alliances (pp. 210–14). Jervis lodges his account of these international actors within their shared history and the multiple affiliations into which they are already locked. Nevertheless, there are a number of caveats, as Jervis himself argues and as our foregoing discussion of network dynamics would lead us to expect.

The first is that in any complex network any local adjustment – for example, former enemies resolving their differences in order to achieve greater balance in the larger web of relations that each enjoys – is liable to set a train of secondary adjustments in motion. Some of these adjustments may turn into cascades or avalanches of wider reconfiguration. Social actors – in this case, nation states – may have limited capacity to anticipate such dynamics. The extent of these secondary adjustments will vary; they may be confined to some particular region – the Balkans, East-Central Africa – or they may pervade a much larger arena, even engulfing the entire international system. In all of this, sequence matters. Depending on which local adjustment occurs first, the chain of adjustments that follows is liable to vary, as also the final ecology of enemies and friends.

Second, it is by reference to the preferences and strategies of social actors that we must interpret instances of structural imbalance. It is they who assess the threats from different enemies and decide which should be courted as friends (pp. 221ff.). If the demands of larger alliances are muted, it may be possible to maintain dissonant local friendships and enmities (pp. 234–5). If, however, those demands are strong, local adventures may be ruled out; the state in question finds itself in a frozen forcing structure, downstream of the Great Powers. Such a country may nevertheless remain on the lookout for unfreezing such structures from below and discovering extra degrees of freedom.

More generally, rather than adjusting its alliances so as to secure structural balance, a country may tolerate some inconsistencies, as the price of securing positional leverage. This may involve some postponement of the structural balance they might otherwise achieve; time matters, not least the strategic horizon and sequence by reference to which such balance is sought. Meanwhile such strategic choices may bring imbalance to rivals, sidelining and disrupting them. Jervis is sensitive to the race for positional advantage in which these actors are involved and the 'runaway loops' for which they search, depending on how they expect the future to unfold. This is of course precisely the race for international advantage that John Darwin and Arrighi depict, as we saw in the previous chapter. A structural balance model need not, therefore, treat actors as simply reacting to the immediate strains in their alliances; it can acknowledge the autonomy and discretion that they enjoy, albeit limited, as they manage this balance over time and seek to build positional advantage.

Jervis shows how signed networks can be used to explore how nation states may seek structural balance, on the one hand, runaway loops of positional advantage, on the other. However, it is not obvious that 'the enemy of my enemy is my friend' is a useful measure of balance and imbalance across the larger range of social connections and dynamics with which we are concerned. We must find a more appropriate alternative. We again recall the deontic operators of requirement, prohibition and permission we introduced in Chapter 5. Following Ostrom (1990), we suggested that these could be taken as the basic rules of social interaction variously enjoined in different institutional settings. Institutions confer entitlements (permissions) and impose obligations (requirements and prohibitions) (see similarly Streek and Thelen, 2005: 9). Indeed, the two often come into existence together. Any entitlement that is institutionally offered typically imposes also an obligation: not only on others, to respect the entitlement conferred on the person in question, but also on the recipient, if only to be a law-abiding citizen. This is the case whether we speak, for example, of the family and informal associations, or of formal organisations, such as the state and the corporate sector.

Any social actor will typically be enmeshed in a variety of institutions, embodying such links of entitlement and obligation. Some will consist of financial debits and credits; others will involve transactions of power, prestige and deference. Some are embodied in formal contracts; some involve legal undertakings in the shadow of the state; some rely largely on moral commitments and sanctions. They will have different timescales. Obligations differ moreover in their 'fungibility': the scope for converting one into another. Entitlements vary in the opportunities they open for building capacity and leverage on the various institutional terrains on which the actor in question is engaged.

The social actor can be thought of as managing these entitlements and obligations, so as to maintain – and if possible to strengthen – their positional advantage: discharging or re-scheduling obligations, mobilising entitlements so as to take advantage of new opportunities for runaway loops. Of course, many of these entitlements and obligations may be fixed and non-negotiable; like Jervis's nation states, an individual or a local community may find itself in a 'frozen forcing structure', downstream of the 'Great Powers' of the society in question. More generally, however, what is of interest empirically is how actors re-weave these entitlements and obligations in time and social space and the consequences that follow for the institutional micro-eco-systems of others, with cascades of wider re-balancing and reconfiguration.

For modelling purposes it may prove convenient to assign positive and negative signs, respectively, to these entitlements and obligations and to map the imbalances thereby revealed. It may also be possible to draw insights from the dynamic models of networks reviewed in this chapter. Nevertheless, the detail of the model must always be subordinate to the sociological and policy questions of interest. We consider in Chapter 15 how such an approach might be applied.

11.5   CONCLUSION

Our ontology of connections guides our search for analytical and computational modelling tools. None of the network models as yet available is entirely sufficient to the task; we may need to use several in tandem. Nevertheless, even if the available tools are only partially suited, we do at least have a standpoint from which to appraise their suitability and improve them. It is far better to be in this position than to practise 'dandyism', investing in methodological tools merely because they are readily available and widely used, rather than because they are suitable for our purpose.

We also now have tools for empirical investigation and data analysis of connections. Doreian has encouraged us to be ambitious in the deployment of blockmodelling, although how far this can be developed for the sort of ontology we have advocated remains a somewhat open question. Certainly any blockmodelling of empirical connections will need to move from its traditional concern with network statics to the treatment of network dynamics, including, for example, the ways in which the reconnection of social sub-systems can 'switch' their trajectories of development. It must also be accompanied by qualitative institutional analysis and investigation of the subjective logic of the situation for the actors in question.

We have touched on the significance of system parameters and thresholds for understanding system dynamics, but we have not offered any summary metrics in place of those traditionally used in static network analysis. This will move centre-stage in Part 3, concerned with policy-making. There we will, for example, be interested in the robustness and resilience of connections and, where they suffer breakdown, the scope for recovery.

It will by now be evident that Part 2 of this book has a somewhat different logic from Part 1. There we were building a coherent and integrated ontology, a conceptual framework in which the rest of this investigation could then be grounded. Here, in contrast, we review a variety of modelling approaches, assessing their relevance and utility by reference to that ontology, but only to a lesser extent offering a cumulative progression from one chapter to the next. Indeed, while our ontology must be coherent, we will be rather eclectic in the models and methods we use. Nevertheless, these individual chapters are not without relevance for each other and in subsequent chapters we build on this discussion of networks and graphs.

As noted in earlier chapters, we approach institutional and technological connections by reference to the systems of rules they embody, but also their populations of carriers. It is on these populations that Chapter 12 will focus. We locate these populations within the social structure – in particular, the affiliations of social class – and the entitlements and obligations these affiliations involve. We consider how, from these socially structured locations, these populations variously reach out to re-weave the connective geometry, building advantage in the positional struggle. It is thus by reference to our discussion of connections – underpinned of course by the ontological and conceptual discussion of Part 1 – that we now turn to the modelling and measurement of population dynamics.

12 Mobility on social landscapes

12.1 INTRODUCTION

Social scientists are generously endowed with social survey data, which provide the basis for much of their research and policy advice. With this substantial comparative advantage, there is no need for them to be laggards in the application of dynamic analysis, quite the opposite (Byrne, 1998: Ch. 4). Indeed, it may be that some social scientists are already 'speaking prose' – more precisely, investigating society as a complex system – without knowing it and without being appreciated for this by the larger community of complexity science.

In this chapter we review the use of social surveys for purposes of social analysis. We are after all concerned here in Part 2 with models and empirical methods; we can hardly avoid assessing existing practices in empirical social enquiry. The techniques we will appraise are moreover those which Byrne highlights, in his pioneering work on complexity and social science, as being of particular interest (Byrne, 1998: 82–5).

It is social surveys of households that are most commonly used by sociologists and social policy analysts (although surveys are also of course possible in relation to firms and other organisations, both public and private). Such surveys typically investigate the number, age and gender of the members of the household (demographic characteristics); their skills, occupations and employment; their incomes and assets; their health and housing; their social contacts. The data they furnish as to the social characteristics of populations can be cross-tabulated, to show how these characteristics are distributed and how they change over time (Gilbert, 1981).

Over recent decades it is sociological investigations of social mobility that have used household surveys with a particularly impressive conjunction of theoretical, methodological and empirical rigour. Patterns and rates of social mobility are of course highly relevant to social policy debates, concerned, for example, with trends and mechanisms of inequality, the relationship between equality of opportunity and equality of outcome, or the optimal utilisation of human resources. Whether, therefore, our interest is primarily sociological or social policy related, this body of work merits attention.

Central to this scholarship has been the work of Goldthorpe and his colleagues, concerned principally with inter-generational mobility. We review first the analytical methods he deploys; we then proceed to the empirical findings and their theoretical explanation. We deal only in passing with other contributors such as Hauser, Hout and Sørensen (see, for example, Hout and Hauser, 1992; Sørensen, 1992; Beller and Hout, 2006). Although there is much critical exchange among these various scholars, this is concerned with methodological refinements and substantive interpretations which do not significantly affect the line of analysis which the present chapter seeks to develop.

We will, however, question whether the patterns and dynamics of mobility this work reveals have been adequately theorised. We argue instead for an account in terms of 'self-organised criticality', as expounded in earlier chapters of this book, but also for more adequate modelling of institutional entrepreneurship. In this way we seek to bring together the methods of measurement and the substantive findings of these mobility studies with the conceptual and modelling approaches we have developed in this book.

12.2 ANALYTICAL METHODS

Goldthorpe groups occupations into social classes according to the CASMIN scheme of which he has been the principal developer.[1] Movements from particular class origins to class destinations are cross-tabulated (Erikson and Goldthorpe, 1993: Ch. 2). These flows can then be analysed using log-linear modelling (Hauser, 1978; Hout, 1983; Sloane and Morgan, 1996). This has permitted a clearer critique of the distinction formerly drawn between 'structural' and 'exchange mobility', leaving that between 'absolute' and 'relative' rates much to be preferred. It has also enabled much more rigorous examination of the extent and degree of cross-national and inter-temporal differences in mobility.

Consider a mobility matrix whose rows refer to origins, the columns to destinations. The matrix is symmetrical, with the same class categories applying to both. Individual cell values are denoted f_{ij} (where i and j each ranges from 1 to N). Now let us express the value f_{ij} thus:

$$f_{ij} = a * b_i * c_j * u_{ij} \qquad (12.1)$$

where a is the total number of – in this case – persons sampled, b_i and c_j are, respectively, the row and column marginal totals (expressed as proportions of the sample total) and u_{ij} expresses the interaction between row and column variables.

This may be turned into the linear logarithmic equation

$$\log f_{ij} = \log a + \log b_i + \log c_j + \log u_{ij} \qquad (12.2)$$

If $\log u_{ij}$ is zero (and thus u_{ij} is 1) there is no association or interaction between origins and destinations; the value of f_{ij} is determined wholly by the corresponding marginal totals and the overall population. This provides a convenient null hypothesis against which other situations – for non-zero $\log u_{ij}$ – can be compared. These are situations where row and column variables interact: where the chances of moving into different destinations depend in part upon social origins. Log-linear models provide us with a convenient and appropriate means of laying bare such u_{ij} interaction effects and examining whether, for example, they vary over time or between countries (Goldthorpe, 1980: 80).

Equations (12.1) and (12.2) represent the simplest case. Additional variables enter these equations when we seek to make comparisons over time, between successive cohorts, or between countries. The possible interaction terms also grow in number: first the bilateral interactions between any two variables in the equation, then those of higher order. Such equations completely specify the value of f_{ij} and reveal the extent to which f_{ij} is determined by the various marginal totals and interaction effects.

However, while such an equation can offer a perfect 'fit', it does so without any economy in the range of explanatory variable employed: everything that could be mobilised has been. The next task, therefore, is to try for a more parsimonious explanation of the f_{ij} cell values, aiming for a less than perfect fit, but one which is nevertheless sufficient. As we have already seen, one approach is to check whether there is a good enough fit when we entirely disregard u_{ij} (the interaction element): when, in other words, we adopt the null hypothesis of no interaction between origins and destinations. If this is rejected, we then have to consider how to develop a model which includes a substantial amount of the u_{ij} interaction but with some parsimony.

Log-linear analysis allows us to posit different degrees (or 'density') of interaction – thus different values of u_{ij} – for different zones of the matrix. On the one hand, this recognises that the null hypothesis has to be rejected: on the other, in the interests of parsimony it is content to capture the main features of the interaction topography and to forego a finer-grained account. Thus, for example, we might posit a relatively high level of interaction down the leading diagonal (self-recruitment by each class) but lesser degrees everywhere else: thus two zones or levels of interaction. Progressively more refined designation of zones is then possible, assessing at each stage the goodness of fit that the model affords. For a given target level of goodness of fit, we will then prefer on grounds of parsimony the model with the fewest zones – these will in general be the zones that offer the highest levels of interaction, the highest values of u_{ij} – as being the most elegant and powerful of the models that meet our requirements.

Nevertheless, while parsimony and goodness of fit are the two principal criteria as far as modelling procedure is concerned, what also matters is that the model with which we end up makes sense in theoretical terms, in relation to the subject matter in question (Hauser, 1978: 937; Goldthorpe, 1980: 98; Erikson and Goldthorpe, 1993: Ch. 2; Sloane and Morgan, 1996: 335–6). Social scientific judgement is therefore required: simple formulaic procedures in terms of fitness and parsimony will not do.

12.3   THE DYNAMIC ANALYSIS OF SOCIAL MOBILITY

Goldthorpe first draws attention to the significant variation in overall (or absolute) rates of social mobility as between different industrial societies and, indeed, the variations within any one of these societies over time. This is scarcely surprising, given the wide variations in occupational and employment structures of different industrial nations and in the rate and phasing of their development (Erikson and Goldthorpe, 1993: 23–4). These structures are shaped by a multitude of wider 'economic, techno-logical and demographic circumstances' (p. 24), including changes in inter-national political economy, trading relations and patterns of economic dominance and dependence (p. 103). There have also been great variations in the extent to which structural change has resulted from specific political interventions by a modernising state.

The result has been quite different development paths, shaping the patterns and rates of absolute mobility: differences that persist long term (pp. 189–204). This is of course fully consistent with the argument of Chapter 10 above: in social, economic and institutional change, timing and sequencing matter and their effects persist. Goldthorpe concludes that the best that can be hoped for is a qualitative, historically oriented case study approach (pp. 61, 188–9). Despite this, we leave open the question of whether the contingent relationships between structural change, on the one hand, and overall mobility rates, on the other, can be formally mod-elled: and how, more generally, we should conceptualise and model what, borrowing from Pierson, we earlier referred to as the 'abrasions' between dynamically coupled social processes.

Goldthorpe now proceeds to use log-linear modelling to abstract from such structural changes and variations, allowing him to examine mobility

Table 12.1   Log-linear interaction parameters (log u_{ij}) for the core model of inter-generational class mobility

		I+II	III	IVa/b	IVc	V+VI	VIIa	VIIb
I+II	Service class	1.24	0.24	0.24	−1.25	−0.22	−0.64	−2.44
III	Routine non-manual/white collar	0.24	0.43	0.00	−1.03	0.00	−0.22	−1.25
IVa/b	Small employers/petty bourgeoisie	0.24	0.00	1.24	−0.57	0.00	−0.22	−1.25
IVc	Farmers	−1.67	−1.25	−0.79	1.98	−1.25	−0.57	0.00
V+VI	Foremen and technicians and skilled manual workers	−0.22	0.00	0.00	−1.03	0.43	0.24	−1.25
VIIa	Semi-skilled and unskilled	−0.64	−0.22	−0.22	−1.25	0.24	0.43	−1.03
VIIb	Agricultural workers	−2.44	−1.25	−1.25	−0.22	−1.25	−0.57	0.43

Source: Reproduced from R. Erickson and J.H. Goldthorpe, *The Constant Flux*, p. 135, Table 4.4, with kind permission of Oxford University Press, © 1993.

net of such effects. Net or relative mobility measures the mobility chances of sons from different classes *relative to each other*.[2] Relative mobility thus refers to what Goldthorpe terms the 'endogenous mobility regime', as distinct from the rates of absolute mobility which sons in different classes enjoy, as a result of both relative mobility and the mobility effects of the aforesaid structural changes. In the above equations, it is the u_{ij} interaction terms that measure this relative mobility and the others that capture the mobility effects of wider structural changes.

Goldthorpe finds that relative mobility rates show a rather high level of stability over time in the various industrial societies his data cover, even if there are some transient variations (pp. 86–96, 147, 175). Following Featherman et al. (1975), he also finds that as between different societies, there is a high degree of commonality, with the various 'zones' of log-linear interaction revealing a very similar topography. Table 12.1 displays the resulting values of log u_{ij} in this 'core model' (Erikson and Goldthorpe, 1993: Ch. 4 and especially Table 4.4). The rows give class of origin, the columns class of destination. The shaded cells are those with positive values, where there is a positive association between the origins and destinations in question.

There are some national variations by reference to this core model. In Sweden the contours of the mobility landscape in the 'core model' are maintained, but they tend to be gentler, especially along the leading diagonal of self-recruitment, with a relatively high degree of openness. In Germany, in contrast, the contours are harsher, especially as between manual and white collar occupations, and indeed between skilled and unskilled manual workers; the zone of white collar self-recruitment (the 'northwest' of the shaded area in Table 12.1) is, however, somewhat enlarged, to include flows between routine non-manual and petty bourgeoisie. Meanwhile in the countries of eastern Europe, the period of communist rule modified the contours in a variety of discrete ways, tending to equalise mobility chances. Nevertheless, overall what is most striking is the degree of commonality in the contours across all of the countries studied, even if the relative 'heights' of those contours vary somewhat (Erikson and Goldthorpe, 1993: Ch. 5).

As we have already noted, fitting these models involves not only considerations of parsimony and goodness of fit, but also theoretical plausibility. It is therefore to Goldthorpe's theoretical account that we now turn.

12.3.1   The Stability of Relative Mobility

If the pattern of relative mobility rates, as captured by log-linear analysis, is so invariable, why is this? Why, in particular, have expectations of a more open society, with 'more universalistic, achievement-oriented processes of social selection', not materialised, notwithstanding the efficiency benefits that this would presumably bring to advanced industrial societies? Goldthorpe argues that countervailing pressures from those who are already advantaged, so as to secure the life chances of their own children, have frustrated any such efficiency requirements (Erikson and Goldthorpe, 1993: 368–9, 393–7). It is these countervailing pressures that he seeks to understand.

Goldthorpe points out that occupational hierarchies are very similar in different industrial countries, producing similar relativities of advantage and power (pp. 24, 376). To understand how these relativities are converted into differential mobility chances, it is necessary to take account of three factors (Goldthorpe, 1980: 98–9; Erikson and Goldthorpe, 1993: 122–3, 302, 391ff.). Across the populations of different industrial societies there is, first, a widely shared perception of the occupational destinations that are most desirable. There is therefore no reason to explain class variations in mobility experience by reference to differences in their assessments of such desirability; on the contrary, aspiration for rather similar occupational destinations must be expected. Differential chances of reaching those destinations must instead be explained, on the one hand, by reference to the relative advantages enjoyed by individuals of different class origin, in terms of their economic, cultural and social resources, and, on the other hand, the relative barriers to access that different class positions present, in terms of those same resources. (The most recent summary of his position is to be found in Goldthorpe, 2007b: Ch. 7.)

A mobility matrix summarises the outcome of a competition for valued positions. However, the mobility matrix itself is agnostic as to the processes involved; it simply offers the truism that if one person attains a highly valued position there is in consequence one less place for others. This may be sufficient if our aim is simply to calculate and compare mobility rates. Nevertheless, if we are properly to explain such rates – and to understand the relationship between agency and structure – we need a theory of positional allocation, identifying the process by which one person's mobility reinforces another's immobility.

Some elements of such a theory are evident in Goldthorpe's own account. Those who are relatively advantaged, in terms of the resources and networks of influence at their disposal, can if necessary bring these reserves to bear, in order to secure key positions and careers for their offspring. They thereby trump the bids of other social classes and oblige them to make do with unoccupied – and less attractive – positions. Indeed, these reserves may also allow them to shape the rules which define what the trumps are. They are thus able not only to throw greater reserves into the fray, but also to establish the priority of their claims.

These are fundamentally status claims, albeit made in the shadow of their greater resources and their greater scope for exit and voice.[3] Thus, for example, the harsh contours of the German mobility landscape, to which we have already drawn attention, involve long-entrenched sub-cultural and status divisions between white collar and manual workers, as well as between skilled and unskilled manual workers, reinforced through the system of vocational education and training and apprenticeships. These are rooted, not least, in the institutionalised differences in employment relations deriving from Bismarckian social policy and German public law (Erikson and Goldthorpe, 1993: Ch. 5). Such status divisions constitute *par excellence* institutionalised first mover advantage and adverse incorporation in a positional competition (Hirsch, 1977), a Stackelberg game of the sort that has figured at various points in preceding chapters, with the same quality of self-reinforcement which we have repeatedly highlighted as being significant for social inertia.

This supplements, rather than contradicts Goldthorpe's own position. He does, after all, give particular attention to those positional resources which grant more advantaged groups an enhanced capacity to exclude

(Goldthorpe, 1980: 100). He also, by reference to Lieberson (1987), recognises the importance of the capacity to 'write the rules' of the positional game (Erikson and Goldthorpe, 1993: 394). Throughout, indeed, his focus is on strategic action by the advantaged, with others reduced to being mere change takers. It is also worth noticing that in his subsequent treatise *On Sociology*, Goldthorpe offers a model where each social class aims at all costs to avoid downward mobility on the part of its offspring (Goldthorpe, 2000: 238–43). Thus while relatively advantaged actors have greater resources in reserve, to throw into the positional fray, the minimum outcome which they are ready to tolerate – the *Verdun* which at all costs they defend – is also set higher. This also is in effect a first mover model: the more advantaged are ready and able to raise the stakes to whatever level is necessary in order to secure their minimum demands, out-bidding less advantaged competitors, who are thus placed in the position of 'last mover' or 'change taker').[4] It follows that we must think of the 'relative barriers' involved in gaining access to different class positions not simply in terms of the economic, cultural and social resources that such access requires but also the institutional rules involved; and we must recognise that the power to maintain or change those rules – and thus to re-design the barriers – is itself socially distributed. Not least, the institutional rules which govern the systems of social selection and express these first choice privileges come to the centre of attention, including in particular the system of education and training and the award of credentials.

Finally, however, Goldthorpe argues that the empirical evidence reveals some scope for purposive political action that could, in principle, modify these relativities of advantage and disadvantage – and, we might now add, the institutional rules of the positional competition (Erikson and Goldthorpe, 1993: 26). This he adduces from some of the aforesaid national variations in the general pattern of commonality (Ch. 5). In Sweden, as we have seen, the landscape of the mobility matrix is generally gentler. This Goldthorpe explains by reference to the lesser inequalities that characterise Sweden, as a result of strongly egalitarian Social Democratic policies; this reduces the scope for more advantaged groups to shape the positional competition. Changes in the institutional rules of educational selection have also helped (Goldthorpe, 2000: 180). Meanwhile, in the cases of Hungary, Poland and Czechoslovakia Goldthorpe finds deviations from the common pattern which are associated, as in Sweden, with political interventions, albeit not according to a standard pattern of 'state socialism'. It is the Swedish and east European cases that lead Goldthorpe to conclude that relative mobility chances may be susceptible to modification through deliberate and sustained political action, albeit still within the broadly common topography of relative mobility chances that his log-linear modelling has otherwise revealed (Erikson and Goldthorpe, 1993: 176–80).

12.3.2   Individual Mobility Strategies and the 'Natural History' of Classes

As we have seen, for Goldthorpe it is the pattern of relative mobility – and in particular its stability over time and across a variety of industrial nations – that is of the greatest sociological interest. Nevertheless, it is the overall pattern of inflows and outflows among social classes – and thus absolute rates of mobility – that dictates whether, for example, a given class grows or shrinks in numbers and whether it becomes more or less homogeneous in its origins. It is this 'natural history' of different classes that tends moreover to shape the subjective experiences of individuals: their readiness, for example, to make common cause with those of the same class and the response they make to shrinking opportunities for their offspring (Goldthorpe, 1980: Ch. 9; Erikson and Goldthorpe, 1993: Ch. 6).

In contrast, 'trends and patterns in relative mobility rates represent aspects of inequality that are of extremely low social visibility' (Goldthorpe, 1980: 266), whatever their significance for sociological analysis. Moreover, notwithstanding the invariance of relative mobility rates, inter- and intra-generational mobility can, from the standpoint of the individual, appear as a series of critical junctures which have arisen variously from personal effort, good or bad luck and general collective progress. Goldthorpe here adopts what is essentially a Weberian method of *Verstehen*, in terms of the 'rational intelligibility' of action (p. 221) and the 'subjective logic' of the choices that individuals make (in his more recent work this is couched in terms of rational action: see especially *On Sociology*).

Goldthorpe recognises that in making these choices, individuals develop 'mobility strategies' for themselves and their offspring adjusted to the specificities of institutions in their particular societies. To this extent, the lifetime trajectories that they follow are likely to display significant cross-national variations. Such variations have been taken by some scholars embracing a life-course perspective as putting in question an account in terms of inter-generational mobility tables (see, for example, Sørensen, 1992). Nevertheless, as Goldthorpe counters, notwithstanding these diversities of route and mobility strategy, the cross-national stability of relative mobility rates attests to overriding constraints on mobility outcomes.

It is of course those who are more advantaged who have the variety of resources that a flexible mobility strategy requires and knowledge of the institutional routes that are most promising. In addition, they are the ones whose experience has, we might say, most disposed them to see themselves as agile 'first movers', rather than simply adjusting to changes imposed by their wider situation (Goldthorpe, 1980: 234–5). This has also made them ready to defend their positions of advantage and that of their offspring through a variety of 'strategies of exclusion' (p. 276): strategies that may involve individual but also collective responses.[5] Such strategies of defence, exclusion and institutional contestation are, as Goldthorpe argues elsewhere, liable to range across a variety of socio-economic terrains: from education to the labour market, to the social security system and the housing market (Goldthorpe, 1974, 1978, 1984, 1985). An advantage gained by changing the terms of one settlement will shift the balance of forces which can contest another; old and relatively stable institutional arrangements are liable to be set in turmoil and new opportunities for leverage to emerge.

Nevertheless, this still leaves us with a puzzle. If individual mobility strategies are framed by reference to absolute mobility flows – flows that vary greatly, over time and between countries – how are we to explain the stability of *relative* mobility rates?

12.4   THE CONTINGENT BALANCE

It may be, as Goldthorpe proposes, that the stability of relative mobility rates is the central sociological puzzle that emerges from these data and that calls for explanation. Nevertheless, he argues that this stability is itself contingent. The class structures of industrial societies tend to sustain and, indeed, to reinforce inequality and to subvert, resist or by-pass political interventions aimed at promoting greater equality of opportunity. If in much of the post-war period relative mobility chances have been stable, rather than worsening, this has been because efforts in social and educational policies have been sufficient to offset the efforts of the advantaged to defend and reinforce their position and that of their offspring. In their absence, relative mobility rates might well have worsened (Goldthorpe, 1980: 275; Erikson and Goldthorpe, 1993: 368). The puzzle is why, across so many countries, travelling along such diverse development trajectories, and over such an extended period, these two effects have apparently balanced each other out so neatly?

It is of course possible that Goldthorpe has over-stated the stability. The data sets he used in his work with Erikson were obtained at various points in the 1970s. Breen (2005) in his more recent study of European countries finds greater cross-national variation in relative mobility rates in the later decades of the twentieth century, as well as a general temporal trend to greater openness. This is not however confirmed, for Britain at least, by Goldthorpe's own most recent findings (Goldthorpe and

Jackson, 2007; Goldthorpe and Mills, 2008). Only in the case of Hungary does Goldthorpe himself acknowledge significant shifts in relative mobility rates: see both *The Constant Flux* (Erikson and Goldthorpe, 1993: 94–5) and his analysis of Hungarian trends before and after the fall of the socialist regime (Bukodi and Goldthorpe, 2009). He demonstrates a steady fall in the inequality of such rates for those cohorts educated and entering the labour market during the socialist period, but a reversal of this trend thereafter. Goldthorpe again explains this by reference to the vigorous efforts of the socialist regime to counter class inequalities, but the retreat from such interventionism post-1989. These departures from stability underline the contingent nature of the relationship between changing mobility opportunities, arising in part from social and educational policies but also from the unanticipated consequences for mobility of other public policies, and the strategies pursued by more advantaged groups to consolidate their dynastic privileges.

For our present purposes, therefore, we take as given the general stability of relative mobility patterns within the various countries with which Goldthorpe deals. How then is the contingent balance to be explained? It is, as we have seen, to the enduring and cross-nationally uniform inequalities of advantage that different classes are able to confer upon their offspring that Goldthorpe himself points, including in particular the inequalities that spring from the contrast between those who enjoy a 'service contract' and those engaged through a 'labour contract' (Erikson and Goldthorpe, 1993: 376, 391; Goldthorpe, 2000: Ch. 10; Goldthorpe and McKnight, 2006).[6] This is, however, only one side of the 'contingent balance': it is surely necessary for any model to encompass both sides. It is to this challenge that we now turn.

12.4.1 Modelling the Contingent Balance

The models developed in the preceding chapters afford further insights. The system of social and occupational recruitment would seem after all to be rather well characterised as an open and 'far from equilibrium' system. As Goldthorpe argues, 'a class structure cannot be regarded as something . . . essentially passive . . . but as [one] . . . through which inequality is actively . . . generated' (Goldthorpe, 1980: 275).

Consider, in particular, the potential application of Bak's account of self-organised criticality, as discussed in Chapter 2. We saw in Chapter 10 that this was deployed by Solé and Bascompte (2006) in their account of percolation across ecological spaces, with reference, for example, to forest fires. Here there is, on the one hand, the slow development of local connectivity (abutting local neighbourhoods of forest); on the other, a recurrent source of instability (spontaneous ignition) which causes general discon-nection. These two factors can bring the landscape in question to a state of 'self-organised criticality'.

The system of social and occupational recruitment described by Goldthorpe embodies a similar set of elements. Consider first the strat-egies of those in the more advantaged social classes. Faced with the widening intrusion of working class families into traditionally middle class institutions (selective schools, white collar and professional occupations), as egalitarian policies by the state take effect, we might posit a critical threshold to such widening. (This does not of course imply that all states engage in egalitarian policies, nor that all the policies of a given state will tend to be equally egalitarian. On the contrary, state policies may – intentionally or otherwise – serve to reinforce inequalities, including of mobility chances.) Here more advantaged families bestir themselves in outflanking strategies, whose effect will be to block and disconnect – or at least constrain – existing access routes, as used by working class families, in favour of new institutional by-passes that the more advantaged expect to reserve for themselves. These institutional by-passes may remain at the individual level (with individual parents, for example, coaching their children in the period leading up to secondary school entry); however, they may become generalised in new institutional arrangements (shared networks of private tutors) or in wholesale adjustments in local and national policy (selection policies for secondary school places, tax breaks for education in private schools). There is plenty of empirical evidence of such positional competition and institutional entrepreneurship by more advantaged families (Lauder and Hughes, 1999: Ch. 5; Ball, 2003: Chs 4–6; Power et al., 2003: Ch. 11; Swift, 2003; Smithers and Robinson, 2010). The consequences may be limited and specific; or they may produce cascades of larger and unforeseen transformations in the terms on which different social classes gain access to these more privileged opportunities.

Such efforts at institutional entrepreneurship are by no means limited to the educational sphere, even if it is from there that we have drawn these illustrations. They are, rather, liable to encompass the whole range of life chance distributing mechanisms, including housing, fiscal and occupa-tional welfare, investment of capital and health security. Indeed, not the least of the skills which more advantaged families are able to deploy – or which they are able to purchase from others – is the agile re-weaving of the interdependencies among these various mechanisms, so as to optimise the return they achieve.

This is self-organised criticality: on the one hand, the progressive widening of access by working class families; but then, as some critical threshold is reached, new institutional routes blazed by more advantaged households, so as to limit that access. Close to such thresholds, interaction dynamics may change dramatically. We saw this in the case of forest fires: as forestation connects ever more neighbourhoods and the 'percolation threshold' is reached, the scope for a global rather than merely local blaze increases dramatically. In discussing such thresholds with reference to social behaviour, Pierson likewise notes that it is when there are, so to speak, just a few valued positions still vacant that the competition among those poised to occupy them will increase in dramatic and non-linear fashion; he makes this comment with reference to Hirsch's notion of 'positional competition', but also as an explicit analogy to the models of avalanches in the physical sciences which were of course central to Bak's account of self-organised criticality (Pierson, 2004: 83).[7]

These 'dramatic and non-linear' effects encourage the use of a model of discontinuous change, such as self-organised criticality, by reference to critical thresholds. So does Goldthorpe's argument that each social class is risk averse, fearing above all the downward mobility of its offspring (see also Breen and Yaish (2006), presenting such risk aversion even more strongly in terms of a model of threshold effects). Efforts to stave off these risks are after all not costless and they involve careful strategic consideration, before they are undertaken. Nevertheless, once that fear has reached a critical level, these efforts are liable to open up a succession of new institutional fronts in the positional struggle, in a race against time: a race, therefore, which may need to be measured not only in quantitative terms, as the private resources such parents are willing to throw into the balance, but also in qualitative terms, the degree of institutional 'deepening' and differentiation in which they are ready to engage.

Consider, on the other hand, the state, faced with the persisting efforts of the more advantaged to block or at least constrain working class access routes. Here we might similarly posit a critical threshold in such blockages, at which the state bestirs itself in new outflanking strategies, designed to open to all (or, alternatively, to close down altogether) the new institutional by-passes that the advantaged have developed for their offspring. Here again, such strategies may be rather limited in their scope (scholarships for working class children to go to private schools); or they may be more general and wide-ranging (common schools for all), with cascades of wider and much less predictable institutional change thereby set in motion.

Solé and Bascompte demonstrate that self-organised criticality depends upon the system parameters in question falling within some intermediate range. The same will presumably apply to the social mobility processes with which we are here concerned. Thus, for example, in regards to the egalitarian strategies of the state, we may conjecture that if the critical threshold is low, with any new middle class initiatives bubbling up from local initiative (for example, parent teacher associations) being stifled for fear that they will disadvantage working class families and pupils, innovation and adaptation within the education system may diminish. If the critical threshold is high, with the state slow to react to the undermining of working class opportunities, working class children and their families may conclude that investment of effort in education is hardly worthwhile.

Nevertheless, even as mere conjectures, meriting empirical investigation, all this requires a strong caveat. In the case of forest fires, it may be possible to produce some useful models of percolation and fire risks. In the case of social dynamics, in contrast, there are many more possible responses than those just indicated, involving various strategies of exit, voice and loyalty (Hirschman, 1970). Which of these is employed will depend in part on fateful choices by political leadership. It is precisely because of the institutional creativity of social actors, to which we have repeatedly pointed, that simple models of the sort deployed above are only ever of limited value (albeit this arguably applies to all models of social interaction).

While simple, the model we have suggested is nevertheless already somewhat more elaborate than those of Bak, or of Solé and Bascompte, inasmuch as two countervailing processes of social action are involved, involving, on the one hand, the advantaged and, on the other, the state, acting as particular thresholds are breached. Depending on how we construct the model, we might see these countervailing projects as offsetting each other to some degree, leaving only the stronger to exercise some net effect. More likely, however, we should regard each as modifying the terrain on which the other henceforth unfolds, with political egalitarianism serving not so much to block as to displace the terrains on which the advantaged will henceforth seek to secure their own position. The respective contenders – the advantaged and the egalitarian policy-maker – thereby lock each other into a 'race against time', with both seeking to weave their own preferred pattern into the life chance distributing institutions of the society. We may have started with Bak's model, drawn from physics, but we have ended with the model of positional competition with which Chapter 8 concluded, and which Chapter 9 captured in the metaphor of intertwined Cantor staircases.

Finally, the model seems to throw possible light on two additional questions.

The first relates to some of the national variations in endogenous mobility regimes to which Goldthorpe refers. His argument, it will be recalled, is that while the general topography of the endogenous mobility regime is to a large extent invariant, its ruggedness varies, being gentler in the case of

Sweden in particular. It seems plausible to relate this to the various critical thresholds to which we have just referred. We might in particular posit that in those countries where the critical threshold for state intervention in the face of working class exclusion is rather low and/or the critical threshold for action by the more advantaged to resist working class incursion is rather high, levels of inequality will be reduced and the topography more subdued. This is of course a matter for empirical investigation – and suggests one of the ways in which this model of self-organised criticality might be operationalised for purposes of empirical enquiry.

Second, our model assists in making 'rationally intelligible' the mobility strategies in which individuals and their families engage. This we earlier set in the context of Goldthorpe's account of the 'natural history' of social classes. We saw that while it is *relative* mobility chances that have been stable – and this stability is what is of greatest sociological interest – they are of 'extremely low social visibility'. It is more likely that individuals frame their mobility strategies by reference to the much more visible changes in *absolute* mobility rates, including the overall patterns of inflow and outflow among different social classes: this, at least, would give a 'subjective logic' to those strategies. The puzzle is how individual strategies that are addressed to absolute mobility flows – flows that vary greatly, over time and between countries – can help us explain the stability of *relative* mobility rates.

In the model of positional struggle we have proposed, it is more advantaged parents – those in what Goldthorpe refers to as the 'service class' – who have the motivation, the resources and the opportunities to ensure with high probability that their children will avoid downward mobility from their class positions. Those born into other classes then variously find a place in their wake. At some point – but this will depend upon whether the overall number of service class positions is growing or declining – the remaining such positions will become few in number, relative mobility chances become visible and inter-class clashes occur. We again recall Pierson's argument that it is when just a few valued positions are still vacant that there will be a non-linear increase in the intensity of competition for them.[8] It is at this point that the goal of securing benefit for offspring in the absolute levels of opportunity – and continuing thereby to participate as a family in the status privileges and cohesion of the service class – is liable to be re-defined by reference to *relative* opportunities and the imperative of excluding intruders from other social classes.

The question remains as to the signals by means of which individuals become alert to such 'tightening' of the positional competition and to the locales in which this competition is played out. It is perhaps here that the education system is of particular significance. It is here that parents can see the social mix of a school – not least in conversation with fellow parents at the school gate – and can form judgements as to how this is changing; can judge, indeed, whether participation in the school concerned by those of other social classes has or has not breached some 'rule of thumb' threshold; can judge – rightly or wrongly – whether such breaches are responsible for changes in the school's performance as measured by published league tables; and can express in practical terms the 'inter-class clashes' to which we have hitherto referred only in abstract and hypothetical terms.

12.4.2 Validation and Testing

Goldthorpe's principal concern has been to explain the stability in the endogenous mobility regimes of different industrial countries. Consistent with this, we have focused attention on the 'contingent balance' that this stability reveals, between the efforts of the more advantaged to preserve their dynastic privileges and such countervailing social and educational policies as the state pursues. Goldthorpe is content to explain this balance in terms of the enduring inequalities of advantage that different classes can mobilise in the interests of their offspring; we, however, have argued that an explanatory model must encompass both sides of the equation. We have found such a model in 'self-organised criticality'.

To use such a model – drawn originally from the physical sciences – does not of course preclude instantiating it by reference to a range of available social science theories: not only those to which we have already referred (including Hirsch's positional competition and Hirschman's exit, voice and loyalty), but some not so far addressed (dealing, for example, with class interests, power resources and state capture). These would, however, now be deployed by reference to a simple but arguably generic model of 'far from equilibrium' processes. Nevertheless, even if the model is of some value in this regard, we should not be over-hasty in embracing it. How might its robustness and validity be checked?

One empirical development, in terms of 'micro-motives', would be to complement the survey questions that are now standard in social mobility enquiries informed by Goldthorpe's approach with questions relating to household strategies of institutional entrepreneurship. Which *Verdun* has been put under threat? In what race against time are these households thereby involved? What additional arrangements have they put in place to protect and secure the opportunities that they want their offspring to enjoy? Have these arrangements been made in conjunction with other households – and, if so, which? What critical thresholds – and what signals of such thresholds – do households variously employ in regards to the tightening of opportunities and the looming risks of downward mobility for their offspring? How stable are these over time and between different countries? How far can variations in these thresholds be related, as we have suggested, to cross-national contrasts in the ruggedness of the endogenous mobility regime? This would, admittedly, amount to a not insubstantial research programme: the more so, if it were then extended to include also the thresholds and interventions adopted by policy-makers seeking to make an egalitarian response.

Such an investigation of 'micro-motives' is consistent with the account of agile action we offered in Chapter 8. Households on the one hand, policy-makers on the other, bestir themselves to an agile response when they detect anomalous patterns. These might include, for example, a threshold level of intrusion by working class offspring into those educational and occupational milieux traditionally dominated by the more advantaged. Whether these agile responses remain rather limited and specific, or produce larger transformations, will depend on the larger institutional re-connections they trigger.

Alongside this, it should surely also be possible to assess, at the level of 'macro-behaviour', whether the self-organised criticality that we have posited is evidenced – as Bak would anticipate – by a power law distribution. Drawing on the analogy of the avalanche, in Bak's sand pile experiment, we might expect – and might set out to test empirically – whether the scale of threshold-related events displays a power law: advantaged households bestirring themselves against the steady encroachment of working class families, state policy-makers bestirring themselves to counter the steady growth in institutional by-passes that more advantaged households have been building for themselves.

Nevertheless, there is a more immediate and obvious point of reference in Goldthorpe's own data. A power law attests to a micro-interaction effect among the elements whose macro-behaviour we seek to explain. It is also of course with interaction effects that Goldthorpe's investigation of the u_{ij} parameters is concerned, in equations (12.1) and (12.2) above. Where interaction is absent, u_{ij} has a value of one and log u_{ij} is zero. Where log u_{ij} departs from zero, interaction is present, either positive or negative.

Table 12.1 reproduced Goldthorpe's matrix of log u_{ij} parameters. First and foremost, this reveals positive interaction parameters all along the lead diagonal: each class in some degree self-recruits. This is most marked in the case of the service class, the petty bourgeoisie and farmers. Nevertheless, in all other classes self-recruitment also obtains. Thus, we might conclude, Goldthorpe's data – in particular, the positive values for all log u_{ij} down the lead diagonal – reveal self-recruitment to be 'scale-free': and this is the case even for skilled and unskilled manual workers and agricultural labourers, the 'change takers' rather than the 'change makers' of industrial societies. It may of course be objected that among these various categories of blue collar workers, such self-recruitment is hardly evidence of agile and successful positioning on their part; rather, it is thrust upon their offspring by their lack of resources and the barriers that they face in the positional competition. Nevertheless, mobility among these different categories is far from random. Albeit on this reduced canvas, skilled workers are able to ensure that their offspring have a better chance of entering skilled occupations than do the children of unskilled workers: here there is evidence of a positional competition no less than we find 'scaled up' across the matrix as a whole.

This is not, however, the whole story. Under self-organised criticality, a single power law pervades the whole system and its exponent is a global property of the system in question. We might therefore expect that the interaction effects revealed by Goldthorpe's u_{ij} parameters might also be 'of a piece': and in an important sense this is the case. True, the values of those parameters vary markedly across the matrix of inter-generational cross-tabulations reproduced here as Table 12.1. Nevertheless, when it comes to comparing national deviations, it is possible for Goldthorpe to speak globally of how rugged or muted this topography is. It seems that in general, a country does not reveal greater ruggedness here, greater gentleness there, as compared with the broader range of countries: the endogenous mobility regime of each country is, rather, woven to a uniform pattern, a single 'power law'.

12.5 CONCLUSION

As we have seen, Goldthorpe demonstrates a remarkable stability in the endogenous mobility regimes of different industrial societies. The egalitarian efforts by the state do not reverse these inequalities so much as mute their harshness and forestall the efforts of the more advantaged to intensify them. Across different industrial societies, such efforts by the state seem in general to have balanced out the countervailing efforts of the advantaged, producing what we have termed the 'contingent balance'.

Goldthorpe explains this topographical stability by reference to the advantages that different classes are variously able to confer on their offspring: in particular those associated with the contrast between a 'service contract' and a 'labour contract'. He does not, however, offer an explanation of the 'contingent balance' between the efforts of the state and the advantaged. It is this theoretical deficit that we have sought to fill, using Bak's model of 'self-organised criticality'.

Bak's model is drawn from physics. We have noted the dangers of applying such simple models to social phenomena, especially given the institutional creativity of social actors. We have also been at pains to argue that the struggle in which they engage must be seen not simply in terms of differential resources; it also involves differential scope, as 'agile first movers', to re-shape the institutional rules of the game. Previous chapters provide us with possible models for depicting this, in terms of evolutionary dynamics, now however couched as a struggle for positional advantage. Agile institutional entrepreneurs, from within their existing institutional anchorages, weave new affiliations and institutional configurations. This they do in order to secure and strengthen their leverage over key institutions; to shift barriers to access so as to improve their own mobility prospects; to by-pass and outflank the existing mechanisms of transformation of origins into destinations. The result is that the offspring of different groups are after all hardly in the same game; this is a landscape of 'non-integral' and incompletely connected spaces, fragmented canvases on which the less advantaged have little choice but to pursue their ambitions on adverse terms.

This is a positional struggle in relation to opportunities and threats posed by the larger social, economic, technological and political transitions through which countries pass. These transitions Goldthorpe acknowledges, in terms of their implications for shifts in employment and for patterns and rates of absolute mobility. However, with his attention mainly on relative mobility chances, they remain somewhat in the background. Nevertheless, it is precisely the 'abrasions' of these larger changes that produce new openings for agile first movers. Or, to use another of the languages that have figured in earlier chapters, we might describe the system of occupational recruitment as an open system pushed 'far from equilibrium' by these larger transitions but then reorganised by the advantaged, so as to extract maximum positional benefit for their offspring. This is 'self-organisation' driven by differential power.

As structural change alters the landscape of positional competition, it is therefore in general those who are already advantaged who are best placed to take advantage of the new opportunities and to avoid the new insecurities. It is they who, as we described it in Chapter 8, are able to 'occupy the future', making sure that they and their offspring have the resources and the institutional leverage to enjoy a place in the sun, whatever the new dispensation of the world, and that others are incorporated on less favourable terms. It is they who, in a sort of Stackelberg game, are in general able to reach first for the most favourable positions, leaving others to compete for the crumbs that they leave.

Potts provided us with an evolutionary account of the successive economic regimes which such transitions involve. Fligstein argued that it is the successful first movers of a given period – the masters of the latest economic regime – who are able to re-shape the macro-institutional settlement and drive the new institutional abrasions of state and market architectures, in what is for them a positive co-evolution. This is a positional struggle, forever renewed but forever path dependent, on the terrain of production and political economy, as the competing protagonists seek to climb their respective 'perilous paths'. What the present chapter has added is an account of how the positional advantage thus conferred in terms of class position spills over onto the terrain of reproduction (even if the state then instigates new interventions to moderate their inegalitarian consequences).

These national dynamics are by no means insulated from each other. Goldthorpe himself points to their dependence on changes in international political economy, trading relations and patterns of economic dominance and dependence (Erikson and Goldthorpe, 1993: 103). We recall Abbott's similar discussion of the 'natural histories' of national welfare regimes, emphasising the need to identify their abrasion against international environing factors. In Chapters 16 and 17 we shall be concerned with this larger international environment, the positional struggle playing out there and the consequences spilling onto the more local terrains on which most ordinary households seek to make ends meet.

Amidst this larger turbulence, what Goldthorpe's use of log-linear analysis lays bare are the deeper and stable patterns of inequality that nevertheless persist, in terms of relative mobility chances. We have in this chapter argued that the theorisation of these patterns can benefit from the conceptual framework we have developed, combining complexity science and institutionalism. Just as important, however, we have confirmed the role that log-linear methods can play in investigating society as a complex system.

13　Towards a generic methodology

13.1　INTRODUCTION

This study aims to enhance our understanding of social dynamics in a complex and turbulent world. It does so in part as a contribution to knowledge, but also as the basis for an improved policy analytics.

Part 1 was concerned with the conceptualisation – the ontology – of social dynamics. Our ontology centred on the evolution of connections – technological and institutional – in a struggle for positional advantage: what we have described as 'deepen-widen-warp'. It is with the search for models and methods appropriate to this ontology that Part 2 has been concerned.

We began with the mathematical modelling of linear and non-linear systems. This included some treatment of specific models – for example, logistic growth – which have been widely applied in the social sciences; and others – including Turing instabilities – which have not. We saw that depending on the model, we may be able to solve the mathematics, in terms, for example, of the model's eigenvectors and eigenvalues; alternatively, a computational approach may offer an approximate solution. Even where mathematical solutions are not possible, and it is not possible to predict the state that the system will attain at any given moment, its trajectory or orbit can often be described in general terms, saying whether it is confined to the region of particular 'attractors' and the extent to which it is dependent on the initial conditions. We extended this discussion to chaotic dynamics, fractals and strange attractors. This then served as a mathematical representation of some of the dynamics discussed in Part 1: in particular, the treatment there of dynamic systems evolving and self-organised between order and chaos.

Our models and metaphors have drawn on the larger legacy of the complexity paradigm, across the physical and biological sciences, not just from mathematics. Nevertheless, whether such models and metaphors are appropriate depends on whether they help in identifying the generative processes at work. The institutionalist tradition in social and political science provides a qualitative account of these generative processes; we seek to combine this with the formal modelling of the complexity paradigm. Nevertheless, there is a trade-off between the dynamics revealed by formal models and the subtlety of qualitative accounts. This was, for example, evident in Chapter 11, in Jervis's use of structural balance theory to understand international relations, and in Chapter 12, in our use of Bak's self-organised criticality to illuminate Goldthorpe's 'contingent balance'. In both cases the models chosen offered important insights; nevertheless, human reflection and creativity introduced additional degrees of freedom, which placed limits on these.

Modelling is not an end in itself; it must be validated and calibrated empirically. For the physicist it may be sufficient to make a few careful measurements of, for example, the temperature and volume of a gas, in order – in combination with the relevant equations – to make a prediction of its pressure which can then be checked empirically. The measurement of such macro-variables is of course also common in the social realm: national rates of poverty, morbidity, price inflation and so on. Nevertheless, many of the aggregate patterns of interest derive from dynamic interactions among heterogeneous social actors on complex institutional terrains. In the social sciences we have at our disposal micro-data sets that enable the investigation of such patterns. As seen in the preceding chapters, techniques such as blockmodelling and log-linear analysis can be used to bring parsimony to the patterns these data sets exhibit. Even then, however, the data do not speak for themselves; we cannot analyse and explain except on the basis of specific theoretical commitments and analytical models, albeit these must remain forever provisional.

Ontology, models and empirical enquiry belong together. Modelling and measurement have not, however, always maintained contact with each other. Modellers have produced a profusion of elegant and intriguing models with only limited empirical reference, while the measurers have been somewhat slow to deploy dynamic models. In this chapter we seek to develop an integrated and generic methodology out of the various elements that previous chapters have supplied. While, however, the ontology must be coherent, there may need to be a selective eclecticism in the models and methods we use: eclectic because there may be no single all-encompassing method and model that will handle the ontology we have elaborated; selective, because the methods and models we use must be chosen not by reference to their elegance or availability, but always having regard to that ontology and the strengths and limitations it identifies within them. (For a similar argument for 'creative methodological *bricolage*', see Boero and Squazzoni (2005: para. 1.10), in regards to agent-based modelling, and Hall (2003), in regards to comparative politics).

The wisdom of such methodological pragmatism was already evident in the discussion of mathematical modelling in Chapter 9. Thus, for example, linear models often provide some initial clues as to the likely dynamics of their non-linear counterparts: a base-camp from which more ambitious if difficult forays can then be attempted. There is of course an enormous difference between assuming that the world is linear and recognising that while it is not, linear models can offer a first and provisional approximation. Likewise, when faced with coupled dynamic systems, 'considerations of tractability often dictate treating the systems as separate, with each affecting the other by determining the values of some of its parameters' (Bechtel and Abrahamsen, 2002: 242–3); this however carries the danger that in treating such systems separately, key aspects of their overall dynamics will be missed, precisely because the latter are more than the sum of their components (Parker and Stacey, 1994: 12–13). These are the hard choices of practical empirical research.

13.2   EXPLANATION AND ONTOLOGY

A fundamental task in any science is to explain the empirical phenomena of interest: to explain, that is, the patterns and regularities they exhibit, how these are generated and how they can be expected to unfold, in response to changes that take place within them or external shocks.

In social science, it may be no mean task even to establish what the patterns and regularities are (Lieberson, 1987: 153). Thus Goldthorpe (2001a) insists on the first and essentially descriptive scientific task of 'establishing the phenomena': demonstrating that, notwithstanding the imperfections of the data and the imprecision of measurement, there are indeed robust regularities that call for explanation. As we have seen, a major part of his contribution to comparative studies of social mobility has been to develop data instruments and methods of analysis that are sufficiently robust to map endogenous mobility regimes and their stability in time and space. In relation to far from equilibrium dynamics, of the sort with which this study has been principally concerned, the regularities of interest have as their signature a power law, of the sort discussed first in Chapter 2 and most recently in Chapter 12, attesting to agile struggles for positional advantage.

The second task is to decide what will count as an explanation of such social regularities. We broadly follow Weber's argument that such an explanation must satisfy two criteria (Weber, 1949). First, it must account for the observed pattern of outcomes, as measured by quantitative statistics: this Weber referred to as 'causal adequacy'. Second, it must be 'adequate at the level of meaning', making sense to us as empathetic observers of the social situation, and being consistent with the reasons that actors provide for their actions, in response to our interrogation. This allows for explanation of macro-social regularities, but within a framework of social action and methodological individualism.

In this section we do not aim to survey the whole range of social scientific writing on explanation and related matters, but simply to consider how we should view the task of explanation, given the conceptual and methodological discussion of the preceding chapters. We draw on various of the writers already discussed in Part 2, but also on Lieberson (1987) and Hedström (2005).

13.2.1 Lieberson: Making It Count

Lieberson starts by emphasising the importance of time and sequence (Lieberson, 1987: Ch. 4). His argument is similar to those of Pierson and Abbott. While some social processes are – like those of classical mechanics – reversible, many are not; they are replete with ratchets and path dependencies. Lieberson also (Ch. 9) echoes many of the other arguments encountered in Chapter 10, concerned with time lags, punctuated equilibria and the scope for small causes to produce large-scale consequences.

Lieberson proceeds to criticise much of contemporary quantitative social science: sociological research in particular. Geared as this is to various sophisticated forms of correlation and regression analysis, it may appear to be well adapted to the first of Weber's criteria of sound explanation. Nevertheless, Lieberson is dissatisfied on two counts. First, he challenges the readiness of sociologists to view their research as a quasi-experiment, enjoying the rigour that a laboratory experiment affords by virtue of the researcher's ability to control the variables and parameters involved. In sociological research it is usual for such variables to be interrelated in complex ways, fatally undermining the investigator's efforts to control for variations in some of them, so as to measure the independent influence of another. These interrelations in many cases also involve irreversible processes of the sort discussed above; this too undermines the logic of the quasi-experiment. Abbott (2001b: Ch. 1) and Goldthorpe (2001a) offer not dissimilar critiques.

Second, Lieberson questions the readiness of researchers to take the regression coefficients that emerge from such analysis as 'speaking for themselves' and able to adjudicate, on the basis of the variance they explain, as to the importance of different explanatory variables (Lieberson, 1987: Ch. 5). Against this, he argues that it is only by reference to a specific theoretical question that we can make sense of the variables involved and set about assessing their joint influence on the 'dependent variable' in question.

One of the main illustrations that Lieberson uses (pp. 164–8, 187–95) is drawn from the area of social mobility. Given its relevance to the substantive subject matter of the previous chapter, it deserves attention here. He takes the case of racial inequalities in the USA, in schooling and in occupational destinations. He assembles and reviews a range of empirical studies that have evaluated the weight of different 'variables' in determining those destinations. He also notes that these findings have served as the basis for a variety of policy proposals. However, his central point is this: that whatever weight racial inequalities in educational performance are found to have on subsequent inequalities in occupational outcomes, this is a poor basis for policy. This is because any success in reducing those educational inequalities is unlikely to reduce corresponding inequalities in occupational outcomes, because more advantaged groups are likely to switch to other institutional means – other causal routes – to sustain their position.

Lieberson therefore calls on researchers to explore the 'basic' or underlying causes of (in this case) racial inequalities in occupational attainment and not to rest content with identifying the more 'superficial' causes, such as the educational inequalities through which the basic causes are currently expressed. He asks us to appreciate the complex networks of causal processes that underpin particular social regularities and that enforce the interdependence of variables, undermining any 'experimental' rationale: interdependencies and linkages that may themselves change in consequence of some other 'upstream' variable changing (Chs 4, 11). This is of course strongly reminiscent of our discussion of network connectivity and dynamics in Chapter 11; recall, for example, the treatment by Solé and Pasator-Satorras (2003) of complex sub-networks within biological cells as switches, triggers and suppressors, enforcing hierarchy and regulation. It is no less reminiscent of our discussion in Chapter 3 of the switching of genetic sub-systems, activating and deactivating potentialities and their chains of consequences. Lieberson is alerting us to the contingent and labile nature of these causal connections and the cascades of larger reconfiguration to which they may be subject, as a result of policy interventions that may have an apparently far narrower and more specific focus.

What then is this more 'basic' or 'substantive' cause of racial inequalities in occupational attainment? Lieberson adopts a position that approximates to the one we developed in Chapter 12, in our application of Bak and 'self-organised criticality' to Goldthorpe's mobility analysis. There is a positional struggle, in which 'whites will give blacks as little as they can', consistent with the need 'to maintain the system and avoid having it overturned'. The means used to pursue this goal 'may however be highly variable and . . . modified by the idiosyncratic history of that setting'. They are also fraught with uncertainty, forever liable to set unanticipated cascades of larger causal reconnections in train (pp. 189–91). This is quite different from any traditional functionalist account of system stability.

In significant respects Lieberson is a precursor of complexity analysis applied to the social sciences. Throughout his study, he is at pains to argue that it is rare for a single causal process to be in operation; 'no equilibrium is really possible between the different causal forces'; there is only a 'constant flux' (p. 190). This brings him close to the discussion of 'far from equilibrium' systems which we introduced in Chapter 2. He explicitly cites Prigogine (p. 67); and like Bak, he takes river basins as a physical example of a dynamic system: one which, although it may well produce a constantly varying configuration of local waterways, is nevertheless forever driven by gravity and dissipated by erosion, as the basic or underlying causal processes (p. 163). More generally, his insistence on the importance of identifying the 'basic' causal force, whose presence or absence will dominate the outcome, whatever the specific path taken, is close to the interest taken by complexity scientists in the 'attractors' of a dynamic system. So is his discussion of 'transformational' causal principles which 'bend a variety of inputs . . . into the same output', albeit he notes – as we have done throughout this study – that this depends always on the system parameters falling within particular bounds (pp. 214, 233–5).

13.2.2   Hedström: Dissecting the Social

Lieberson, as we have seen, starts with the first of Weber's criteria for the explanation of social regularities: causal adequacy. At first glance he says rather less about 'adequacy at the level of meaning'. Nevertheless, in going behind and beyond the superficial causes that present themselves for regression analysis, and seeking the more basic causes that are anchored in strategic positional competition, he shows how to lay bare the socially meaningful processes that underlie persisting inequalities and other social regularities.

Hedström (2005) starts from the opposite end. His approach to explanation is in terms of generative mechanisms: that is, the processes and causal linkages by means of which 'one thing leads to another'.[1] In the case of social phenomena, such mechanisms must, he argues, involve meaningful action and interaction.[2] As he further insists, such mechanisms must correspond to those that are empirically at work and must not therefore merely be convenient fictions. This is broadly consistent with our own account of scientific method, according to which we seek, through modelling and theorisation, to capture in abstract form the real world processes that generate the patterns and regularities that we observe. It follows of course from Lieberson that these mechanisms may well involve both more 'basic' and more 'superficial' elements and that the linkages between them may be contingent and labile.

For Hedström, the challenge is how to move from meaningful action and interaction to the 'causally adequate' explanation of social patterns and regularities. His approach is where possible to use formal mathematical modelling. Thus, for example, he uses the logistic function we deployed in Chapters 2 and 9 to model diffusion processes, according to a variety of assumptions as to micro-level interactions, and he explores the corresponding variety in macro-patterns (pp. 87–92).

When, however, faced with non-linear systems that are not tractable by formal mathematical methods, Hedström turns to computational methods. Agent-based modelling is his main interest, in the tradition *inter alia* of Schelling and Holland. What is more, he recognises that such models must not involve mere 'dandyism', preoccupied with 'their intrinsic elegance, refinement or subtlety', regardless of their substantive relevance (Goldthorpe, 2004). They must therefore be empirically grounded and calibrated. Hedström offers a demonstration of how this might be done, by reference to transitions out of youth unemployment in Stockholm during the 1990s (Hedström, 2005, Ch. 6).

Hedström is interested in the extent to which such transitions depend upon the unemployment level among the peers of the individuals concerned. This he treats as a form of 'social interaction' which may help to explain the rate of transition in terms that are 'adequate at the level of meaning'. This is consistent with, for example, Granovetter's emphasis on the role of informal social contacts in providing information and encouragement about job opportunities.

Hedström first uses social survey data to estimate the likely rates of youth unemployment in each neighbourhood, taking into account the demographics of the areas. Such rates vary more than expected. Hedström proceeds to explore whether 'excessive' rates can be accounted for by the aforementioned social interaction effects. His statistical analysis of the survey data reveals that even after controlling for individual and labour market attributes, the unemployment level among neighbourhood peers remains of substantial significance.

Lieberson has warned against rushing to causal explanations on the basis of regressions alone; consistent with this, Hedström now uses agent-based modelling to ensure that his explanatory account is 'adequate at the level of meaning'. Just as Schelling uses cellular automata to demonstrate homogeneous clustering of racial groups, Hedström seeks to develop agent-based models of young people adjusting to the unemployment experience of their neighbours. He assesses how far this produces clustering that approximates to the spatial maps of youth unemployment that the Stockholm statistics reveal. Rather than dealing in the homogeneous cellular automata of Schelling, his model reproduces in each neighbourhood the youth demographics already derived from the Stockholm statistics. In particular, the regression weights established by reference to these demographics are used to define the interaction rules incorporated into the agent-based model. Hedström reports that after allowing the simulation to run, the correlation between predicted and actual neighbourhood unemployment level was 0.84. This would suggest that his explanation of these variations meets both of Weber's criteria of adequacy.

Nevertheless, in both his theoretical and methodological discussion and in his empirical example, Hedström leaves the matter incomplete in three respects.

First, as one reviewer has argued, agents are hardly present in the model: 'no beliefs, no desires, no heterogeneity' (Squazzoni, 2006). Still less are the agents he presents and the rules of interaction that they follow checked empirically for their 'adequacy at the level of meaning'.

Second, while Hedström gives a central place to social interactions it is not entirely clear how social interactions relate to social institutions and structure. As we noted in the conclusion to Chapter 2, there is a tendency in agent-based modelling to treat institutions as emergent from the rules of interactions and therefore as arising endogenously. Here there is little or no place for varied institutional contexts among which agents can 'shop' and which they can also, as 'institutional entrepreneurs', re-weave into novel patterns and opportunity structures. Nor does Hedström find it useful to employ concepts such as class; these may 'be useful as descriptive typologies' but they add nothing of explanatory value to social mechanisms couched in terms of meaningful action (Hedström, 2005: 153). It is noteworthy that when, in his study of Stockholm, he controls for the effects of neighbourhood demographics on rates of youth unemployment, neither class nor occupation figure.

It is true that at various points in his study Hedström discusses institutional contexts and the scope for individuals to re-weave them. Thus, for example, (following Granovetter) he discusses the strong and weak ties in which individuals are anchored and (following White) the 'catnets' or networks of social categories to which an individual may be affiliated (Hedström, 2005: 93–4; White, 2008: Ch. 2). He also stresses that the structural configurations in which actors are embedded are fateful for the social outcomes that emerge; and that agents interact 'under conditions inherited from the past' (Hedström, 2005: 98–9), mirroring our own stress on path dependency. Nevertheless, these insights hardly enter into his formal modelling; he has provided an empirically – but not an institutionally and historically – grounded complexity perspective.

Third, in Chapter 2 we saw that while Schelling, for example, has his agents interact with their neighbours according to some simple rules, Holland goes further, allowing agents to modify the rules, searching for those which work best. These are complex adaptive systems, with rules that evolve. Hedström leaves such evolutionary dynamics unexplored. It is, however, with such complex adaptive systems and dynamically coupled systems that our own study has been largely concerned, with particular reference to the role of first movers, their position in relation to 'hyperstructures' of institutions, their efforts to change the opportunity structure and the 'far from equilibrium' dynamics that these activities then set in motion. Hedström is right to place social action at the heart of the causal mechanisms that underlie social phenomena; nevertheless, the models that we employ must recognise that social action is agile and entrepreneurial and the terrain is complex.

It is nevertheless easier to point to the limitations in Hedström's efforts than to improve on them. It behoves us to consider how far, on the basis of our own discussion, we are able to offer the 'institutionally grounded complexity perspective' that we promised at the start of this work, in a manner which respects Hedström's altogether worthy goal of being empirically calibrated and providing robust explanations of social phenomena.

13.3   AGENT-BASED MODELLING

Computational modelling has played a key role in the development of complexity analysis, in part because of the limits faced by mathematical analysis in handling non-linear dynamics. It takes a number of inter-related forms. In Chapter 3, for example, we saw how Kauffman used computational modelling for exploring evolutionary dynamics, using genetic algorithms. In Chapter 11 we saw that computational modelling has also been applied to network dynamics, including various types of network evolution. We have also made a number of references to agent-based modelling (ABM), starting with Schelling and Holland in Chapter 2. However, only in the present chapter, in our discussion of Hedström, have we presented any specific example of ABM and the challenges that it faces. Nevertheless, for many of its practitioners, ABM is *par excellence* the generic methodology of complex dynamics. It is therefore incumbent on us to evaluate it by reference to the central issues of the present study (for more general treatments, see, for example, Gilbert and Troitzsch

(2005), Gilbert (2008), Miller and Page (2007), Squazzoni (2009) and, in a somewhat more applied vein, North and Macal (2007)).[3]

ABM offers an ontology of micro-agents. This would seem especially well suited to the investigation of social systems. Micro-agents have an intuitively appealing 'ontological correspondence' with real world actors such as the household, the enterprise, the nation: the classic actors with whom the economic, social and political sciences have been concerned (Gilbert, 2008: 14). ABM can also demonstrate the emergence of macro-behaviour from their micro-interactions, as the work of Schelling elegantly illustrates. It can thus respect the principle of methodological individualism – a concern common across much of social science – while demonstrating how micro-behaviours can contribute to macro-patterns and regularities. This suggests that ABM should be an ideal tool for exploring the sorts of 'generative mechanism' that underlie those regularities and with which much of the discussion in this chapter has been concerned (Moss and Edmonds, 2005).[4]

The agents depicted in ABM typically employ if/then algorithms of action, which reflect deontic rules of prescription, prohibition, permission. This involves simple pattern recognition, assessing situations by reference to standard templates and making an immediate and appropriate response. This is consistent with much of the account of individual action that has appeared in previous chapters. Thus, for example, Schelling assumes social actors to have a threshold of tolerance for members of other racial groups; if this is breached, they withdraw to alternative social milieux. Potts depicts entrepreneurs as searching for improved technologies using 'schematic preferences'. These provide a simplified template against which the technologies being scanned can be matched: initially on a broad brush basis, with many elements that are # ('don't care'), but then progressively refined. So also in Chapter 11, in our discussion of structural balance, social actors were assumed to have a threshold level of imbalance that they could tolerate, before taking remedial action.

This pattern recognition, with accompanying responses, is what Chapter 8 presented as 'habitual' action. Nevertheless, this was only part of the story. Faced with novel situations, uncertainty and turbulence, human actors deploy mental models that embody conjectures as to how the world will unfold; on this basis they wager their ventures. This is 'agile' action. Empirically it is when actors detect anomalous patterns, including, for example, those that fall outside certain critical thresholds, that they make such an agile response. It was, for example, in these terms that we sought in Chapter 12 to understand the conditions under which advantaged households bestir themselves to action, to defend their educational and occupational preserves against working class intrusion. What the if/then rules in this case prescribe is that the matter be removed from the if/then realm of the habitual. However, whether such agile action is something that ABM can handle remains to be seen.

Scientific modelling, as we have seen, poses a double challenge: formal modelling and empirical validation. Gilbert and many of the other writers on ABM convincingly address the former challenge; the second, however, is more worrisome. The claim is that ABM is a new and important form of experimentation in social science, conducted in the 'virtual laboratory' of the computer. Its exponents stress also its value in terms of theory building and in suggesting new and fertile lines of empirical enquiry. Thus, for example, as noted in Chapter 2, Schelling's modelling of racial segregation invites enquiry into the levels of racial antipathy which exist empirically, sufficient to prompt residential mobility, and the sorts of countervailing policy measure that city authorities might pursue. More generally, ABM may serve – at the level of ideal types – to elucidate the typical but counter-intuitive consequences of particular patterns of interaction, as the prelude to more conventional empirical studies.

Nevertheless, if the goal is to advance our understanding of the social dynamics of the real world, simulation and theory building *in silica* are surely insufficient; the empirical calibration and validation of such models remains essential, and if possible more than in terms of just 'qualitative resemblance' of the model and empirical cases (Gilbert, 2008: 42). For this purpose, Boero and Squazzoni (2005: para. 5.3) argue the need 'to embed ABMs within the entire set of empirical methods for social science', including qualitative interviews and questionnaires and large-scale statistical surveys. In regards to the latter, Gilbert himself has been active in developing and promoting methods for the analysis of tabular data (Gilbert, 1993); however, there are as yet few bridges between those methods of handling large quantitative data sets and the theory building and 'virtual experimentation' of ABM. As noted earlier, this leaves ABM open to the charge of 'dandyism', no less than, for example, much of the formal but empirically rather sterile modelling that characterises mainstream neoclassical economics.[5]

Consider, therefore, some of the challenges in turning ABM into an empirical research strategy.

First, it is necessary to check the macro-behaviour of the model against the regularities that have been established empirically, notably as evidenced by power laws. The empirical evidence of macro-regularities that is typically deployed is, however, rather scanty. This is arguably because ABM has been used in particular by economists, working in a tradition where empirical work means econometrics and econometrics means 'mere curve fitting' against a few key variables of the macro-economy (Ormerod and Rosewall, 2009). Contrast this with the approach to empirical enquiry exemplified by Goldthorpe's mobility studies, where a substantial task is to establish the macro-regularities which require explanation.

Second, it is necessary to validate empirically the assumptions that the model makes as to the micro-interactions and behaviours of the agents. Among many of the practitioners of ABM there is admittedly the wide-spread assumption that 'once a macro-empirical validation has been found . . . the micro-foundations can be considered validated' (Boero and Squazzoni, 2005: para. 2.11). Nevertheless, as many of those practitioners also readily concede, a variety of rules of micro-interaction could in principle generate the same macro-regularities; even if the latter prove empirically well attested, this may therefore not in general suffice to validate the model's chosen algorithm of micro-interaction. Gilbert recommends sensitivity analysis to explore how such macro-regularities change when the rules of micro-interaction are varied (Gilbert, 2008: 31–2, 41–2): however, this hardly meets the point. More promising is the use of participative or 'companion' modelling, where the model is built and progressively checked through continuous discussion and negotiation with the social actors in question (North and Macal, 2007: Ch. 9; Gilbert, 2008: 13–14; Moss, 2008).

Third, ABM locates agents within an environment, a virtual world. This might, for example, be a geographical space, with the aim to illuminate urban policy in a particular city. Nevertheless, ABM generally models the environment in only rudimentary terms (Gilbert, 2008: 26–7, 68–70). We, in contrast, have highlighted the importance of the institutional and organisational – and indeed the technological – environment: the 'connective geometry' within which actors find themselves enmeshed and which they commonly seek to re-weave, as they seek to secure and maintain first mover positional advantage. This of course was central to our evolutionary ontology of 'deepen-widen-warp'. It is less obvious whether ABM can model this with sufficient 'ontological correspondence'.

Gilbert (2008: paras 3.1, 4.3) offers an example of an ABM of positional competition. He is concerned with communities in which those of high status seek to maintain and reinforce their distinctiveness, while those of lesser status seek to adopt the behaviours of their betters. This approximates, therefore, our own interest in the dynamic relationship between first and last movers. Gilbert's model seeks to represent this dynamic as a two-fold pattern of movement across a space, with high status individuals moving into under-populated space and the rest moving into spaces that are already well populated. The model reveals the emergence of population 'clumps' that drift around the space, with some turnover of membership.

The model fails, however, to incorporate certain elements that have been fundamental to our own ontology. In particular, those who move into an under-populated region – the first mover innovators – do not thereby exert any extra leverage over the landscape on which others must henceforth live; there is no extraction of rent or profit, no barriers to entry, no scope for those first movers to reinforce their advantage in subsequent rounds. Nor, therefore, does 'status' or positional advantage have any real meaning in this model, beyond a description of under- and over-populated areas at any given moment.

It is, however, arguable that in making these demands, we risk missing and muting the distinctive contribution that ABM can make. ABM is concerned first and foremost with interactions between micro-agents: it is fellow agents who constitute *par excellence* the 'environment' in which each agent is located and via which the micro-behaviours of individuals 'emerge' into the overall macro-outcome. Institutions can be included, but only insofar as they are the product of those interactions: norms of cooperation, for example. In contrast, pre-existing institutional hyper-structures, making for a finely variegated terrain for social interactions, constitute a confounding influence which the investigator must keep within strict bounds, if ABM is to deliver its analytical promise. This is a counsel of modesty for the practitioners of ABM, who are perhaps too prone to overlook its limitations as a method for studying a world whose connectivity is in part inherited, rather than being constructed by the interacting agents who are being modelled.

By recognising the limitations of ABM, in relation to the institutional environment, we can also identify more precisely its contribution. ABM can reveal how, under a variety of algorithms and models of human cognition, simple micro-level interactions can lead to self-organisation in terms of macro-segments. The Schelling model is the classic example. This is what in Chapter 10, by reference to Turing instabilities, we referred to as 'symmetry breaking'. Put humans together in a shared and undifferentiated social space and they will self-organise into distinct camps; and, we then add, they will typically express this in terms of new and more complex institutional arrangements, by which this self-organisation can be given some permanency. This was, for example, a key finding in our account of social mobility in Chapter 12, where white collar families found 'affinity' in their shared lifestyles, not least around efforts to mobilise a collective positional struggle against blue collar incursion that might threaten the educational and professional futures they seek to retain for their off-spring. ABM helps us to model the self-organisation; it does not deal with the strategies of institutional reconstruction that follow. This is both its strength and its limitation.

There is one other standpoint from which this discussion may also and finally be reconsidered. The criticisms that we have made of ABM are by reference to its role in explaining the social patterns and regularities that empirical enquiry reveals. To explain, however, is only part of the task of social science. What is also required is to illuminate possible futures; to elaborate a range of possible scenarios of change; to inform the 'mental models' by reference to which policy-makers intervene in a complex and turbulent world. It may be that it is here that more generic models of social dynamics – of the sort that ABM seeks to develop – are of particular value, in the portfolio of tools that agile policy-makers will need. To this we return in Part 3.

13.4 MODELLING OUR ONTOLOGY

It is worth repeating: we adopt an ontology of social dynamics that is integrated and coherent. There may, however, be no single all-purpose model and method by which this ontology can be operationalised empirically. We may therefore need to be somewhat eclectic in our approach.

Our ontology is of positional dynamics on institutionally complex terrains. It is in these terms that we seek to understand what Leiberson describes as the 'basic' or underlying causes of the patterns we observe. In general the level of complexity this implies defies formal modelling. Nevertheless, we draw insights from physical and biological model-making wherever this can be done appropriately, but always having regard to the perils of applying such insights to socio-economic action and dynamics.

We heed the advice of Macy and Willer (2002: 162): 'models should start out simple and complications should be added one at a time'. For example, self-organised criticality is a simple model of energy inflow, on the one hand, abrasion and dissipation, on the other. We applied it to Goldthorpe's endogenous mobility regimes. The latter abstract from long-term structural development, the marginal totals of the gross mobility matrix; they are to this extent as 'timeless' as the sand pile. By itself, however, the model is very limited in illuminating the variety of responses that social actors may develop and their institutional creativity. Nor can it help us understand how their positional struggles shape long-term structural change. In relation to these matters, other models are needed; nevertheless, self-organised criticality can provide the starting point. In the same way, physical scientists often use linear models as a point of reference from which to explore the properties of non-linear systems; and network theorists use random networks as a starting point for exploring non-random networks.

This general principle, as enunciated by Macy and Willer, applies also to the specific case of computational models. We began in Chapter 2 with Schelling and his cellular automata on a lattice. These are the 'atoms' of a dynamic system, whose simple interactions with their immediate neighbours – in terms of attraction and repulsion – can produce global patterns, such as the racial segregation of an urban space. Here the rules of interaction are fixed for any one 'run' of the model. However, we saw that Holland then offers a second option, with the cellular automata changing the rules or algorithms, searching for and choosing those which work best. This is an 'adaptive walk' in which the rules of interaction themselves evolve, as we also saw in the work of Kauffman and Potts. Finally, we saw that Holland enhances the cognitive capacities of his agents still further, endowing them with 'internal models' of the world and 'lookahead'. He also looks for 'lever points' where interventions, although local, can produce changes in global patterns and trajectories. This is the stuff of a human world of positional competition and policy interventions, although as Holland himself recognises, the scope for modelling is here much tougher. Nevertheless, as we concluded in the previous section, in our review of ABM, it may be better not to risk over-stretching a given method, if this means missing and muting its distinctive contribution.

The ontology that emerged from Part 1 of this study was summarised in Figure 8.1. This depicted the combinatorial dynamics of Potts and Crouch, nested in an evolutionary framework of 'deepen-widen-warp', and involving processes of agile struggle for positional advantage. If our ontology is to dominate our selection of models and methods, Figure 8.1 should help us to re-visit and resolve the outstanding methodological dilemmas and conundra revealed in Part 2.

13.4.1   Sequence Analysis

We first re-visit Abbott's efforts to identify and compare sequences, as a tool in social analysis. We questioned whether this is in itself useful, unless the potential significance of those sequences – as dependent or independent variables – in social dynamics is made clear and placed at the centre of any empirical enquiry. We noted that elsewhere in his work – for example in his review of social dynamics in Chicago – Abbott is ready to address these larger temporal and socio-structural dynamics. We also noted that his critique of the 'general linear model' insists, not least, on understanding causation by reference to temporally complex processes.

Abbott asks us, in effect, to examine and compare sequences of elements in isolation from any larger evolutionary process. In reference to Figure 8.1, this means taking the sequence of lower case letters that are successively combined – for example a, b, c, d – but neglecting the significance of the upper case hyperstructures M, N, P or any wider macro-abrasions. It is true that in applying our ontology we may have to be content with a variety of partial insights, gained by applying in eclectic fashion a variety of investigatory tools; nevertheless, Abbott's focus on sequence viewed in isolation loses too much.

Consider again, therefore, Abbott and DeViney's analysis (1992) of the sequence according to which major welfare programmes were established in different industrial countries during the nineteenth and twentieth centuries. One of the hypotheses they examine is that a process of contagion or diffusion was at work. Already in Chapter 6, in our treatment of Crouch's 'institutional entrepreneurs', to which our own ontology has been strongly indebted, we recognised the importance of such cross-national institutional borrowing or imitation. Nevertheless, this must always be set in the context of adaptation to local and national institutional legacies and to abrasions against other local, national and international dynamics of socio-economic change. We can hardly expect to learn much simply by noticing that similar welfare programmes have been adopted according to the same sequence across several countries.

Figure 8.1 has provided us with a template for a more appropriate strategy of empirical enquiry. It invites us to identify the elements – in this case welfare programmes – which are adopted or re-deployed, in what sequence and with what consequences. This sequence matters because it dictates which sub-systems are made available and when, for incorporation into larger hyperstructures and for abrasion against other systems. It matters, therefore, in relation to the triggers and switches that get turned on and off, creating critical junctures, thresholds and tipping points and setting novel dynamics in motion. It is, in other words, not sequencing *per se* that matters but the sequencing of those switches, unlocking potential or closing it down and forging the 'connective geometry' of socio-economic space.

We might consider a group of countries with a broadly common mix of welfare programmes at some historical juncture. We might then ask what variations to those programmes have been subsequently introduced and how these have variously performed. Here we take as the unit of analysis the shared trajectory of welfare development, its dispersion or divergence into a number of offshoots and their respective fates. With Abbott we would ask how far these divergences in welfare programmes display a limited number of typical sequences; this is, however, of interest only as a starting point for investigating whether these programmes have been similarly deployed (connected) in relation to other welfare and public policies and how they abrade against other socio-political actors and processes, both national and international. We may, for example, with the 'varieties of capitalism' writers, be interested to see whether the scope for variation on all these fronts is limited. This does not, *pace* Abbott, fall into the error of treating sequence in itself as being of interest; but nor does it seek 'to substitute variables for nations' as Abbott and Goldthorpe both rightly decry, in their attack on the linear casual model. Instead it identifies contingent trajectories and their outcomes and consequences: the heart of our evolutionary model.

This is close to the project in which Thelen and her collaborators have been engaged. Thus, for example, Palier investigates the 'Bismarckian' welfare states and their recent variations in precisely these terms, challenging the conventional wisdom that they are institutionally 'frozen' (Palier and Martin, 2008: Ch. 1; Palier, 2010). He maps the welfare reforms that different Bismarckian countries have introduced and considers how each reform impinges upon other elements of the welfare mix and, beyond that, upon employment structures and relations. More than this, Palier uses Thelen's evolutionary model – involving layering, conversion and so on – to make sense of the sequence of actions – the switches – by which policy-makers have set new dynamics in motion, undermining interests in the existing welfare settlement and building coalitions in support of change. Not that this has happened everywhere; whether because of the political strategy and sequencing chosen, or the depths of the institutional 'freeze', a country such as Greece seems fated to tragedy (Petmesidou and Mossialos, 2006).

13.4.2   Evolution of Social Structure

Several of our chapters have been concerned with the evolution of social structure, starting with the institutionalist writers on whom we drew in Part 1. At various points in Part 2 we have been faced with the question of how to model such processes of structural change.

As we saw in the last chapter, Goldthorpe wrestles with this question in the context of rates of absolute mobility. Variations in such rates – over time and between countries – are considerable. They are associated *inter alia* with shifts in employment from primary to secondary and eventually tertiary sectors. These shifts have, however, had very varied speeds and phasing in relation to other aspects of structural change, including national social and economic policies and larger changes in international political economy. As we saw, Goldthorpe considers that with timing and sequence of such significance, it is misguided to venture any macro-sociological explanation of the consequences of these structural shifts for patterns and rates of absolute mobility.

Certainly we cannot hope to explain the differences in such rates by reference to systematic variations among nations in their other macrosocial attributes, or in terms of successive 'developmental stages' (Erikson and Goldthorpe, 1993: Ch. 11). Nevertheless, Figure 8.1 again provides us with a template for thinking about these contingent causal chains. Abbott was wrong to imagine that sequences of lower case letters could be compared in isolation from the upper case hyperstructures in which they are embedded; and Goldthorpe is right to dismiss explanations of absolute mobility rates in terms of variables deracinated from these causal chains. Nevertheless, this still leaves scope and value for an explanatory account which identifies critical junctures in this evolution and the typical responses by key actors; the thresholds and tipping points; the divergent trajectories along which hitherto similar evolutions then lead. While this may constitute a somewhat 'softer' version of causal explanation than that which is enjoined in much of quantitative social science, it is consistent with Lieberson's exhortations.

The evolution of social structure was also addressed in Chapter 10, albeit in rather different terms. There we were interested in the emergence of temporal and spatial patterns. Turing instabilities provided a simple but generic model. We saw that Kauffman had applied Turing to the morphogenesis of *Drosophila*. At critical junctures in the development of the embryo, new 'symmetry breaks' or 'bifurcations' emerge, in a succession triggered or suppressed by regulatory genes, switching other genetic circuits in sequence. Figure 8.1 is again a helpful point of reference, with lower case letters now referring to the actions of these regulatory genes, the upper case to the resulting morphologies.

We suggested that Turing might equally be applied to the 'morphogenesis' of social structure, driven by the positional struggles between agile first movers (the 'activators' of the Turing model) and the larger population of second and last movers (the 'inhibitors'), as they seek to contest and re-shape the boundaries and barriers of advantage and the rules by reference to which new lines of 'symmetry breaking' are to be ordered. In reference to the work of Thelen and Palier, for example, or Goldthorpe's treatment of national development trajectories, this would involve a historical treatment of the positional struggles that wove the distinctive social structures of the countries concerned; and the critical junctures at which political actors activated or suppressed particular forms of self-organisation, sending the countries in question along one trajectory of development rather than another. Nevertheless, any modelling exercise must pay its way in analytical and explanatory terms; whether Turing is more than an intriguing metaphor of socio-political morphogenesis would require a more thorough demonstration than can be offered here.[6]

13.4.3 Agile Actors on Complex Terrains

Finally, we review our efforts to model agile actors on complex terrains, again by reference to the ontology of Figure 8.1. This has the social actor combining new elements of the present with the heritage of the past; switching and re-working hyperstructures of connections; building positional advantage in the socio-economic 'eco-system' of the future.

Much social action is habitual, applying the templates we develop during our lifetimes and those encoded within social institutions. However, faced with anomalous situations we deploy 'mental models' of how these are likely to play out and we set about re-weaving the 'connective geometry' of our institutional and technological space. The anomaly may offer self-reinforcing co-evolutionary dynamics by which we can build positional advantage: in short, an opportunity to be seized and nurtured. It may alternatively pose a threat: one which must be resisted, so as to stabilise and reinforce the existing order of things, the 'niche' by which we seek to 'buffer' ourselves against turbulence.

Social actors typically recognise anomalies by reference to the crossing of some critical threshold. Dissonance triggers action, aimed at controlling the disruptive consequences of the anomaly, while at the same time making use of the new opportunities for positional advantage that it may afford. This dual concern, on the one hand to stabilise, on the other to seize dynamic opportunities, was evident in Chapter 11, in our efforts to model connections. There we gave pride of place to notions of 'structural imbalance', involving the recognition and resolution of dissonance. Jervis provided our template. We saw how he uses signed networks to explore how nation states may seek structural balance, but how they may also pursue runaway loops of positional advantage, along the lines depicted by John Darwin and Arrighi.

Nevertheless, 'the enemy of my enemy is my friend' seemed in any case of only limited relevance to the policy world with which we are concerned. In Chapter 11 we therefore proposed an alternative approach, in terms of the institutional entitlements and obligations in which social actors are enmeshed and which they seek to manage and re-weave, with a view to defending – and if possible strengthening – their positions. We emphasised that any such model must take account of the complex and interdependent time frames within which social actors manage these dynamics and the extent to which they have to dance to the rhythms of others. This management of time frames is also the management of sequence: activating, switching and re-combining entitlements and obligations, so as to navigate perilous institutional paths to maximum advantage. It is thus that we seek to combine the qualitative insights of institutionalist analysis with the formal models made available by the complexity paradigm: what at the start of this book we described as an institutionally grounded complexity perspective. We will – in some modest degree – apply this perspective in Part 3.

This approach is of course consistent with our more general treatment of institutions. In Chapter 5 we spoke of institutions as embodying rules of social interaction. These rules impose constraints (North, 1990: Ch. 1) but they also activate capacities (Crouch, 2005: Ch. 5) – for example, by granting access to particular education and training opportunities. This dual face of institutions we have now characterised in terms of obligations and entitlements. We then saw in Chapters 6 and 7 how Crouch characterises the institutional entrepreneur, weaving institutional forms together into a complex governance hyperstructure, with a view to producing a particular mix and distribution of constraints and capacities across the population in question (whether on a small or a grand canvas). Thus if individual institutions apply rules which activate and constrain social actors, systems of governance combine and organise those institutional elements into larger ensembles.

This is well depicted by Figure 8.1. It is of course no simple matter of adding institutions Lego-like. The constraints and capacities that different institutional forms contribute will blend and interact in complex ways, just like the K-connections on Kauffman's rugged landscapes. The entrepreneur's efforts are moreover likely to be contested by a variety of other protagonists. This is the struggle over governance that Crouch seeks to put on a clear analytical basis, using a combinatorial ontology we have been eager to borrow.

13.5   CONCLUSION

Part 1 of this study elaborated a conceptual model of social dynamics which draws on complex adaptive systems and institutionalism. Part 2 has considered how this conceptualisation of social dynamics can be handled analytically, in terms of formal models and measuring instruments. We have offered a number of such approaches, all inspired by and consistent with our conceptual approach, but serving a variety of substantive purposes. The journey towards a generic methodology is incomplete, as with any adaptive walk; we have, however, provided a vantage point from which the dilemmas, challenges and unexplored opportunities of an institutionally grounded complexity perspective and policy analytic can be systematically addressed. We now have a basis for asking more appropriate questions about complex and turbulent policy terrains, even if the answers we can reasonably hope to provide are less precise than those to which traditional methodologies aspired. It is, however, better to have imprecise answers to the right questions than precise answers to the wrong ones.

Part 2 has re-visited some of the methodological approaches current in the social and policy sciences, reassessing their significance in light of this perspective on social dynamics. It seems that some social scientists have already if unwittingly been 'speaking prose', making use of dynamic perspectives which match those drawn from complexity science.[7] This has in turn provided us with a critical standpoint from which to assess the added value that complexity science brings and to identify its inappropriate uses. We have, for example, questioned whether ABM as commonly applied to social science is sufficiently well grounded empirically or is at risk of 'dandyism', notwithstanding the claims that its great merit is to advance theory rather than be a tool of empirical enquiry.

We may find that given the complexity of the phenomena under study, we need to splice various methods together and cross-check or triangulate their insights. Self-organised criticality as modelled by Bak comes from physics, but Ludwig and Abell show how it can be placed in an evolutionary setting. Ludwig and Abell themselves were modelling structural balance, but by reference to Jervis we argued for an extension of structural balance methods to include the drive for positional advantage. We borrow and combine and re-deploy and hone methods, in a creative methodological *bricolage*, and we see pragmatically whether they are fit for purpose. Our methodological odyssey is itself therefore well represented by Figure 8.1.

This chapter has been centrally concerned with causation and explanation. We therefore conclude by considering in what degree we now have a general causal framework for the analysis of social dynamics. It was with Lieberson that our discussion began. He asks us to appreciate the complex networks of causal processes that enforce the interdependencies among variables: linkages that may themselves change in consequence of changes in some other 'upstream' variable (Lieberson, 1987: Chs 4, 11). This is why, while some social processes are reversible, many are not; they are replete with ratchets and path dependencies (Lieberson, 1987: Ch. 4). We must expect time lags and punctuated equilibria and not be surprised if small causes produce large-scale consequences.

Lieberson asks that we identify the 'basic' or underlying causes of the social regularities in question. At first glance it might seem that this must refer to whichever variable is furthest 'upstream' within the aforesaid network of causal connections. However, in the examples he cites, Lieberson seems to mean something more than this: in particular, the competing drives by social actors for positional advantage and control, as captured in the first mover dynamics elaborated in earlier chapters. These drives provide the 'generative mechanism' rooted in meaningful action, the energy that drives the system far from its present equilibrium. Only in these terms does the complex network of causal variables that we model and measure hang together as an explanatory framework.

Figure 8.1 can be taken as a general representation of such a causal account. At any given moment, causal variables and sub-systems of variables are organised into a particular hyperstructure, the interdependence of whose elements we may wish to measure using the established methods of statistical analysis. Nevertheless, this hyperstructure of relationships among measurable variables is also a hyperstructure of social relationships which are perennially contested in the real world. Statistical analysis can explore the relationships among the measured variables by reference to their past values; it cannot anticipate how in the real world these relationships will change, when the hyperstructure is re-fashioned as a result of the positional struggle, or indeed as the result of public policy interventions.

As we observed in Chapter 8, to disentangle and understand this messy history of successive reconnections and contingencies is the central task of dynamic causal analysis. This need not mean that the task has now become impossibly complicated. Thus, for example, as we saw in Chapter 12, Goldthorpe insists that what matters is not so much the diversity of mobility routes that individuals follow, within the institutional settings of their particular societies, but rather the commonality of the pursuit of positional advantage which drives this. To follow Lieberson's advice and identify the 'basic' or underlying causes may provide precisely the analytical key that is needed to unlock and simplify the causal complexities among the variables that we measure.

Finally, our causal framework also seems robust by reference to the larger literature in the philosophy of science. We have argued that what matters is the sequence in which sub-systems are connected to each other and to larger hyperstructures, as also when it is that triggers and switches get turned on and off – all serving to unlock potential or close it down, creating critical junctures, thresholds and tipping points and setting novel dynamics in motion. In like manner, Harré would have us think of causal processes as releasing or blocking potentialities (Harré, 1972: 121–2). In relation to evolutionary processes more particularly, Harré argues for a causal framework which acknowledges contingency and which explains adaptive change without attributing 'positive causality' (Jensen and Harré, 1981: 164). By this he means that evolutionary change involves several linked processes of mutation, selection, self-organisation and co-evolution. We can explain each process – each generative mechanism – and identify how it permits or prevents other processes unfolding; even so, contingency remains.

Causal chains are also, however, of political concern. They are constructed institutionally and historically. If they are complex and contingent, subject to cascades of reconfiguration, this is because they are forever being contested and re-shaped by agile entrepreneurs, in the race for positional advantage. Moreover, it is in part by keeping others in 'forced structures' of adverse incorporation – by controlling the rules of entitlement and obligation – that first movers consolidate and stabilise their positions of advantage. This is their 'niche construction', buffering them against turbulence, but constraining and determining the lives of others: a determination that social scientists then capture in the arithmetic of structured inequality. Harré's account of potentialities unlocked or closed down, critical thresholds and novel dynamics, can be read as much as an account of this historical and political struggle as a contribution to the philosophy of science.[8]

PART 3

Policies

14 Agile policy-making

14.1 INTRODUCTION

As argued in Chapter 1, conventional approaches to the conceptualisation and measurement of dynamic change are weak. Policy researchers are therefore ill-equipped to provide critical illumination and advice for policy-makers and the wider public. What is needed is a new policy analytics: tools to illuminate the world of public policy-makers and the interventions they make on complex and turbulent landscapes.

We saw in that same introductory chapter that policy-makers are being exhorted to base their decisions on sound evidence. This cannot but appeal to any social scientist concerned to promote rational argument and enlightened politics; indeed, it would seem to be an obvious area of common interest and fruitful collaboration across the policy-science divide (Goldthorpe, 2004). Nevertheless, as we also saw, much of the argument for evidence-based policy-making takes for granted a rather stable and linear world. How to cope with complex and turbulent terrains is not at all clear.

There is a view that this complexity is being reduced world-wide, as markets are extended and common rules established for a widening range of interactions. In Thomas Friedman's phrase, globalisation makes for a flat world (Friedman, 2006). Our analysis suggests otherwise. The extension and intensification of global rules and interactions, abrading against domestic institutional path dependencies and local political choices, are more likely to produce turbulence. Once we recognise the human world as a complex adaptive system driven by the struggle for positional advantage, we abandon such simple prognostications and face up to the hard policy choices of the real world, both domestically and internationally.

Policy-makers cannot but act; they must use whatever tools they have to hand. Part 3 assesses some of these tools and considers how they might be developed and honed.

14.2   THE IDEA OF THE POLICY-MAKER

There have been several ideas of the policy-maker lurking in previous chapters. Each will provide a point of reference in Part 3.

14.2.1   The Policy-maker as Tuner

As we have seen throughout this study, real world dynamic systems – whether physical, biological or social – are often far from equilibrium, non-linear and not entirely predictable. Their behaviour typically varies between three zones: order, chaos and an intermediate zone of complexity, where spontaneous self-organisation is possible. In which of these zones the system finds itself depends on the values assumed by the underlying system parameters; at the transition points there are discontinuous 'phase changes' and 'tipping points'. We have traced such transitions across a wide range of physical, biological and social processes, including sand piles, speciation processes, forest fires, network dynamics and social segregation.

For the physical scientist, the question then arises, of the extent to which the system parameters can be 'tuned' so as to steer the trajectory of the system; not necessarily in fine detail, but sufficient to avoid tipping points into zones and forms of system behaviour that are not desired. We referred in Chapter 9 to Stewart's discussion of such control systems in engineering and medicine, and the scope for tuning system dynamics by continuous adjustment of the relevant parameters.

In referring to system parameters, the term must of course be interpreted appropriately. In physical processes we may be speaking of the ambient temperature, acidity, atmospheric pressure. In agent-based models we refer to the underlying algorithms. In relation to networks or fitness landscapes we refer to the connections, whether in the form of Kauffman's K and C parameters, for example, or the percolation thresholds of eco-systems (Solé and Bascompte, 2006). Tuning may also involve decomposing the system in new ways, switching and modifying the connections among its sub-systems, in a strategy of 'decomplexity' (Simon, 1996: Ch. 8; Stewart, 2001).

This raises the question as to whether social systems can similarly be tuned and if so, by reference to what range of possible futures. It is, however, necessary to remember that social processes are different from the control systems applied in engineering and medicine. Human agents reflect upon their world and are agile in re-weaving its elements, contesting the attempts of policy-makers and others to exercise control, and instead seeking to drive it in their own preferred direction. In the social world, therefore, control systems are forever being imposed but also forever contested, exploited and by-passed. This makes for a strong element of uncertainty, additional to the uncertainty that may in any case be bound up with the complex dynamics of the system concerned. This also means that the task of policy tuning is unavoidably political; it involves not only anticipating patterns of human behaviour, but also promoting more enlightened consideration of the possible futures that they face and among which they can in some degree choose (Toulmin, 2001: 93).

It is in these terms that we might read Pierson's call for policy researchers to advise as to the various trajectories of institutional development that are possible, given particular institutional histories. This is rather different from seeking to predict the most likely impact of a given policy. This advice, Pierson adds, should take account of the tight couplings between different institutions that produce 'deep equilibria' of long duration (what Kauffman, it will be recalled, discussed in terms of frozen components and forcing structures) (Pierson, 2004: 157–62).[1] Nevertheless, the institutional couplings and trajectories thus unearthed by the policy researcher are always contingent, for the reasons discussed in the previous chapter.

Such policy advice would also identify the 'runaway loops' and eddies of self-organisation likely to result from any re-working of the institutional architecture. Indeed, the exploitation of such loops lies at the heart of the policy task. Chapter 7 brought centre-stage the efforts of the agile entrepreneur to find co-evolutionary dynamics for technological and institutional change, in a single self-reinforcing process. The same may now be said of the policy entrepreneur, looking for a fleeting policy window which will open opportunities for self-reinforcing advance. Kingdon (1984: Ch. 8) describes well the purposeful opportunism this involves: watching for openings, whether created by sudden crises or by the regular abrasion of policy-making calendars; seizing on new precedents and widening their application; hooking policy solutions onto particular problems and both onto current political fashions; building coalitions for reform, undermining coalitions of resistance.[2] The policy-maker must persuade his or her constituency that policy reform need not involve risky long-jumps of uncertain outcome: the landscape can be re-fashioned to allow a step-wise walk that will ensure their well-being and enable them to 'occupy the future'. This is advocacy, in which the policy-maker may point to demonstration projects and pilot schemes, or to shocks and scandals, as demonstrating that the walk is both necessary and feasible. And of course, persuasion, by building a constituency for reform, itself helps to make those steps more feasible (Marris, 1974).

14.2.2   The Policy-maker as Energiser

Potts and Crouch share a combinatorial ontology, with entrepreneurs weaving novel technological and institutional designs. This makes human creativity central to a dynamic socio-economic system. To support this creativity is therefore similarly central to public policy. This includes 'second order' policies concerned with education, innovation and the growth of knowledge (Dopfer and Potts, 2008: Ch. 7) and policies that expand the opportunities for institutional entrepreneurs to draw models from their neighbours and from the *bricolage* of the past (Crouch, 2005).

This suggests an analysis of public policy in terms of the creation, sharing and organisation of knowledge. Thus, for example, the literature on national innovation systems is concerned with the ways in which institutional linkages connect knowledge resources, facilitating new technological and institutional designs, and the scope for public policies to accelerate such connections (Nelson, 1993). The same goes for the literature on knowledge management and knowledge society indicators: this will be our concern in Chapter 16.

This is the policy-maker as energiser of creativity. For some of the scholars to whom we have referred, this is quite sufficient. Beyond this, 'micro-meso-macro' in a vibrant and creative economy will self-organise so as to bring growth and prosperity. It follows that policy interventions that interfere with self-organisation are misguided and likely only to reduce welfare. Self-organisation may impose costs on some groups – those whose innovations fail and those 'last movers' who get left behind on low fitness peaks – but these costs are outweighed by the benefits that it brings to society in general. Among some writers on complexity, including those influenced by Schumpeter and Hayek, the conclusion is clear: modern societies are over-regulated by the state and must be 'liberated' so that they can self-organise (Parker and Stacey, 1994). For Hayek himself, capitalism is a self-organising system and, as Desai and Ormerod (1998) summarise, 'the complex interaction of individual agents implies, for example, that government intervention is not needed to revive the economy in a depression. The natural rhythms of the system itself ensure that a recovery takes place.'

Nevertheless, as we have had frequent occasion to note, even if a social system self-organises it does not follow that the outcome is necessary, efficient or desirable. Moreover, within the range of system parameters where self-organisation is possible, this may take a variety of different forms. In any case, the capacity of human beings to take note of the system in which they live and to modify their behaviour will itself tend to change that system; whether they are policy-makers intervening *de haut en bas*, or ordinary citizens seeking in more local contexts to modify the 'connective geometry' of their socio-economic environment. Indeed, there may be a multitude of social actors seeking to make such modifications, racing to impose their preferred order upon a shifting landscape, but with self-organisation for one producing disorganisation or adverse incorporation for others.

14.2.3 The Policy-maker as Steward

The policy-maker is in a world pushed 'far from equilibrium' by competing projects for positional advantage. Agile and creative first movers produce swarms of technological and institutional novelty, variously taken up by the larger population, and then setting larger abrasions and macro-dynamics in motion, warping the landscape on which the positional struggle is pursued.

Like Darwin's gardener or pigeon breeder, the public policy-maker both wittingly and unwittingly shapes this struggle and the forms of self-organisation that emerge. This is husbandry of the social fabric: the arts of civilisation, rather than those of the hunter-gatherer. This is the policy-maker as umpire or steward, civilising the struggle between competing 'evolutionary logics' and seeking to build what Kristensen and Zeitlin describe as a virtuous circle of trust, respect and mutual commitment. This is what, in our discussion of Ostrom (1990), we termed a negotiated moral community, capable of nurturing the terrains of our collective life.

Civility must be built, it does not organise itself. So also, stewardship is not merely reactive, applying a shared normative framework and enforcing the rules of the game. It involves encouraging creativity and energising diversity; but then also and inevitably judging the various evolutionary logics that manifest themselves and deciding which should be favoured and encouraged to flourish. Indeed, the policy-maker may be not only the steward of a race but also its instigator, cultivating novelty and driving the community in new directions. The policy-maker must also, however, decide what limits to place on the race, so that the struggle does not get out of hand.

Indeed, we might pose this in terms of the double challenge that the policy-maker as steward confronts. On the one hand, the diverse evolutionary logics championed by the various protagonists pose a challenge to social stability and may even bring war and chaos. On the other hand, it may sometimes be the policy-maker, the community leader, who seeks to reinforce this diversity, as a means of breaking out from the institutional log-jams of the past, challenging stasis and the collusive veto that the self-satisfied occupants of favoured positions may seek to impose. These two challenges echo a recurring theme of earlier chapters: that complex systems hover between the realms of order and chaos, Red Queen and evolutionarily stable state, but can also find an intermediate realm of adaptability and self-organisation.

No steward can be entirely even-handed. His or her actions fatefully re-shape the landscape on which the positional struggle will henceforth unfold and variously affect the leverage which the different protagonists can bring to bear. The policy-maker as steward strikes an always contingent balance among their competing projects: a socio-political settlement that allows each some scope for activation, but also imposes constraints.

If the policy-maker is the umpire and steward of a community, he or she is also a policy entrepreneur, promoting its interests and goals within the larger world and reaching out for new opportunities and resources. This is an 'external' task as protagonist, whether the policy-maker is champion of a business, a university, a local community, a nation or an international organisation. Here the policy-maker has no choice but to 'ride the fitness landscape', as one among many agile actors (Pascale, 1999; Bovaird, 2008; Klijn, 2008).

Other actors within the community – the very actors whom our policy-maker seeks to civilise and steer – may also conduct their own 'foreign policies' within that wider world. Indeed, it is on their relations with actors in the larger world that their creativity in considerable degree depends, as also therefore does the resilience of the community or organisation in question. Turbulence in that external environment may, however, regularly shift their interests and stakes, inciting them to new lines of action and upsetting stable patterns of interaction among them, adding to the difficulties that face the policy-maker as steward. Think, for example, of the efforts of local authorities and civil society organisations to take advantage of EU programmes and processes, including the Open Method of Coordination (OMC), to expand the leverage they can exert in the domestic struggle (Zeitlin and Pochet, 2005).

Of course, the policy-maker may prove a poor steward, in regards to this wider world. As Kristensen and Zeitlin discover, community stewards may be distracted by some local 'village' – in their case, the shareholders and investment bankers who hold the levers of accountability to which these stewards are most immediately subject. Predators are on the prowl, ready to incorporate vulnerable communities on adverse terms, within their own 'forcing structures' and timescales.

14.2.4 Policy-making and Governance

In this book we have ventured little into the scholarly literature on governance, sharing somewhat with Rhodes the view that the latter 'has too many meanings to be useful' (Rhodes, 1997: 15). In a treatise that is already theoretically dense, additional families of concepts can be entertained only if they contribute substantial added value.

Nevertheless, the ideas of the policy-maker as tuner, energiser and steward sit well with much of the governance literature, and its presentation of the policy-maker as steering society 'at a distance', rather than undertaking what Weber referred to as 'imperative coordination'. The scholarship on governance also draws attention to its roots in cybernetics and in 'autopoeisis', another of the strands of the complexity paradigm to which Chapter 2 briefly alluded. The governance literature also makes reference to the way that interdependent organisations form self-organising networks (Rhodes, 1997: Ch. 3; Pierre and Peters, 2000: Ch. 2).

Pierre and Peters argue that the main governance problem is to how redefine the relationship between the political and administrative branches of the state so as to allow market-based models of reform (Pierre and Peters, 2000: 5). Our own view does not privilege markets in this way; the debate on governance should properly be concerned with the appropriate place for markets but also for negotiated moral communities and common pool resources, as well as hierarchical organisation in the shadow of the state.

The present study may well prove of value to those governance debates; nevertheless, to demonstrate that value is not among its own core tasks.

14.3   THE REAL WORLD OF POLICY-MAKING

The preceding discussion has been couched in perhaps rather abstract terms. However, these ideas of the policy-maker as tuner, creative energiser and steward can serve as points of reference for analysing the real world policies and interventions of specific public agencies and departments: a local authority, a regional health organisation, a central government department. Thus, for example, in relation to the professional officers within such an organisation, or in relation to the larger population which it serves, each such agency plays a role in ensuring civility and in championing the community's interests in the larger struggle. It may be that most departments play such a role only in conjunction with their political bosses; and that even these, save at the highest level, have little scope for independent action. Nevertheless, they have some; social and political structures are in some degree fractal; the challenges of maintaining civility and avoiding stasis are to this extent scale-free.

In Chapter 8 we took stock of the capacities that agile agents require in a complex and turbulent world. That discussion applies no less here. Organisations that make and deliver public policies need skills and leverage that go beyond habit, simply 'rolling out' policies that are known to work. Evidence of what works – including what works elsewhere and could be imitated here – is of course necessary. It is not, however, sufficient. There is, first, the challenge of applying that knowledge – matching and combining a variety of possible templates – to the specificities of particular situations, in a world that is far from flat. In addition, policymakers must consider how this particular world is likely to unfold. They must select from among a range of mental models those that may enable them to peer through the murk, 'satisficing' rather than optimising. Not only will they need mental models of their own, they will also need to be aware of those being used by others, including the wider population of 'last movers', upon whose expectations and responses the effects of their policy interventions will crucially depend. Thus, for example, Breakwell examines the implications of popular perceptions of health hazards for policy interventions, and for the sequencing of communications about such risks. In exploring these dynamics, she uses 'hazard templates' not dissimilar to the 'schematic preferences' of Holland and Potts, which have informed our own discussion of mental models (Breakwell, 2001; Barnett and Breakwell, 2003).

We will give particular attention to policy indicators of social, economic and technological conditions and patterns of change. In the contemporary world of public policy, such indicators are commonly endowed with a dual significance (Kingdon, 1984: Ch. 5). They reveal first the state we are in, the specificities to which our various policy templates must be matched and how we stand in relation to the various drivers of change. They also provide us with clues as to the trajectories along which we are travelling and the choices and trade-offs that will face us – the thresholds and tipping points of virtuous and vicious change. We will evaluate this dual significance in a number of policy fields.[3]

The real world of policy-making may be so turbulent that there are few familiar patterns by reference to the regularities of the past, even fewer plausible 'mental models' or conjectures for the future. Public policymakers may be able to reduce this uncertainty by actively shaping the future, rather than just attempting to predict it; however, even they are limited in the capacity and knowledge of which they dispose. This is in part the stuff of scenario-building and forecasts, whether in relation to climate change, energy security or the threat of terrorism. It is also the stuff of ideas, intellectual paradigms and metaphors for seeing the world, the stock in trade of scholars and teachers.

14.4 CONCLUSION

The chapters that follow examine the complex and turbulent dynamics of social disadvantage, the knowledge economy and the financial crisis, re-examining their respective policy landscapes by reference to the conceptual framework developed in this book. They consider the public policy responses, the adequacy of the tools that policy-makers deploy, the institutional constraints within which they operate and the mental models of the world in which their expectations appear to be nested. They recognise that policy-makers may themselves be protagonists, predators or prey.

We will be concerned not only with the tools that policy-makers deploy but also how they may best see the world to which they apply those tools (Schön, 1993). Parts 1 and 2 left us not only with methods and models but also with larger perspectives and metaphors of the social world. It is these that, consciously or otherwise, shape our selection of the 'stylised facts' of that world and our efforts to explain the regularities and patterns we observe. Thus the metaphors of a mechanical equilibrium, a biological eco-system, a positional struggle among first movers in a race against time, will 'frame' the way that we 'see' a policy 'problem' in quite different ways.[4] This does not mean that the choice is arbitrary; we will typically find that one metaphor or frame proves sterile in terms of the explanatory and policy illumination it offers, while another offers insights that have broader resonance. Our metaphors also we must select for their fitness. This applies, however, not just to the policy-makers of the day but also the larger populations they serve. The metaphors and meaning systems that are in general currency shape popular responses to public policies; they influence which programmes of reform are perceived as plausible, which not, and what constituencies of support can be mobilised; they are therefore central to the political contest (Marris, 1974).

It is neither possible nor particularly useful to separate the analysis of policy problems, tools, options and trade-offs. In the chapters that follow we make clear with which of these we are concerned at any given point; nevertheless, the way we 'see' problems, the evidence of 'regularities' that we investigate and the range of policy options we identify are closely interrelated, as indeed they are to the tools of intervention that we take to be politically and technically feasible. Each chapter therefore ranges variously across these connected themes.

We have seen that in human affairs at least, the appeal to self-organisation does not release us from fundamental choices of public policy. A capitalist economy may self-organise at various levels of unemployment, with the level of public investment being fateful for the forms of self-organisation that emerge. However, it is not just in relation to the economy that public policy shapes the forms of self-organisation that emerge, the projects of positional advantage that prosper. Thus, for example, as Goldthorpe demonstrates, social and educational policies are fateful for the 'ruggedness' or otherwise of the mobility landscape across which different social classes self-organise inter-generationally.

We will consider how public policies affect the ability of different households to organise themselves and the various institutional systems in which they are enmeshed, so as to meet their needs, appropriate opportunities and buffer themselves against instability and turbulence. We will consider how such policies empower and connect some communities while undermining others. Public policies shape whose hopes are realised, which metaphors of the social world have general resonance and plausibility; which lines of social differentiation harden, which shared institutions are nurtured. They thus define our collective value choices. Self-organisation can thus be taken as a normative vantage point from which to appraise the policies in question, by reference not to the goals of economic policy so much as the social well-being of different groups.

These chapters thus make a start in applying to the policy world the institutionally grounded complexity perspective which previous chapters have developed. The Postscript distils this provisional wisdom into a compendium of practical tools for agile policy-makers. This also, however, is only a first step, which it is for others to hone and extend.

15 Poverty and social exclusion

15.1 INTRODUCTION

Chapter 1 described the unsatisfactory state of social policy research, as far as the conceptualisation and measurement of dynamic change are concerned. I illustrated this argument by reference to two areas of policy research in which I have been involved over a number of years. In the present chapter and that which follows, I consider the implications of the present study for research and policy in these two areas. This makes perhaps for a somewhat heterogeneous agenda – the dynamics of social exclusion and policy indicators of the knowledge economy. Nevertheless, Part 3 does not pretend to be a systematic application to the policy world of the concepts and methods developed in Parts 1 and 2.

A substantial body of research has been undertaken in recent decades, both nationally and internationally, into poverty and social exclusion. This reveals some broadly similar shifts in the map of poverty in the second half of the twentieth century, as far as the advanced industrial societies of the West are concerned (for example, the shift in the risk of poverty from the older population to those of working age) but also some stability (for example, the league table of national poverty rates across the countries of the EU) (Room, 1990: Ch. 3; Ramprakash, 1994; Marlier et al., 2007). Nevertheless, these have been turbulent times, with global economic restructuring, welfare 'recalibration' and concerns about new lines of social polarisation.

Scholars have investigated these stabilities and shifts in part through the longitudinal analysis of household circumstances, using cohort and panel studies (Leisering and Walker, 1998; Goodin et al., 1999). However, as argued in Chapter 1, these circumstances are mediated by institutions and policies; these must be included in the analysis, if appropriate policy inferences are to be drawn. This means, on the one hand, analysing the goals and strategies of key institutional actors – employers, public policy-makers, social service managers, for example – and, on the other, those of individuals and households, as they seek to shape, resist or by-pass institutions and extract benefit from their operations. It also means understanding how the outcomes secured by these various actors spill over onto other terrains and the circumstances under which this produces self-reinforcing processes of social inclusion or exclusion. However, as Chapter 1 noted, in general the longitudinal national data sets that have been established do not themselves allow us to say much about these social, political, economic and institutional dynamics and the larger changes in political economy within which they unfold.

We now consider how far the conceptual framework and methodological tools developed in this study equip us for this analytical challenge and in what degree they illuminate the task of policy-makers. We focus in particular on access to education and employment and the risks of incorporation on adverse terms faced by different households variously located in the social structure.

15.2   TOLERANCE SCHEDULES AND SOCIAL POLARISATION

Policy-makers frequently trumpet the importance of extending educational opportunities to the whole population: both as a social policy priority, concerned with equality, and as an economic priority, developing human resources to support national economic advance. Certainly this became a central theme in the UK, under the Labour Government after 1997, and its oft-stated concern to combat persisting lines of social exclusion.

Policies that affect access to schools by different sections of the population are therefore centre-stage. In the UK, under reforms introduced by Kenneth Baker, Education Minister in the Conservative Government, and continued after 1997 by Labour, parents have been given the freedom, in principle at least, to send their children to the state school of their choice. To assist them in making this choice, government has given increased attention to publishing details of the performance of schools, by reference to the test and examination results of their pupils.

Le Grand (2007: Ch. 3) argues that this policy shift to a quasi-market has led to competition among schools, driving up educational standards, to the benefit of everyone. The counter-argument is that the policy has locked schools into vicious and virtuous spirals of decline or expansion, with deleterious consequences for equality of educational opportunity. Indeed, a considerable but not uncontroversial literature has developed, concerned with competition for entry to schools on the part of families endowed with different resources and capacities for institutional agility, and able to express this not only through the support that they give to their children but also their ability, where this aids entry to the most sought after schools, to access housing in the school's immediate vicinity (Butler and Robson, 2003; Burgess et al., 2007b).

The level of demand for places that each school attracts is highly consequential, not least because school budgets depend heavily on the number of pupils recruited. Recruitment, resources and reputation march in step. It is hardly surprising, therefore, that schools make efforts to exclude difficult pupils and market themselves to affluent homes, in the hope of boosting school examination performance, because this will tend to produce a self-reinforcing boost to budgets and also to future recruitment (Davies, 2000).

Lauder and Hughes (1999) investigate the consequences of similar reforms in New Zealand. Like Davies, they point to the spirals of success or decline in which schools find themselves, as they compete to attract middle class pupils. Using multi-level modelling, Lauder and Hughes show that variations in educational attainment, as between different schools, are shaped not only by the social background of pupils and school level characteristics such as pupil turnover and school management and practice; there is an additional effect relating to the social mix within schools, so that those schools with disproportionate numbers of middle class children deliver an even higher level of educational attainment than the social class backgrounds of their intake and their school management characteristics would lead one to expect. This is consistent with cross-national comparative work by Willms, using the OECD PISA data, which highlights social class segregation in schools as a key factor exacerbating social class differences in educational attainment (OECD, 2001a: Ch. 8).

Davies gives a qualitative account of the processes of social and educational polarisation. Lauder and Hughes weigh the various influences on school performance once this polarisation has run its course. Our interest is in modelling the dynamics of polarisation which Davies describes, as the basis for understanding the pattern of outcomes that Lauder and Hughes measure.

In an article published in 2006, I sought, in collaboration with Nick Britton, in our Department of Mathematics, to model these processes of polarisation (Room and Britton, 2006). This work was subsequently developed by Perdita Robinson, a dissertation student working with Julian Padget in our Department of Computer Sciences. This work illustrates how three of the modelling approaches discussed in the present book can be used to illuminate these exclusionary dynamics and potentially to inform policy.

15.2.1 Qualitative System Dynamics

First, under the guidance of John Powell, in our School of Management, we made use of signed directed networks, as discussed in Chapter 11. Powell has developed this as a form of qualitative system dynamics to analyse organisational strategies. By mapping organisational processes and their interdependencies in terms of such directed graphs, Powell can identify those sub-graphs which are liable to produce self-reinforcing circles or 'runaway loops' and which may then, depending on how well connected the sub-system in question is to the system as a whole, have a much wider influence.

Figure 15.1 maps the signed graphs embodied in the quasi-market of secondary education, as described by Davies and by Lauder and Hughes. Each sign indicates whether the relationship is direct or inverse: whether, in other words, an increase in the 'upstream' variable causes a change in the 'downstream' variable that is positive or negative. In this case we see a whole system of positive and therefore mutually reinforcing links. This brings out starkly the tendency of such a quasi-market to generate a runaway loop, as high-performing schools attract excess demand and can then pick pupils from middle class homes in particular. This is a complex adaptive system, in which middle class parents – and their children's peer group – self-organise through school selection processes (Burgess et al., 2007a). We might even describe this as 'co-evolution' of this middle class clientele and the sub-group of high-performing schools that serve them.

15.2.2   Mathematical Modelling

Qualitative system dynamics is useful in mapping the dynamics to which such an educational quasi-market may be vulnerable. We next considered what mathematical models might be appropriate for modelling the 'runaway loops' thereby exposed. School selection involves a two-sided process of competitive assortative mating. On the one hand, parents strive to send their children to schools of high reputation; on the other hand, schools draw on their reputations to compete for middle class pupils. Human mating has been modelled as just such a two-sided strategic search for desirable partners (Bloch and Ryder, 2000); this can in principle be extended to school selection. More generally, indeed, it can be applied to other situations where recruiting organisations compete for particular sub-groups of the population, and where those sub-populations target the recruiters: insurance companies, for example, in search of low-risk clients and prepared to offer them reduced premia (Daykin, 2003).

Nevertheless, a model similar to that of Schelling seemed both simpler and more fruitful. As will be recalled from Chapter 2, Schelling models the development of racial segregation in cities by reference to the 'tolerance schedules' of whites and blacks: their readiness to live in a neighbourhood with more than a certain proportion of the other race. Parental strategies

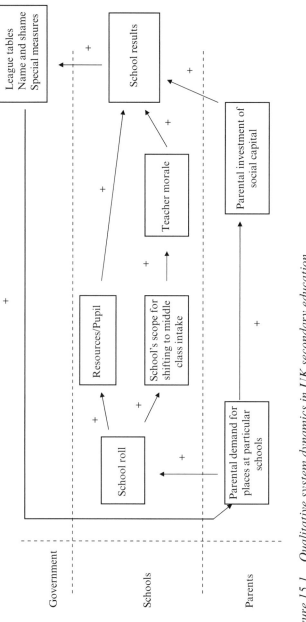

Figure 15.1   Qualitative system dynamics in UK secondary education

251

can be modelled analogously: parents have 'preference schedules' which treat schools with high proportions of middle class pupils as the most attractive. This preference is taken as being common to middle class and working class parents, although stronger among the former, given that they have the resources if needed to move into the catchment areas of other schools, if those available locally are insufficiently attractive.[1] The model allows us to study how the strength of this parental preference affects the dynamics of the system.

This involves a simplification of the process mapped in Figure 15.1. There it was school league tables that drove parental demand for places at different schools. However, school results – and hence position in the league table – benefit from the proportion of middle class pupils; here therefore we treat the object of parents' preferences as being not the league table results themselves but the social class composition of the school directly – more particularly the proportion of middle class pupils.

Schools must have strategies as to how they should allocate places, when demand exceeds supply. The model allows us to explore two such strategies. In the first, schools are blind to social class. In the second, schools are class-sensitive: they prefer middle class pupils and those from the working class are accepted only to the extent that schools would otherwise have unfilled places. Davies argues that it is towards this second strategy that schools have been pushed by the logic of the quasi-market.

The model examines the conditions under which runaway loops can develop through the dynamic interaction of these parental and school strategies.[2] In particular, it suggests that with strong parental preference for schools with a high proportion of middle class pupils, and school allocation policies which are class-sensitive, preferring middle class pupils, the 'equity state' – one where each school has a representative cross-section of the population – becomes unstable in face of even minor perturbations. Once any school gains an advantage in terms of its league table performance, movement towards an 'inequity state' follows, and this is likely to be highly stable. Twin polarisations are likely to develop: social class polarisation among schools and polarisation of school results, as captured in league tables.

However, what is also clear from the mathematics of the model is that these developments depend critically upon the strength of these parental and school preferences. If school allocation policies are class-blind, polarisation will develop only if parental preferences for schools with a high proportion of middle class pupils are very strong indeed, and even then the polarisation will be only partial. In contrast, if school allocation policies are class-sensitive, it will take only moderately strong parental preferences to produce polarisation, and this polarisation will be total.

15.2.3 Computational Modelling

Robinson (2007) uses agent-based modelling to explore these dynamics further.[3] The mathematical model used above focuses on the 'equity' and 'inequity' states and their stability under different values of the system parameters. Multi-agent simulation can model the dynamic processes involved. It can also introduce stochastic shocks (associated, for example, with an unexpectedly good or bad inspection report of the school, or the arrival or departure of a particularly good head teacher).

Robinson shows, first, that her simulation is consistent with the mathematical model used above. She goes on to introduce a variety of elaborations: these would render the mathematical model intractable, but can be readily handled by simulations of this sort. She explores the scope for schools to develop distinctive niches – for example, around particular specialist subjects, or in terms of a commitment to socially inclusive 'class-blind' entry, even when other schools are competing for middle class entry.

Thus, for example, with schools class-sensitive in their selection policies, she allows those schools entering a downward spiral to revise their entry policies to be class-blind, and finds that in some degree this does indeed arrest that decline and the social class polarisation between schools. This is contingent, of course, on her adoption of a more heterogeneous model of parental preferences than was ever possible in the mathematical model discussed above: some parents have a positive interest in sending their child to such a class-blind school, they are not swayed solely by league table performance. So also, with schools class-blind in their recruitment, Robinson allows any school that gains a league table advantage to switch to a class-sensitive strategy, so as to capitalise on that advantage and reinforce it. Only if parents are strongly in favour of class-blind schools, with league table performance merely secondary, does this strategy fail.

By introducing these threshold-related strategy changes, and simulating their evolution for different parameters, Robinson powerfully demonstrates the value of experimentation *in silica*, as a tool of policy analysis on these dynamic terrains.[4]

15.2.4 Overview for Policy and Policy-making

It was by no means unreasonable for UK policy-makers to see choice in education and competition among schools as a way to expand opportunities and improve performance. In this book we have after all made much of institutional inertia and 'frozen structures'. Moreover, the critics of the reforms can hardly argue that the pre-existing system was a model of social equity. Reforms which challenged this inertia, unleashed the energies of parental choice and set schools in a race against each other, even a struggle for their very existence, might reasonably have been expected to produce improved outcomes.[5]

Of course, what one person deems system inertia another may see as resilience; these can involve highly contested educational and political judgements. In addition, with the new reforms as much as with the existing system, it was to be expected that the various protagonists would seek to subvert, resist, exploit or by-pass these well-meant intentions (albeit these are perhaps overly harsh and pejorative terms to describe what, for many parents, involve difficult moral choices and conflicting loyalties: see Swift (2003)). Schools can themselves become the vehicles by which the more advantaged and agile self-organise for these purposes. The result can be to frustrate the policy intent.

It is on the scope for such self-organisation for positional advantage that our various models have focused. The qualitative system dynamics with which we began, using signed directed networks, takes the 'stylised facts' of the educational reforms and displays the strong potential for self-reinforcing 'runaway loops' of school pupil selection. It helps us map the points where action might be taken to dampen down – or indeed to accelerate – these loops. These include the rights of parents to exercise free choice of school, rather than being confined to the local school; the scope for schools to select pupils by methods whose consequence is to maximise middle class intake; the publicity which policy-makers give to the relative performances of schools, in league tables and policies of 'naming and shaming'; and the allocation of budgets by reference to school pupil numbers, with only limited regard for the additional challenges which are faced by those schools, which find themselves with large proportions of disadvantaged pupils.[6]

The mathematical and computational models explore the dynamics of these 'runaway loops'. The mathematical model gives a central place to school allocation policies, on the one hand (whether or not they are 'class-blind') and, on the other, the strength of parents' preference for schools with a high proportion of middle class pupils. The computational model adds a variety of 'evolutionary' developments within the educational 'eco-system': elaborations that again express alternative national policies in regards to parental choice, school resources, opportunities for schools to develop niche specialisms and so on. It also tracks the degree of social class polarisation across the schools concerned, as the eco-system develops. All of these models are however limited, insofar as they ignore the extent to which parental preferences and school policies may themselves be shaped by the insecurity created by the Baker reforms, as schools are set in open competition with each other, a 'race against time' which threatens to polarise school performances. They therefore also ignore the scope for political leaders to reduce turbulence and bring civility to this 'struggle for existence'.

In all of this, it may be helpful to recall the example of the Millennium Bridge, discussed in Chapter 2. When pedestrians began walking across, their steps were uncoordinated. However, the slight sway that they produced served to orchestrate their subsequent steps, which in turn only reinforced the sway. Here also slight sways in the reputational league table of schools induce movements on the part of parents (and especially of agile middle class parents) which reinforce those sways. Particular schools emerge as middle class territory. The insecurities this creates for those involved – and the strategies they then respectively adopt – are 'emergent' properties of the chosen educational architecture, no less than with the design of the bridge. On turbulent terrains parents can hardly but be agile opportunists, stampeding after whichever school appears to be best: to behave otherwise, as we saw in Chapter 8, is hardly rational. To examine this as primarily a question of personal morality hardly meets the point (Swift, 2003).

15.3 INSTITUTIONAL ENTREPRENEURS ON COMPLEX TERRAINS

Across most advanced industrial societies, lone parents and their families comprise one of the major population groups at risk of poverty and social exclusion. In the UK the Labour Government elected in 1997 made it a priority to raise the incomes of such households, by moving them from dependence on social benefits into employment. This involved a number of major new investments, including a dedicated labour market programme (the New Deal for Lone Parents), increased financial support for those in employment (the Child and Working Tax Credits) and an expansion of childcare services (the National Childcare Strategy).

My colleagues Jane Millar and Tess Ridge have been following a sample of lone parents, as they move from social benefits (Income Support) into work. Compared with the previous regime, where means-tested social benefits were available to those not employed, entitlements have changed markedly and lone mothers now find themselves on an institutionally more complex landscape. It is also one with stronger obligations to seek employment. The work requirements placed on lone mothers may still be less than those in many other countries; nevertheless, the pressures to work – including the requirement that all lone mothers receiving social benefits should have a work-focused interview and agree an action plan

– have undoubtedly increased (Millar, 2006). In 2010 all lone mothers with no child below seven years were moved onto Jobseekers Allowance, not Income Support, and were required to be available for employment.

Millar (2006) contrasts the relative security and familiarity of Income Support with the delays and uncertainties involved in the various financial supports now available, as mothers take up employment. Any improvement in their financial situation depends not only on the level of their wages relative to Income Support, but also on tax credits and various short-term bonuses, paid as they move back to work. There may be new costs of childcare and travel to work. Improvements in their incomes may move them beyond the eligibility threshold for other allowances they receive, for example, in relation to free school meals, housing benefits and Council Tax remission. Tax credits and other allowances can moreover be heavily affected by changes in family composition (for example, as children pass particular age thresholds or leave home). In all, therefore, for these mothers their incomes are much more unstable and uncertain than with a normal wage or salary, or than Income Support benefit had been previously (Ridge and Millar, 2008: 27–9, 84). Personal advisers at job centres make calculations as to whether on balance the mother will be better off if she takes a particular job; however, because of the aforesaid complexities, these are often inaccurate (Millar, 2008: 7).[7]

These mothers are nevertheless required to make some critical calculations and choices in relation to employment opportunities. They seem able to comment on those choices *ex post* and when pressed by an interviewer; they are less able to stand back and make such calculations *ex ante* with any degree of confidence. Step-wise adjustments at particular decision points are more likely. It is not just that information about the likely financial gains and losses is embedded in somewhat opaque administrative regulations; it is also the difficulty of predicting the various path dependencies which the decision to take a given job will set in motion and the ways this may abrade against other elements of their 'family-work projects'.

First, there is frequently the hope that the move into employment will be a 'foot in the door', leading eventually to further improvements, in terms of greater job security and maybe promotion, for the day when children move beyond school age and tax credits are reduced (Millar, 2006); albeit in the short term at least, such improvements are somewhat rare (Millar, 2008: 7–8). It is, however, also possible that taking a given job will close off other opportunities for job search and/or re-training and lock the mother concerned into a long-term sub-optimal trajectory.

Second, the sustainability of such employment depends crucially upon the informal patterns of social support that emerge – we might say self-organise – both at home and at work: the 'niche' which the mother constructs out of her various social relationships. Millar and Ridge stress the importance of friends and parents, in making the family-work project viable for these mothers. No less important is a work environment sufficiently stable to allow the mother to plan her childcare arrangements, but sufficiently flexible and resilient to allow her to cope with fluctuations in the children's needs, for example, when they are ill (Millar, 2008: 9–10, 54–5, 59; Ridge and Millar, 2008: Ch. 3; Millar and Ridge, 2009).

In the language of earlier chapters, these mothers live under conditions of enforced myopia, where step-wise adjustments may bring some improvement (or stave off a deterioration of conditions) but longer-range jumps are too risky to consider. The uncertainty of their world means moreover that the 'mental models' they use to map their institutional landscapes give only limited guidance as to future possibilities. Only those mothers with strong informal support can take full advantage of the new opportunities that the reforms offer, as distinct from merely 'keeping the show on the road'.

This is the lone mother as agile institutional entrepreneur, re-weaving the complex web of formal and informal social affiliations in which she is enmeshed, albeit on a rather limited canvas and without easily predictable results (Ridge, 2007: 409). This is her 'institutional micro-ecosystem', involving competition and cooperation, niche differentiation, hierarchy and adverse incorporation. These are her efforts to cope with the abrasions consequent upon the policy reforms launched by the Labour Government: efforts that allow her some scope as agile first mover, but that leave her still in large measure a change taker. It is these dynamics that we seek to analyse, so as to illuminate the policy options and trade-offs involved.

15.3.1 Modelling the Institutional Entrepreneur

Abstract economic models depict the household as a Robinson Crusoe, who arrives ready equipped with skills, tools, seeds and a plot of land, unencumbered by rights and obligations and free to take up new opportunities as they arise. In general, however, we should not think of households as possessed of resources and capacities in some absolute or unmediated sense, apart perhaps from the produce grown in the vegetable garden. Rather, resources are drawn down through a variety of institutional channels; they depend therefore on the resilience and stability of those institutional arrangements. Households may re-weave these institutions; this may in turn change the landscape for other households also, just locally or maybe on a larger scale. The institutional landscape is therefore in constant flux.

This perspective has been at least implicit in much of the slow and painstaking fieldwork of empirical social policy studies. This predominantly qualitative tradition may have been somewhat upstaged by the more recent quantitative emphasis in longitudinal cohort and panel studies, but it should not be neglected (Millar, 2007). It was, for example, evident in the research by Kempson and Rowlingson (1994) into household strategies for coping in situations of insecurity and uncertainty, and the use they make of the various assets, relationships and rights at their disposal. Steinert and Pilgram (2003) likewise provide analyses of 'welfare policy from below', with households re-weaving the *bricolage* of their resources and relationships, in an effort to resist exclusionary pressures. This perspective is also well represented in development studies, especially qualitative studies of household livelihood strategies. These investigate the ways in which households make their consumption and investment decisions; how, in highly precarious situations, they cope with shocks; the importance of maintaining diversified stocks of physical, human and social capital; and the adverse economic, social and political fates into which households may be forced, in order to survive at all. These studies also offer potent indicators – tipping points – of impending catastrophe: for example, when households are found eating the seed corn for next year (Chambers, 1989; Bevan and Sseweya, 1995; Indra and Buchugnani, 1997; Carney, 1998; Moser, 1998).[8]

Lone mothers inhabit a complex institutional micro-eco-system. This enmeshes them in a number of social networks: their friends and relatives, helping with childcare; the public officials who administer benefits and support them in entering the labour market; their employers and work colleagues. Each of these networks embodies a complex structure of rules of entitlement and obligation. Miller and Ridge investigate mothers' efforts to navigate and re-weave these. What they find can be readily understood using the analytical framework for networks and connections deployed in the final sections of Chapter 11, reinforced in the penultimate section of Chapter 13.

In Chapter 11 we took Jervis's analysis of international relations as our template. The analytical framework had three elements. We recognised, first, that social actors have multiple affiliations within a social structure: a legacy which both shapes and limits their capacities. The networks to which they attach themselves and the ways in which these may be re-woven are strongly path dependent. Chapter 12 was then concerned in particular with the affiliations of social class. The inequalities of class that our social structure embodies – and the ways in which they combine with the inequalities of gender – have long been at the heart of research into lone parents by Miller and by Ridge, including the studies under review here.

Second, we saw that social actors make new connections and discard old ones, by reference to their fitness for purpose. Much social action is of course merely habitual, 'following the rules' and applying well-established responses to familiar situations. Nevertheless, when anomalous situations arise, perhaps crossing a certain critical threshold, actors may bestir themselves to be agile change makers. This, we argued, can be modelled using structural balance theory. Within an action frame of reference, this allows us to explore the strains that social actors discover in their institutional connections and the actions they take to re-weave and reconcile them. This depends of course on the subjective meanings that social actors give to the connections and rules, both formal and informal, in which they are enmeshed. To the elucidation of these Millar and Ridge's use of qualitative longitudinal panels is particularly appropriate.

Third, and again as in our treatment of Jervis, we recognise that social actors may seek virtuous 'runaway loops' in their institutional hinterland, accepting some persisting strain in their institutional connections, but building positional leverage for the future. Nevertheless, as Millar and Ridge reveal, the scope for venturing such strategic risks is itself socially structured. Many lone mothers lack the necessary informal support for enduring such strain; the priority is 'stability and consolidation rather than change and advancement' (Millar, 2007: 542).

Meanwhile other and more advantaged households bestride a larger world and are more able to undertake these agile ventures, not least because of the wealth of 'weak ties' (in Granovetter's sense) on which they can call.[9] Positional advance may be taken for granted in their 'family-work projects', ranging beyond the confines of the local job centre, benefits office and neighbourhood. Their efforts may then substantially re-shape the terrain on which those less fortunate must henceforth survive, forcing cascades of institutional change upon them, and plunging them into a struggle for survival which leaves little escape. Thus, for example, the agile business leaders depicted by Kristensen and Zeitlin (2005), having left home in the morning and dropped off their children at school, then spend the day re-structuring corporations and the local communities in which those corporations are variously embedded: including no doubt the lives of not a few lone mothers and their families. It is these abrasions against the larger structure of stratification and inequality that in large measure dominate the more confined lives of Millar and Ridge's sample.

15.3.2 Overview for Policy-making

The policy reforms discussed here were part of the Labour Government's goal of 'opportunity for all'. As Millar and Ridge demonstrate, the reforms achieved significant improvements in the circumstances of many lone parent families. Nevertheless, these depend critically upon the 'institutional micro-eco-system' in which the mother is rooted. The aim may be opportunities for all, but these mothers are heterogeneous in their micro-eco-systems and in their ability therefore to take up these opportunities.

The biological metaphor is therefore well taken. We saw in earlier chapters that when new opportunities for fitness ascent arise in the evolutionary process, different elements of the population of a given species will vary in the ease with which they can adapt or 'migrate'. Typically the result is progressive divergence into distinct sub-species. New socio-economic opportunities tend likewise to break up old solidarities, while enabling others to form. The policy-maker committed to 'opportunity for all' will therefore need to have a policy that is itself capable of evolving, to take account of these heterogeneities. As Ostrom, for example, argues, with an enormous diversity of institutional rules available, no optimal combination can be designed *a priori*; what is needed is a process of evolutionary adaptation and self-organisation (Ostrom, 2005: 245).

As with much of the social research in this area, policy-makers have given particular attention to the resources which different households typically command and how these vary over time. They have given much less attention to these institutional micro-eco-systems (but see Atkinson and Carmichael (2007), for example, on some policy initiatives in this direction, in the UK and elsewhere in Europe). This is somewhat surprising, given the European – and especially French – provenance of the language of 'social exclusion' which the Labour Government so eagerly embraced. Unlike the language of poverty, with its focus on the distribution of resources, that of social exclusion has a focus on social relations, rights and obligations, and the risks of their erosion (Gallie and Paugam, 2002: Ch. 3). It also directs attention to the shared resources and services within communities, collective investments, and not just the resources and investments of the individual household (Room, 1995: Chs 1, 13). Perri 6 (1996) offers just such a perspective on anti-poverty policies, focused on institutional micro-eco-systems and the range of social connections on which disadvantaged households can call. More policy analysis along these lines is needed.

This focus on social and institutional connections and networks brings centre-stage a range of new policy questions. There is, first, the robustness and resilience of social systems – in this case, the 'systems' constituted by families and their institutional networks – and, where they suffer breakdown, the scope for recovery. How far is such resilience – and indeed the scope for resolving structural imbalance – itself socially distributed? How far are lone mothers and other vulnerable groups obliged to concentrate on building defensive resilience, rather than striking out with new family-work projects? Our earlier discussion has also drawn attention to the ways in which the reconnection of sub-systems can 'switch' their development along new trajectories. How far do the family-work projects of the advantaged create an unstable world for the less advantaged, leaving them in a turbulent wake, or locking them into adverse 'forcing structures'? What reconnections might unlock these and produce a dramatic cascade of change? What practical implications follow for a public policy of 'opportunity for all'?

The answers to these questions will of course depend on the institutional and policy context of the country in question, the welfare regimes that it variously combines (Esping-Andersen, 1990). It is these that structure the canvas on which people re-weave their institutional micro-eco-systems, and whose abrasions present them with both opportunities and threats. It is in these terms that future comparative research on institutional and welfare regimes could usefully be re-framed: and not only, of course, in relation to lone mothers.[10]

15.4   POVERTY, EXCLUSION AND POSITIONAL DYNAMICS

At the outset to this chapter, we recalled the difficulties involved in drawing policy inferences from longitudinal studies of household circumstances. Nevertheless, it has become commonplace to analyse earlier events in the person's life course – for example, in relation to the labour market, or in terms of household formation or break-up – as the 'triggers' or 'drivers' of subsequent changes in household circumstances (for example, descending into or escaping from poverty); and to identify such drivers by reference, in part at least, to their weight in statistical regressions (Social Exclusion Unit, 2004). It is against this overly simple identification of the most significant causal factors and policy variables that Lieberson warns, as we saw in Chapter 13 (see also Millar, 2007). A more complex array of causal processes – and therefore also policy levers – commonly operates.

Accordingly, the two preceding sections offered accounts of policies and processes of social exclusion, by reference, on the one hand, to existing empirical studies and, on the other hand, to some of the conceptual models deployed in earlier sections of this book. Admittedly the treatment was illustrative rather than comprehensive. Nevertheless, from this somewhat limited canvas we now draw some more general inferences.

Section 15.2 modelled parental strategies within the quasi-market of UK secondary education. In some degree at least, middle class parents colonise particular schools in processes of competitive assortative mating. By 'sorting' schools in this way, they construct new lines of institutional differentiation, which cement their positional advantage. This was consistent with the conclusion to our discussion of ABM in Chapter 13: put humans together in a shared and undifferentiated social space and they will self-organise into distinct camps; they will typically express this in terms of new and more complex institutional arrangements, by which this self-organisation can be given some permanency. It was also consistent with the argument of Chapter 12: inter-generational mobility chances involve a positional competition among households in different social classes, by reference not only to the resources with which they are differentially endowed, but also their differential scope for adjusting the institutional rules of the competition, through strategies of defence, contestation and exclusion. This 'tilts' or warps the landscape on which the educational race is run, in favour of the offspring of the more advantaged, albeit as Goldthorpe argues, vigorous public policies can mute those inequalities and the degree of 'tilt'.

Section 15.3 modelled the 'family-work projects' of lone mothers on low incomes, as they weave new institutional micro-eco-systems of formal and informal support. This model or metaphor alerts us to the complex web of interdependencies in which these mothers are enmeshed, but also the likelihood that competition for niches will force them into those that are least attractive. Millar and Ridge make clear that these mothers live a precarious and over-stretched existence. They survive in institutional niches which leave them little resilience and no 'slack' for risk-taking in search of larger opportunities and virtuous 'runaway loops'. Instead they find it hard to avoid incorporation on adverse terms, for example, into the labour and housing markets.

Both of these discussions resonate with T.H. Marshall's pronouncement that 'in the twentieth century, citizenship and the capitalist class system have been at war' (Marshall, 1950). Nevertheless, we may now view that statement through the accounts of far from equilibrium systems we have developed here. In particular, we give a central place to the institutional entrepreneurship of more advantaged groups and not just the weight of their superior material and financial resources. Class differences persist and a common citizenship is undermined because of the continuing and dynamic re-weaving of institutional space, the twisting and tilting of the positional landscape. Public policies may aim at opening opportunities for all citizens; social groups differ, however, in their scope for exploiting such opportunities and incorporating them into their family-work projects. It is hardly surprising if societies which allow greater scope for such twisting and tilting end up with greater inequalities of outcome.

Although our discussion has been no more than preliminary, some implications emerge for the data sets and indicators that might serve policy-makers. First, and to repeat, it is not enough to track the changing circumstances of households over time and from this to infer policy lessons, without also capturing the mediation of these circumstances by social institutions. The interactive dynamic of institutions and social actors has been evident throughout this chapter. One approach to such interactions is that of Statistics Canada, which over recent years has run a two-level panel survey of employing organisations and their employees, precisely in order to track the ways in which enterprise strategies shape the lives of their workers (Krebs et al., 2000; Statistics Canada, 2004). Among the issues included are some – payments systems, training, flexible working – which are of central interest for studies of social exclusion. This approach could, in principle, be extended to other key institutions which shape such risks, including schools and health services. This would admittedly pose practical and methodological challenges, for example, in relation to data availability and sample design; however, these should not be insurmountable.

Second, our discussion suggests a range of survey questions concerned not just with the sums of money in people's pockets and their sources, but also with the resilience and stability of the institutions by which household resources as mediated. This has potential implications for the main social surveys and statistics on which much of our social policy analysis draws. Not that these are robust even in relation to financial resources. With an increasingly complex array of institutional arrangements for household savings and wealth, even the measures used in our system of national accounts are incomplete (Daffin et al., 2009). At the same time, our injunction to examine changes in household resources by reference to the institutions that mediate them suggests that we should not rely on surveys alone. There may be scope for mining administrative records, so as to understand and track the trajectories along which institutions send individuals, the sorting and classification to which they are subject, and maybe even their counter-strategies, designed to subvert, contest and re-shape these institutional architectures (on the opportunities for mining data sets gathered by a wide variety of public and commercial institutions, see Savage and Burrows (2007)).

Finally, there are implications for the policy indicators – in particular of social exclusion – that are used both nationally and at European level. The latter refer, on the one hand, to financial resources, on the other, to various 'dimensions' of deprivation, such as joblessness, poor housing, educational disadvantage and so on. They serve as the principal reference points for 'benchmarking' the national policies of member states in combating social exclusion, with reference to children in particular (Marlier et al., 2007; European Commission, 2008; Social Protection Committee, 2008: Part II, Section II). Nevertheless, in general these indicators only offer national rates for each aspect of disadvantage taken separately. Only to a limited extent do they map the exposure of households to multiple deprivations, even though this multiplication of disadvantage is the typical result of the struggle for existence we have traced.

Moreover, these indicators say little or nothing about the institutional micro-systems, formal and informal, on which households depend and which mediate their life chances. As already noted, this hardly squares with the importance that European debates on social exclusion attribute to social relations and to the shared resources and services available within communities: childcare facilities and health clinics, but also shops and banks, parks and recreation spaces. It is their strength – and the terms on which different households can access them – that shape household resilience and the forms of exclusion and adverse incorporation to which they are subject. No less important are the institutional rules of public and private organisations – schools, benefit offices, employers and many others – and the ease with which households can navigate and negotiate the entitlements and obligations these embody.[11]

To develop corresponding indicators is admittedly no simple matter. Nevertheless, it has been clear from our discussion that patterns of social inclusion and exclusion are closely associated with the extent to which institutions tend to integrate or separate the opportunities available to different groups of the population. We have referred, for example, to the cross-national comparisons undertaken by Willms, using OECD PISA data, which highlight the extent of social class segregation between schools as exacerbating social class differences in educational attainment (OECD, 2001a: Ch. 8). Here is one plausible indicator of the institutional pathways that households face, which is significant for social inequality and risks of exclusion and which is moreover available on a comparative basis.[12]

Nevertheless, no indicator speaks for itself; its significance must be assessed by reference to the models we have of the socio-economic dynamics involved. Thus, for example, in our discussion of quasi-markets in education, we saw that a variety of factors in the policy mix play a part in producing the 'runaway loops' of social class polarisation; and we acknowledged the policy trade-offs that policy-makers face, in expanding opportunities and choice while avoiding new inequities. Here we have models of dynamic change which, given appropriate empirical grounding, may yield insights into the 'tipping points' which policy-makers may wish to avoid, as they 'tune' the educational system. Indeed, the comparisons between European countries which the EU social inclusion process involves could usefully focus precisely on developing such insights, rather than simply recording a league table of national outcomes.[13]

15.5 CONCLUSION

Chapter 14 offered three ideas of the policy-maker, distilled from earlier chapters: as tuner, energiser and steward. Each finds some resonance with the discussion of poverty and social exclusion in the present chapter, but all three also have limitations.

The policy-maker as tuner acts upon the underlying system parameters, seeking to adjust them by reference to critical thresholds which correspond to 'tipping points' and 'phase changes'. It was in terms of such thresholds that we modelled the dynamics of school selection and the patterns of social polarisation that can unfold; critical were the admission policies ('class-blind' or otherwise) and the 'tolerance' thresholds of parents. The former may be amenable to policy change; the latter may not be immutable, but are likely to depend on complex currents of popular opinion and specific local circumstances and traditions.

Policy tuning may also mean switching and modifying the connections between sub-systems. The introduction of a quasi-market substantially changed the 'connective geometry' of the UK education system. Figure 15.1 maps the landscape following the reforms; prior to the changes many of those positively signed connections were absent and the various sub-systems operated in some degree separately from each other. As in Abbott's Chicago, different neighbourhoods and their schools in some degree had their own local 'natural histories'; after the reforms, the larger interactions of the quasi-market brought abrasion and turbulence to all. So also, the UK reforms since 1997 in support for lone parents build new connections to the world of employment, which then abrade in complex ways against other connections within the family's institutional micro-eco-system.

The policy-maker as energiser supports agile creativity. This creativity tends, however, to accrue disproportionately to the advantaged, the agile first movers, enabling them to reinforce their position. New opportunities, even if open to all, rarely accrue to all. To energise the less agile last movers, those with lesser resources of knowledge and only limited connections, is likely to require a major countervailing effort of public policy. Without this, the advantaged are well able to organise themselves within the new 'connective geometry' of the school system or the 'family-work' project, leaving the less disadvantaged to be incorporated on adverse terms. This is a 'social regularity' whose generative mechanisms we are by now well able to appreciate.

The policy-maker as steward brings civility to a world of competing projects for positional advantage. This can, however, never be even-handed. The policy-maker fatefully re-shapes the landscape on which the struggle for existence will henceforth unfold, the leverage which different protagonists can bring to bear. Thus, for example, the Baker educational reforms seem to have unleashed a 'race against time' which intensifies insecurity and positional competition. The reform of support for lone mothers may advance their family-work projects but it also exposes how these are conducted on highly adverse terms relative to those of the more advantaged. In short, as we argued in Chapter 14, public policies affect which households are able to organise themselves so as to meet their needs, appropriate opportunities and buffer themselves against instability and turbulence. 'Self-organisation' may be an 'emergent property' of complex systems but it also now refers to the positional leverage which different sections of the population are able to exert. It can therefore serve as a nor-mative vantage point from which to appraise the policies in question, by reference to the social well-being and self-development of different social groups and communities.

16 Social dynamics of the knowledge economy

16.1 INTRODUCTION

This chapter turns to the second area of policy research, by reference to which Chapter 1 called for a more adequate conceptualisation of dynamic change. This was concerned with the policy indicators being used by governments and by the EU, OECD and United Nations (UN), to track the development of the new 'knowledge economy', ranging across its social, technological, economic and organisational aspects (Room, 2005a). In Chapter 14, when introducing Part 3, we noted that such policy indicators have a dual significance for contemporary policy-making. They reveal the state we are in; and they provide clues as to the trajectories along which we are travelling, the choices and trade-offs that will face us, the thresholds and tipping points of virtuous and vicious change.

We first recall the context, both scholarly and political, for indicators of the 'knowledge economy'. The closing decade of the twentieth century saw widespread claims of economic and social transformation through the development of a knowledge economy. Of course, the very phrase 'knowledge economy' is arguably over-simplistic, even trite; all economies involve the application of knowledge and inventiveness. Nevertheless, at least in signifying a shift of emphasis, the phrase has merit. A number of key elements emerged as the focus of academic theorising (see, for example, Rubenson and Schuetze, 2000; Castells, 2001, 2004). These included:

- the role of the new information technologies as a 'general purpose technology' pervading all areas of production, distribution, consumption and governance;
- the growing importance of knowledge as a factor of production, requiring investment in human resources and life-long learning;
- the new and more flexible organisational architectures associated with the 'network economy';
- the accelerating pace of innovation – both technological and organisational – and the consequent restructuring and volatility of social and economic relations;

● the challenge of ensuring both security and transparent governance for these new institutional forms.

This was also a debate about globalisation. Some writers claimed that globalisation – economic but also political and social – was bringing about (or was closely associated with) a new phase of industrial or post-industrial development, towards which most if not all countries would be drawn (Giddens, 1990; Castells, 2001; Friedman, 2006). This was in some degree a re-working of longer-established convergence theory, with a strong dose of neoliberal ideology. Against this were ranged scholars for whom national differences in socio-economic institutions and political settlements remained crucial prisms through which the effects of globalisation would be mediated; there were good theoretical and empirical grounds for expecting that diverse trajectories of socio-economic development would persist (Esping-Andersen, 1990; Crouch et al., 1999; Brown et al., 2001; Goldthorpe, 2001b; Hall and Soskice, 2001).

Second, there was the political context, of the EU in particular. The EU has long been preoccupied with the fear of falling ever further behind the economies of the USA and East Asia. During the 1980s the fragmentation of different national markets was seen as the main barrier to European economic development; the policy response was the Single Market, to be completed by 1992 (Cecchini, 1988). With a single home market, European enterprises would, it was hoped, be able to operate on a scale to match their American and Japanese rivals. During the 1990s economic and monetary union consolidated the project.

During the late 1990s the focus of attention shifted to the new information technologies and their associated economic transformations. The fear now was that the USA would run away with the knowledge-based industries of the new economy, while East Asia – China in particular – would capture manufacturing industries. However, even the hope that China would concentrate on the 'old economy', and leave the 'triad' of Europe, North America and Japan to divide out the new economy, began to look increasingly forlorn (Schaaper, 2004).

The Lisbon European Summit of March 2000 therefore set a new strategic goal for the EU: 'to become the most competitive and dynamic knowledge-based economy in the world, capable of sustaining economic growth with more and better jobs and greater social cohesion' (European Council, 2000b: para. 5). This not only asserted the ambition to play a central role in the development of the new knowledge-based industries. It also reaffirmed a long-standing goal of European policy and – implicitly at least – a critique of the American model: to temper the flexibility and insecurity of the market with high quality social protection and an active social policy. Nevertheless, the Lisbon Summit recognised that the accelerating pace of change, while it opened up new employment opportunities, also rendered traditional patterns of employment precarious and might place a heavy burden on systems of social protection. The so-called European social model would have to be reconfigured, consistent with the new knowledge economy and itself making use of the new information technologies (European Council and European Commission, 2000).

In support of this strategic goal, the Lisbon Summit established a new approach to concerted policy development by the member states, the 'Open Method of Coordination' (OMC). Central to this was the notion of policy benchmarking, using appropriate policy indicators which would compare national performances, both within the EU and by reference to the USA in particular. Such indicators would illuminate points of leverage – triggers and catalysts – which national policy-makers could use to move their countries along trajectories of sustained socio-economic development and away from stagnation and decline.

The chosen strategy involved the EU in moving beyond the traditional demarcation of national and Community competence and responsibility. Even well-entrenched areas of national policy competence – in relation to social policy, for example – were now brought together in a common and cooperative endeavour. In these respects the OMC was inspired in part by the Maastricht process of monetary union and the Luxembourg employment strategy; both had involved closer coordination of national economic and employment strategies, with member states reporting their performance within a clear and rule-based system, using quantitative indicators (De la Porte et al., 2001; Room, 2005b).

At the same time the OMC was meant to embrace a much wider range of actors. Lisbon recognised that in order to develop a knowledge-based economy, the member states would need to pool best practice and accelerate the transfer of technological and organisational know-how from the best performers to the rest of the Community, energising innovation capacity and competitiveness. Policy benchmarking was to serve not only as a tool of collective discipline, but also as a means of coordinating intelligence about different national experiences and enriching national debates. This was more of a bottom-up logic, allowing economic and institutional entrepreneurs on the ground to drive the process of comparison and policy learning, depending on their specific needs and interests (De la Porte et al., 2001: 300–2; Arrowsmith et al., 2004; Room, 2005b). Against a background of fears about the democratic deficit of EU policy-making, the OMC was also meant to build and nurture public support for the social and economic transformations that were in prospect (Lebessis and Paterson, 2001; Room, 2007).

Although, therefore, the EU drive for a knowledge-based economy was at first glance concerned with technological change, innovation and productivity growth, it was from the start set in the context of social policy broadly conceived. Hence the emphasis placed upon the European social model and its reconfiguration for the knowledge economy; social cohesion and the risk of new social divides; policy learning and the governance of socio-economic change. The goal was to energise competitiveness, but not at the price of tearing society apart: to husband civility was no less important a priority of public policy (for a general overview of the state of the Lisbon strategy, see Rodrigues (2009)).

16.2   INDICATORS OF THE KNOWLEDGE ECONOMY

The knowledge economy poses a challenge for the systems of official statistics by reference to which national policy-makers have attempted to track and steer socio-economic development through the post-war period. The OECD – the club of the richest industrial countries – has been the principal international forum within which these debates have taken place. Some of its earliest reports on the knowledge-based economy confirmed that fundamental changes were underway, associated with the new information and communication technologies (ICT) and making for higher levels of productivity and economic growth (OECD, 2001b, 2002b, 2003). However, investing in ICT would in itself achieve little; this would facilitate productivity growth only when accompanied by appropriate investment in human skills, organisational change, innovation and entrepreneurship. Technological and institutional innovation needed to be woven together. Meanwhile other OECD studies underlined the importance of the regulatory and competitive environment and of national innovation systems, in providing the impetus for firms to be radically innovative, at the same time providing a climate of stable expectations (OECD, 2002a). They also warned of the dangers of a 'digital divide' which could leave some countries, regions, businesses and households lagging behind (OECD, 2000).

There has also been a succession of OECD reports concerned more specifically with statistical indicators of these developments (Arundel et al., 2006). Following the OECD lead, the EU has also developed a number of indicator sets for regularly monitoring and benchmarking the development of the knowledge economy. These have included three in particular:

● The eEurope action plan was an early initiative in pursuit of the Lisbon goals (European Council, 2000a; European Commission,

2001a, 2002b). The indicators focused on the levels of connection to the internet by consumers and business and the development of e-commerce, e-government, e-health and e-education.

- The European science and technology indicators aim to capture research capacity and activity levels in different member states (European Commission, 2007). They refer, for example, to R&D expenditure (both public and private), human resources (such as the numbers of science graduates) and the volume of venture capital investment. They also refer to the impact of this research activity, for example, in terms of the number of patents registered and the weight of high-tech industries within each national economy.
- The European Innovation Scoreboard (European Commission, 2009) covers much of the same ground. It also, however, includes a number of additional indicators of innovation, including innovation activities by small and medium-sized enterprises (SMEs), which are particularly important as sources of new employment.

As already noted, Lisbon established a new process of 'soft' governance that extended well beyond the policy areas that were a European mandate, into all those that were key for building a Europe-wide knowledge economy that would be socially cohesive. In practice, however, each policy area has been developed by reference to more proximate goals, with the link to this larger vision left somewhat in the background. Moreover, the policy benchmarking that was central to such governance was seen in rather crude terms, once it moved away from its intellectual progenitors. Comparisons of national performance by reference to agreed indicators would enable governments to see what were their comparative strengths and weaknesses; this would then – through a process of self-examination and imitation of the best – enable them to make the necessary reforms and to improve their national performance. This was a rather simplistic theory of policy learning and of how individual governments might impel – or at least nudge – their social and economic systems along the desired trajectory. In the event, improvements and 'catch-up' during the subsequent decade were patchy; and in any case it was not clear that they were the fruit of Lisbon (European Commission, 2004a).

Initially at least, the indicators were chosen because they were readily available from national statistical systems that were still geared largely to the 'old economy'. There was of course a tension between making use of existing statistics to capture these novel dynamics and investing in new and more appropriate statistical tools.[1] However, there was in any case no general consensus as to what would be valid indicators of socio-economic progress towards this new 'knowledge economy'. National policy-makers have tended to view the chosen indicators as a checklist of points for reporting and comparison, but without reference to any model of socio-economic dynamics which might itself be appraised and improved.

Nevertheless, Eurostat at least was aware that the indicators served up to national policy-makers for purposes of benchmarking and reporting should not be an undifferentiated checklist. Instead it adopted a framework (originally proposed by Statistics Canada and the OECD) by reference to which these various indicators could be organised – a framework which carried with it, implicitly at least, a model of socio-economic dynamics. This drew on the logistic curve as used by Rogers (2003), in his studies of innovation and its dissemination; it distinguished indicators of 'readiness' for innovation, 'intensity' and eventual 'impact'. As we saw in Chapter 1, Rogers had applied this curve to individual technological innovations (recall Figure 1.1); it was now applied to total economies. Research teams under contract to Eurostat developed this framework in various ways, for example, with the addition of a fourth phase of 'outcome' indicators (Room, 2005a: Ch. 4). This left the framework still rather crude, albeit not wholly without value.

In this chapter we draw on the conceptual framework and methodological tools developed in the present study to mount a more substantial appraisal of some of these indicators. Potts has of course been one of our major points of reference, with his account of 'micro-meso-macro'; he urges that this conceptual work now serve as the vantage point, from which new and more appropriate indicators of innovation are developed, in terms, for example, of 'the resources devoted to each source of creativity and the competences developed' (Potts, 2007a: 14). Nevertheless, we should not forget that multiple processes of 'micro' are forever in train, across the many different elements of the socio-economic system; that only some are retained as 'meso'; and that the macro-abrasions and co-evolutions that are then set in motion can have multiple feedback effects. We will need to make trade-offs between the rather crude frameworks employed in the Rogers tradition and the more elaborate accounts of 'micro-meso-macro' or 'deepen-widen-warp' developed in the preceding chapters.

16.3   MICRO: DEEPENING AND INNOVATION

16.3.1   Knowledge and Creativity

Some of the statistical indicators used in the Lisbon process are intended to measure the 'knowledge' component of a 'knowledge economy'. In

Eurostat parlance, these are indicators of 'readiness' for innovation. They include national indicators of R&D expenditure, high-tech patent applications and the numbers of science and engineering graduates. These statistics are readily available; they illustrate how old indicators are being re-deployed to provide insights into the new economy. However they may not be entirely appropriate.

Knowledge is no 'manna from heaven' (as in the accounts of technical progress offered by some neoclassical economists), descending freely on all whom may wish to make use of it. It emerges from human creativity and it can be 'capitalised'; that is to say, it is an asset from which others can be excluded, for a period at least, and which is therefore capable of yielding an income stream.[2] In terms of the challenges this poses for measurement and accounting, knowledge is part of a larger class of 'intangible' assets that also include reputations and brands: yielding an income stream as much by constraining rivals and customers as by innovation.

Knowledge-related intangible assets form a very substantial and growing part of the resources held both by individual enterprises and by nations; it is around the control of such assets that competitive struggles increasingly focus. Among the major intangible assets of corporations are those associated with intellectual property, some of which – patents, licenses and so on – can be bought and sold, licensed and traded, just like physical goods.[3] These are now being given explicit and standardised recognition through the International Financial Reporting Standards (IFRS) which have applied to listed EU companies since January 2005, after being piloted in the USA (Eustace, 2007). Knowledge in the form of education is an intangible asset held within households, even if national accounts still treat expenditures on education as a form of consumption rather than investment.

These assets are increasingly important for the economy and for individual businesses. Difficulties in measuring them are a growing impediment for business accountants, public policy-makers, official statisticians and academic researchers (Hill, 2004). These difficulties are compounded by the rapidity with which existing patents and innovations are 'creatively' destroyed by new ones, and by the continuous dissolution and reforming of the teams in which much of this knowledge – tacit as well as formal – inheres. If such intangibles are measured as investment rather than just as intermediate consumption, estimates of national investment can double (Clayton et al., 2008) (see also Marrano et al., 2007 and, for the USA, Corrado et al., 2006). This can also dramatically change the measurement of productivity growth. The statistical picture also shifts if account is taken of the software that firms develop for themselves, not just what they purchase from software manufacturers.

How we account for such intangibles depends on how we understand the growth, significance and boundaries of knowledge in a modern economy. It is therefore worth recalling that knowledge was also central to the discussion in Part 1, notably in relation to Potts and Loasby. For Potts, economic growth was first and foremost the growth of knowledge: knowledge of the 'specific connections that . . . work in a particular environment' (Potts, 2000: 59). Firms are the 'repositories' that create, coordinate and deploy knowledge, thereby setting in motion the dynamic of 'micro-meso-macro' that Potts has made the conceptual and analytical centrepiece of his economics. Similarly, Loasby was concerned with the role of institutions and culture as the carriers of such knowledge, and with its local application by individual firms.

This reveals a convergence between two very different clusters of economists: on the one side, the economic statisticians, on the other, the evolutionary economists. For both, the key to economic growth is not so much capital accumulation as the growth of knowledge. This depends on investment in knowledge as capital but also, as Potts insists, on appropriate institutional innovation (Potts, 2007a: 7). Like Clayton, Potts is actively re-drawing the boundaries of intangible knowledge assets (Potts, 2007b). His recent work is focused on the cultural and creative industries, now seen not in terms of consumption, a luxury for those with sufficient income and leisure time, but as a key element of the knowledge economy. These industries, he argues, are integral to the creative energy on which that economy is based; entrepreneurs have more in common with the artist than the capitalist financier, on whom they must however rely, if their inventions are ever to come to market (Potts, 2008a).[4] Even so, Potts leaves the boundaries of these creative industries – and their relationship to the knowledge economy as a whole – somewhat unclear. Not all the cultural industries, it seems, offer this benefit (museums, galleries, some of the performing arts) (Potts, 2007a); on the other hand, universities hardly figure. For Potts as for Clayton, this remains work in progress.

Knowledge and creativity, however, also have a dark side. Knowledge of whom to bribe when negotiating arms deals can bring rich returns, albeit the public disclosure of such knowledge can pose a broader threat to national reputational capital. The creative industries, as Potts shows, have been prominent in spawning the young super-rich, including celebrity artists such as Madonna (Potts, 2006); what remains unclear is the sense in which this wealth represents a return on creativity, as distinct from fashion-driven and volatile 'herding' or 'flocking' behaviour (as discussed in Chapter 2) in the global consumer market. What this all suggests is that knowledge and creativity, while they may indeed be the source of economic growth and cultural change, are not in consequence necessarily a good; they may imperil human well-being as well as enhancing it and public policy cannot avoid making such evaluations.

16.3.2   Selection and Innovation

The preceding discussion dealt with the knowledge assets that enterprises – and indeed nations – have developed. This concerned, therefore, their capacity to invent: to produce novelties. Whether inventions get taken to market, in what Schumpeter referred to as 'swarms of innovation', is however a separate matter.[5]

The European Innovation Scoreboard includes indicators of the proportion of enterprises (small and medium-sized enterprises in particular) that are involved in product and process innovation (either in-house or in cooperation with others) (European Commission, 2003a; for general discussion, see Mairesse and Mohnen, 2009). This is on the basis of their self-reporting. There is, however, widespread agreement in the academic, business and policy literature that innovation is a complex process, involving interactions at the level of the enterprise between technological investment, organisational change, entrepreneurship and workforce development (Pettigrew et al., 2003, especially Part 2; Vidgen and Wang, 2004). Indeed, if innovation is limited to just one of these aspects, it may even depress performance; enterprises need to discover and promote the self-reinforcing processes that allow these different aspects to co-evolve. This was of course central to the argument of Chapter 7, in our treatment of agile first movers, driving the co-evolution of technologies and institutions.

The OECD (2003, Ch. 3, 2004) reviews evidence on the importance of these firm-level complementarities for processes of innovation. The introduction of information technologies is unlikely to enhance business performance, without corresponding organisational development and workforce skills. These findings are reinforced by Clayton and his colleagues, who explore the interdependencies at the level of the enterprise between ICT investment, ICT use and the innovation process, by linking together a variety of data sets (Clayton et al., 2005; Franklin et al., 2009). Clayton emphasises that exploitation of these interdependencies is closely bound up with investment in the knowledge-related intangibles discussed earlier. Evident once again is the convergence with Potts, stressing the importance of enterprise knowledge of 'what connections work in particular environments'.

Although the technical questions raised by these debates are considerable, and the empirical work by which they might be resolved is still incomplete, some of the implications for policy indicators of innovation are fairly clear. If indicators are to capture the self-reinforcing processes that innovation evidently involves, longitudinal analysis and data linking at the level of the enterprise will be needed (OECD, 2003: Annex 1). Questions that may help capture the complementary investments required for successful innovation are gradually being included by Eurostat in its business surveys (Franklin et al., 2009).[6] Again, however, this is work in progress.

There is one further aspect of innovation that these studies highlight. The OECD review discussed above reveals that ICT investment, if accompanied by appropriate and concomitant organisational and workforce development, not only enables process and product innovation but can also produce substantial spill-over effects, in terms of the functioning of markets and the general exchange of information across the economy. Clayton points to similar externalities, for example, as enterprises replicate successful ICT-related innovations across a variety of different markets. Innovation tends to bring enhanced market share and indeed to create new markets; and thus, indeed, to confer the self-reinforcing positional advantage that has been at the heart of our analysis through the preceding chapters. Enterprise is not just about bringing technologies and skills together; it is also about refashioning the market terrain on which the action then unfolds. This is the 'micro' testing of what 'Surtseys' may be available, so as to spill over into 'meso' and indeed 'macro'.

Brynjolfsson et al. (2006) reinforces this argument, demonstrating the ease with which companies can replicate ICT-enabled improvements in business processes across widely diverse settings. This is tending to produce increasing concentration within ICT-intensive industries, but also their increasing turbulence and riskiness. This is a 'winner take all' dynamic. The European Innovation Scoreboard already includes indicators of the proportion of enterprises whose innovations enable them to reinforce their position, in terms of increased market share or reduced labour and other input costs (European Commission, 2003c, 2004b). This needs to be accompanied by analysis of associated changes in market structures, patterns of market dominance and turbulence, along the lines that Brynjolfsson suggests.

16.3.3 Innovation Systems

Innovation depends on the growth and application of knowledge. However, this requires that there be appropriate institutional channels for enterprises to tap into global best practice and then to apply and develop this knowledge for their own specific circumstances. Both are key to effective systems of knowledge management and the gaining of competitive advantage.

In some ways enterprises are in a situation similar to the households we encountered in the previous chapter, with the financial resources and knowledge they require being accessed through the 'institutional micro-ecosystems' and collaborations in which they are involved. These institutional connections are the concern of the literature on regional, national and international innovation systems (see, for example, Nelson, 1993). This stresses the role played by research institutes and other 'knowledge institutions'; the speed and accuracy of communications; the transparency of markets and the trustworthiness and security of transactions. It also emphasises that notwithstanding processes of globalisation, local and country-specific contexts influence knowledge sharing (OECD, 2001b: para. III.5; European Commission, 2003c).

We might view innovation systems by reference to our earlier discussion of agility. Potts and Crouch present us with entrepreneurial agents engaged in 'adaptive walks', by which they recombine and reconstruct technological and institutional space. In doing this, these entrepreneurs make connections with their neighbours, so as to build up the stocks of knowledge on which they can draw. This is, however, by no means limited to step-wise walks; the institutions of the national innovation system (or what Potts (2007a) prefers to see as a 'creative system') give access to more distant neighbours. They span – but also contest – taken-for-granted boundaries; and it is this transfer and testing of knowledge between contexts that is the key to creativity (Seltzer and Bentley, 1999).

National – and regional and international – innovation systems may, however, be anything but systematic. They may be of wide or narrow extent, effective or ineffective in supporting the assimilation and building of knowledge by enterprises. Each component is regularly transformed through processes of technological change and the 'system' is little more than the untidy outcome of these diverse transformations. It is also an arena of socio-economic struggle, with protagonists striving for first mover positional advantage and re-shaping the landscape of the national innovation system accordingly. This is not always sufficiently central to the scholarly discussion (Lorenz and Lundvall, 2006; Lundvall et al., 2006). This literature risks also perhaps being seduced by the language of self-organising systems, so as to neglect the necessary role of public policy, both in 'civilising' such struggles and in capturing the external economies essential for economic growth (Toner, 1999: para. 7.1).

The research literature on national innovation systems makes clear that these are systems of 'distributed knowledge'. It is wrong to look for 'best practices' that are universally applicable; practices that work have to be understood in relation to specific contexts and circumstances. Cross-national policy learning must therefore enable local and national actors to draw lessons appropriate to their own circumstances. Thus, for example, from the early days of the European Innovation Scoreboard, the European Commission foresaw that as well as the indicators and benchmarks of the scoreboard, there would be a database of comparable information on national policy measures and workshops for sharing best practices in innovation policy. These would be the tools for 'intelligent' policy benchmarking. Benchmarking would thus be accompanied by 'bench-learning', involving the exchange of narratives, case studies and 'stories' of what works where (European Commission, 2001b: Part III; European Commission, 2002a: 5–6; European Commission, 2003b: para. 2.4). This is consistent with broader debates on innovation and policy learning (Room, 1986, 1993; Senge, 1990; Bennett, 1991; Dolowitz and March, 1996; Evans and Davies, 1999; Lundvall and Tomlinson, 2002).

16.3.4   The Ontology of Innovation

To conclude this review of the indicators of 'micro', we make explicit – insofar as this may not already be clear – how this discussion is grounded in the ontology we developed in Part 1 of this study.

Potts and Crouch provided us with an account of entrepreneurs, weaving new combinations of technology and institutions, so as better to achieve their purposes. This was the entrepreneur as practitioner of artificial selection, like Darwin's pigeon breeder or horticulturalist. This presupposed knowledge of what works in different settings and some imagination (mental models and informed conjectures) as to how new combinations are likely to perform; albeit the range of this imagination will always be constrained by the ideational legacy of the community in question. The first of the sub-sections above reviewed the search for indicators of such knowledge, as an intangible asset for the enterprise and the nation.

Potts was concerned with the entrepreneur and technology; Crouch with the entrepreneur and institutions. In Chapter 7 we brought these together, arguing that entrepreneurs typically transform technologies and institutions in a single self-reinforcing process. This insight is now confirmed by the academic, business and policy literature reviewed here, that innovation requires complex interactions between technological, organisational and workforce development at the level of the enterprise. In the second of the sub-sections above, concerned with selection and innovation, we have reviewed the search for indicators of such interactions.

Darwin's breeders and horticulturalists depended on their peers. They shared their experience and learned from each other's successes and failures, even while they also sought to steal a march on their rivals by thinking 'outside the box'. Nor of course was this limited to watching their immediate neighbours; they drew lessons from a much wider and diverse range of experience. Crouch similarly highlights the proximity of a diversity of neighbours as crucial to institutional innovation; also, indeed, the availability of a rich *bricolage* of past endeavours, the waste left by forebears but available for potential re-deployment. The third of the sub-sections above dealt with innovation systems, enabling entrepreneurs to learn from their neighbours but also from the past. We ended with the policy-maker, nurturing innovation systems and energising creativity.

16.4 MESO: WIDENING THE TRAILING EDGE OF INNOVATION

Some of the statistical indicators of the knowledge economy that are commonly used by EU and national policy-makers track the diffusion of the new information technologies across society: for example, the proportion of enterprises, universities or households who have adopted a particular technology. These are indicators of 'diffusion' and 'impact'. They were, for example, used by the eEurope action plan following the Lisbon Summit. They reveal the extent to which a given technology has 'widened' to even the least reachable. They have featured extensively in global surveys of the 'digital divide'. They define new risks of social polarisation and as such are of interest to social policy-makers (Room, 2005a: Ch. 7).

It is often assumed that the diffusion of a given technology will follow a logistic or S-curve (recall Figure 1.1). Rogers (2003) is the most widely cited authority as far as social scientists interested in such diffusion are concerned, although his own account is more nuanced. First and most obviously, only a minority of technological innovations get very far along the diffusion curve (these processes of selection and retention are at the heart of Dopfer and Potts's account of 'meso'). In addition, however, if innovation requires a complementary mix of technological, organisational and workforce development, at the level of the enterprise and more broadly, it is indicators of these mixes that will be of most use to policy-makers, rather than of individual technologies.

We recall moreover that any population is somewhat heterogeneous, with some elements more able and ready to embrace a particular innovation than others. As an innovation widens across a population, it tends to prompt the emergence of new sub-populations and niches, which then confront each other in new 'eco-systems' of competition and domination. Yesterday's winners may be best placed to move first, exploiting the new innovation and the opportunities it offers, leaving others to adjust as best they can, in a Stackelberg game. Nevertheless, the opportunities and risks attached to being a first mover will depend on the particular empirical case. The first mover can sometimes leave others struggling in the turbulence of his or her wake; in other situations, to adopt the same metaphor, second movers can move easily into the slipstream of the first mover and from there at low cost develop profitable (if initially subsidiary) opportunities of their own. This is quite different from a simple S-curve.

Beyond the first and second movers are the 'last movers' (including many of the lone mothers who figured in the previous chapter). Technological and institutional changes may lead to the progressive erosion of the institutions and technologies on which they depend; the turbulence of 'winner take all' is liable to impose the costs of change on them disproportionately, leaving them more vulnerable to incorporation on adverse terms. Thus, for example, across Europe there have been protests from associations of older people, when banks offer incentives to customers using electronic services and internet accounts (Room, 2005a: Ch. 7). With many of the new technologies accessible only to those who are already well equipped in terms of ICT, these gaps between social groups can be cumulatively reinforced. This increasingly raises dilemmas for government about the political trade-offs that might have to be made between the costs of delivering 'trailing edge' services and the marginalisation of their users. The acceleration and intensification of such risks are part of the larger positional struggle through which advantage and disadvantage is reproduced; this is the 'dark side' of the knowledge economy.

This raises fundamental questions for public policy: in terms of buffers to insulate and protect; the building of resilience; and the deliberate re-tuning of macro-dynamics so as to support last movers, rather than excluding them. This is why the Lisbon process emphasises social cohesion as a goal and benchmarks national policies to combat social exclusion, using the indicators we discussed in the previous chapter; and why, indeed, those efforts to combat social exclusion have been given the importance they have within the European policy agenda.

16.5   MACRO-DYNAMICS OF THE KNOWLEDGE ECONOMY

Taken as an ensemble, the indicators that are being used for the Lisbon process are meant to reveal the progress made by different member states in establishing a dynamic knowledge economy, with sustained economic growth, more and better jobs and greater social cohesion. They are moreover meant to guide national policy-makers, in making such interventions as will bring their own national performance closer to the level of the best. This is policy benchmarking.

This leaves unclear, however, whether these comparisons of national performance are intended to track the progress of member states towards a single common future, and one which can be defined in terms of common economic and technological requirements; or whether they are meant to provide different scenarios of potential development, so as to enrich national political debates and guide the policy interventions that might be made, in order to achieve one future rather than another. In the former case, the role of policy-makers is to ensure as rapid and comfortable an adjustment as possible to that common future. In the latter case, in contrast, there are real political choices and trade-offs to be made, on the basis of coordinated intelligence about different national experiences.

EU reports which track and compare progress towards knowledge-based economies give little sense of alternative patterns of socio-economic development and the trade-offs that these may involve: what in previous chapters we referred to as competing evolutionary logics. The language used is that of laggards catching up with leaders, with the implication that those leaders hold out the future to which the laggards must aspire. Only in relation to the European quest for a socially cohesive trajectory of development, distinct from American market liberalism, is there much sense of alternatives. Nevertheless, in principle, many of the selected benchmarking indicators could be used to explore these trade-offs and the variety of possible futures they imply. Do higher rates of competitiveness through technological innovation have to be traded against higher risks of social exclusion? Do high rates of social inclusion in the knowledge economy presuppose high rates of investment in human capital? This type of exercise is consistent with studies such as that by Ferrera et al. (2000), undertaken in the lead-up to Lisbon, analysing the policy trade-offs of precisely this sort that have been made by different EU member states. It is also, of course, common in comparative policy studies, where policy outcomes are examined by reference to a variety of antecedent factors.

Such policy trade-offs and choices could be more explicitly addressed within the Lisbon process; indeed, they could be made central to it. Nevertheless, they are mediated by complex dynamics of the sort that have figured through the preceding chapters of this book. There is no simple calculus of substitution among these various public goods: competitiveness, social inclusion, and so on. What is also needed is some sense of the feasibility of different policy trajectories for a given country, given the distinctive institutional, technological and political path dependencies in which it finds itself, both internally and externally.

16.5.1   National Trajectories and Attractors

If much EU reporting seems to posit a convergent future for the countries of Europe, some of the principal academic literatures on which the present study has drawn take precisely the opposite standpoint. The institutionalist scholarship to which we have referred commonly insists on the path dependency of national socio-economic development. National pasts are distinctive and they will in turn colour different national futures. Path dependency and institutional lock-in limit the scope for subsequent policy variation and shape the trajectories along which organisations, institutions and nations are constrained to move. Indeed, for many of those working in the 'varieties of capitalism' tradition, this lock-in moves countries towards one of just a few typical configurations – what we might indeed refer to as 'attractors'.

Thus, for example, Alber (2006) compares the macro-economic performance of European countries. The Scandinavians and the 'Anglo-Saxons' have achieved the highest rates of employment growth, notwithstanding the differences in their social policy mixes. He argues that here are two distinct pathways of successful socio-economic development. In contrast, it is what he calls 'countries of the middle way' – such as Germany and France – that face difficulties in adapting to the contemporary economic environment. A very different national trajectory is traced by Petmesidou and Mossialos (2006), in their book *Social Policy Developments in Greece.* Here the picture is much gloomier. Greece seems to be institutionally deadlocked, a landscape frozen in pre-modern forms of social and political organisation, unable to respond to processes of modernisation within the European mainstream.

What Alber and Petmesidou are arguing is that countries develop along distinctive socio-economic trajectories, involving dynamic feedback and path dependency. Both employ qualitative institutional analysis, coupled with relevant quantitative indicators of national economic performance. Nevertheless, they leave unclear how these trajectories might be more formally modelled; what scope the less successful countries have for steering development along more positive lines; what indicators policy-makers might employ to guide such developmental choices.

The key policy question for Lisbon is how to move the member states of the EU out of the evolutionarily stable states in which many of their economies seem at risk of being caught. In Kauffman's language, policy-makers seek guidance as to how best to 'melt' these frozen structures and move to some new regime of more fluid elements. The process of Europeanisation itself abrades continuously against these frozen structures and opens new opportunities for agile policy entrepreneurs, as we noted in our discussion of Fligstein. The Lisbon process provides countries with greater visibility into the institutional practices of their neighbours; inspired by these examples, national policy-makers may be able to re-weave and re-deploy the institutional *bricolage* of their past and give them new resonance. Even in the supposedly frozen wastes of the Bismarckian welfare systems, Palier shows that melting is proceeding apace and may indeed produce more dramatic cascades of reconfiguration (Palier and Martin, 2008; Palier, 2010).

This provides us with an alternative standpoint from which to view the Lisbon process: focusing less on the benchmarks, more on the processes of cross-national comparison and learning it has set in motion. Here is the 'diffusion' that Pierson identified as a key mechanism of institutional change; the connections with neighbours which Crouch highlighted. Now benchmarking provides intelligence about different national experiences; it brings hitherto unconsidered options into each national debate; it accelerates the transfer of technological and organisational know-how. Benchmarking is now accompanied by the 'bench-learning' discussed earlier, involving the exchange of narratives which integrate these indicators into coherent accounts of how change can be introduced practically (Lundvall and Tomlinson, 2002).

16.5.2 The Global 'Eco-system'

The policy choices that are available to a given country are constrained not only by the distinctive institutional, technological and political path dependencies involved in its own socio-economic development, but also their abrasion against those of the international environment.[7] This is not immediately apparent from the way that the Lisbon process is couched. Benchmarks and indicators are defined in terms which enable national comparisons; national governments are at the centre of attention and are responsible for their own choices and progress. The Lisbon method itself makes no reference, however, to their management of the international – or even indeed the European – arena within which such choices are made. This absence is remarkable.

The knowledge economy is unfolding on a global terrain. 'Micro-meso-macro' transcends national borders and the policy environment is multi-tiered (Gereffi, 2005). In developing their national economies, it is on a crowded stage that national governments are choosing among alternative futures. Here again, it is misleading if Lisbon leads us to think of laggards catching up with leaders. The futures that are available for laggards to choose are constrained by the institutional and technological 'eco-system' of niches which the leaders have already occupied. There is little chance that Bulgaria or Rumania will be able to mimic Germany, if only because

Germany is already occupying that niche. This is a Stackelberg game, in which imitation of the front-runners is likely to be a flawed hope; if they are to thrive and prosper, the laggards must discover some distinctive niche amid the interstices of the powerful. If policy benchmarks and indicators are to be of practical use, they must assist in that search, rather than just providing overall league tables. They must be rooted in an understanding of the institutional and technological 'food webs' in which countries are enmeshed and the new niches that are opening for them: niches for which, however, there may be only a fleeting window of opportunity and which therefore place countries in a race against time.

The picture is of course more complex than this. States are not monolithic entities; they encompass a variety of interest groups, each in search of a viable niche in this global eco-system. Indeed, some of these groups are transnational rather than national actors. This includes, for example, the ethnic diaspora significant both in the European expansion of the eighteenth and nineteenth centuries and the recent resurgence of China (see the discussion in Chapter 10 of John Darwin (2007) and Arrighi (2007); and, more generally, Chua (2003)). Most obviously, however, it includes the multinational enterprises (MNEs) who dominate the knowledge economy (Room, 2005a: Ch. 10).[8]

We must therefore understand national economic strategies and goals by reference to a global political economy within which these various actors – and many others – jostle to construct niches for positional advantage. This is a complex institutional and technological eco-system of the sort we encountered in Chapter 10, involving colonisation, hierarchy, competition and extinction. Nevertheless, these are dynamic processes; the eco-system is by no means frozen and change is not limited to late arrivals seeking some marginal niche for themselves. Eco-systems may remain stable for a period; but as they abrade against each other and as the struggle for positional advantage continues, wide-ranging cascades of reconfiguration are possible. Fears of such change were, as we have seen, only too evident in the establishment of the Lisbon process, as European leaders took stock of the new information technologies and the industries they were spawning and the resulting risk of a global economic reconfiguration, in which Europe might secure few of the spoils. It was in order to recover some control over that global process, build European resilience and ensure that European economies would not be forced to dance to the rhythm of other economic powers, that the Lisbon strategy was launched.

Indicators of global development are commonplace. Thus, for example, the World Bank publishes an annual *World Development Report* and the UN a *Human Development Report*. Both give due attention to the knowledge economy and its central place in global development. The World Summit on the Information Society has been active in producing indicators and statistics of the global digital divide and the prospects for extending to the developing world some of the benefits of the knowledge economy. Meanwhile the World Economic Forum has been producing a series of *Global Information Technology Reports*, which monitor and compare the 'networked readiness' of different countries, by reference to indicators of ICT infrastructure and internet use (World Economic Forum, 2004). Nevertheless, as with the Lisbon process, these all report the progress of individual nations in respect of a list of common indicators of social, technological and economic progress. This is valuable, indeed indispensable for public debate and policy-making. However, these indicators inadequately capture the global transformations which in considerable degree shape the fates of these nations and the place that they occupy within the international division of labour and welfare.

First, indicators are needed that capture the enmeshment of national economies within the European and global 'eco-system' of international political economy, conceived first and foremost in terms of structural relations of positional advantage, only secondarily in terms of factor endowments and choice of technologies. Snyder and Kick (1979) and Held et al. (1999) offer some possible indicators: nevertheless, when we reviewed them in Chapter 10, we found them severely limited.[9]

Second, indicators are needed of the networks and knowledge agglomerations within this global economy.[10] The knowledge economy involves networks of unrivalled scope and speed. Databases are, for example, available, updated throughout the year, concerned with the world's largest internet backbones, the traffic they carry and the providers who operate them (Meijers, 2003; PriMetrica, 2010). These serve to identify those cities that are the hubs, interconnecting the major economic blocs. These could provide indicators, albeit crude, of the relative power positions of different cities and regions within the global knowledge economy (on the underexploited value of such commercial databases for research and policy, see Savage and Burrows (2007)).

Agglomerations of knowledge resources determine which communities are at the leading edge of new waves of innovation and reap the benefits of economic change.[11] Indicators of dependency upon these agglomerations are also important; there is a growing literature on the forms of 'adverse incorporation' experienced by developing countries (see, for example, Humphrey et al., 2003). Similar effects may also become apparent among the new EU member states, where levels of infrastructural development are significantly poorer from those of longer-standing members. It is not self-evident that benchmark indicators measuring national performance against common standards will readily pick up these unequal relationships and the constraints they place on the socio-economic futures facing peripheral economies.

Finally, indicators are needed of transnational movements of capital, skilled labour and services. National governments and international organisations have been slow to include these mobile factors in their systems of statistics. This is, however, now changing. The OECD is spearheading this drive; recent publications grapple with the methodological problems involved and provide such data as are currently available. Thus, for example, OECD *Science, Technology and Industry Outlook*, appearing biannually, deals with the globalisation of science and technology and with cross-border human capital flows. The OECD (2005) *Handbook on Economic Globalisation Indicators* is concerned with MNEs in relation to trade, international investment and technology transfer. It proposes indicators that will disentangle the cross-national transactions between parent companies and affiliates, the flows of investment and the patterns of ultimate beneficial ownership. It does the same in relation to the internationalisation of industrial R&D, the international diffusion of technology and trade in high technology products.

These are indicators not just of economic dynamics but of power and dependence in the shared institutional and technological eco-systems of international political economy. They help capture flows of economic resources and production chains but they also reveal the race for positional advantage, domination and control.

16.6   CONCLUSION

This chapter has been concerned with the policy indicators used in the Lisbon process. As we saw in Chapter 14, such indicators are commonly taken as revealing where we stand in relation to the various drivers of change, the trajectories along which we are travelling, the choices and trade-offs we face.

To select appropriate indicators – and to assess those in use – presupposes an understanding of the processes of socio-economic change that are underway. Indeed it is only by reference to a qualitative and institutionally grounded account of such processes that these indicators have any meaning. That is why our discussion has been as much about the models of change that are appropriate to the knowledge economy as about the technical details of the indicators themselves. As we have seen, the indicators chosen will then have major implications for macro-economic measurement; they will also shape the comparisons that Lisbon benchmarking encourages and the directions of cross-national policy learning that are possible.

The Lisbon process and the policy indicators it deploys can to some extent be seen as empowering national and European policy-makers, enabling them to 'tune' socio-economic development. Nevertheless, these indicators are hardly being used to illuminate the trade-offs and tipping points which diverse national experiences may reveal. Instead, tuning consists principally in encouraging 'laggards' to catch up with 'leaders'.

The Lisbon process was meant to promote innovation. This is the policy-maker as the energiser of creativity. There was, however, always the recognition that the drive for knowledge economies would bring turbulence and disruption. This places the policy-maker in the role of umpire or steward, civilising the struggle and building civility.[12] From the start, therefore, the Lisbon process was meant to embrace a much wider range of actors and to involve them in the social and economic transformations that were in prospect: enterprises and business associations but also labour organisations, the 'third sector' and citizens in general. Benchmarking would involve not only accountability 'upwards', but also transparency 'sideways' to enable cross-national learning between economic and social practitioners and accountability 'downwards' to the public in general. It would improve hierarchical direction and facilitate mutual adjustments within markets but it would also build the civility of a shared community. That at least was the stated intention, even if its realisation has been limited (Room, 2007).

However, the policy indicators and statistics that are available are still in considerable degree geared to national industrial economies, not yet to global knowledge economies. Even at a European level, the focus remains on the national state and its 'performance', rather than on the larger 'eco-system' within which those nations construct their niches, the varied terms on which they are incorporated, the unequal division of labour and welfare. EU innovation policies will help shape the emerging balance of power and positional advantage in the European knowledge economy, the prosperity that it brings to some and the instability it offloads on others: these should surely be an explicit point of reference for the Lisbon strategy and the policy indicators it deploys. Beyond Europe, our discussion raises similar questions for the governance of global socio-economic development, as well as the governance of global economic and statistics (Room, 2005a: Ch. 10). The countries of Europe may seem relatively well protected and resilient; nevertheless, predators lurk and their continued well-being will depend in considerable part on European efforts to civilise the global commons.

A decade on from Lisbon, the EU has set out the successor strategy, Europe 2020, covering the next ten years (European Council, 2010). This retains much of the Lisbon strategy. However, the new strategy has of course been formulated amidst the global economic crisis, as the European economy struggles to avoid prolonged recession. The countries of Europe have proved less resilient than they might have hoped to the financial crisis of the global commons and the predatory activities of the financial institutions. The much vaunted European social model will now be put to the test. In particular, will the member states be able and willing to protect the more vulnerable against the insecurity of the liberal market; or will the European social model be revealed as no more than a device to hide the gross inequalities of the social division of welfare?[13]

17 Global turbulence and crisis

17.1 INTRODUCTION

This study started by recognising that the world of the policy-maker is complex and that our conventional methods of illuminating that world, as policy analysts, have their limitations. However, the policy world is not only complex, it seems also to have become increasingly turbulent, with the international financial and economic crisis spilling over to affect many areas of public policy. Government leaders acknowledge that conventional methods of policy intervention seem no longer to work; new models of a dynamically interconnected world are needed, so as to anticipate, steer and control this turbulence; but as yet they are lacking.

This chapter does not compete with the many accounts that have appeared of the origins of this crisis or the policy reforms that have been proposed. Instead it draws on previous chapters for templates with which to make sense of this new situation and tools for policy-makers to navigate and steer it.

17.2 CREATIVITY AND INNOVATION IN THE FINANCIAL SYSTEM

The previous chapter was concerned with the knowledge economy that moved centre-stage in the 1990s and 2000s. The development of the new information technologies had, it seemed, changed the social and economic landscape. The pace of technological and institutional innovation was accelerating, promoting new forms of globalisation and non-inflationary growth. Even so, the 'dotcom' bubble of the early 2000s gave warning that the new economy might also bring turbulence. Moreover, policy-makers were all too aware – as our discussion of EU policy indicators has revealed – that the tools at their disposal for monitoring and steering these developments were hardly fit for purpose, having been framed for national industrial economies rather than global knowledge economies. Our discussion laid out the range of technical and policy challenges and the search for more appropriate indicators.

There are significant parallels with the financial turbulence that unfolded in the later part of the 2000s: not just parallels, however, also connections. If the globalisation of the post-Cold War period marched in step with the new information technologies, the same went for the rise of global finance. In finance as in the new technologies, entrepreneurs displayed their creative energies and, in Schumpeter's phrase, brought 'swarms of innovation' to market, with hedge funds, derivatives, securitisation and many other weird and wonderful new products and services (Soros, 2008a: especially Chs 2, 4, 5). In finance as in the new technologies, entrepreneurs have won huge rewards.

The new financial products and services have been invented in part to exploit the different expectations, time horizons and risk stances of different market actors. They may serve to bridge those differences and thereby improve market functioning. Nevertheless, what is also well documented is that some of these new instruments were designed to evade the regulators (notably their rules on the capital base that banks must maintain on their lending) and by their complexity to conceal the riskiness of the assets which they represent (notably in the case of sub-prime lending) (Soros, 2008b: Ch. 4; Brummer, 2009; Tett, 2009: Ch. 2). Goldman Sachs stands accused of making huge and successful bets against junk assets that it was enthusiastically selling to clients (*Guardian*, 19 April 2010). Knowledge of tax regimes and creative re-deployment of a bank's assets between countries, so as to maximise tax benefits, can be similarly lucrative, as the Structured Capital Markets division of Barclays Bank has, for example, demonstrated (*Guardian*, 19 March 2009). Also not in dispute are the efforts of the major banks to assist the use of offshore accounts and tax havens and to tolerate complex and deliberately obscure international arrangements for the ownership of companies by persons of questionable repute (Cable, 2009: Ch. 2).

This is the dark side of financial invention, far removed from what Schumpeter had in mind and tending instead to undermine the very rule of law on which, as he recognised, capitalism depends. More than this, however, it has destroyed trust between financial institutions and the scope for collective self-regulation which they had hitherto trumpeted as sufficient, in opposition to statutory regulation. It was the loss of such trust – and the inability of financial institutions to assess the riskiness and value of the assets they had themselves created (even their own, never mind those of others) – that led the financial system to freeze up during the later part of 2008. This has been creative destruction on a huge and suicidal scale.

If there are parallels between the inventiveness and turbulence of the new information technologies and those associated with the financial world, the connections do not end there. Galbraith points out that during the 1990s the entrepreneurs of the new information technologies had broken free from the corporations of mainstream America, but only with the aid of the financiers of Wall Street. Technological innovation and institutional innovation (in the form of new financial products and markets) co-evolved. Growing income inequality, in the USA at least, was dominated by these two interrelated constituencies, growing rich together (Galbraith, 2009: Ch. 7).

Meanwhile, as both developments unfolded, the tectonic plates of global political economy were shifting, with the rise of the Asian economies and the recycling of their trade surpluses through the international financial system: recycling that in part fed the aforementioned new financial instruments, including securitised sub-prime mortgage loans. (On the relationship between financial innovation and financial globalisation, see Watson (2007) for a theoretical account, Peston (2008a) for one more practical.) The struggle for geopolitical control of the technologies of the knowledge economy saw Europe fearing for its eclipse; the USA now found itself in no less perilous a position as regards its reserve currency and its international financial deficit. Both Europe and the USA were now, arguably, locked in a 'race against time' with the rising powers of Asia, an ironic sequel to John Darwin's account of the earlier struggle for Euroasia (see Chapter 10) (Cable, 2009: Ch. 5; Galbraith, 2009: Ch. 6).

Policy-makers who sought to monitor and steer the knowledge economy found themselves with inadequate and antiquated tools. The same went for the regulators charged with steering the new systems of international finance (still relying, for example, on the Basel Accords, setting standards for the capital reserves that banks must hold). Complex processes of change driven by the animal spirits of opportunistic entrepreneurs left both sets of policy-makers floundering in their wake, with inappropriate 'world models', outdated indicators of dangerous tipping points, inadequate capacity to act and an insufficiently well-defined view of the value choices and political trade-offs involved.

17.3   ADVERSE INCORPORATION

Creativity and innovation are driven by first movers; this is the realm of 'micro' and 'deepening'. The first mover can then build advantage in the positional struggle and force others to accept incorporation on adverse terms. This is the realm of 'meso' and 'widening'.

Those who have commented on the financial turbulence of recent times have focused in general on the risk-taking of the financiers and the efforts of governments to rescue the banking system and to stave off recession (Blackburn, 2008; Krugman, 2008; Peston, 2008b; Soros, 2008b; Brummer, 2009; Cable, 2009). Contrasts have been drawn in the media with the lack of support to businesses, coping with the recession and the continuing lack of credit: 'second movers' struggling to construct a niche for themselves amidst the destruction wrought by the first movers. If the circumstances of ordinary households – the broad mass of 'last movers' – are discussed at all, it is as payers of the taxes that have rescued the banks, and as beneficiaries of public services whose budgets have now to be cut. This inequality in the distribution of pain and gain has evoked strong indignation but little redress. (As Watson (2009) points out, in the UK at least, such redress as has happened has been geared to the more articulate among these 'last movers': for example, the middle classes, panicking lest their housing equity be threatened after a generation of steadily rising house prices.)

Galbraith is one of the few to have attempted an overall analytical account.[1] This is couched in terms of predation on the major institutions of society – corporations, banks, housing finance, education and health, pensions – for purposes of private gain at public expense. Galbraith argues that this is present-day America, the 'Predator State' (although he does not claim that the same story can necessarily be told of the other 'varieties of capitalism'). He traces the progressive erosion of the corporate and public ethic which underpinned these institutions through much of the twentieth century; he argues that the financial entrepreneurship discussed above has produced a new class of oligarchs who are devoted to rapacious looting (Galbraith, 2009: Chs 7, 9). This, he further argues, tends to crowd out and demoralise ordinary businesses, just as it also tends to divert and distort the social goals of public institutions, to the detriment of the mass of ordinary households and their 'institutional micro-systems' as discussed in Chapter 15.

The argument can be re-stated in terms of security and risk. The institutions of which Galbraith speaks have traditionally provided ordinary people with security against the risks of a turbulent urban-industrial society. The first bulwark was that of secure employment through the corporation or public service employers; the second was the social security system, meeting the risk of interrupted earnings as a result of industrial accident, unemployment, sickness and so on. These are risks that at any moment affect only a minority of individuals; insurance is a device for pooling those risks. Larger-scale risks affecting whole populations – mass unemployment, flooding, pandemic, climate change – require other responses.

The financial crisis resulted from high levels of risk-taking, but of a rather unusual sort. First, if only because of the novelty of the financial instruments involved, it has been difficult or even impossible for outsiders – or even for insiders – to assess the level of risk or the range of institutions and activities through which any malfunction might spread. Such risk assessment is of course a precondition for any insurance scheme. Second, the assets placed at risk have not been those of the agents concerned (the market dealers) but those of their bank and its shareholders and customers. If the risk paid off, both would gain; if it failed, the agent lost nothing (save the opportunity for a premium or bonus) because the loss fell entirely upon the third party. Third, whereas in classical social insurance schemes the risk was an interruption in the flow of future earnings, what was here at risk, for bank customers and shareholders alike, were assets built up over many years (housing equity, pension funds entitlements and so on).

This was asymmetric risk-taking on highly turbulent terrains (Watson, 2007: Ch. 1). As Galbraith argues, the institutions which had traditionally provided security for the mass of the population – including the lone mothers and their families we encountered in Chapter 15 – have (in Thelen's sense) been 'converted' to new purposes, captured by the financial institutions and warping the institutional micro-eco-system within which those mothers seek to 'keep the show on the road'. Thus, for example, the mortgages taken out by sub-prime buyers were institutionally obscure and deliberately so, notwithstanding the rhetoric of 'empowerment' that sometimes accompanied this ostensible extension of home ownership. 'Securitisation' bred insecurity. It is to this that Galbraith refers as predation. It is also perhaps an example of the 'exclusion, extinction, domination or enslavement' to which Potts too briefly alludes, as a possible outcome of 'micro-meso-macro' (Dopfer and Potts, 2008: 115).[2]

Predation did not, Galbraith argues, begin with the financial crisis. The latter is just the most dramatic and visible manifestation of the re-working of the institutions of collective security, from protection of the many to predation by the few. He exposes the ways in which shifts in public policy over recent decades have opened opportunities for commercial interests to prosper at the expense of citizens: the expansion of the sub-prime housing market, the shift to funded pensions, public subsidies to private health providers. In the Predator State much wealth creation depends not on technological inventiveness but on leverage over – and access to – public expenditure programmes. Depending on how public policy develops, with growth in public expenditure successively focused on healthcare, technology, defence and so on – the menu of looting opportunities available to the new oligarchs will also shift (Galbraith, 2009: Chs 7–10).

The final twist is that the many are now called upon to provide protection for the few. Whatever the situation of individual banks, governments were clear that the financial system as a whole must be preserved.

In general, they therefore decided – after some initial fumbling – that no major bank should fail, because of the likely knock-on consequences. Whether the actions taken over the last decade or more by individual banks were reasonable or reckless – and whether the risks these posed to the financial system as a whole were foreseeable and preventable – are still matters of heated debate.[3] What is not in doubt is that they have exposed to grave risk the health of the larger economy and the well-being of the wider public. These are of central social policy concern.

The consequences have been hugely expensive. First, there is the past and future looting involved in the payments that bankers have paid themselves: payments that might alternatively have gone to their customers, their shareholders and their staff, or in reimbursement of government support.[4] These are the gains accruing to their micro-innovations, their 'deepening' of the world of financial services. Second, there is the seizing up of the whole financial system and the losses falling on the financially less agile, including businesses and consumers. This is meso, the trailing edge, as the effects of such innovation widen. Finally, these mesos warp the macro-economy. There is the cost to the public finances of supporting the financial system; of maintaining a fiscal stimulus to the economy; of supporting those who become unemployed; and of forfeiting the tax revenues associated with the years of lost economic growth. Here also are the reduced standards of living that will, it seems, have to be borne by the mass of the public. As noted already, this has all been against a background of growing income inequality, especially in the USA and the UK: in particular, between the super-rich and the least well off (Lankester, 2009).

As institutions evolve, they embody a shifting mix of obligations and entitlements for the various sub-populations of their 'carriers', as we saw in Chapter 6. It is around these different mixes that much of the political contest revolves; after all, one person's entitlement presupposes another's obligation. As the financial crisis widened, it saw a very unequal struggle to rearrange these entitlements and obligations, as between the financial institutions, government and the mass of households. It is in large measure those least able to cope who are now left to adjust perforce to new institutional rules and to re-weave their 'micro-eco-systems' in the hope of making ends meet. As we noted in concluding Chapter 10, it is thus that first movers consolidate and stabilise their positions of advantage and construct their niches, buffering themselves against turbulence, but constraining and determining thereby the lives of others.

This distribution of public burden and largesse is what Titmuss famously analysed in terms of the 'social division of welfare' (Titmuss, 1963: Ch. 2). That essay pointed out that the public pursue offered financial support to citizens, in their various situations of need, not only in the form of the social benefits distributed to welfare recipients, but also through tax reliefs ('fiscal welfare'), which were, however, much more regressive in their impact. In addition, the non-wage benefits ('occupational welfare') available through employers (pensions and various 'fringe benefits') were often subsidised through tax relief but were, again, regressive in their impact.

By taking this larger view of the social division of welfare, and the support of the public purse, Titmuss brought centre-stage the multiple institutional channels through which households gain access to the public finances, but on very different terms, depending upon their location in the social structure and the skills, knowledge and agility with which they are able to weave and re-weave their institutional eco-system. Now, however, it seems necessary to take a still larger view, to encompass not only the financial support to individual households – the social division of welfare – but also the support given to the corporate and banking sector, the tax burden involved and the political balance struck between the two. Not that this 'corporate division of welfare' is unconcerned with households: on the contrary, it has major consequences for the households of the executives concerned, notably by enabling banks to continue to offer those households the levels of remuneration to which they have become accustomed.

In another of his essays, 'The Irresponsible Society', Titmuss showed he was well aware of such corporate interests and their influence on the uses of the public purse (Titmuss, 1963: Ch. 11). In terms which in some degree anticipate Galbraith's account of the Predator State, he pointed to the growing power of the pension funds and private insurance companies: a power that they were reinforcing through their accumulation of share ownership in an ever-wider range of public companies. This economic power – and the massive investments involved – had major consequences for social priorities and public policy. Those who managed these funds had thus become 'arbiters of welfare and amenity for larger sections of the community'. Such power was, however, being exercised invisibly and without any public accountability: hence Titmuss's claim that this was an 'irresponsible society'.

Titmuss through these essays redirected social policy research along new lines and sowed the seeds of the new scholarship in social policy that emerged in the 1970s, much more attuned to political economy (George and Wilding, 1976; Gough, 1979; Room, 1979). There is a similar need now for research that maps the financial flows involved in the 'social' and 'corporate and banking division of welfare'. Also needed is analysis of the contrasting language and presuppositions of public policy debate, as far as these very different groups are concerned, and the terms in which political actors seek to establish the legitimacy and appropriateness of the financial settlement.

In Chapter 7 we made reference to Butler's study of the role of scandals in the development of British public policy (Butler and Drakeford, 2005). His focus was on mental health institutions and childcare; but these may offer some wider insights. Butler shows that administrative failings or institutional brutality do not suffice to generate a public policy scandal. A scandal must also evoke alarm at the 'assault . . . upon the collective sense of security' (p. 227). There must also be 'claim makers' who contest the status quo and can develop an alliance for reform. Nevertheless, Butler shows that scandals can also provide opportunities to divide consensus, with a wide range of moral entrepreneurs seizing the opportunity to drive public concern in new directions. Thus, for example, childcare scandals were used to re-energise the debate about the death penalty; now, Butler argues, they are invoked to question multiculturalism, welfare dependencies or other forms of 'broken Britain'.

Some of these elements seem present in the financial crisis: most obviously, institutional brutality and an assault upon the collective sense of security. Nevertheless, 'claim makers' seem to speak with mixed voices and there is no alliance for reform. In the UK, the media seized on publicity around the expense claims of Members of Parliament and for months this eclipsed discussion of the financiers' far larger spoils. Meanwhile the main opposition party increasingly blamed the recession on 'big government'. A study is needed to complement that of Butler. It is not enough for researchers to lay bare the social and corporate division of welfare or the anatomy of the irresponsible society: they must also analyse the politics of scandal generation and extinction.

17.4   WARPING THE REAL ECONOMY

The financial system is not isolated; it is dynamically coupled to the 'real economy'. Here too there has been 'creative destruction' on a massive scale. However, these couplings are not everywhere the same. There are 'varieties of finance capitalism', with different countries experiencing the financial crisis through the prism of their own distinctive banking and regulatory institutions. The consequences for real economies have been correspondingly varied.

In the previous chapter, concerned with knowledge economies, the central policy question for national economies related to institutional inertia and the scope for national policy-makers to 'melt' frozen structures into more agile and adaptable forms. Here the central policy question has shifted to the resilience of national and international institutions, in the face of financial turbulence, and the extent to which those institutions 'buffer' the real economy, limiting its exposure to 'tipping points' and cascades of wider destruction.

Among those who have picked over the debris of the financial crisis, views vary as to how it percolated across the 'connective geometry' of the economic system. They join, however, in pointing to the US interest rate increases of 2004–06, the associated downturn in house prices, the resulting defaults and the sub-prime crisis; all then triggering wider financial disorder and eventually the larger crisis in the real economy (Krugman, 2008; Peston, 2008b; Cable, 2009; Skidelsky, 2009). Nevertheless, as we saw in Chapter 13, causal chains are rarely simple. As Lieberson argues, the more 'basic' or underlying causes must be laid bare, in terms of the typical strategies that social actors pursue to gain positional advantage and the macro-patterns to which these give rise.

For the broad range of economists who study the economy as a complex adaptive system, the strategic situation of economic actors facing such turbulence is readily understandable. The modern economy presents a rather high level of uncertainty and requires economic actors to make conjectures as to how their decisions will play out. This uncertainty can then produce the 'flocking' or 'herding' behaviour discussed in earlier chapters. This in turn makes for agglomerations or 'bubbles' of trading activity which are highly unstable: the 'fat tails' of a non-Gaussian distribution, where extreme events are far from unlikely (Watson, 2007: Ch. 3; Soros, 2008b; Skidelsky, 2009: Ch. 2). This goes quite counter to neoclassical confidence in 'rational expectations' and in the ability of market traders to predict and manage risk. It is with uncertainty rather than risk that a turbulent economy confronts us: the future is not limited to the well-behaved tails of the Gaussian distribution (recall our discussion in Chapter 2).

As we saw in Chapter 2, the fat tails attest to interaction effects. Risk assessment that assumes something like the Gaussian distribution is inappropriate because no one market functions in isolation. The crisis arose in part from the high level of coupling between systems: global connections make not for a flat and stable world but one of dynamic turbulence. The policy inference that many have drawn is what we earlier referred to as 'decomplexity' (Stewart, 2001, 2003): these connections should be reduced, perhaps by separating 'retail' and 'investment' banks, and the different sub-systems should have independent back-up, so as to ensure resilience and robustness (Kay, 2009a). Alternatively or in addition, more buffers or 'firebreaks' might be inserted, perhaps by means of a 'Tobin tax' on international financial transactions. These would involve major changes in the overall governance of the financial system.

Here is a strong convergence with the work of Keynes, both in the significance he attributes to uncertainty and his desire to harness the financial institutions to the common good (Keynes, 1936: Ch. 24; Skidelsky, 2009: Chs 2, 4, 5). Nevertheless, Keynes goes further in drawing out the implications for public policy. We previously distinguished Keynes's position – compared, for example, with Potts and Schumpeter – by emphasising that for him, a modern economy was unlikely to self-organise without the active intervention of the state, at least at a level which secured full employment. He also however argued that such intervention – in particular, in the form of public investment projects – would project certainty into an otherwise uncertain future and limit the destabilising effects of flocking behaviour. This – and not just the adjustment of overall levels of effective demand – was the centrepiece of his economic strategy.[5] Meanwhile, with capital investment plentiful, interest rates would be low. Speculation would disappear and finance capital would enjoy no more than a modest 'rent'. This would be tantamount to the 'euthanasia of the rentier' (Keynes, 1936: Ch. 24; Tily, 2007: Ch. 2).[6]

Nevertheless, Keynes was fully aware that national policy is dynamically coupled to what in the previous chapter we referred to as the global 'eco-system' of international political economy. He sought to establish an inter-governmental financial system in which none of the major national economies would be obliged to dance to the rhythm of any other; each could then adopt a domestic policy which would maintain full employment and steady growth (Skidelsky, 2002: Ch. 6). At Bretton Woods, however, this was achieved only in part; all would henceforth dance to the dollar. Even Bretton Woods was by-passed in the 1980s, however, as financial liberalisation and deregulation shifted the locus of these dynamics from the inter-governmental to the commercial world. Domestic policies were now exposed to the speculative flocking of global finance (Davidson, 2009: Ch. 8; Hudson, 2010).

Keynes's hopes for the 'euthanasia of the rentier' now appear forlorn. It has in particular been the recycling of East Asia trade surpluses back to the West that has fuelled this growth in the finance sector, which has in turn exposed the global economy to crisis on such a large scale. Those who manage this recycling extract a slice of the proceeds as their remuneration. Nevertheless, as Tily notes, 'Finance has grown to such an extent only because the *choice* was taken to re-position the world economy as servant to these interests' (Tily, 2007: 324, emphasis in original; see also Watson, 2007: 217–20). These are fundamental choices of global governance.

17.5   CIVILITY AND THE FINANCIAL SYSTEM

This chapter has offered an account of the international financial and economic crisis and the dilemmas it poses for public policy. The crisis has focused attention on the governance of the financial system and has re-ignited debates around public policy and social citizenship.

In the conclusion to Part 1, we argued that the struggle for positional advantage poses fundamental choices for public policy, reconciling these animal spirits and building civility. At the start of Part 3, we returned to this argument, in terms of the policy-maker as umpire and steward, encouraging creativity and civility but resisting predation and despoliation. It is to these most fundamental of policy questions that we now return.

In Chapter 5 we distinguished three contrasting institutional settings: markets, hierarchical direction and 'negotiated moral communities'. As we saw, Ostrom (1990) elaborates the third of these in relation to the 'commons': natural resources which are fixed in supply but easy to access, and whose progressive depletion by self-interested individuals has ultimately tragic consequences for society as a whole. She argues that here at least, neither markets nor hierarchical direction by the state are effective or sustainable.

The general question for public policy is where and how to apply the principles of common pool regimes, and how far to rely instead on markets or hierarchical direction. These offer alternative principles of institutional design, alternative models of civility. How they are blended and applied to the governance of particular terrains will drive the self-organisation of the socio-economic system, variously affecting the social and economic well-being of different social groups and communities. This provides a normative vantage point from which to appraise the policies in question.

The international financial system may not be a natural resource but it is part of the 'commons' of the contemporary world. The tragedy of the commons is the tragedy of the hunter-gatherer whose predatory capacity outruns the capacity of the eco-system to replenish itself. The tragedy of the meltdown of 2007–08 involved predatory risk-taking that ran away with itself and brought a collapse of trust across the financial system. State regulation and hierarchical direction may be costly and ineffective but markets have proved unable to regulate themselves by reference to the social and economic well-being of the larger community.

As we saw in Chapter 5, Ostrom (1990: Ch. 3) argues that common pool resources must respect certain design principles. The participants must be clearly identifiable; the operational rules must be customised to local circumstances; monitoring and enforcement must be embedded in the community of participants; and the arrangements must be underpinned by the governmental authorities. We now ask whether and how these design principles could be applied to the international financial system.[7]

The participants must be clearly identifiable. For Ostrom, this design principle is important as the basis for trust and 'norms of proper behaviour'. However, in the global – or even just the national – financial system this is not unproblematic. The bankers will interpret the principle as implying self-regulation. However, taxpayer support to the banks establishes a much wider stakeholder interest, even if governments have been slow to articulate this in new rules of governance of the financial institutions. The crisis also raises questions about the role of shareholders in publicly listed financial companies and the place of private equity companies. This is a complex eco-system with a multitude of sometimes shadowy participants, many with the power – it is now apparent – to destroy the financial commons.

The difficulty does not end there. As we have seen, the tectonic plates of the global financial system are shifting and new – predominantly Asian – players are staking their claims to be full participants in international financial governance. China's central bank has called for a new international reserve currency instead of the dollar, a proposal originally mooted by Keynes at Bretton Woods (Skidelsky, 2002: Ch. 6). These developments are incomplete and of uncertain outcome.

Ostrom develops her design principles principally by reference to long-established rural communities with clear boundaries and natural resources – most notably water – for which all have an enduring need. In the global financial system in contrast, we find multiple interlocking communities, with fluid boundaries and the mediation of needs by money – but money which comes in new and weird forms, whose trustworthiness is as precarious as it is essential. The cast of participants is therefore ill-defined. This is in part because some of them lurk in the shadows, but also because they are forever changing, as innovation and the restructuring of the global economy bring new stakeholders into play, in terms of both financial institutions and governments.

Nevertheless, Kay's proposals for the separation of retail and investment banks would bring some clarity as to the key participants in each. In particular, retail banks, no longer seduced by the incentives of 'casino' operations, would tend to compete in providing customer service with good value for money (Kay, 2009a: Ch. 9). With such a separation, consumer markets could thus be expected to do much of the regulatory work of the financial commons. As already argued, in public policy we must in general expect to forge some blend of 'negotiated moral community', market and hierarchical direction, rather than relying on any one 'pure' type.

The operational rules must be customised to local circumstances. For Ostrom, this second principle allows for subtly different rules for different local circumstances. Within the UK, some local authorities have established new local banks for precisely this purpose. This principle could also herald a reversal in the decline of the mutuals – the building societies in particular – many of which have in recent decades converted into public companies (Kay, 2009a: 45). Utility banking by local mutuals and credit unions, the institutional *bricolage* of the past, might also be given a new and key role, re-building customer trust from the bottom up and providing access for the excluded.

New initiatives of this sort, albeit developed in the niches left by much larger institutions, might set in motion a cascade of wider reconfiguration and help to re-build – or at least re-balance – the larger financial architecture. This reform is, however, unlikely to develop on a large scale unless there is positive state encouragement to local experiments and appropriate support in terms of a favourable legal and regulatory framework. Existing financial institutions, however, are likely to resist changes that undermine their position and their political power is substantial (Peston, 2008b; Galbraith, 2009: 102).

Monitoring and enforcement with graduated sanctions must be embedded in the community of participants. This third design principle is important in securing compliance and commitment to the rules of the commons. However, many of the studies of the financial institutions at the heart of the recent crisis paint a very different picture: 'the unifying theme is one of boys behaving badly' (Kay, 2009b). The question therefore is how to design a new system of financial regulation embedded not in the narrow community of financial entrepreneurs but in the larger community of participants to which we have just referred: customers, shareholders and taxpayers, long-developed nations and newly industrialised countries, rich and poor, change makers and change takers.

The challenge is two-fold. The first is technical. We saw in the previous chapter that policy-makers seeking to monitor and steer the knowledge economy found themselves with inadequate and antiquated tools: 'rear view mirrors' that use the statistical tools of yesterday. The same goes for the regulators of the new financial economy. Nevertheless, as Kay stresses, detailed supervision of the operations of banks by the public authorities is undesirable and is likely in any case to be ineffective; what is needed is regulation by reference to specific and clearly identified public policy concerns. Beyond this, with retail and investment banking separated, self and market regulation can deliver what is needed (Kay, 2009a: Ch. 4).

The second challenge is political. A country such as the UK, central to the global financial system, is key to the reform of financial regulation; it is, however, also desperate not to lose that central role by incurring the disfavour of the bankers. Hence the pusillanimous efforts it has made (at least at the time of writing) and the refusal to countenance any significant sanctions, graduated or otherwise.

Finally, *the arrangements must be underpinned by the governmental authorities.* Recovery from the financial crisis requires a central role for the public authorities, not just in 'bailing out' the banks but in constructing a new order: for example, registering and approving new financial 'products' before they can be used (Soros, 2008a).

During the summer of 2009, even as the recession in the 'real economy' continued and unemployment mounted, some of the banks began returning to profit. However, their returning prosperity was derived in part from predation on the destruction wrought by their earlier financial recklessness. The extinction of some competitors enabled them to raise the fees that they charged; meanwhile, with banks continuing to restrict lending, companies and governments around the world needed to tap other markets to raise funds, bringing extra work to the investment banks, for which they have charged handsomely (Treanor and Inman, 2009). They even took fees from governments around the world, for advice on what to do with their stakes in the bailed-out banks (Hargreaves, 2009). State authorities that lend their support to this reconstruction of a predatory order are complicit in the continuing tragedy of the financial commons (Galbraith, 2009: xii–xv).

This discussion of Ostrom's design principles hardly confirms that the global financial system can move easily towards a 'common pool resource': its governance arrangements would be hotly contested. Nevertheless, far from appearing utopian, the crisis of 2008 arguably demonstrates that the challenge must be addressed. True, this is no small and self-contained farming community, quite the opposite. Nor, however, was the Slashdot virtual community, our example in Chapter 5 of a self-regulating 'common pool resource'. There as we saw the openness of the community's boundaries – apparently incompatible with Ostrom's design principles – was addressed by the earning and expenditure of 'karma', in a moral economy nicely customised to the 'virtual commons'.

We might equally point to the 'common pool resource' offered by universal healthcare systems, as part of social citizenship. Recall, for example, *The Gift Relationship*, Titmuss's study of the UK national health system and its system of blood donation, serving a common citizenship service that was free to all. These were donations experienced as moral obligations by those involved, a broad cross-section of the British population, but obligations willingly accepted (Titmuss, 1973).

In short therefore, providing that we heed Ostrom's injunction to customise the operational rules to the circumstances of the common pool resource in question, there seems no reason to shirk the attempt, even in apparently unpromising environments.[8] As Ostrom and Kay both argue, no optimal combination of institutional rules can be designed *a priori*; what is needed is a public policy led process of evolutionary adaptation and self-organisation (Ostrom, 2005: 245; Kay, 2009a: Chs 3–4). Nevertheless, any such process is always at risk of predation.

17.6 CONCLUSION

This chapter has been concerned with positional dynamics on a global canvas. The institutional entrepreneurship, by which more advantaged groups shape and tilt the positional struggle, here involved financial products and services. These were novelties offered to the world-wide population of investors; they also however incorporated particular sub-populations – most obviously, the clients of sub-prime housing – on new and highly risky terms. This was the result not just of the 'creativity' of these financial entrepreneurs, but also of the specific regulatory and public policy regime within which this creativity proved so lucrative.

The positional struggles with which this whole book has been concerned are set in an essentially dynamic context. True, today's victors may seek to consolidate and cement their position and secure some 'stasis'; nevertheless this is always contingent and liable to be contested. We have presented this in terms of an evolutionary model of 'deepen-widen-warp': not the blind evolution that Darwin himself depicted, more a process which strategically oriented agile entrepreneurs seek to seize and tune, not least by re-shaping public policy. In this positional dynamic, the race for perennial novelty or 'deepening' brings customers and profits, enforces new forms of domination, evades and re-shapes public regulation, offloads uncertainty and secures leverage within the future disposition of the world. Any slackening in the pace and the regulators will catch up, rivals will regain their poise and mount a challenge, profits will dissipate. Accelerate the deepening, however, and the danger is social turbulence and political backlash.

At each stage of this race, the victors will typically seek to cement and reinforce their advantage by strategies of institutional differentiation, by which the defeated can be assigned thereafter to a separate and poorer array of life chances. This was why in Chapter 15, drawing on the work of Willms, we argued for policy indicators of the extent to which institutions tend to integrate or separate the opportunities available to different groups of the population. We do not claim that a turbulent environment or a high rate of 'deepening' will necessarily give rise to greater inequality; it is rather where they allow new and fateful lines of institutional differentiation that those inequalities are more likely. It is from this stand-point that we recall Tawney's argument that 'social institutions . . . should be planned, as far as is possible, to emphasise and strengthen, not the class differences which divide [people], but the common humanity which unites them' (Tawney, 1931 [1964]: 49). This is also consistent with the findings of scholars such as Goldthorpe and Esping-Andersen (1990), that vigor-ous social democratic policies aimed at inclusive institutions tend both to reduce inequalities and to expand opportunities for all. As we have seen, however, such opportunities remain forever exposed to predation by the advantaged.

This is an essentially dynamic account of the relationship between positional struggle, institutional differentiation and inequalities of life chances. It is quite different from the account offered by Wilkinson and Pickett (2009), for example, concerned with the consequences of overall levels of inequality for general levels of well-being, and giving a central explanatory role to psycho-social processes. That work has been subject to various methodological critiques (Goldthorpe, 2009). Even if we accept Wilkinson's empirical finding, that higher levels of inequality depress levels of well-being for most social groups, there are a variety of pos-sible explanations alongside those which Wilkinson himself advances. Nevertheless, our own account of the financial crisis confirms how the positional struggle, and the institutional differentiation to which it tends to give rise, can produce gross inequalities of life chances and wreak general havoc with the well-being of the society. Again therefore we echo an argument recurring through earlier chapters: even insofar as we can regard the socio-economic system as 'self-organising', this in no way excuses us from confronting the public policy choices posed by the result-ing pattern of outcomes and the scope for re-tuning these by appropriate policy interventions.

James Galbraith describes this society as 'predatory'. He stands in the robust tradition of Veblen and John Kenneth Galbraith. Recall, for example, Veblen's account of the 'leisure class', associated not with indus-try but with finance (of whose contribution he was as sceptical as Keynes) (Veblen, 1899). They advertise their success through their conspicuous consumption, which reinforces their social and economic distance from the larger society. This also provides ever-renewed symbols of the good life, to which that larger society is enjoined to aspire: the perennial crea-tion of new consumption 'needs'. It was, however, only on the basis of bur-geoning consumer debt that this injunction could be heeded, something that has been highlighted in post-mortems on the recent financial crisis, but which Galbraith senior had already made central to his analysis of the 'affluent society' in the 1950s (Galbraith, 1958: Chs 5, 14).

To describe such a social dynamic as 'predatory' invokes the language of hunters and food webs, the 'struggle for existence' and the destruction of life that this entails (Darwin, 1859: Ch. 3). It is precisely this metaphor of the evolving eco-system that we have found appropriate, in the previous chapter and now here, for viewing the global economy within which national and other actors carve their respective niches and struggle to survive. The predators who roam our social and economic world feed on the livelihoods of the vulnerable. Nevertheless, the fog of complex interconnections conveniently obscures their responsibility for the suffering that results; genteel civility masks the predatory brutality of global finance.[9] Lotka and Volterra remind us that predators in the natural world depend ultimately on their prey surviving and thriving. In contrast, the financial predators of today are not specialised eaters but omnivores, who can devastate one population of prey but then move on to another. This is slash and burn and the tragedy of the commons, whose costs then fall on the public purse and those least able to bear them.[10]

Many of the writers on whom we have drawn offer a bleak assessment of the prospects for democratic politics. Citizenship is in retreat before the power of a predatory kleptocracy. Wealth buys political power (Peston, 2008b; Galbraith, 2009: 102) and the organisational basis for resistance is weak (Galbraith, 2009: 143). Nevertheless, in complexity science as in politics, prediction is perilous; agile humanity is forever able to devise new challenges to the prevailing order; nothing is incontestable; human beings can in some degree choose their futures. Our task as scholars is to illuminate this process; and it is to this that the conceptual and methodological framework offered in this book is meant to contribute.

Its contribution is an institutionally grounded complexity perspective. It is evolutionary in inspiration, but without the biology. Its ontology is of agile actors locked in a race for positional advantage and leverage. An evolutionary model directs our attention to the local novelties that emerge 'bottom up' and are then variously adopted by the population, in turn abrading and co-evolving with the larger technological and institutional 'eco-system'. Viewing this as a complex adaptive system means looking for order to 'emerge' as the system 'self-organises'. A model of positional leverage directs us no less to order that is imposed. It asks which social actors have secured leverage in the husbandry of society's energy and resources and which other actors are now incorporated on adverse terms: on terms indeed that may amount to organised predation. It recognises that social processes are complex and that to understand them, we may usefully draw on models taken from the physical and biological sciences. We cannot, however, escape from the fundamental social and political choices of our time.

Postscript: Tools for policy-makers

This Postscript offers a practical guide for agile policy-making, rooted in the conceptual, methodological and policy approaches developed through the preceding chapters.

Policy toolkits abound. Among contributions from academics, Bardach (2005), for example, offers a toolkit for policy analysts. His 'eight-fold path' includes the following steps:

- Define the problem
- Assemble some evidence
- Construct the alternatives
- Select the criteria
- Project the outcomes
- Confront the trade-offs
- Decide
- Tell your story.

It would not be particularly useful to work our way through each of these steps, assessing their appropriateness and limitations. Suffice to say, however, that Bardach's toolkit is geared more to the policy-maker who, in the language of Chapter 1, is on a stable putting green, rather than a bouncy castle.

Toolkits developed by organisational consultants and geared to policy practitioners are also plentiful. Heijden (1996) is one of the most widely cited. This treats organisations as complex adaptive systems, seeking to survive and prosper in uncertain and often turbulent conditions. It is addressed to business leaders but it has also been widely deployed for public policy development.

We might summarise Heijden's advice in terms of three injunctions:

- Identify and nurture your organisational strengths
  Heijden asks an organisation to be clear as to the distinctive competencies which provide it with competitive advantage. This is, however, set in a dynamic context: the organisation must discover how, within the specific circumstances it faces, these competencies

can produce self-reinforcing cycles that build further strength, and how these virtuous dynamics can be nurtured.

- Undertake a strategic conversation
  Heijden asks the business leader to instigate a 'strategic convers-ation' within the organisation, so as to develop a 'mental model of the forces behind its current and future success' and identify the key leverage points available to managers. This will enable organis-ational leaders to interpret their environment and identify early signs of significant change (van der Heijden, 1996: 59–60).
- Formulate scenarios of development
  Scenarios provide 'virtual laboratories' for the ideas that emerge from the strategic conversation (van der Heijden, 1996: 56–7). The aim, however, is to empower managers, not to provide them with the false comfort of implausibly precise – if technically sophisticated – forecasts (Wack, 1985). The greater the uncertainty, the more these scenarios will focus on building strength and readiness, with distinctive competencies but also some diversity, so as to remain agile and adaptable.

This may serve as an appropriate script for Heijden, as he engages with individual organisations and their leaders. As already noted, his approach has also been widely deployed in public policy treatments of scenario development. It resonates well with our own account of a complex and turbulent world. Nevertheless, it also has limitations. First, there is little discussion of the institutional and technological path dependencies in which organisations may find themselves trapped. Second, there is little on the interactions with other change makers and change takers, re-shaping and warping each other's terrains; nor on the dangers of predation or of getting locked on adverse terms into the 'forcing structures' and timescales of others.

Policy toolkits are also available from government. The UK government provides several for its own staff but makes them available for anyone else who wants to improve policy practice. One, from the Prime Minister's Strategy Unit, offers good practice in developing an evidence base for policy.[1] As we noted in our opening chapter, this has to some considerable extent become the accepted gold standard of good policy making. The Cochrane and Campbell collaborations, reviewing and pooling evidence on the effectiveness of particular interventions, are notable exemplars.[2] There are many other sources – government departments, policy institutes and so on – offering similar guidelines.[3]

Evidence-based policy-making is based on reviews of 'what works'. There is also a UK government toolkit concerned with international policy comparisons, assessing 'what works elsewhere'.[4] This guides officials and policy analysts as to how, starting from a particular domestic policy problem, they may best identify other countries whose experience is of particular interest and proceed to gather relevant evidence, in a form that can illuminate domestic policy initiatives. The toolkit does not under-estimate the difficulties of translating lessons between different national policy environments, notwithstanding international efforts – for example, through the EU and the OECD – to facilitate the international comparability of policies. (For a cautionary account of how toolkits such as this have fared in cross-national policy transfer, see Duncan (2009).)

All these government toolkits tend to assume a stable environment and well-defined policy problems, by reference to which specific interventions can be framed. They may be less appropriate in uncertain and turbulent conditions. There is, however, yet another UK government toolkit, part of their 'Strategy Survival Guide', concerned with scenarios of future development, and drawing upon Heijden and related management literatures.[5] Much of what Heijden advocates in relation to scenario building and its use in a 'strategic conversation' is retained. The toolkit also emphasises the importance of understanding the societal, technological, economic, environmental and political 'drivers' of change in the organisational environment, so as to hone the 'mental models' that the organisation employs. Nevertheless, the links to other tools of policy-making are left implicit.

We now offer a toolkit of eight elements for the practice of 'agile policy-making'. It is accompanied by four worked examples, drawn from preceding chapters. The toolkit builds on the conceptual, methodological and policy approaches developed in this book. It may help if we recall their key points.

First, the world of the policy-maker cannot be thought of tending towards some stable equilibrium, whether market-based or otherwise. Social actors continually drive it away from equilibrium; in doing so, they sculpt the world in new and fateful ways. True, societies can get locked or frozen into inertia; there is always the weight of existing institutions and technologies; nevertheless, change is always possible. The policy-maker can nudge and in some degree even tune and steer these processes, re-shaping the world of tomorrow.

Second, the world of the policy-maker involves complex processes of adaptation. Creative innovations by economic, institutional and policy entrepreneurs are variously taken up across the wider society; they then abrade against larger currents of social and economic change, tipping them in new directions. This is an evolutionary model, albeit one in which the actors are not blind; they can in some degree anticipate and nurture co-evolutionary dynamics that will bring them positional advantage. Nevertheless, with different actors pursuing such projects, they are thrust into a struggle or race, opening and closing windows of opportunity for each other. The policy-maker can set the terms of this race and seek to civilise it, so that it does not develop into open warfare or expand the scope for predation, but instead builds general resilience and well-being. Or indeed, where the society in question is frozen into inertia, the policy-maker may be the one who sets the race in motion in the first place, energising the protagonists to be active entrepreneurs.

The policy-maker faces political choices in regards to the well-being of different sections of the society and the trade-off between alternative conceptions of the good society. With social actors struggling for positional advantage, and endeavouring to re-shape the larger social landscape, the policy-maker is no mere umpire. Many writers have admittedly drawn a rather different conclusion: the policy-maker may encourage creative energies and innovation but must then be content to leave economic markets and social networks to select those which shall prosper (Beinhocker, 2007: Chs 15, 18). Nevertheless, policy-makers cannot but shape this selection process, by the expenditure programmes they undertake, the regulatory mechanisms they set in place, the support and direction they give to the national innovation system. Insofar as we think of society as a complex adaptive system, the policy-maker will unavoidably shape how – and by reference to whose advantage and well-being – it self-organises.

Many of the toolkits to which we referred earlier start out by asking the policy-maker to be clear as to his or her strategic goals. All else depends on this. However, it is also possible to argue that strategic goals can be clarified only as business leaders or policy-makers come to understand the landscape on which they find themselves, the protagonists with whom they are locked in struggle, the path dependencies of particular courses of action, the interdependence and trade-offs between different objectives. This is in some degree the position of Heijden, concerned primarily with business leaders; it is no less true for policy-makers, whether at local, national or international level. Any policy-maker will need to bring some initial commitments in terms of broad policy objectives and will of course have to engage with the legacy of existing commitments; but only through practical engagement will a new statement of strategic goals become possible.

The toolkit comes with three caveats.

First, the eight elements should not be seen as a simple linear sequence, as, for example, in Bardach's 'eight-fold path'. Instead, they should be used iteratively: not just in the sense of being ready to go through the sequence again and again, but more fundamentally allowing each element to evolve in tandem with the others. The toolkit decomposes the complex process of policy-making into eight sub-processes, so as to render them practically manageable, but the agile policy-maker must continuously weave them together, adapting them to specific situations.

Second, the turbulence of the real world means that the policy-maker must be ready to deal with unpredictable and exogenous shocks; with crises that extinguish years of patient work by some policy actors, while opening windows of opportunity for others; with new fashions and fads that have captivated political leaders and must now be turned into practical policies. It is also important never to lose sight of the larger political projects by which policy is shaped: the politics of retrenchment as against the politics of expansion (Pierson, 1994); the politics of choice and of equity (Le Grand, 2007); the politics of scandal and moral indignation (Butler and Drakeford, 2005). Each can variously consolidate, reconfigure or launch a new struggle for positional advantage.

Finally, the toolkit is only provisional, leaving others to hone and rework it, as their own particular circumstances demand. Any good tool must after all be fine-tuned by a collective wealth of experience far beyond what any one person can bring: a wealth that can then be progressively incorporated into its very design (Pollan, 1997: Ch. 5).

For further resources and development of the toolkit, readers are referred to the website http://www.bath.ac.uk/soc-pol/people/gjroom-policy-making.html.

AGILE POLICY-MAKING TOOLKIT

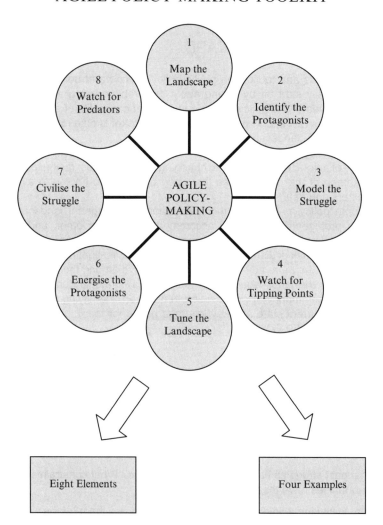

Eight Elements

---

1   MAP THE LANDSCAPE

The textbooks and toolkits on public policy-making and policy assessment typically start off by asking about the problem being addressed,
the objectives of the policy-maker, the costs and benefits of alternative
policies. This tends to assume that the policy-maker is on a rather stable
– even static – landscape.

Many policy-makers, however, confront a turbulent landscape, with a
variety of actors trying to adapt to changing circumstances, racing to take
advantage of the opportunities that open up, but also hoping to avoid
disasters and dead ends.

Some policy-makers find themselves facing a stagnant landscape,
where protagonists have long accommodated to each other, and are
therefore ill-prepared for new challenges from outside. The policy-maker
then has the task of disrupting this collusive inertia, instigating a race that
will unleash the more adventurous and innovative among them.

Mapping the landscape may be aided by a 'strategic conversation'
within the community or organisation in question, identifying the forces
behind its current state and key leverage points for the future (van der
Heijden, 1996: 59–60).

Questions to ask

Is the policy landscape stable or turbulent? Do you wish to challenge
the stability or reduce the turbulence?

Does the landscape connect to others? How far are you locked into
stasis – or plunged into perpetual turbulence – because of those larger
connections?

What past struggles have shaped the landscape? What constraints and
opportunities have these left?

What institutional rigidities and frozen structures are there? If the
landscape is one of stasis, is this because the protagonists view the
risks and costs of change as too great? Or is it because those who are
in a weak position see little scope for challenge?

What routes towards change are most readily available? Are there
'runaway loops' by which processes of change can become self-
reinforcing? What levers does this offer the policy-maker?

2   IDENTIFY THE PROTAGONISTS

Policy-makers live on crowded landscapes, with interest groups and stakeholders of varying agility and power: not least the wider but heterogeneous public, upon whose expectations and responses the effects of their policy interventions may crucially depend.

Social and economic change continually re-shapes the interests of these protagonists and the opportunities that they face. New protagonists may emerge as the race unfolds. A dynamic understanding is therefore required.

Protagonists have competencies and vulnerabilities shaped by their respective pasts. Each is, however, able to explore how these vulnerabilities can be turned into strengths, the competencies used to produce self-reinforcing cycles that build further strength.

Each protagonist will focus on particular strategic concerns. It is here that they concentrate their efforts to transform, by-pass or subvert the landscape they face. Elsewhere they are content to be change takers. Nevertheless, the agenda of strategic concerns can readily change, as everyday matters become turbulent and trigger thresholds of concern.

Questions to ask

Who are the main protagonists? Who are the likely first movers and last movers? What new actors are likely to emerge? How are they likely to re-shape the struggle and its direction?

Which of the protagonists will the landscape favour? What patterns of cooperation among them is it likely to foster?

How do you rate their respective competencies and vulnerabilities? How strong are the institutional, professional and political positions that each holds?

Which objectives and concerns will each defend? What traps will they seek at all costs to avoid? What thresholds of concern do they employ and what 'mental models' of how their world is likely to unfold?

3   MODEL THE STRUGGLE

Policy-makers must consider how the struggle is likely to unfold. It is important to anticipate the critical junctures: points at which the race could move in a number of different directions. It is also important to identify the interventions by which the policy-maker might exercise leverage at these critical points.

This does not mean that policy-makers can forecast the future. Nevertheless, it may be possible to delineate a range of possible scenarios. Local policy experimentation may allow scenarios to emerge progressively (Marris, 1974; Room, 1993; Sanderson, 2006). Agent-based modelling may likewise serve as a 'virtual' laboratory.

Generic – and often simple – models of dynamic systems may help in formulating likely scenarios. These include Schelling's model of cellular automata and social polarisation; Bak's self-organised criticality; Turing's instabilities; Kauffman and Maynard Smith's arms races, Red Queens and evolutionarily stable states; Volterra-Lotka's predator-prey; Jain and Krishna's model of network dynamics, with cascades of catastrophic collapse but then recovery. They also include the positional dynamics of 'deepen-widen-warp' presented in this book and incorporating elements of all the aforementioned models.

It is commonplace to use formal models in this way, as a means of anticipating possible social futures. Equilibrium models drawn from classical mechanics have long been used to this effect, as have models of negative feedback and homeostasis. So have various iconic models in game theory, such as Prisoner's Dilemma and Battle of the Sexes. So also have formal mathematical models, for example, involving the logistic function (or S-curve). What we are doing here is to enlarge the repertoire of such models, with specific reference to the dynamics of 'far from equilibrium' systems elaborated in this book.

Questions to ask

How is the race or struggle likely to unfold? What are the critical junctures?

What would drive the race in a different direction? What are the possible trajectories and their outcomes?

What are the key 'system parameters'? What feedback loops and eddies of self-organisation are likely to develop?

What models can usefully capture these dynamics?

4 WATCH FOR TIPPING POINTS

Social and economic change does not necessarily take place in a continuous and smooth fashion. It may be 'punctuated' with periods of apparent stability followed by periods of turbulence: not because of exogenous shocks, but because slow and perhaps unnoticed changes in background factors eventually cross some threshold and trigger larger changes.

It may be possible to identify 'tipping points', where the dynamics of change shift dramatically. In general these shifts are not readily reversed.

Policy-makers must keep track of how a particular race or struggle is developing in real time. Publicly available statistics and indicators may help – but they may be geared to yesterday's problems. The struggle may play out in particular key arenas which the policy-maker can watch: particular local communities or services, for example. All relevant information sources must be mobilised eclectically, but always having due regard to their respective validity, timeliness and accuracy.

Questions to ask

What will mark the key stages and critical junctures in the race or struggle?

What indicators or signals allow you to track the race in real time – the changing landscape of the race and the progress and dominance of the various protagonists?

Can you see when and where the struggle among the protagonists tightens and becomes particularly intense?

Do you anticipate particular tipping points into desirable or undesirable trajectories? How will you recognise these?

5 TUNE THE LANDSCAPE

The policy-maker may be able to 'tune' the policy landscape and the struggle or race that unfolds, so as to re-shape the patterns of self-organisation that develop. This obliges the policy-maker to make political and normative judgements, deciding what forms of self-organisation should be allowed to develop and for whose benefit.

Tuning may involve modifying the 'system parameters'. It may also mean changing the connections among its sub-systems. Thus for example, 'decomplexity' involves unpicking hierarchical connections and decentralising management responsibility, so as to encourage adaptability, innovation and dynamism (http://www.decomplexity.com/).

Tuning may mean coupling the policy landscape to new and external landscapes, for example, those of the EU or of global political and market institutions; or decoupling, as, for example, in the case of Scottish and Welsh devolution.

Tuning is, however, an imprecise art; the tools available give only modest leverage or traction on social dynamics. It is also unavoidably political; it involves not only anticipating patterns of human behaviour, but also promoting more enlightened discussion and understanding of the possible futures that can be chosen. The policy-maker must persuade his constituency that the landscape need not involve risky long-jumps of uncertain outcome: policy reform is necessary but it is also feasible.

Questions to ask

How might you tune the landscape, so as to set in motion particular runaway loops, particular patterns of self-organisation?

For the race or struggle that is underway, what trade-offs and conflicts are becoming apparent among policy goals and the value commitments that underpin them? These goals may be multiple, interrelated and with different time horizons. Who could benefit and who suffer from the outcome?

Which forms of tuning are available to you? What levers do you have to steer the race?

To what policy landscapes and communities might you re-couple your own? From which might you decouple?

How can you construct for your community a step-wise path to their betterment, capable of building their support without having to embrace risky leaps in the dark?

6 ENERGISE THE PROTAGONISTS

The policy-maker can build capacity and knowledge among the members of the organisation or community, so as to promote and channel their creativity. This could include policies concerned with education, innovation and the growth of knowledge. It could also include policies that expand opportunities for learning from neighbours and from past experience.

Nevertheless, human creativity can also have a dark side, producing new forms of domination, exploitation and conflict. Energising the protagonists does not therefore release the policy-maker from fundamental choices as to the sort of society that should be fostered.

The policy-maker can also build resilience for times of stress and turbulence. This means widening and diversifying capacities and strengths and the skills required to address and adapt to new challenges.

Questions to ask

How can you help those within your organisation or community to develop their creativity and enterprise? How can you help them draw on external expertise?

In energising them, what undesirable forms of social organisation and outcome do you risk promoting?

How can your organisation or community build its strength and readiness, with distinctive competencies but also diversity, so as to remain agile and adaptable?

7   CIVILISE THE STRUGGLE

Policy-makers are umpires and stewards within their communities or organisation, civilising the struggle for positional advantage.

The policy-maker faces a double challenge. The diverse projects championed by the various protagonists may be so intense as to challenge the stability of the community, bringing war and chaos. The policy-maker must decide what limits to place on the struggle, so that it does not get out of hand. On the other hand, there may be an institutional log-jam of collusive vetoes. Here the policy-maker must re-energise the protagonists, build a constituency for reform and undermine the constituency opposed to change.

This is civility, between stasis and chaos. It involves the policy-maker in negotiating forms of cooperation and community customised to local circumstances, monitored by the participants but also underpinned by the public authorities (Ostrom, 1990). It shapes the terms on which different communities are empowered and self-organise. It gives plausibility to the hopes of some (but also perhaps to the fears of others). In some degree at least, it builds common institutions that unite, as against the barriers that divide (Marris, 1974; Obama, 2008: Part 2).

Questions to ask

How can the struggle for positional advantage within your organisation be civilised, so as to avoid both stasis and chaos?

How may a shared moral community be negotiated, with rights and entitlements respected by all stakeholders but underpinned by government authority?

8   WATCH FOR PREDATORS

The policy terrain with which a policy-maker deals is rarely an isolated one. As it abrades against others, the policy-maker may be forced to dance to their rhythms.

Policy-makers may operate at different tiers of government: local and regional, national and international. They compete and cooperate with policy-makers from other domains and jurisdictions. This may involve the adoption of shared 'technologies' of policy intervention, not necessarily attuned to the local peculiarities of the policy-maker's own community.

At each of these levels there is a multitude of other economic and social actors seeking to shape public policy for their own interests. Policy-makers may reach out, as protagonists and entrepreneurs for their communities, seeking to promote their well-being and opportunities; they are also, however, at risk of exposing them to predation.

Questions to ask

Across what other policy tiers and terrains are you active? How far do developments there constrain and dictate your own?

In what forms of cooperation and competition across policy terrains are you involved? How far do shared systems of policy governance limit your ability to deal with local particularities?

With which economic and social actors do you engage in order to promote well-being and opportunities for your community? What are the risks of predation?

How far can you outflank, trap or control these predators?

Four Examples

Example one: choice, equity and polarisation in education
Chapter 15 (Section 15.2) was concerned with policies for expanding educational opportunities. In the UK competition among schools has been increased, in the hope of driving up standards, and parents have been given greater choice of school. We saw, however, that this can encourage 'competitive assortative mating' by schools and middle class parents and produce social class polarisation.

1.   Map the landscape   We used qualitative systems dynamics to map the quasi-market of secondary education (Figure 15.1). This revealed the strong potential for self-reinforcing 'runaway loops' of school pupil selection. It also helped identify the points where action might be taken to dampen down – or indeed to accelerate – these loops. These included the rights of parents to exercise free choice of school; the scope for schools to select pupils by methods which maximise middle class intake; the publicity which policy-makers give to the performances of different schools; and the extent to which school budgets take account of the numbers of pupils from disadvantaged backgrounds.

2.   Identify the protagonists   The protagonists are readily identified: the parents and the schools. Parents seek schools with a good reputation; schools seek pupils likely to enhance that reputation. Nevertheless, it was also evident that this cast of actors was also in some degree 'emergent' from the educational quasi-market that policy-makers had created. Small movements in school reputations can induce 'flocking' by agile middle class parents which reinforce those movements and allow some schools to emerge as middle class territory. The result can be higher levels of insecurity for all.

3.   Model the struggle   We used mathematical and computational models to examine the dynamics of 'competitive assortative mating': the self-reinforcing spirals that are likely to be set in motion, the stability of the distribution of social classes across schools, the consequences of exogenous shocks. We modelled school admission policies and parental preferences; and the conditions under which these would produce stronger or weaker degrees of polarisation. The dynamics these models revealed were consistent with the stylised facts; nevertheless, we could have drawn on a wider range of models; and our efforts at empirical validation were only preliminary.

4.   Watch for tipping points   Policy-makers face the task of expanding opportunities, raising school performance and promoting social cohesion. It is not self-evident what mix of these goals – and in what form – quasi-markets will tend to produce in different local circumstances. It is necessary to watch out for critical junctures and tipping points, and to intervene appropriately, so as to limit the degree of social class polarisation that develops. It was in this context that we discussed the EU social inclusion indicators. We recommended that these should include indicators of the extent of social class segregation between schools, as exacerbating social class differences in educational attainment. This could be used not just for reviewing national performance *ex post*, but also for timely monitoring of educational policies at national and indeed local level, subject to appropriate data systems being made available.

5.   *Tune the landscape*   We took as the underlying 'system parameters' the admission policies of schools ('class-blind' or otherwise) and the 'tolerance' thresholds of parents. The former may be amenable to 'tuning'; the latter may not be immutable, but are likely to depend on complex currents of popular opinion and specific local circumstances and traditions. We also however noticed that the introduction of a quasi-market had involved substantial change in the 'connective geometry' of the educational system: previously the various sub-systems had operated in some degree separately from each other. These connections are a matter of public policy: the 'runaway loops' are not inevitable and could be modified, to produce a different trade-off among policy goals.

6.   *Energise the protagonists*   We saw that some protagonists are already highly energetic. Middle class parents tend to be more skilful in discovering which schools are high performers and what 'inside tracks' to entry may be available. Policy-makers give publicity to schemes that are intended to raise working class aspirations; but the constraints that face children from such families mean that low aspirations are in many ways entirely rational.

7.   *Civilise the struggle*   Educational policy-makers are faced with competing champions for different social goals: choice versus equity, competitive improvement versus community solidarity and resilience. To establish a quasi-market is not enough: policy-makers must keep track of the lines of inequality and division that develop among both schools and pupils, modifying policies as appropriate, so as to secure the social well-being and self-development of all. Instead of being a merely reactive umpire or steward, the policy-maker must actively nurture civility.

8.   *Watch for predators*   Any head teacher who succeeds in raising the performance of his or her school makes it a target for agile middle class parents. The temptation is to welcome their attentions, even at the cost of disregarding the school's traditional catchment, leaving them to do the best they can with lower performing schools. Only if public policies tilt the educational system against these pressures is it likely that head teachers and school governors will be able to resist them.

Example two: lone parents and their family-work projects
Chapter 15 (Section 15.3) was concerned with policies in the UK for improving the circumstances of lone parents and their families, notably by moving them from dependence on social benefits into employment. We saw, however, that this involves them in managing a complex institutional 'eco-system'. Many live a

precarious and over-stretched existence, with little 'slack' for risk-taking in search of larger opportunities for their 'family-work' projects.

1. Map the landscape   The landscape the policy-maker faces is the institutional 'eco-system' in which lone parent households develop their 'family-work' projects. This can be mapped in terms of the institutional connections in which each lone mother is enmeshed and the entitlements and obligations these involve. These institutional connections include, on the one hand, the extended family and the friendship and neighbourhood contacts that provide a 'hinterland' of pre-existing affiliations; on the other hand, the public bureaucracies and private corporations she faces. It also, third, includes the 'family-work' projects of more advantaged households, who bestride a larger world, and may wittingly or otherwise force cascades of institutional change upon her, plunging her into a struggle for survival with little escape.

2. Identify the protagonists   The protagonists are the mothers themselves, their children and their network interlocutors. We saw that with the move from welfare to employment, mothers must juggle more complex arrangements for child-care, but in a situation of greater uncertainty as to their incomes and prospects. Employment income helps, but mothers who lack strong informal support cannot take full advantage of the new opportunities that the reforms offer, so as to build their capacities and improve their future employment prospects. Instead they must concentrate on building defensive resilience and 'keeping the show on the road'.

3. Model the struggle   Like any social actor, these mothers may be thought of as seeking to maintain some balance in their institutional entitlements and oblig-ations: avoiding critical thresholds, re-scheduling obligations, mobilising entitle-ments so as to take advantage of new opportunities. We may model the imbalances that mothers face, the corrective actions they take and the larger dynamics that their actions set in motion. Some of the dynamic models we reviewed in Chapter 11 may then be useful. Ludwig and Abell (2007) provided one such, where networks are faced with a regular stream of changes that produce structural imbalance, which if above a certain threshold led to connections being discarded. This invites us to identify the imbalances that families typically encounter and the types of 'discard' in which they then engage.

4. Watch for tipping points   Policy-makers aim to expand opportunities and improve the circumstances of lone parents and their families. This may set them on virtuous 'runaway loops' of greater job security and promotion: virtuous tipping points. There is always, however, the risk that taking a given job will close off other opportunities for job search or re-training and lock the mother concerned into a long-term sub-optimal trajectory. The extent to which lone mothers are able to take up these opportunities depends on their institutional eco-systems; policy-makers must be able to adjust policies to take account of these local heterogenei-ties. It was in this context that we discussed the EU social inclusion indicators and their national and local counterparts. These remain concerned principally with household resources, hardly with institutional eco-systems. We recommended that they should include timely indicators of social relations and the risks of their erosion; of shared resources and services within communities; of the robustness and resilience of social supports.

5. *Tune the landscape*   The 'New Deal' for lone parents re-worked the institutional connections between welfare and work. As we have seen, this has in many cases meant improved outcomes for the families in question; however, the extent to which this is the case has depended on the agility with which these mothers have been able to re-weave these new connections into their own institutional hinterland. Many live a precarious existence and are easily incorporated on adverse terms into the landscapes and 'family-work projects' of others.

6. *Energise the protagonists*   The UK policies of 'welfare to work' aim to energise lone mothers in relation to employment: providing them with incentives but also with advice and institutional supports to this transition. Nevertheless, what is also crucial is the network of informal support on which the mothers concerned can call: these are protagonists whom such policies largely neglect. Larger policies of support, reinvigorating community services and networks, may well be of significance here.

7. *Civilise the struggle*   Public policies may aim at opening socio-economic opportunities, but social groups differ in their scope for exploiting them. This depends in part on the resilience of the informal solidarities on which they can draw. Policies must themselves be capable of evolving, to take account of these heterogeneities. This is what it means to civilise the struggle: ensuring that the social well-being and self-development of different social groups and communities does not depend on existing differentials of advantage.

8. *Watch for predators*   Even as they move back to work, lone mothers remain vulnerable and may have to content themselves with subordinate and insecure positions in the labour market. As such, they share with other groups of marginal workers the risk of exploitation and poor treatment by employers, especially at times of labour market insecurity and recession. Public policies to ensure minimum working and employment conditions are just as important as policies to move lone mothers back to employment: in hard economic times the prospect for such protections seems bleak.

Example three: social dynamics of the knowledge economy
Chapter 16 was concerned with European policies to promote competitive and dynamic knowledge economies that are socially cohesive. The Lisbon process and the Open Method of Coordination (OMC) established policy indicators by reference to which national progress can be compared, leaders and laggards identified and cross-national policy learning encouraged. We saw, however, that these

indicators were hardly predicated on a well-grounded understanding of the processes of socio-economic change that are underway.

1. Map the landscape The knowledge economy involves a new connective
geometry – new technologies, new forms of organisation, new networks of communication. In large measure and to an increasing extent, it is a global geometry.
Nevertheless, this does not make for a flat landscape. The abrasion of the new
global geometry against national and local connections is likely instead to produce
turbulence. It involves the development of a global 'eco-system' within which
national, local and transnational communities, multinational enterprises and
many other protagonists jostle for a niche and make their own choices and trade-
offs. This landscape cannot be depicted as one across which leaders and laggards
make a uniform journey, albeit at different speeds. Policy indicators deployed and
applied on this assumption serve only to shroud the landscape in uncertainty.

2. Identify the protagonists The protagonists include the European and national
policy-makers who seek tools with which to steer social and economic development; the entrepreneurs and businesses whose knowledge-based innovations they
seek to support; the casualties of rapid socio-economic change with whom they
aim to maintain social cohesion; the wider public, unsure about the risks and costs
of change. The policy indicators selected were intended to serve their respective
needs and contribute to innovation, policy learning and public accountability. The
intent was sound; the achievement however has been paltry.

3. Model the struggle We understand the knowledge economy in terms of the
positional dynamics of 'deepen-widen-warp' presented in this book. This cannot
be captured in a simple model solved mathematically or computationally. It
can, however, be visualised as a monotonic ascent across a moderately rugged
landscape, with entrepreneurs re-weaving and deepening the local connective
geometry, these novelties then variously widening across the larger population and
warping the larger geometry. The policy indicators of the OMC, suitably revised,
could in principle track these processes, as Chapter 16 demonstrated.

4. Watch for tipping points Policy-makers face the task of promoting and
steering the European knowledge economy. This presupposes real time information, to establish the state we are in, the trajectories along which we are moving,
the choices and trade-offs that will face us, the thresholds and tipping points of
virtuous and vicious change where policy-makers can usefully intervene. It was
with reference to these tasks that the indicators we reviewed have been included in
the OMC. However, the policy indicators and statistics that are available are still
in considerable degree geared to national industrial economies, not yet to global
knowledge economies.

5. Tune the landscape The key policy question for Lisbon is how to 'melt' the
frozen socio-economic structures of the EU member states into more agile and

adaptable forms. The Lisbon process connects countries in new ways and encourages comparison and learning. With the institutional practices of their neighbours more visible, national policy-makers may be able to re-weave these with the institutional *bricolage* of their own past and give them new resonance. Even in the supposedly frozen wastes of the Bismarckian welfare systems, melting is proceeding apace and may produce more dramatic cascades of reconfiguration (Palier and Martin, 2008).

6. Energise the protagonists Enterprises and national policy-makers require appropriate institutional channels for tapping into global best practice. We may think of the OMC of the Lisbon process as aiming to provide a public policy-led European innovation system: energising, organising, building competence. Nevertheless, innovation systems are systems of 'distributed knowledge'. There are few if any 'best practices' that are universally applicable; they must be understood in relation to specific contexts and circumstances. Cross-national learning must involve local and national actors drawing lessons appropriate to their own circumstances, from the pool of collectively calibrated experience that the Lisbon process furnishes.

7. Civilise the struggle It was always recognised that the drive for knowledge economies would bring turbulence and disruption. This places the policy-maker in the role of umpire or steward, civilising the struggle. From the start, therefore, the Lisbon process was meant to embrace a much wider range of actors and involve them in the social and economic transformations in prospect: enterprises and business associations but also labour organisations, the 'third sector' and citizens in general. Benchmarking would involve not only accountability 'upwards', but also transparency 'sideways' to enable cross-national learning between economic and social practitioners and accountability 'downwards' to the public in general. It would build the civility of a shared community and ensure social cohesion and social progress, not just economic. That at least was the stated intention, even if its realisation has been limited (Room, 2007).

8. Watch for predators The knowledge economy is global. European policy-makers therefore engage with their international counterparts, reaching for new opportunities and resources for European businesses and communities. Whatever the civility inside Europe, this global arena is somewhat anarchic. European well-being will depend in part on efforts to civilise the global commons, including the development of an appropriate global regime of public statistics and indicators. The challenge for the EU is to construct an international order which is transparent, rule-governed and accountable (Room, 2005a: Ch. 10)

Example four: global turbulence and crisis
Chapter 17 was concerned with national and international policies to address the global financial crisis and the ensuing recession. Policy-makers intervened to prevent collapse of the banking system and the cascade of destruction that

has swept across the real economy. We saw, however, that the costs have been enormous; they have fallen on the larger public and have brutally assaulted any collective sense of security.

1. Map the landscape The connective geometry of the financial system is global. Local stresses are readily transmitted across the system as a whole and have cascaded into the real economy, where there has been 'creative destruction' on a massive scale. Nevertheless, the landscape is not uniform. There are 'varieties of finance capitalism', with different countries experiencing the financial crisis through the prism of their own distinctive banking and regulatory institutions. The consequences for real economies have been correspondingly varied. Chapter 17 reviewed the now extensive literature that maps the detail of this landscape and the connections through which the credit crunch percolated globally.

2. Identify the protagonists The protagonists include national policy-makers, facing the collapse of the banking system and the costs for the real economy; financiers and their asymmetric risk-taking; businesses and the wider public, coping with the recession and the credit famine. It has been the financiers who have been the first movers, the change takers to whom all the other protagonists have had to respond. It has been their 'animal spirits', their pursuit of financial advantage, their design of new financial products and services that has made for a new and turbulent landscape. It is they who have now buffered themselves against turbulence, whatever the costs for others.

3. Model the struggle Modern financial markets have proved highly volatile. It is more appropriate to model them in terms of the 'flocking' or 'herding' behaviour discussed in earlier chapters, rather than neoclassical 'rational expectations'. We may also model the crisis in terms of the positional dynamics of 'deepen-widen-warp' presented in this book. This can be visualised as a monotonic ascent across a moderately rugged landscape, with financial entrepreneurs crafting new financial products and services, these novelties then percolating across the wider financial system and warping the economy at large. Within this positional dynamic, the race for perennial novelty or 'deepening' brings customers and profits, enforces new forms of domination, evades regulation, offloads uncertainty and secures future leverage in financial markets.

4. Watch for tipping points The regulators charged with overseeing the system of national and international finance have found themselves with inadequate and antiquated tools. Complex processes of change left them floundering, with outdated indicators of dangerous tipping points, inadequate capacity to act and an insufficiently well-defined view of the choices and trade-offs involved. As tipping points, commentators point to the US interest rate increases of 2004–06, the associated downturn in house prices, the resulting defaults and the sub-prime crisis; all then triggering wider financial disorder and eventually the larger crisis in the real economy (Krugman, 2008; Peston, 2008b; Cable, 2009; Skidelsky, 2009).

5.   *Tune the landscape*   The global financial crisis put in question the resilience of national and international institutions, in face of financial turbulence, and the extent to which those institutions 'buffer' the real economy, limiting its exposure to 'tipping points' and cascades of wider destruction. The crisis attests to the high level of coupling between systems: global connections that make not for a flat and stable world but one of dynamic turbulence. The policy inference many have drawn is that these connections should be reduced, perhaps by separating 'retail' and 'investment' banks (Kay, 2009a). Alternatively or in addition, more buffers should be inserted, perhaps by means of a 'Tobin tax' on international financial transactions. These would involve major changes in the overall governance of the financial system.

6.   *Energise the protagonists*   There would seem little need to energise the financial innovators and entrepreneurs whose risk-taking produced the global crisis; quite the contrary. Instead there is a need to energise, organise and build competence in the regulatory systems.

7.   *Civilise the struggle*   The international financial system is part of the 'commons' of the contemporary world. The global crisis brought turbulence, disruption and the destruction of the commons. This places the policy-maker in the role of umpire or steward, seeking to civilise the struggle between financial entrepreneurs and the wider community. We followed Ostrom (1990: Ch. 3) in arguing that the financial commons must be organised as a moral community, with rights and entitlements respected by all stakeholders and underpinned by international governmental authority. We drew on a wide range of critical commentators on the financial crisis, including Galbraith and Kay.

8.   *Watch for predators*   Recent decades have seen financial predation on the major institutions of society – corporations, banks, housing finance, education and health, pensions – for purposes of private gain at public expense. This entrepreneurship has produced a new class of oligarchs devoted to rapacious looting. This tends to demoralise ordinary businesses, just as it distorts the social goals of public institutions, to the detriment of the mass of ordinary households. The global economic crisis is the culmination of this process. This is slash and burn and the tragedy of the commons, whose costs then fall on the public purse and those least able to bear them.

Notes

CHAPTER 1

1. Throughout this book I use the term 'policy-maker' to mean public policy-makers. I use other terms, for example, 'business leader' elsewhere.
2. Of course, even 'first movers' typically make their moves only in response to a perceived opportunity or threat.

CHAPTER 2

1. There is a range of good texts for the general reader – and for the social scientist approaching these matters for the first time – which can be consulted for elaboration of the exposition offered here (Waldrop, 1992; Buchanan, 2000; Johnson, 2001; Ball, 2004). The paradigm is admittedly somewhat inchoate, even among the Sante Fé community (Cowan, 1994), as perhaps befits any lively and novel enterprise; nevertheless the elements highlighted here would probably command general assent. A more comprehensive review might also have included some discussion of 'autopoeisis' as elaborated by Maturana and Luhmann, for example, or some of the 'softer' strands of complexity writing in cultural studies: see, for example, Cilliers (1998).
2. This should be distinguished from internal economies of scale associated with large-scale production, allowing enterprises to produce at lower unit cost, as their fixed costs are spread across a larger volume of output.
3. Myrdal's original use of this term (Myrdal, 1944) was by reference to the dynamics of urban disadvantage faced by African-Americans: the self-reinforcing process of social exclusion with which this book began. Young was heavily influenced by Veblen: see, for example, Veblen (1898).
4. Arguments for punctuated equilibria are sometimes seen as being in tension with Darwin's own account of evolution, seen as stressing continuous and incremental change. Nevertheless, Darwin was also concerned to emphasise that in the 'struggle for existence', even in the long run the forces may be 'so nicely balanced, that the face of nature remains uniform for long periods of time', although a mere trifle may then give 'victory to one organic being over another' (Darwin, 1859: 58).
5. Darwin (1859: Ch. 2) argues at some length that the distinctions between a variation, a sub-species, a species and a genus are somewhat arbitrary: all develop from the same underlying evolutionary dynamics.

CHAPTER 3

1. This process of mutation and recombination can be modelled in terms of a genetic algorithm. Genetic algorithms are widely used and they provide a major point of reference for computational modelling, not only by those interested in the modelling of biological evolution and other complex natural and social phenomena, but also

those seeking to develop computer software embodying simple iterative searches for best solutions (Mitchell, 1996). Actual biological processes of point mutation and cross-over are, however, much more complex than those used in genetic algorithms; and the version of the latter that we adopt here is only very simple. It is, however, sufficient as the starting point for our own analytical approach to complex adaptive systems.

2. Recent exponents of fitness landscapes include Kauffman (1993, 1995a) and Gavrilets (2004). The origins of the metaphor are to be found in R.A. Fisher (1930) and Sewall Wright (1932).

3. For a computational implementation and assessment of Kauffman's models, see Vidgen and Padget (2009).

4. Darwin himself was of course writing before the development of genetics. Nevertheless, in his examination of 'correlation of growth' he offers a parallel account of the way in which, during the course of evolution, variations in one aspect of an organism produce variations in other aspects (Darwin, 1859: Ch. 5).

5. Darwin (1859) likewise insists that variations and adaptations are short-range: as he declares repeatedly, *Natura non facit saltum* – nature makes no leaps.

6. Kauffman finds that landscapes are characterised by such *Massifs Centrals* when N is very large relative to K (Kauffman, 1993: 60–3, 114–15).

7. For example, mammalian cells (and indeed all eukaryotic cells – cells with nuclei) at an early stage of evolution incorporated elements of the DNA of bacteria and viruses; these perform crucial functions in various tracts of the host's body (Kauffman, 1995a: 215–16). On the major evolutionary transitions, with more complex organisms evolving in what is normally an irreversible process, see Maynard Smith and Szathmáry (1995).

8. In the NK(C) model Kauffman introduces not only C but also S, the number of such species (Kauffman, 1993: 262). However, the introduction of S does not greatly affect the main argument here and it is therefore ignored for our present purposes.

9. Kauffman reserves the designation of Red Queen to an extreme version of such arms races, where those involved are 'forever doomed by their own best efforts to . . . deform . . . their own landscapes' (Kauffman, 1995a: 223). However, some evolutionary biologists would use the term somewhat more generally, to mean evolutionary change that is continuous due to antagonistic feedbacks between two co-evolving partners.

10. 'A population is said to be in an evolutionarily stable state if its genetic composition is restored by selection after a disturbance, provided the disturbance is not too large' (Maynard Smith, 1982: 204). This corresponds to a Nash Equilibrium in game theory.

11. Bak, we might add, is critical of both the phrase and the argument: he prefers his own notion of 'self-organised criticality', as discussed in the previous chapter (Bak, 1997: Chs 7–8).

12. This is not unlike the notion of 'structural deepening' elaborated by Arthur (1994b).

13. This conversion of peaks into saddles was recognised by Fisher, whom Gavrilets (2004: 36–7) however criticises, for suggesting that the new ascents thus made available would enable a population to move towards a single global fitness peak. Whether such a global peak exists is of course a quite separate matter. Nevertheless, having criticised Fisher on the question of a global peak, Gavrilets does not himself pursue the implications of successive monotonic ascents, as new dimensions of genotypic space open up.

14. This is no coincidence. It seems that it is these deep-seated structures that drive ontogeny, that is, the successive developmental stages of individual organisms. More particularly, they play a key role quite early in the development of an organism (the 'phylotypic' stage), in activating particular gene sequences at key stages. This produces similarities between immature organisms across different species, even if subsequent developments then hide these similarities (Maynard Smith, 1998: 15). As Maynard Smith argues, random mutations in such deep-seated processes would pose major risks to evolutionary survival.

15. This can be seen as a version of the 'minority game' we encountered in Chapter 2.

16. Like Kauffman, Gavrilets (2004: Ch. 4) conceives of fitness landscapes in rather static terms, instead of adopting the relativistic and dynamic perspective on landscape construction advocated here. Nevertheless, his mathematically more rigorous analysis in terms of 'neutral networks' and 'holey fitness landscapes' is not without interest for our own discussion of speciation and 'widening' and 'perilous paths'.

17. Surtsey is a volcanic island that appeared off the southwest coast of Iceland in November 1963 and that then, over several years, suffered a succession of changes in height and extent, as a result, on the one hand, of a series of new eruptions, on the other, of settlement of the volcanic material and general erosion. It is now a United Nations Educational, Scientific and Cultural Organisation (UNESCO) world heritage centre and a scientific preserve for the study of newly developing eco-systems. For an eye witness account of some of the eruptions, see Tilman (1987).

18. The 'holey network landscape' that Gavrilets presents may provide a static map of the pathways that are possible: however, which of these actually emerge depends on a race against time. His map is timeless, as are the connections it displays.

19. Nevertheless, under some circumstances niche construction may become exhausted as a means of buffering environmental selection pressures; beyond some critical threshold – and thus with time lags – such buffers may fail and cascades of dramatic genetic reconfiguration may be unleashed, affecting other species in the eco-system no less dramatically (Odling-Smee et al., 2003: para. 7.3.3).

20. This is a system of distributed information of course, in the sense discussed in the previous chapter: a system that takes particular local expressions but whose value resides in the ensemble as a whole.

21. We should nevertheless recognise, again following Noble, that DNA itself provides no more than a database: it is a 'nonsense . . . until it is interpreted functionally . . . by the cell-protein machinery [of the organism] . . . and by the system-level interaction between proteins' (Noble, 2006: 21).

22. It is for this reason – as much as the relatively slow pace of many evolutionary processes – that we are entitled for the purposes of the present study to ignore the biology of human evolution.

CHAPTER 4

1. Other scholars in evolutionary economics on whom Potts draws include Hodgson (2004), Loasby (1999), Metcalfe (1998), Metcalfe and Foster (2004), Nelson and Winter (1982) and Witt (2003). See also the essays collected together in Nelson (2005). For a more popular treatment, see Beinhocker (2007).

2. Kaldor (1985: 61–2) likewise contrasts neoclassical notions of equilibrium, which assume that exogenous variables, stable over time, constrain the operation of economic forces, and the recognition that 'the only truly exogenous factor is . . . the heritage of the past'.

3. Pollan (2006: Ch. 5) captures this combinatorial ontology vividly in relation to the modern industrial food chain, where plants and animals are broken down into their component parts and then recombined and re-assembled into new food products with high 'added value', in commercial if not nutritional terms. Various writers on the financial collapse of 2008 describe 'securitisation' in similar terms: see, for example, Skidelsky (2009: Ch. 1).

4. Similarly Potts examines the family – and policies to support the family – by reference to the decomposibility of the complex set of connections between the family and other social systems. This is an approach on which we shall build in Chapter 15 of this book.

5. Others who have sought to apply Kauffman's landscape models to populations of enterprises include Frenken (2006), McKelvey (1999), Stewart (2001) and indeed Kauffman himself (Kauffman, 1995b).

6. Recall our discussion in Chapter 1 of the dynamic relationship between first and last movers. The first mover makes a novel but fateful choice (Ebbinghaus's 'road juncture'); this choice, if it proves a winner, gives the instigator a positional advantage to which others then aspire. The more 'last movers' make this walk, the more it becomes Ebbinghaus's 'well-trodden path', the taken for granted low cost option for everyone. Widespread use may dissipate the positional advantage that the first mover temporarily enjoyed, although this may for a time be prolonged by restraints on entry (through patent laws, for example), allowing the first mover to extract rent. However, 'second movers', instead of imitating, may instead seek to differentiate their 'product', establishing a niche of their own.

7. Dopfer and Potts applaud the efforts of such predecessors as Marshall, Schumpeter, Penrose, Nelson and Winter, in revealing the meso dynamics of innovation in relation to particular industries and technologies. However, they question whether this work gives sufficient insight into the macro-dynamics of co-evolutionary structural change and regime transition (Dopfer and Potts, 2008: para. 6.3).

8. This view that the growth of knowledge drives change is common among evolutionary economists (for example, Loasby, 1999). For Potts such knowledge refers in particular to the growth of 'connections' (Potts, 2000, 2001, 2003). Among the most significant of these connections are those that provide actors with diverse technological and institutional templates to enhance their own creativity. It is in these terms that much of the research literature on national and international innovation systems has developed.

9. There is larger literature applying complexity perspectives to organisational development: see, for example, Morel and Ramanujam (1999) and Meyer et al. (2005).

CHAPTER 5

1. There are, in short, two ways of analysing situations where the outcomes of actions are interdependent. One is in terms of an 'oligopolistic' game, with a small number of actors, the other is in terms of the dynamics of increasing returns, as in self-organising systems. These are of course the two main alternatives which mainstream economics identifies to the perfect competition on which much mainstream economic analysis of equilibrium depends.

CHAPTER 6

1. For an overview of the literature on such cross-national policy learning, using an institutionalist perspective, see Dwyer and Ellison (2009).

2. We add – although this is not something that Crouch himself stresses – that these hybrids are typically forged to meet local circumstances, even if subsequently they are extended across a broader terrain. This contrasts with the readiness of many authors, not just within the 'varieties of capitalism' literature but also those we cited in Chapter 5, in our discussion of institutional diversity, to treat institutional contrasts without regard to these local-global dynamics.

3. Among institutionalist writers Crouch is not alone in this approach. There are, for example, significant parallels between Crouch's account of institutional 'recombinance' and Ostrom's account of institutional reconfiguration and self-organisation (Crouch, 2005: Ch. 8). The same goes for Aoki's game-theoretic account of institutional change and novelty in terms of institutional 'unbundling' and 're-bundling' (Aoki, 2001: Ch. 10). More generally, there are resonances with the larger literature on governance: see, for example, various of the essays in Barnes and Prior (2009).

4. Similar treatments of the role of such mental models can be found in Ostrom (2005:

104–9) and Aoki (2001: 239), who like Potts explicitly links this to Holland (1995). See also Breakwell (2001) and Barnett and Breakwell (2003). Crouch and Potts leave somewhat unclear, however, what limits there may be on the range of such models. Contrast Weber's discussion of the directions and limits of exploitability and adaptation of different ideological (in his case primarily religious) heritages (Weber, 1965). See also Ostrom (2005: 104–9) on the role of symbols in stabilising shared mental models.

5. Potts's treatment, involving progressive refinement of the schematic preferences, may in part reflect the aim of advancing this evolutionary micro-economics through computational simulation. Crouch in contrast, as we saw in Chapter 1, models actors' choices through a series of elaborations of the Polya urn.

6. Obama (2008: Part 2) is as nice an account as any.

7. The interpretation and application of these modes offered here diverges somewhat from that in Thelen's own most recent work (Mahoney and Thelen, 2010: Ch. 1). This is not necessarily a cause for concern; we are adapting her ideas and combining them with others in order to serve our own analytical purposes, which do not necessarily coincide with those which she and her most recent collaborators have set themselves.

8. In relation to poverty and social exclusion, there is a long tradition of action-research 'experiments' that may be construed as 'layering': testing not only the effectiveness of novel interventions but also the institutional malleability of the status quo and the scope for building a 'constituency for reform' (Marris, 1974). Institutional innovation can also involve applying established precedents in new ways, most obviously in quasi-legal situations. We referred in the previous chapter to the efforts of the European Commission to apply Community law and majority decision-making in such a way as to extend its mandate; such institutional entrepreneurship has been a key driver of European integration (Leibfried and Pierson, 1995). Similarly, the US government in 2009 sought to extend federal control of greenhouse gas emissions by invoking the powers of the Environmental Protection Agency. Such innovations can set a larger avalanche of institutional changes in motion, switching the further development of public policy along a new trajectory.

9. These contiguities between layering and displacement are evidenced by Thelen having initially included some elements of displacement (notably the use of elements borrowed from the past) within her discussion of layering (Thelen, 2003). Nevertheless, on the 'subtle but important' distinction she subsequently draws, see Streek and Thelen (2005: 35, fn. 20).

10. We notice once again that innovation typically starts small-scale, before possibly being taken upon on a larger scale by the population at large. The risks of novelty can thereby be kept at a manageable level. This was why Kauffman's models gave priority to step-wise short range adaptive journeys and why, as Darwin insisted, *Natura non facit saltum* – nature makes no leaps. This makes an evolutionary ontology a rather special type of combinatorial ontology, with differential population dynamics selecting certain combinations over others. It is because Crouch's focus is on the novel combinations that entrepreneurs forge – and not on the differential population dynamics that then select among these combinations – that he is not included in Table 6.1.

11. Some of the forms of institutional change identified by Pierson also appear in Ostrom's study, discussed in the previous chapter. In her account of the development of ground water regimes in California, Ostrom (1990) highlights the role of diffusion, as voluntary associations shared information between different polities and borrowed models of cooperative governance which associations in neighbouring communities had trail-blazed (pp. 137–9). Local initiatives of this sort were, moreover, uploaded into state-wide legislation, once their credibility at the micro-level had been established and publicised. Generalisation of a particular set of local agreements can however mean that local specificities are overlooked. Thus, for example, in her discussion of institutional failures and fragilities, Ostrom points (Ch. 4) to the fisheries of Nova Scotia, where a single fisheries policy for the whole of the Canadian east coast, embracing both

deep-sea and inland fishing, failed to respond to the specific needs and circumstances of the latter, and unwittingly undermined local efforts at negotiated cooperation.

12. Even if it has focused on recent scholarship in historical institutionalism, our account has a much wider resonance. This includes, for example, Weber's treatment of the role of religious ideas in particular: from 'charisma' as a source of novel ideas (deepening) to the 'routinisation of charisma', as it widens across the population, and the consequences that then follow for economic activity, as religious ideas abrade against the secular sphere (Weber, 1965: not least, see the introduction by Talcott Parsons, which brings out this evolutionary perspective).

CHAPTER 7

1. The term 'adverse incorporation' I borrow from my colleague Geoff Wood (2003).
2. Potts provides a generic if rather abstract account of all these possible forms of co-evolution: not only between social rules (institutions) and technical rules (technologies) but also between subject rules (rules for interaction between agents) and object rules (rules for organising things and people) (Dopfer and Potts, 2008: Ch. 1).
3. The detailed architecture of European and global governance depends crucially upon the specific historical junctures through which this institutional capacity is built (Fligstein, 2005). See, for example, the legacy of World War II for the development of the EU and of global financial institutions (Room, 2004); and the legacy of the 1990s global financial crisis and the scandals surrounding Enron for the development of international financial accounting standards in the early years of the new century (Porter, 2004). It remains to be seen what institutional legacy in global governance emerges from the current economic crisis: see Chapter 17.
4. It is sometimes the case that the fate of some technological novelty (the Sinclair C5 mini-car, for example) may discourage the wider population of entrepreneurs from going down the same path. This is unlikely, however, to lead to a broader public soul-searching about the whole thrust of entrepreneurial activity. On the other hand, the recent fate of risky practices in financial markets has in some degree produced precisely such public anguish: see Chapter 17.

CHAPTER 8

1. In physical systems that self-organise far from equilibrium, this maximisation of positional advantage and fitness have as their counterpart the maximisation of entropy production (Martyushev and Seleznev, 2006).
2. We are concerned with human agents in 'far from equilibrium' systems. Physicists and others have considered more generally what properties agents must have to drive systems far from equilibrium. This debate began in 1871 when the Scottish physicist Maxwell undertook a thought experiment. He conjectured that it might hypothetically be possible for a microscopic agent (a 'demon') to select, from among the particles of a gas, those that were heading in one direction rather than another and to separate them. This would allow the agent to drive the system far from equilibrium, so that it might, for example, be used to power a machine, which could then provide energy free of charge: something that contradicts the laws of thermodynamics. In Maxwell's thought experiment what prevents this is that the demon must itself employ energy, in order to undertake the selection process; in a closed system, there is no such energy source. Only an open system, where energy is drawn from outside, can be driven away from equilibrium (Ball, 2004: Ch. 3). Odling-Smee et al. (2003: 172ff.) draws on this debate in order to understand the processes of 'niche construction' in which he is himself interested.

The properties he identifies have close parallels with those we discuss here in relation to agile human agents.

3. As we saw in Chapter 5, with reference to Jones and Sergot (1996), this is most obvious in quasi-legal situations, where a given case may fall under a variety of possible provisions and procedures.

4. It may be objected that rational action theory in at least some of its forms is far from 'timeless'; 'rational expectations' theory, for example, is centrally concerned with future events. Nevertheless, the whole basis of rational expectations theory – as applied to financial markets in particular – is that the probabilities of those future events can be calculated and uncertainty (as distinct from risk) can in principle be disregarded (Skidelsky, 2009: Ch. 2). 'Nobody tries to shape pricing structures to their own ends, because the fact that everyone else also holds rational expectations means that such attempts will be fully anticipated and will therefore stand no chance of success' (Watson, 2007: 66).

5. This difference in ontology and focus goes wider than this of course. Thus, for example, debates over rational action and choice (including game theory) have given central attention to the conditions under which it may be rational for actors to cooperate or even to behave altruistically: see, for example, Axelrod (1984) and Ball (2004) Chs 17–18. For us, it is certainly important to understand the conditions under which cooperation develops, rather than competition or conflict. Nevertheless, once we move from rational choices on relatively stable terrains to agile choices on turbulent terrains, it is the positional struggle that moves centre-stage. Competition and cooperation, solidaristic as distinct from individualistic advance, domination and adverse incorporation are contingent expressions of that struggle and must be understood in relation to it.

6. Nevertheless, as we noted in Chapter 4, Potts in his more recent work, concerned with the creative industries, does bring institutions centre-stage, and in a manner that is consistent with our own treatment of institutions in Chapters 5–7 above. We make further use of his analysis of the creative industries in Chapters 16 and 17.

7. At various points we have pointed to Kaldor as an economist who anticipated many strands of our argument. We now further notice that Kaldor's account of technical progress closely matches our account here at the interface between two surfaces (Kaldor and Mirrlees, 1962; Kaldor, 1972). On the one hand, entrepreneurs 'learn by doing' as they invest in new machines, at the same time discarding or re-deploying more ancient vintages. This is innovation and adaptation in technological space. On the other hand, in pursuit of positional advantage entrepreneurs search for and seize new markets: markets for the new and superior products which these new technologies promise to meet; markets whose anticipation induces the investment in the first place. The first of these arguments rejects the neoclassical notion that technical progress descends like 'manna from heaven' across technology in general: it is instead the hard won fruit of embodied learning, hastening the obsolescence of earlier vintages. The second argument embraces Allyn Young's thesis that the scale of different markets drives the degree of specialisation in an economy and therefore the pace and direction of investment (Young, 1928; Kaldor, 1985: Part III). Both walks involve path dependency, discontinuous steps and threshold effects of the sort discussed in Section 8.2 of this chapter. Kaldor's 'technical progress function' depicts the results of this two-fold walk (albeit the investment that it captures is just that which the entrepreneur makes in new machines, ignoring the investment required for developing new markets).

8. Other species engage in farming (for example, there are ant colonies that farm fungi, including nurturing particular varieties), but only humans engage in deliberate hybridisation and selection with a view to obtaining improved varieties. This means of course that human beings and the flora and fauna they select themselves co-evolve: see, for example, Pollan, *The Botany of Desire* (2003).

9. Crouch and Potts leave it somewhat unclear what limits there may be on the variation of such models. Contrast Weber's discussion of the adaptability of different ideological (in his case primarily religious) heritages; and the typical direction in which religious

innovation tends in different heritages: inner- or other-worldliness, asceticism or mysti-
cism (Weber, 1965: Ch. XI). See also Ostrom (2005: 104–9) on the role of symbols in
stabilising shared mental models; and Denzau and North (1994) on the role of cultural
learning in such model sharing.

10.   To elaborate on just one of these: Gadamer depicts the reader as coming to a particular
work (for example, a text, a piece of music) with a set of distinctive prejudgements and
anticipations: these give this particular 'reading' its novelty. Through engaging with
the work, the reader checks and judges how far this particular reading 'works' – and
whether, indeed, it works 'better' than other readings. The reader goes on to check this
reading against the wider range of works by the author in question: this may expose
weaknesses in existing interpretations and readings; equally, however, it may reveal
that the new reading is flawed. The process of interpretation thus involves correction or
confirmation of earlier stages of the process.

     This is rarely a solitary activity by one reader; it will normally involve a conversa-
tion in a community. New readings will regularly appear, some being adopted by the
community but many rejected. This selection is however rarely of concern only to the
aficianados of the author in question. The author engaged in a range of wider debates;
so therefore must they. A new reading requires the re-assessment of those wider abrasions. These controversies may remain at the intellectual and aesthetic level, but they
may also have consequences in terms of institutional power and interests.

     This account of the hermeneutic process can, not least, be applied to Darwin
himself. The conventional picture is of a man who went to the Galapagos and came
back with a theory of evolution. However, his *Origin of Species* consists, in large
part, of a re-visiting of the extensive literature on species, their variations and their
adaptations, but now on the basis of Darwin's novel prejudgements and anticipations,
rooted both in his appreciation of husbandry and breeding (the arts of artificial selection) and his observation of the results of natural selection. The length of time that
he took in finalising the volume – brought to a head by the gentlemanly competition
with Wallace – was the result of his reluctance to publish until his arguments were
fully worked out by reference to that community of knowledge. But of course, once
the book had been published, it was exposed to a larger struggle for survival by reference to the intellectual and cultural controversies it stirred and the interests on which
it intruded.

11.   This orientation to the world, and to positional security within the uncertain dispensation of the future, was central to Weber's account of Occidental capitalism, in particular the 'inner-world asceticism' that emerged from Protestant Christianity (Weber,
1930). He contrasts this with the orientations to the world enjoined by the cosmologies
and soteriologies of other world religions (Weber, 1930; Weber, 1965: especially Chs
XI–XII).

12.   The distinction between 'material' and 'positional' goods was not original to Hirsch: it
appears, for example, in Keynes (1952), 'Economic Possibilities for our Grandchildren'
(albeit not using those precise terms).

13.   Neoclassical economics might lead us to expect that such oligopolies are rare, compared
with competitive markets. However, proponents of 'cumulative causation' and increasing returns such as Kaldor, discussed in Chapter 2, argue that under such conditions
oligopoly is the more likely market structure (Toner, 1999: Ch. 6).

14.   Michael Pollan (1991) provides an eloquent account of his own gardening, which perfectly expresses the relationship between humans and nature that Darwin depicted.
In his final chapter, he takes us on a walk up the path that ascends through his
garden. This is a path that weaves connections between one space and the next; that
from each such space affords us a novel and distinctive vantage point for viewing the
garden at large and the journey so far made; that creates tensions and twists between
the vistas thus juxtaposed, but then allows the walker to resolve them in a still larger
view; that tells a unique story about Pollan and his garden and his relationship with
his neighbours; that distinguishes this particular garden from convention, on the

one hand, the wilderness, on the other; but that always acknowledges and works with the topography and particularities of this piece of land, including the residues left by previous occupants. This is the best – if unwitting – parable I have found of the 'perilous path' which has been at the heart of our ontology. It also offers an ethical vision no less powerful than that other classic parable of a perilous journey, Bunyan's *Pilgrim's Progress*.

CHAPTER 9

1. Harré argues that such selection is integral to all scientific enquiry. Kaldor in his discussion of 'stylised facts' adds that in the social sciences, the aim must be to discover and explain empirical regularities pertaining to particular aspects of economy and society, rather than aspiring to the sorts of universal law that are the goal of the natural sciences.
2. This section draws heavily on Bertuglia and Vaio (2005), Chs 1–3 and Stewart (1997).
3. Notice that in the case of linear dynamics, we can either have continuing sensitivity to initial conditions but unbounded orbits (no attractor); or limited orbits (ordinary attractor) with insensitivity to initial conditions (no memory). Here, in the case of chaotic attractors, we have orbits that are limited by attractors but with continuing sensitivity to initial conditions (Bertuglia and Vaio, 2005: 133).
4. It might be objected that the Cantor function has fractal structure: we would therefore expect that if the analogy is well founded, the evolutionary timeline should reveal this fine structure of 'deepen-widen-warp' at all scales. This is, in a sense, what we find. Recall first that as Darwin himself repeatedly notes (1859: Ch. II), variation and selection continue at all scales – sub-species, species, sub-genera, genera and so on. Notice also that even below the level of the organism, we find similar processes driving cell diversification and specialisation (Arendt, 2008).
5. It is not of course only in the language of fractals and complex systems that we can describe such nested structures. In Chapter 8 we introduced Stackelberg's account of positional competition in a situation of 'asymmetric oligopoly', where there is one lead producer, to whom lesser rivals must adjust. With producers arrayed into several categories by size, Stackelberg depicts a nested structure to the resulting market.
6. This point has obvious affinities with Goodhart's law: see Goodhart (1975).

CHAPTER 10

1. Pierson notes that the current focus on short-term and immediate causes and effects was not always so: he cites the modernisation literature (Pierson, 2004: 98), and its collapse in face of the critique it faced in terms of functionalism and teleology.
2. Contrast the argument that in the UK the administrative capacity built for purposes of total war could then be deployed for the extensive intervention of the welfare state (Titmuss, 1963: Ch. 4).
3. This can be readily likened to the three zones of order, complexity and chaos that we have encountered at various points in the preceding chapters, depending on degrees of connectedness to wider societal dynamics.
4. None of this means that Kauffman leaves behind his interest in genetic endowments. On the contrary, he highlights the interface between this molecular chemistry of pattern formation and those genetic endowments as a crucial area of further research (Kauffman, 1993: 611ff.). These genetic endowments include in particular the deep and ancient genetic structures that we highlighted in our earlier discussion of Kauffman, as driving ontogeny by switching other genetic circuits in sequence.

5. Krugman offers a parallel – if mathematically more elaborate – application of Turing to socio-economic dynamics, in particular the development of urban structure or 'urban morphogenesis' (Krugman, 1996: Ch. 4, 1997).
6. There are strong parallels with Weber's discussion of religious communities and their boundaries: see Weber (1965: Ch. V).
7. Much of Arrighi's discussion is a debate, on the one hand, with Adam Smith, on the other, with a variety of neo-Marxists. The best bits – on which we draw here – are neither. We may nevertheless notice that for Arrighi, one of the central propositions made by Smith was that 'the widening and deepening of exchanges in the global economy would act as an equaliser of power between people of European and non-European descent' (Arrighi, 2007: 5). This seems to embody some notion of an underlying tendency towards equilibrium or balance. Contrast that with the position of John – as indeed of Charles – Darwin: there is no such tendency towards equilibrium, in biological or societal evolution; instead, it is an unending race against time, red in tooth and claw.
8. It may be worth pausing to consider the relationship of the foregoing to the account of economic development offered by economists such as Myrdal and Kaldor, who as we saw in Chapter 2 give central attention to external increasing returns and cumulative causation. Myrdal and Kaldor bring the domination of international markets centre-stage, rather than the supply or scarcity of factors of production; and it is this domination of markets that for them may be said to define positional advantage. The international political economy of John Darwin and Arrighi and the 'far from equilibrium' growth economics of Myrdal and Kaldor both highlight dynamic struggles for positional advantage and seek analytical methods by which these may be illuminated (Toner, 1999: paras 5.4.2, 6.2.4, 7.1).

CHAPTER 11

1. For general overviews of network analysis from the standpoint of social scientists, see Wasserman and Faust (1994), Scott (2000) and Carrington et al. (2005).
2. It would be more precise – if more wordy – to entitle this 'Graphs with random behaviour under specified constraints'.
3. The time frame used can also make a big difference: whether, for example, when studying social networks, we include all the contacts in which an individual has ever been involved, or only those within a certain recent time period (Bornholdt and Schuster, 2003: para. 2.1).
4. Much of the literature on directed networks to which we have referred – including Jain and Krishna – makes extensive use of computational modelling. Nevertheless, there is also a literature which develops the formal mathematics of directed networks and the non-linear dynamics associated with different network architectures. Thus, for example, Golubitsky and Stewart (2006) explore such dynamics by reference to a number of the themes of interest to the present study, including symmetry and synchrony in networks (see our discussion of time and space in Chapter 10) and the non-linear dynamics of networks (including periodic and chaotic attractors and the bifurcations of network dynamics as parameters change). They also treat mathematically the question of structural equivalence in networks, something to which we return below in our discussion of empirical analysis through blockmodelling.
5. http://www.arschile.cl/ucinet_ing/index.html.
6. http://www.analytictech.com/Netdraw/netdraw.htm.
7. We approach the modelling of connections at a similar level of generic abstraction. There is, however, also a more specific literature on economic networks, concerned with the connections of loyalty and trade in which economic agents find themselves, and again drawing on the approaches to networks as complex systems which the present chapter has reviewed: see, for example, Kirman (2003).

CHAPTER 12

1. The classes distinguished in the CASMIN framework comprise:
   I   Service class – professionals and managers and large employers
   II   Service class – lower professional and managerial
   III   Routine non-manual/white collar
   IVa/b   Small employers/petty bourgeoisie
   IVc   Farmers
   V   Foremen and technicians
   VI   Skilled manual workers
   VIIa   Semi-skilled and unskilled
   VIIb   Agricultural workers
2. Goldthorpe has undertaken a substantial amount of work on the mobility experience of women: see, for example, Erikson and Goldthorpe (1993: Ch. 7). Nevertheless, given the data sources at his disposal, the bulk of his work concentrates on sons, and it is on these therefore that we also concentrate.
3. We here use the notion of status in the sense employed by Weber – and indeed Goldthorpe himself – to refer to claims to social honour, as expressed in patterns of shared lifestyle and socialisation (Chan and Goldthorpe, 2007). Goldthorpe is always at pains to distinguish this from notions of 'socio-economic status', as commonly used by sociologists in the USA, a notion which he rather convincingly argues is vacuous.
4. Notice also that the occupational destinations which service class parents target for their offspring tend to be in the long upper tail of the distribution: the rational parent may judge that some extra investment on their part may well be worthwhile if it moves the likely destination significantly along that tail. Contrast the situation of a parent from, let us say, the skilled working class, where not only are spare resources more modest, but also the range of occupations which are potential targets offer a narrower 'spread' and thus a lesser likely return on any extra investment.
5. Goldthorpe argues, *pace* Lieberson, that the efforts of the more advantaged to write the rules of the positional game need not be purposive, foresightful and concerted (Erikson and Goldthorpe, 1993: 394). This is likely to depend in part on the strategies pursued by political and opinion leaders, but also on the forms of group action that develop. Not least, we have seen how social groups can self-organise within complex and turbulent environments: recall from Chapter 2 the dynamics of flocking behaviour, as also the tale of the Millennium Bridge. We return to these dynamics, in particular within the education system, in Chapter 15.
6. Goldthorpe distinguishes a number of channels through which this advantage is mobilised: these he discusses in terms of 'hierarchy', 'inheritance', 'sector' and 'affinity' and 'disaffinity' (Erikson and Goldthorpe, 1993: 121–31). If there are national deviations from the contours of the 'core model', he explains these in terms of the weighting that should be given to these different elements and he provides a theoretically grounded justification for each of these adjustments (Erikson and Goldthorpe, 1993: Ch. 5).
7. Pierson takes the example of a game of musical chairs, commenting that 'adding a few more players may alter the social dynamics dramatically'. Beyond the happy state where there are enough chairs for everyone, the addition of each extra player steadily increases the risk of finding no seat. More significant, however, faced with such a prospect, the original players are likely to act collectively, segregating enough chairs for themselves from some cushions on the floor, for which the latecomers are told to compete. It is through such collective strategies of defence that the social dynamics can most significantly change.
8. We have come across this sort of congestion-driven innovation previously: for example, in our discussion of Metcalfe's Law in Chapter 11 or the minority game in Chapter 2.

CHAPTER 13

1. The view that explanation must include some account of generative mechanisms is not of course specific to the social sciences. It is central to the realist tradition in the philosophy of science, as defended and developed by such writers as Harré (1972: Ch. 4). The cause is not merely antecedent to the effect: it generates it, whether by biochemical, physical, social or other processes which it is part of the scientific task to lay bare. Nevertheless, as Harré points out, what happens is generally the outcome of a multiplicity of influences and of generative mechanisms, acting in the context and against the background of certain more or less permanent conditions. This generative view sees entities as having 'causal powers which can be evoked in suitable circumstances' (p. 121). In reference to social behaviour in particular, see Harré and Secord (1972: Ch. 12).

    In all of this, the term 'mechanism' may not be the most appropriate, especially given our oft-stated wish to move away from the intellectual hegemony of classical mechanics. It may, following Harré, be better to speak of blocking or unlocking potentialities; or, following Lieberson, 'transformational' processes.

2. This is, Hedström argues, because (in Popper's words) such actions are the 'animating principles' of the social. This is consistent with our account of dynamic systems, where there is a source of energy driving it 'far from equilibrium'. See also our discussion of Maxwell's demon (Chapter 8).

3. There are also a considerable and growing number of useful web-based resources, including http://econ2.econ.iastate.edu/tesfatsi/abmread.htm and http://www.openabm.org/.

4. It will be evident that ABM is quite different from the various exercises in micro-simulation that have been prominent in social policy research in recent years: see, for example, Evans and Eyre (2004). In these, data relating to a representative sample of the population are re-worked, to see how their financial circumstances, for example, are likely to change, as they age or under specified changes in labour market conditions or national policies. There is, however, no interaction among these agents.

5. For more general discussion of ABM in relation to competing philosophies of social science, see Halfpenny (1997).

6. It is worth noticing the parallels between Turing's model in terms of activation and inhibition and Harré's account, discussed in a previous footnote, of causal powers and the circumstances that constrain or enable these powers to be expressed. This again underlines the generic nature of Turing's model, which we stressed in Chapter 10 and which underpinned the suggestion there that it might fruitfully be applied to the social as well as the natural world.

7. Although we have pointed to cases of such 'prose', it is necessary also to recognise that the language we have used, drawn from complexity science, risks itself creating obstacles to understanding and to the building of links with the wider social science literature. Thus, for example, we have made much use of the language of 'landscapes', and in particular the dynamic landscapes on which policy-makers may find themselves. Similar arguments, however, are advanced by such writers as Blamey and Mackenzie (Blamey and Mackenzie, 2007: 440–1) using the language of dynamic 'contexts'. Nevertheless, we can do little more than acknowledge the risk, and leave the social science community to select and adapt these various languages as appropriate.

8. Marris (1996: Ch. 7) offers a similar account of 'power as the mastery of contingencies rather than the accumulation of assets'. He emphasises that at every level this typically involves the progressive displacement of the burden of uncertainty onto those who are weaker. This is another long-range 'power law', all 'of a piece' like the one we discussed in Chapter 12.

CHAPTER 14

1. This is also consistent with Potts's interest in 'regimes' and the path dependency of transitions from one regime to the next (Dopfer and Potts, 2008: Ch. 6). Much of Fligstein's study can likewise be seen as an analysis of such institutional transitions: see in particular his discussion of the market institutions and employment systems that different power constellations tend to produce and to entrench (Fligstein, 2001: Chs 3, 5).
2. In terms of economic policy, Hirschmann similarly calls on policy-makers to seek not equilibrium and stability but 'chains of disequilibria' – what we might equally refer to as 'runaway loops' of 'structural imbalance' – and to 'maintain tensions, disproportions' as the 'mechanism . . . for . . . the development process (Toner, 1999: 21 and Ch. 4).
3. Scheffer and his colleagues (2009), their eyes primarily on physical and biological systems, argue that there are generic symptoms of complex adaptive systems approaching a tipping point. These include, for example, a slow-down in the recovery rate after small perturbations and increased variance in the pattern of fluctuations. Scheffer suggests that financial markets may exhibit some of these symptoms, but his claims are suitably cautious. We will be alert for such tipping points but equally cautious.
4. See similarly Kaldor (1985) on the contrasting metaphors of mechanism and eco-system for the economy; and Gilchrist and Barnes on community development as 'human horticulture' rather than social engineering (Gilchrist, 2000; Barnes et al., 2003).

CHAPTER 15

1. On the range of such factors which constrain the 'free' educational choices of less advantaged households within a market-like educational system, see Goldthorpe (2000, Ch. 9).
2. The more formal mathematical treatment is available at http://www.bath.ac.uk/soc-pol/people/people-pdfs/GJR_dynamics_of_social_exclusion_annex.pdf.
3. There have been a number of other simulations of school choice, including, for example, Hoyle and Robinson (2002), concerned with school performance, league tables and social class. However, they were not concerned with the two-way processes of 'competitive assortative mating' that are central to our own interest.
4. Burgess and his colleagues at the Centre for Market and Public Organisation (University of Bristol) have a long record of empirically oriented work in the issues raised here; some of their work has already been cited. It is by reference to work such as this that the modelling approaches we have described might fruitfully be developed further.
5. It is salutary to contrast the quite different approach to educational reform attempted two decades earlier by the then Labour Government (Halsey, 1972). This attempted positive discrimination in favour of educationally disadvantaged communities, sufficient to raise the average educational outcomes of their children to a level similar to that for the population as a whole. This was to be achieved by putting extra resources into schools, by building bridges between schools and homes in pre-schooling programmes and by integrating schools into the life of the communities concerned. Schools, homes and communities would co-evolve and build a shared resilience, under the benign stewardship of the public authorities. Much was achieved; but political realities meant that the experiment was small scale and short-lived. The Baker reforms played instead to the aspirations of middle class homes and have become the centrepiece of the national educational architecture.
6. In the UK, the coalition government elected in May 2010 proposes to introduce a 'pupil premium' for school budgets, related to the numbers of disadvantaged pupils.
7. These advisers play a mixed role, both as gatekeepers and advocates. Their counter-

parts in the middle class include tax accountants and financial advisers. Both mediate new institutional combinations and financial strategies for the household in question.

8. We cannot, however, assume that real world actors are fully aware of these rules and organise their actions accordingly. Rules may be obscure or misunderstood or discretionary, needing gatekeepers to interpret them. In situations of turbulence moreover, different rules may come into play, of which those concerned were previously unaware. Resilience in coping with such surprises may be limited and itself dependent on the support systems of the mother in question. It may be easier to 'follow the crowd' rather than to study the rules and devise positional strategies accordingly.

9. In general the empirical tradition in social policy research has focused on families at the margin and has paid little attention to the more advantaged. There is, of course, a tradition of work on fiscal and occupational welfare and its role in consolidating privilege. Rowlingson has been publishing on inheritance and wealth (Rowlingson and Mackay, 2005; Rowlingson, 2008). Toynbee and Walker (2008) have provided a review of the lives of the haves and have-nots in contemporary Britain and of the new institutional mechanisms by which the advantaged escape the redistributive efforts of state policies. The so-called 'credit crunch' has prompted a spate of books that shine a light into some dark corners of privilege (Peston, 2008b). In general, however, the more advantaged can choose the terms under which their family-work projects become visible.

10. A more general observation about comparative research on welfare regimes is appropriate. Much of the work inspired by Esping-Anderson's 1990 study has focused on cash benefits and the extent to which these 'decommodify' workers, by providing them with enough outside the labour market to meet their physical consumption needs. I have in an earlier paper (Room, 2000) argued for equal attention to be paid to 'decommodification for self-development': the extent to which social policies enable people to learn and develop their knowledge and capacities, in relationship to market, society and polity. It is similarly on agile creativity and the growth of knowledge – and the scope of the canvas on which this is exercised – that the present discussion has focused and which indeed underpins this entire study.

11. Those involved in the development and application of the EU social exclusion indicators are well aware of these limitations. Thus, for example, Frazer and Marlier (2007) underline the significance of the extended family, of participation in the local community and of access to social and health services (paras 3.6, 5.3–5.5). The Social Protection Committee (2008: 82–3) likewise recognises the need for such indicators of participation and points to indicators used in particular countries that might be adopted more generally.

12. In the UK the Sutton Trust has, on the basis of its review of social segregation in state secondary schools, argued for just such an indicator (Smithers and Robinson, 2010).

13. Current developments in comparative policy analysis associated with the social inclusion process are centred in Euromod at the University of Essex (http://www.iser.essex. ac.uk/research/euromod). This is a micro-simulation of the national tax benefit systems of the EU countries, using 'model families' defined with respect to family composition and circumstances. It allows policy researchers to compare the interaction between different policy measures and their weights in different countries. They can also conduct 'what if?' experiments, in which the consequences of a tax-benefit change in a given country are simulated on the basis of the known effects of that policy elsewhere. This is, however, a static model: what we are proposing is in some senses a dynamic counterpart.

CHAPTER 16

1. The development of appropriate new statistical indicators can itself be viewed as a process of innovation and evolution. It typically starts with 'layering', whereby 'satellite

accounts' separate from the main system of national accounts can pilot new types of measurement, for example, of intangibles. If these prove workable, they can then in due course be 'mainstreamed', with 'conversion' of the national accounts as a whole to these novelties. See, for example, Ramprakash (2004: Chs 4, 6).

2. For purposes of national statistical accounts it is conventionally required that this income stream should be for at least 12 months, if the asset is to be deemed capitalised. For discussion and investigation of the length of these intangible asset income streams, see Whittard et al. (2009).

3. Notice that under recent trade agreements, intellectual property can refer to the marketable property of an individual or a corporation but not of a tribe or community, for example.

4. Just therefore as Polanyi (1944) reaffirms the social and institutional foundations of the market, Potts reaffirms its dependence on the institutions of social creativity (Potts, 2007a).

5. The distinction is well embedded in conventional wisdom in the UK, where it has long been popularly believed that while our scientists are good at basic research and invention, our businessmen are poor at innovating.

6. These indicators will in some respects therefore amount to so-called 'third generation' indicators of innovation, based on interactive 'chain-linked' models of innovation, with feedback loops and organisational as well as technological change (Kline and Rosenberg, 1986; Orsenigo, 2000; Lundvall and Tomlinson, 2002: 216).

7. Recall similarly Abbott's discussion of Chicago's neighbourhoods (see Chapter 10). The more these are connected to the larger socio-economic system, the more their dynamics must be understood – and indicators of those dynamics devised – by reference to those larger interactional processes.

8. In constructing their niches, these MNEs can use the new information technologies to out-source low value-added activities to developing countries, along with those which are pollution-generating, but tolerated by their lighter regulatory regimes. Thus while MNEs are well placed to range freely across national boundaries, this does not mean that such boundaries are irrelevant in constructing their niche; on the contrary, their global strategies can be carefully chosen, having regard to the different sets of opportunities that are afforded by the conditions in each country.

9. Other sets of indicators of the degree of economic, social and political globalisation of different countries include that of the Swiss Economic Institute (2010).

10. Such agglomerations were central to the discussion in Chapter 2 of external economies of scale, as analysed by Arthur and before him by Marshall, Young, Myrdal, Kaldor and others: all highlighting the dynamic relationship between innovation, the expansion of markets and the path dependency of associated patterns of economic development.

11. There is a substantial literature concerned with the international location dynamics of high-skill, technologically based economies (see, for example, Porter, 1990; Dunning, 1993a, 1993b; Held et al., 1999). What this highlights is that far from capital always seeking low cost countries in a 'race to the bottom', it tends to be attracted by agglomerations of knowledge resources and by national policies which strengthen them (Room, 2002). The development of knowledge economies can be set in this context of analysis, but with the pace of innovation dramatically accelerated and the implications for the trajectories which different communities then follow – whether benign or adverse – potentially much more destabilising.

12. These challenges of public governance in some ways parallel those of corporate governance, as we saw in our discussion of Kristensen and Zeitlin (2005) in Chapter 7; and indeed, this parallel between the OMC and their corporate case study is one which they themselves draw.

13. For a critical review of the new strategy, see Pochet (2010).

CHAPTER 17

1. See also Watson's account of financial innovation and capital mobility, risk-taking and the social burden to which ordinary households are exposed (Watson, 2007, especially the Conclusion). This prescient analysis appeared before the 2008 crisis but discusses *inter alia* the similar distributional consequences of the Asian financial crisis of the 1990s, and the burden in terms of poverty and well-being imposed on the mass of the population.
2. Just as in the previous chapter we traced the capitalisation of intangibles, here there has been a trend towards progressive capitalisation of the public realm. In both cases the aim is to measure assets hitherto left out of account, but also to take them to market.
3. See, for example, the 22 July 2009 letter to the Queen from Besley and Hennessy on behalf of the London School of Economics and the British Academy (http://www.britac.ac.uk/events/archive/forum-economy.cfm).
4. The case of Barclays is particularly noteworthy. They did not take government aid to re-build their capital base but this does not mean that they did not benefit from government support. It is on the contrary because of the government's general support to the financial system that Barclays soon found itself reporting a healthy rate of profits and able to pay out large bonuses again. Meanwhile Barclays told the broad mass of its employees it could no longer afford their final salary pension schemes.
5. The 'stimulus package' of the UK government during 2009–10, involving VAT reductions and 'quantitative easing', although often referred to as Keynesian, was therefore anything but, relying as it did on an increase in the 'money supply' and the revival of business and consumer spending that these measures were supposed to produce. Countries such as France looked more to public investment projects. Without this emphasis in the UK, 2009 not surprisingly saw a dramatic fall in business investment. At the time of writing, the UK appears most sluggish of the major economies in recovering from the recession.
6. The main difficulty with Tily's otherwise valuable study of Keynes is that he identifies the maintenance of low interest rates as being for Keynes the principal lever of economic policy intended to foster full employment and prosperity (Tily, 2007: Ch. 5). Low interest rates are, however, better seen as the *consequence* of the more fundamental policy measures that Keynes advocated, in particular a high level of public investment, along with appropriate inter-governmental institutions to protect domestic economic policy from the vicissitudes of the international economy.
7. Davidson (2009: Ch. 8) offers a complementary discussion of reform of the international payments system, updating Keynes's proposals at Bretton Woods for the twenty-first century. As with the discussion here, his aim is to consider how the larger community, both nationally and internationally, can reassert public policy goals and civilise market anarchy.
8. There is a large literature on the global commons, both academic and practitioner-related, which it is beyond the scope of this chapter to review. See, for example, the pages of *Yes! Magazine* (http://www.yesmagazine.org), starting with its special issue 'Reclaiming the Commons' in summer 2001.
9. We might recall Jonathan Swift's satirical *Modest Proposal* (1729) for solving the problems of poverty in Ireland, by having Irish children served up as food for the rich and genteel: a satire intended to underline the predatory consequences of British policies towards Ireland. It is hardly more far-fetched to describe the perpetrators of the present crisis in the same terms. Eating people is wrong.
10. This havoc we have discussed primarily in terms of the wreckage of the real economy and the public finances. However, the conspicuous consumption of the leisure class and its perennial creation of new consumption 'needs' as the goal of the good life are also key drivers of climate change. As Pochet (2010: 3, 6) argues, in his critique of the new *Europe 2020* strategy of the EU, 'the idea of a green economy is hardly credible, for no one is going to change their behaviour if the most affluent sections of the population

continue to enjoy material prosperity such that they can disregard with impunity the constraints imposed by the environmental crisis . . . and continue to waste resources as much as they like'. Even in the world of higher education, the race for reputational advantage as described by Enders and King – discussed earlier in Chapter 10 – involves universities in carbon-wasteful global enterprises, hardly less over-weaning than those of Barclays' 'masters of the universe' (Enders, 2009; King, 2009).

POSTSCRIPT

1. http://interactive.cabinetoffice.gov.uk/strategy/survivalguide/skills/evidence_base.htm.
2. http://www.cochrane.org/ and http://www.campbellcollaboration.org/.
3. See, for example, the Overseas Development Institute: http://www.odi.org.uk/RAPID/index.html.
4. http://www.nationalschool.gov.uk/policyhub/better_policy_making/icpm_toolkit/index.asp.
5. http://interactive.cabinetoffice.gov.uk/strategy/survivalguide/skills/eb_scenarios.htm.

References

Abbott, A. (1988), *The System of Professions*, Chicago, IL: University of Chicago Press.

Abbott, A. (1990), 'A Primer on Sequence Methods', *Organization Science*, 1(4) (November): 375–92.

Abbott, A. (1991), 'The Order of Professionalization', *Work and Occupations*, 18: 355–84.

Abbott, A. (1995), 'Sequence Analysis: New Methods for Old Ideas', *Annual Review of Sociology*, 21: 93–113.

Abbott, A. (1997), 'Of Time and Space: The Contemporary Relevance of the Chicago School', *Social Forces*, 75(4): 1149–82.

Abbott, A. (2001a), *Chaos of Disciplines* Chicago, IL: University of Chicago Press.

Abbott, A. (2001b), *Time Matters: On Theory and Method*, Chicago, IL: University of Chicago Press.

Abbott, A. and S. DeViney (1992), 'The Welfare State as Transnational Event: Evidence from Sequences of Policy Adoption', *Social Science History*, 16(2): 245–74.

Alber, J. (2006), 'The European Social Model and the United States', *European Union Politics*, 7(3): 393–419.

Aoki, M. (2001), *Towards a Comparative Institutional Analysis*, Cambridge, MA: MIT Press

Arendt, D. (2008), 'The Evolution of Cell Types in Animals: Emerging Principles From Molecular Studies', *Nature Reviews: Genetics*, 9 (November): 868–82.

Arrighi, G. (2007), *Adam Smith in Beijing*, London: Verso.

Arrowsmith, J., K. Sissons and P. Marginson (2004), 'What Can "Benchmarking" Offer the Open Method of Coordination?', *Journal of European Public Policy*, 11(2): 311–28.

Arthur, W.B. (1994a), 'Inductive Reasoning and Bounded Rationality (the El Farol Problem)', *American Economic Review*, 84: 406–11.

Arthur, W.B. (1994b), 'On the Evolution of Complexity', in G.A. Cowan, D. Pines and D. Meltzer (eds), *Complexity: Metaphors, Models and Reality*, Reading, MA: Addison-Wesley: 65–81.

Arthur, W.B., S.N. Durlauf and D.A. Lane (eds) (1997), *The Economy as an Evolving Complex System II*, Boulder, CO: Westview.

Arundel, A., A. Colecchia and A. Wyckoff (2006), 'Rethinking Science and Technology Indicators for Innovation Policy in the Twenty-first Century ' in L. Earl and F. Gault (eds), *National Innovation, Indicators and Policy*, Cheltenham, UK and Northampton, MA, USA: Edward Elgar Publishing: 167–97.

Atkinson, R. and L. Carmichael (2007), 'Neighbourhoods as a New Focus for Action in Urban Policies of West European States', in I. Smith, E. Lepine and M. Taylor (eds), *Disadvantaged by Where You Live?*, Bristol: Policy Press: 43–64.

Avineri, S. (1968), *The Social and Political Thought of Karl Marx*, Cambridge: Cambridge University Press.

Axelrod, R. (1984), *The Evolution of Cooperation*, New York: Basic Books.

Bak, P. (1997), *How Nature Works: The Science of Self-organized Criticality*, Oxford: Oxford University Press.

Bak, P. and M. Paczuski (1996), *Mass Extinctions vs Uniformitarianism in Biological Evolution*, Department of Physics, Brookhaven National Laboratory.

Ball, P. (2004), *Critical Mass: How One Thing Leads to Another*, London: Heinemann.

Ball, S.J. (2003), *Class Strategies and the Education Market: The Middle Class and Social Advantage*, London: RoutledgeFalmer.

Barabási, A.-L. (2003), 'Emergence of Scaling in Complex Networks', in S. Bornholdt and H.G. Schuster (eds), *Handbook of Graphs and Networks*, Weinheim: Wiley-VCH: 69–84.

Bardach, E. (2005), *A Practical Guide for Policy Analysis*, Second edition, Washington, DC: CQ Press.

Barnes, M. and D. Prior (eds) (2009), *Subversive Citizens: Power, Agency and Resistance in Public Services*, Bristol: Policy Press.

Barnes, M., E. Matka and H. Sullivan (2003), 'Evidence, Understanding and Complexity: Evaluation in Non-linear Systems', *Evaluation*, 9(3): 265–84.

Barnett, J. and G. Breakwell (2003), 'The Social Amplification of Risk and the Hazard Sequence: The October 1995 Oral Contraceptive Pill Scare', *Health, Risk and Society*, 5(3): 301–13.

Bechtel, W. and A. Abrahamsen (2002), *Connectionism and the Mind*, Second edition, Oxford: Blackwell.

Beinhocker, E.D. (2007), *The Origin of Wealth*, London: Random House.

Beller, E. and M. Hout (2006), 'Welfare States and Social Mobility', *Research in Social Stratification and Mobility*, 24(4): 353–65.

Bennett, C. (1991), 'How States Utilise Foreign Evidence', *Journal of Public Policy*, 33(4): 31–54.

Berger, P.L. and T. Luckmann (1967), *The Social Construction of Reality*, Harmondsworth: Penguin.

Bertuglia, C.S. and F. Vaio (2005), *Nonlinearity, Chaos and Complexity*, Oxford: Oxford University Press.

Bevan, P. and A. Sseweya (1995), *Understanding Poverty in Uganda*, Oxford: Centre for the Study of African Economies.

Bianconi, G. and A.-L. Barabási (2001), 'Competition and Multiscaling in Evolving Networks', *Europhysics Letters*, 54(4): 436–42.

Blackburn, R. (2008), 'The Sub-prime Crisis', *New Left Review*, 50 (March–April): 63–106.

Blamey, A. and M. Mackenzie (2007), 'Theories of Change and Realistic Evaluation', *Evaluation*, 13(4): 439–55.

Bleicher, J. (1980), *Contemporary Hermeneutics*, London: Routledge.

Bloch, F. and H. Ryder (2000), 'Two-sided Search, Marriages and Matchmakers', *International Economic Review*, 41(1): 93–115.

Boero, R. and F. Squazzoni (2005), 'Does Empirical Embeddedness Matter? Methodological Issues on Agent-based Models for Analytical Social Science', *Journal of Artificial Societies and Social Simulation*, 8(4), available at http://jasss.soc.surrey.ac.uk/8/4/6.html.

Bornholdt, S. and H.G. Schuster (eds) (2003), *Handbook of Graphs and Networks*, Weinheim: Wiley-VCH.

Bovaird, T. (2008), 'Emergent Strategic Management and Planning Mechanisms in Complex Adaptive Systems', *Public Management Review*, 10(3): 319–40.

Bowker, G.C. and S.L. Star (2002), *Sorting Things Out: Classification and Its Consequences*, Cambridge, MA: MIT Press.

Breakwell, G. (2001), 'Mental Models and Social Representations of Hazards: The Significance of Identity Processes', *Journal of Risk Research*, 4(5): 341–51.

Breen, R. (2005), *Social Mobility in Europe*, Oxford: Clarendon Press.

Breen, R. and M. Yaish (2006), 'Testing the Breen-Goldthorpe Model of Educational Decision-making', in S.L. Morgan, D.B. Grusky and G.S. Fields (eds), *Mobility and Inequality*, Stanford, CA: Stanford University Press: 232–58.

Breunig, C. (2006), 'The More Things Change, the More They Stay the Same: A Comparative Analysis of Budget Punctuations', *Journal of European Public Policy*, 13(7): 1069–85.

Brown, P., A. Green and H. Lauder (2001), *High Skills: Globalisation, Competitiveness and Skill Formation*, Oxford: Oxford University Press.

Brummer, A. (2009), *The Crunch: How Greed and Incompetence Sparked the Credit Crisis*, London: Random House.

Brynjolfsson, E.J., A. McFee, F. Zhu and M. Sorell (2006), 'Scale Without Mass: Business Process Replication and Industry Dynamics', Harvard Business School Technology and Operations Management Unit Research Paper No. 07-016.

Buchanan, M. (2000), *Ubiquity*, London: Wiedenfeld and Nicolson.

Buhr, P. and S. Leibfried (1995), 'What a Difference a Day Makes: The Significance for Social Policy of the Duration of Social Assistance Receipt', in G. Room (ed.), *Beyond the Threshold: The Measurement and Analysis of Social Exclusion*, Bristol: Policy Press: 129–45.

Bukodi, R. and J.H. Goldthorpe (2009), 'Market Versus Meritocracy: Hungary as a Critical Case', *European Sociological Review*, doi:10.1093/esr/jcp043.

Burgess, S., R. Johnston, T. Key, C. Propper and D. Wilson (2007a), 'The Formation of School Peer Groups: Pupils' Transition from Primary to Secondary School in England', CMPO Working Paper Series University of Bristol, Bristol.

Burgess, S., C. Propper and D. Wilson (2007b), 'The Impact of School Choice in England', *Policy Studies*, 28(2): 129–43.

Butler, I. and M. Drakeford (2005), *Scandal, Social Policy and Social Welfare*, Second edition, Bristol: Policy Press.

Butler, T. and G. Robson (2003), 'Plotting the Middle Classes: Gentrification and Circuits of Education in London ', *Housing Studies*, 18(1): 5–28.

Butts, C.T. (2001), 'The Complexity of Social Networks: Theoretical and Empirical Findings ', *Social Networks*, 23: 31–71.

Byrne, D. (1998), *Complexity Theory and the Social Sciences*, London: Routledge.

Cable, V. (2009), *The Storm: The World Economic Crisis and What It Means*, London: Atlantic Books.

Carney, D. (ed.) (1998), *Sustainable Rural Livelihoods*. London: UK Department for International Development (DFID).

Carrington, P.J., J. Scott and S. Wasserman (eds) (2005), *Models and Methods in Social Network Analysis*, Cambridge: Cambridge University Press.

Cassidy, C. (2009), 'Rational Irrationality', *The New Yorker*, New York, available at http://www.newyorker.com/reporting/2009/10/05/091005fa_fact_cassidy.

Castells, M. (2001), *The Internet Galaxy, Reflections on the Internet, Business and Society*, Oxford: Oxford University Press.

Castells, M. (ed.) (2004), *The Network Society: A Cross-cultural*

Perspective, Cheltenham, UK and Northampton, MA, USA: Edward Elgar Publishing.

Cecchini, P. (1988), *The European Challenge: 1992: The Benefits of a Single Market*, Aldershot: Wildwood House.

Chambers, R. (1989), 'Vulnerability: How the Poor Cope', *IDS Bulletin*, 20(2): 1–7.

Chan, T.K. and J.H. Goldthorpe (2007), 'Class and Status: The Conceptual Distinction and its Empirical Relevance', *American Sociological Review*, 72: 512–32.

Checkland, P. and J. Scholes (1990), *Soft Systems Methodology in Action*, Chichester: John Wiley.

Christakis, N. and J. Fowler (2009), *Connected: The Amazing Power of Social Networks and How They Change Our Lives*, London: HarperPress.

Chua, A. (2003), *World on Fire: How Exporting Free-market Democracy Breeds Ethnic Hatred and Global Instability*, London: Heinemann.

Cilliers, P. (1998), *Complexity and Postmodernism*, London: Routledge.

Clayton, T., S. Farooqui, G. Gales, M. Leaver and R. Sadun (2005), *IT Investment, ICT Use and UK Firm Productivity*, London: ONS/LSE.

Clayton, T., M. d. Borgo and J. Haskel (2008), *An Innovation Index Based on Knowledge Capital Investment*, London: NESTA (UK National Endowment for Science, Technology and the Arts).

Cliffe, O., M. De Vos and J.A. Padget (2007), 'Specifying and Reasoning About Multiple Institutions', in J. Vazquez-Salceda and P. Noriega (eds), *Lecture Notes in Computer Science*, Berlin: Springer, 4386: 63–81.

Coase, R. (1937), 'The Nature of the Firm', *Economica*, 4(16): 386–405.

Cohen, J. and I. Stewart (1995), *The Collapse of Chaos: Discovering Simplicity in a Complex World*, Harmondsworth: Penguin.

Coleman, J. (1990), *Foundations of Social Theory*, Cambridge, MA: Harvard University Press.

Collingwood, R.G. (1939), *An Autobiography*, Oxford: Oxford University Press (paperback 1970).

Collingwood, R.G. (1942), *The Idea of History*, Oxford: Oxford University Press.

Corfield, R. (2001), *Architects of Eternity*, London: Headline Book Publishing.

Corrado, C.A., C.R. Hulten and D.E. Sichel (2006), 'Intangible Capital and Economic Growth', NBER Working Papers 11948, Washington, DC.

Coyle, R. (1996), *Systems Dynamics Modelling: A Practical Approach*, London: Chapman and Hall.

Croft, D., R. James and J. Krause (2008), *Exploring Animal Social Networks*, Princeton, NJ: Princeton University Press.

Crouch, C. (2005), *Capitalist Diversity and Change: Recombinant Governance and Institutional Entrepreneurs*, Oxford: Oxford University Press.

Crouch, C., D. Finegold and M. Sako (1999), *Are Skills the Answer? The Political Economy of Skill Creation in Advanced Industrial Countries*, Oxford: Oxford University Press.

Daffin, C., S. Levy and A. Walton (2009), 'Improving Measurement of Household Savings and Wealth', *Economic and Labour Market Review*, 3(7) (July): 33–6.

Darwin, C. (1859), *The Origin of Species*, London: Wordsworth (reprinted 1998).

Darwin, J. (2007), *After Tamerlane: The Rise and Fall of Global Empires, 1400–2000*, Harmondsworth: Penguin.

Davidson, P. (2009), *The Keynes Solution*, New York: Palgrave Macmillan.

Davis, C. (2006), 'The Politics of Forum Choice for Trade Disputes', American Political Science Association, Philadelphia, 31 August.

Davies, N. (2000), *The School Report*, London: Vintage.

Dawe, A. (1970), 'The Two Sociologies', *British Journal of Sociology*, 21(2): 207–18.

Dawkins, R. (1976), *The Selfish Gene*, Oxford: Oxford University Press.

Daykin, C.D. (2003), 'Genetics and Insurance – Some Social Policy Issues', Institute of Actuaries and Faculty of Actuaries. London.

De la Porte, C., P. Pochet and G. Room (2001), 'Social Benchmarking, Policy-making and New Governance in the EU', *Journal of European Social Policy*, 11(4): 291–307.

Delong, J.B. and L.H. Summers (2001), 'How Important Will the Information Economy Be? Some Simple Analytics', University of California at Berkeley.

Denzau, A.T. and D.C. North (1994), 'Shared Mental Models: Ideologies and Institutions', *Kyklos*, 47(1): 3–31.

Desai, M. and P. Ormerod (1998), 'Richard Goodwin: A Short Appreciation', *Economic Journal*, 108: 1431–5.

Dolowitz, D. and D. March (1996), 'Who Learns What from Whom: A Review of the Policy Transfer Literature', *Political Studies*, 44: 343–57.

Dopfer, K. and J. Potts (2008), *The General Theory of Economic Evolution*, London: Routledge.

Doreian, P. (2002), 'Event Sequences as Generators of Social Network Evolution', *Social Networks*, 24(2): 93–119.

Doreian, P., V. Batagelj and A. Ferligoj (2005), *Generalized Blockmodelling*, Cambridge: Cambridge University Press.

Douglas, M. (1986), *How Institutions Think*, London: Routledge and Kegan Paul.

Duncan, S. (2009), 'Policy Transfer: Theory, Rhetoric and Reality', *Policy and Politics*, 37(3): 453–8.

Dunning, J.H. (1993a), *The Globalization of Business*, London: Routledge.

Dunning, J.H. (1993b), *Multinational Enterprises and the Global Economy*, Wokingham: Addison-Wesley.

Durkheim, E. (1964), *The Division of Labour in Society*, New York: Free Press.

Dwyer, P. and N. Ellison (2009), '"We Nicked Stuff From All Over the Place": Policy Transfer or Muddling Through?', *Policy and Politics*, 37(3): 389–407.

Earl, P.E. and J. Potts (2004), 'Bounded Rationality and Decomposability: The Basis for Integrating Cognitive and Evolutionary Economics', in M. Augier and J.G. March (eds), *Models of a Man: Essays in Memory of Herbert A. Simon*, Cambridge, MA: MIT Press: 317–33.

Ebbinghaus, B. (2005), 'Can Path Dependence Explain Institutional Change?', MPIfG Discussion Paper 05/2, Max-Planck-Institut fuer Gesellschaftsforschung, Cologne, Germany.

Egidi, M. and L. Marengo (2004), 'Near-decomposability, Organization and Evolution: Some Notes on Herbert Simon's Contribution', in M. Augier and J.G. March (eds), *Models of a Man: Essays in Memory of Herbert A. Simon*, Cambridge MA: MIT Press: 335–50.

Enders, J. (2009), 'Global Rankings and the Academic Reputation Race', Paper presented to the South West Higher Education Forum, Society for Research into Higher Education, University of Bath, 13 November.

Erikson, R. and J.H. Goldthorpe (1993), *The Constant Flux: A Study of Class Mobility in Industrial Societies*, Oxford: Clarendon.

Esping-Andersen, G. (1990), *The Three Worlds of Welfare Capitalism*, Cambridge: Polity Press.

Etzioni, A. (1961), *Complex Organisations*, New York: Free Press.

European Commission (2001a), *Communication: eEurope: Impact and Priorities*, Brussels: European Commission.

European Commission (2001b), *Work Programme for the Follow-up of the Report on the Concrete Objectives of Education and Training Systems*, Brussels: European Commission.

European Commission (2002a), *Commission Staff Working Paper: 2002 European Innovation Scoreboard*, Brussels: European Commission.

European Commission (2002b), *Communication: eEurope 2005: Benchmarking Indicators*, Brussels: European Commission.

European Commission (2003a), *2003 European Innovation Scoreboard: Technical Paper No 5: National Innovation System Indicators*, Brussels: European Commission.

European Commission (2003b), *eLearning: Designing Tomorrow's*

Education: A Mid-term Report, C.S.W. Paper, Brussels: European Commission.

European Commission (2003c), *European Innovation Scoreboard 2003: Technical Paper No 1: Indicators and Definitions*, Brussels: DG Enterprise.

European Commission (2004a), *Facing the Challenge: The Lisbon Strategy for Growth and Employment: Report of the High Level Group Chaired by Wim Kok*, Brussels: European Commission.

European Commission (2004b), *Innovation in Europe*, Brussels: European Commission.

European Commission (2007), *Towards a European Research Area: Science, Technology and Innovation: Key Figures 2007*, Brussels: European Commission.

European Commission (2008), *Portfolio of Overarching Indicators and Streamlined Social Inclusion, Pensions, and Health Portfolios*, Brussels: European Commission.

European Commission (2009), *European Innovation Scoreboard 2008: Comparative Analysis of Innovation Performance*, Brussels: European Commission.

European Council (2000a), *eEurope Benchmarking Indicators*, Brussels: European Council, 20 November.

European Council (2000b), *Presidency Conclusions*, Lisbon: European Council, 23–24 March.

European Council (2010), *Europe 2020: A New European Strategy for Jobs and Growth* (EUCO 7/10), Brussels: European Council, 25–26 March.

European Council and European Commission (2000), *Action Plan, eEurope: An Information Society for All*, Brussels: European Council, 14 June.

Eustace, C. (2007), 'The Intangible Economy: Key Indicators of the "Hidden" Productive Capacities', in T. Wolters (ed.), *Measuring the New Economy*, Amsterdam: Elsevier: 83–101.

Evans, M. and J. Davies (1999), 'Understanding Policy Transfer: A Multi-level Multi-disciplinary Perspective', *Public Administration*, 72(2): 361–83.

Evans, M. and J. Eyre (2004), *The Opportunities of a Lifetime*, Bristol: Policy Press.

Evans, P.B., H.K. Jackson and R.D. Putnam (1993), *Double-edged Diplomacy: International Bargaining and Domestic Politics*, Berkeley, CA: University of California Press.

Everett, M.G. and S.P. Borgatti (2005), 'Extending Centrality', in P.J. Carrington, J. Scott and S. Wasserman (eds), *Models and Methods in Social Network Analysis*, Cambridge: Cambridge University Press: 57–76.

Faris, R.E.L. (1967), *Chicago Sociology 1920–1932*, Chicago, IL: University of Chicago Press.

Featherman, D.L., F.L. Jones and R.M. Hauser (1975), 'Assumptions of Social Mobility Research in the US: The Case of Occupational Status', *Social Science Research*, 4: 329–60.

Fenner, T., M. Levene and G. Loizou (2007), 'A Model for Collaboration Networks Giving Rise to a Power-law Distribution with an Exponential Cut-off', *Social Networks*, 29: 70–80.

Ferrera, M., A. Hemerick and M. Rhodes (2000), *The Future of the European Welfare States*, Report for the Portuguese Presidency of the European Union, Lisbon: European Council.

Fisher, R.A. (1930), *The Genetical Theory of Natural Selection*, Oxford: Clarendon Press.

Fligstein, N. (2001), *The Architecture of Markets: An Economic Sociology of Twenty-first Century Capitalist Societies*, Princeton, NJ: Princeton University Press.

Fligstein, N. (2005), 'The Political and Economic Sociology of International Economic Arrangements', in N. Smelser and R. Swedberg (eds), *The Handbook of Economic Sociology*, Princeton, NJ: Princeton University Press: 183–204.

Franklin, M., P. Stam and T. Clayton (2009), 'ICT Impact Assessment by Linking Data', *Economic and Labour Market Review*, 3(10) (28–30 May): 18–27.

Frazer, H. and E. Malier (2007), *Tackling Child Poverty and Promoting the Social Inclusion of Children in the EU: Key Lessons: Synthesis Report*, Brussels: European Commission.

Frenken, K. (2006), *Innovation, Evolution and Complexity Theory*, Cheltenham, UK and Northampton, MA, USA: Edward Elgar Publishing.

Friedman, T. (2006), *The World is Flat*, London: Penguin.

Gadamer, H.-G. (1980), 'The Universality of the Hermeneutical Problem', in J. Bleicher (ed.), *Contemporary Hermeneutics*, London: Routledge: 128–40.

Galbraith, J.K. (1958), *The Affluent Society*, Harmondsworth: Penguin (reprinted 1962).

Galbraith, J.K. (2009), *The Predator State*, New York: Free Press.

Gallie, D. and S. Paugam (2002), *Social Precarity and Social Integration*, Brussels: European Commission.

Gallie, D., C. Marsh and C. Vogler (eds) (1994), *Social Change and the Experience of Unemployment*, Oxford: Oxford University Press.

Gavrilets, S. (2004), *Fitness Landscapes and the Origin of Species*, Princeton, NJ: Princeton University Press.

George, V. and P. Wilding (1976), *Ideology and Social Welfare*, London: Routledge and Kegan Paul.

Gereffi, G. (2005), 'The Global Economy: Organization, Governance and Development', in N.J. Smelser and R. Swedberg (eds), *The Handbook of Economic Sociology*, Second edition, Princeton, NJ: Princeton University Press: 160–82.

Giddens, A. (1990), *The Consequences of Modernity*, Cambridge: Polity Press.

Gilbert, G.N. (1981), *Modelling Society*, London: Allen and Unwin.

Gilbert, G.N. (1993), *Analyzing Tabular Data: Loglinear and Logistic Models for Social Researchers*, London: UCL Press.

Gilbert, N. (2008), *Agent-based Models*, London: Sage.

Gilbert, N. and K.G. Troitzsch (2005), *Simulation for the Social Scientist*, Second edition, Maidenhead: Open University Press.

Gilchrist, A. (2000), 'The Well-connected Community: Networking to the "Edge of Chaos"', *Community Development Journal*, 35(3): 264–75.

Gladwell, M. (2001), *The Tipping Point: How Little Things Can Make a Big Difference*, London: Abacus.

Goldthorpe, J.H. (1974), 'Social Inequality and Social Integration in Modern Britain', in D. Wedderburn (ed.), *Poverty, Inequality and Class Structure*, Cambridge: Cambridge University Press: 217–34.

Goldthorpe, J.H. (1978), 'The Current Inflation: Towards a Sociological Account', in F. Hirsch and J.H. Goldthorpe (eds), *The Political Economy of Inflation*, London: Martin Robertson: 186–216.

Goldthorpe, J.H. (1980), *Social Mobility and Class Structure in Modern Britain*, Oxford: Clarendon Press.

Goldthorpe, J.H. (1984), *Order and Conflict in Contemporary Capitalism*, Oxford: Oxford University Press.

Goldthorpe, J.H. (1985), 'Problems of Political Economy After the End of the Post-war Period', in C.S. Maier (ed.), *Changing Boundaries of the Political*, Oxford: Oxford University Press: 363–407.

Goldthorpe, J.H. (2000), *On Sociology*, Oxford: Oxford University Press.

Goldthorpe, J.H. (2001a), 'Causation, Statistics and Sociology', *European Sociological Review*, 17(1): 1–20.

Goldthorpe, J.H. (2001b), *Globalisation and Social Class*, Mannheim: Mannheimer Zentrum für Europäische Sozialforschung.

Goldthorpe, J.H. (2004), 'Sociology as Social Science and Cameral Sociology: Some Further Thoughts', *European Sociological Review*, 20(2): 97–105.

Goldthorpe, J.H. (2007a), *On Sociology: Volume One: Critique and Program*, Second edition, Stanford, CA: Stanford University Press.

Goldthorpe, J.H. (2007b), *On Sociology: Volume Two: Illustrations and Retrospect*, Second edition, Stanford, CA: Stanford University Press.

Goldthorpe, J.H. (2009), 'Analysing Social Inequality: A Critique of Two Recent Contributions from Economics and Epidemiology', *European Sociological Review*, doi:10.1093/esr/jcp046.

Goldthorpe, J.H. and M. Jackson (2007), 'Intergenerational Class Mobility in Contemporary Britain: Political Concerns and Empirical Findings', *British Journal of Sociology*, 58(4): 525–46.

Goldthorpe, J.H. and A. McKnight (2006), 'The Economic Basis of Social Class', in S.L. Morgan, D.B. Grusky and G.S. Fields (eds), *Mobility and Inequality*, Stanford, CA: Stanford University Press: 109–36.

Goldthorpe, J.H. and C. Mills (2008), 'Trends in Intergenerational Class Mobility in Modern Britain: Evidence from National Surveys, 1972–2005', *National Institute Economic Review*, 205(83): 83–100.

Golubitsky, M. and I. Stewart (2006), 'Nonlinear Dynamics of Networks: The Groupoid Formalism', *Bulletin of the American Mathematical Society*, 43(3): 305–64.

Goodhart, C.A.E. (1975), *Monetary Relationships: A View from Threadneedle Street*, Papers in Monetary Economics, Canberra: Reserve Bank of Australia.

Goodin, R.E., B. Headey, R. Muffels and H.-D. Dirven (1999), *The Real Worlds of Welfare Capitalism*, Cambridge: Cambridge University Press.

Gough, I.R. (1979), *The Political Economy of the Welfare State*, London: Macmillan.

Gould, S.J. and N. Eldridge (1977), 'Punctuated Equilibrium: The Tempo and Mode of Evolution Reconsidered', *Paleobiology*, 3: 45–51.

Granovetter, M. (1973), 'The Strength of Weak Ties', *American Journal of Sociology*, 78: 1360–80.

Grewal, D.S. (2008), *Network Power: The Social Dynamics of Globalisation*, New Haven, NJ: Yale University Press.

Halfpenny, P. (1997) 'Situating Simulation in Sociology', *Sociological Research On-Line*, 2, 3, available at http://www.socresonline.org.uk/2/3/contents.html.

Hall, P.A. (2003), 'Aligning Ontology and Methodology in Comparative Research', in J. Mahoney and D. Rueschemeyer (eds), *Comparative Historical Analysis in the Social Sciences*, Cambridge: Cambridge University Press: 373–404.

Hall, P.A. and D. Soskice (ed.) (2001), *Varieties of Capitalism: The Institutional Foundations of Comparative Advantage*, Oxford: Oxford University Press.

Hall, P.A. and K. Thelen (2008), 'Institutional Change in Varieties of Capitalism', *Socio-Economic Review*, 7: 7–34.

Halsey, A.H. (ed.) (1972), *Educational Priority: Volume 1: EPA Problems and Policies*, London: HMSO.

Hargreaves, D. (2009), 'Momentum for Reform Falters as Profits Grow', *Guardian*, 4 August.

Harré, R. (1972), *The Philosophies of Science*, Oxford: Oxford University Press.

Harré, R. (2004), *Modeling: Gateway to the Unknown*, Amsterdam: Elsevier.

Harré, R. and P.F. Secord (1972), *The Explanation of Social Behaviour*, Oxford: Blackwell.

Hauser, R. (1978), 'A Structural Model of the Mobility Table', *Social Forces*, 56(3): 919–53.

Hedström, P. (2005), *Dissecting the Social: On the Principles of Analytical Sociology*, Cambridge: Cambridge University Press.

Held, D., A. McGrew, D. Goldblatt and J. Perraton (1999), *Global Transformations*, Cambridge: Polity Press.

Hill, P. (2004), 'Satellite Accounts to Measure the New Economy', in D. Ramprakash (ed.), *NESIS Summative Conference Proceedings Vol 1*, Athens: Informer SA: 55–74.

Hirsch, F. (1977), *Social Limits to Growth*, London: Routledge and Kegan Paul.

Hirschman, A.O. (1970), *Exit, Voice and Loyalty*, Cambridge, MA: Harvard University Press.

Hodgson, G.M. (2004), *The Evolution of Institutional Economics*, London: Routledge.

Holland, J. (1975), *Adaptation in Natural and Artificial Systems*, Ann Arbor, MI: University of Michigan Press.

Holland, J. (1995), *Hidden Order: How Adaptation Builds Complexity*, New York: Basic Books.

Hout, M. (1983), *Mobility Tables*, Beverly Hills, CA: Sage.

Hout, M. and R.M. Hauser (1992), 'Symmetry and Hierarchy in Social Mobility: A Methodological Analysis of the CASMIN Model of Class Mobility', *European Sociological Review*, 8(3): 239–66.

Hoyle, R.B. and J.C. Robinson (2002), 'League Tables and School Effectiveness: A Mathematical Model', *Proceedings of the Royal Society*, DOI 10.1098/rspb.2002.2223.

Hudson, D. (2010), 'Financing for Development and the Post-Keynesian Case for a New Global Reserve Currency', *Journal of International Development*, 22(6): 772–87.

Humphrey, J., R. Mansell, D. Parée and H. Schmitz (2003), *The Reality of E-commerce with Developing Countries*, London: London School of Economics/Institute of Development Studies.

Indra, D.M. and N. Buchugnani (1997), 'Rural Landlessness, Extended Entitlements and Inter-Household Relations in South Asia', *Journal of Peasant Studies*, 24(3): 25–64.

Jain, S. and S. Krishna (2003), 'Graph Theory and the Evolution of Autocatalytic Networks', in S. Bornholdt and H.G. Schuster (eds), *Handbook of Graphs and Networks*, Weinheim: Wiley-VCH: 355–95.

Jensen, C. (2009), 'Policy Punctuations in Mature Welfare States', *Journal of Public Policy*, 29(3): 287–303.

Jensen, U.J. and R. Harré (ed.) (1981), *The Philosophy of Evolution*, Brighton: Harvester Press.

Jervis, R. (1997), *System Effects: Complexity in Political and Social Life*, Princeton, NJ: Princeton University Press.

Johnson, S. (2001), *Emergence: The Connected Lives of Ants, Brains, Cities and Software*, Harmondsworth: Penguin.

Jones, A. and M. Sergot (1996), 'A Formal Characterisation of Institutionalised Power', *Journal of the Interest Group in Pure and Applied Logic*, 4: 429–45.

Kaldor, N. (1972), 'The Irrelevance of Equilibrium Economics', *Economic Journal*, 82(328): 1237–55.

Kaldor, N. (1985), *Economics Without Equilibrium*, Cardiff: University College Cardiff Press.

Kaldor, N. and J. Mirrlees (1962), 'A New Model of Economic Growth', *Review of Economic Studies*, 29(3): 174–92.

Kauffman, S.A. (1993), *The Origins of Order: Self-organisation and Selection in Evolution*, Oxford: Oxford University Press.

Kauffman, S.A. (1995a), *At Home in the Universe: The Search for Laws of Self-organisation and Complexity*, Harmondsworth: Penguin.

Kauffman, S.A. (1995b), 'Technology and Evolution: Escaping the Red Queen Effect', *McKinsey Quarterly*, (1): 119–29.

Kay, J. (2009a), *Narrow Banking: The Reform of Banking Regulation*, London: Centre for the Study of Financial Innovation.

Kay, J. (2009b), 'What a Carve Up', *Financial Times*, 1 August.

Kelly, K. (1999), *New Rules for the New Economy*, London: Fourth Estate.

Kempson, E. and K. Rowlingson (1994), *Hard Times*, London: Policy Studies Institute.

Keynes, J.M. (1936), *The General Theory of Employment, Interest and Money*, London: Macmillan.

Keynes, J.M. (1952), *Essays in Persuasion*, London: Hart-Davies.

King, R. (2009), *Governing Universities Globally: Organizations, Regulation and Rankings*, Cheltenham, UK and Northampton, MA, USA: Edward Elgar Publishing.

Kingdon, J.W. (1984), *Agendas, Alternatives and Public Policies*, Boston, MA: Little, Brown and Company.

Kirman, A. (2003), 'Economic Networks', in S. Bornholdt and H.G. Schuster (eds), *Handbook of Graphs and Networks*, Weinheim: Wiley-VCH: 273–94.

Klijn, E.-H. (2008), 'Complexity Theory and Public Administration: What's New?', *Public Management Review*, 10(3): 299–317.

Kline, S.J. and N. Rosenberg (1986), 'An Overview of Innovation', in R. Landau and N. Rosenberg (eds), *The Positive Sum Strategy*, Washington, DC: National Academy Press: 275–305.

Krebs, H., Z. Patak, G. Picot and T. Wannell (2000), 'The Development and Use of a Canadian Linked Employer-Employee Survey', in K. Rubenson and H.G. Schuetze (eds), *Transition to the Knowledge Society*, Vancouver: University of British Columbia: 411–30.

Kristensen, P.H. and J. Zeitlin (2005), *Local Players in Global Games: The Strategic Constitution of a Multinational Corporation*, Oxford: Oxford University Press.

Krugman, P. (1991), *Geography and Trade*, Cambridge: MA: MIT Press.

Krugman, P. (1996), *The Self-organising Economy*, Oxford: Blackwell.

Krugman, P. (1997), 'How the Economy Organizes Itself in Space', in W.B. Arthur, S.N. Durlauf and D.A. Lane (eds), *The Economy as an Evolving Complex System II*, Boulder, CO: Westview: 239–62.

Krugman, P. (1999). 'Networks and Increasing Returns: A Cautionary Tale', available at http://www.pkarchive.org/.

Krugman, P. (2008), *The Return of Depression Economics and the Crisis of 2008*, Harmondsworth: Penguin.

Kuhn, T.S. (1970), *The Structure of Scientific Revolutions*, Chicago, IL: University of Chicago Press.

Lankester, T. (2009), 'The Banking Crisis and Inequality', *World Economics*, 10(1): 151–6.

Lauder, H. and D. Hughes (1999), *Trading in Futures: Why Markets in Education Don't Work*, Buckingham: Open University Press.

Le Grand, J. (2007), *The Other Invisible Hand*, Princeton, NJ: Princeton University Press.

Lebessis, N. and J. Paterson (2001), 'Developing New Modes of Governance', in O. De Schutter, N. Lebessis and J. Paterson (eds), *Governance in the European Union*, Luxembourg: European Commission: 259–94.

Leibfried, S. and P. Pierson (eds) (1995), *European Social Policy: Between Integration and Fragmentation*, Washington, DC: The Brookings Institution.

Leisering, L. and R. Walker (eds) (1998), *The Dynamics of Modern Society*, Bristol: Policy Press.

Lieberson, S. (1987), *Making it Count: The Improvement of Social Research and Theory*, Berkeley, CA: University of California Press.

Lipsky, M. (1980), *Street Level Bureaucracy*, New York: Russel Sage Foundation.

Loasby, B. (1999), *Knowledge, Institutions and Evolution in Economics*, London: Routledge.

Lorenz, E. and B.-A. Lundvall (eds) (2006), *How Europe's Economies Learn: Coordinating Competing Models*, Oxford: Oxford University Press.

Ludwig, M. and P. Abell (2007), 'An Evolutionary Model of Social Networks', *European Physical Journal B*, 58: 97–105.

Lundvall, B.-A. and M. Tomlinson (2002), 'International Benchmarking as a Policy Learning Tool', in M.J. Rodrigues (ed.), *The New Knowledge Economy in Europe*, Cheltenham, UK and Northampton, MA, USA: Edward Elgar Publishing: 203–31.

Lundvall, B.-A., P. Intarakumnerd and J. Vang (eds) (2006), *Asia's Innovation Systems in Transition*, Cheltenham, UK and Northampton, MA, USA: Edward Elgar Publishing.

Macy, M.W. and R. Willer (2002), 'From Factors to Actors: Computational Sociology and Agent-based Modeling', *Annual Review of Sociology*, 28: 143–66.

Mahoney, J. (2000), 'Path Dependence in Historical Sociology', *Theory and Society*, 29(4): 507–48.

Mahoney, J. and K. Thelen (eds) (2010), *Explaining Institutional Change: Ambiguity, Agency and Power*, Cambridge: Cambridge University Press.

Mairesse, J. and P. Mohnen (2009), 'Innovation Surveys and Innovation Policy', Paper presented at the conference: Advancing the Study of Innovation and Globalization in Organizations, German Federal Employment Agency, Nuremberg, 28–30 May.

Marlier, E., A.B. Atkinson, B. Cantillon and B. Nolan (2007), *The EU and Social Inclusion*, Bristol: Policy Press.

Marrano, M.G., J. Haskel and G. Wallis (2007), 'Intangible Investment and Britain's Productivity', Treasury Economic Working Paper No. 1, HM Treasury, London.

Marris, P. (1974), 'Experimenting in Social Reform', in D. Jones and M. Mayo (eds), *Community Work One*, London: Routledge and Kegan Paul: 245–59.

Marris, P. (1996), *The Politics of Uncertainty*, London: Routledge.

Marshall, A. (1920), *Principles of Economics*, London: Macmillan.

Marshall, T.H. (1950), *Citizenship and Social Class*, Cambridge: Cambridge University Press.

Martyushev, L.M. and V.D. Seleznev (2006), 'Maximum Entropy Production Principle in Physics, Chemistry and Biology', *Physics Reports*, 426, 1–45, doi:10.1016/j.physrep.2005.12.001.

Maynard Smith, J. (1982), *Evolution and the Theory of Games*, Cambridge: Cambridge University Press.

Maynard Smith, J. (1998), *Shaping Life: Genes, Embryos and Evolution*, London: Weidenfeld and Nicolson.

Maynard Smith, J. (2000), *Evolutionary Genetics*, Second edition, Oxford: Oxford University Press.

Maynard Smith, J. and E. Szathmáry (1995), *The Major Transitions in Evolution*, Oxford: Oxford University Press.

Maynard Smith, J. and E. Szathmáry (2000), *The Origins of Life: From the Birth of Life to the Origins of Language*, Oxford: Oxford University Press.

McKelvey, B. (1999), 'Avoiding Complexity Catastrophe in Coevolutionary Pockets: Strategies for Rugged Landscapes', *Organization Science*, 10(3): 294–321.

Meijers, H. (2003), *Using ICT to Measure ICT Use: Facts and Fictions*, World Summit on the Information Society, Geneva: ITU.

Metcalfe, J.S. (1998), *Evolutionary Economics and Creative Destruction*, London: Routledge.

Metcalfe, J.S. and J. Foster (ed.) (2004), *Evolution and Economic Complexity*, Cheltenham, UK and Northampton, MA, USA: Edward Elgar Publishing.

Metcalfe, R. (1995), 'From the Ether: A Network Becomes More Valuable as it Reaches More Users', *InfoWorld Magazine*. 2 October.

Meyer, A.D., V. Gaba and K.A. Colwell (2005), 'Organizing Far From Equilibrium: Non-linear Change in Organizational Fields', *Organization Science*, 16(6): 456–73.

Millar, J. (2006), 'Better off in Work? Work, Security and Welfare for Lone Mothers', in C. Glendinning and P.A. Kemp (eds), *Cash and Care: Policy Challenges in the Welfare State*, Bristol: Policy Press: 171–85.

Millar, J. (2007), 'The Dynamics of Poverty and Employment: The Contribution of Qualitative Longitudinal Research to Understanding Transitions, Adaptations and Trajectories', *Social Policy and Society*, 6(4): 533–44.

Millar, J. (2008), *'Work is Good for You': Lone Mothers, Children, Work and Well-being*, Helsinki: KELA Research Department.

Millar, J. and T. Ridge (2009), 'Relationships of Care: Working Lone

Mothers, their Children and Employment Sustainability', *Journal of Social Policy*, 38(1): 103–21.

Miller, J.H. and S.E. Page (2007), *Complex Adaptive Systems: An Introduction to Computational Models of Social Life*, Princeton, NJ: Princeton University Press.

Mitchell, M. (1996), *An Introduction to Genetic Algorithms*, Cambridge, MA: MIT Press.

Morel, B. and R. Ramanujam (1999), 'Through the Looking Glass of Complexity: The Dynamics of Organizations as Adaptive and Evolving Systems', *Organization Science*, 10(3): 278–93.

Moser, C. (1998), 'The Asset Vulnerability Framework: Reassessing Urban Poverty Reduction Strategies', *World Development*, 26(1): 1–19.

Moss, S. (2008), 'Alternative Approaches to the Empirical Validation of Agent-based Models', *Journal of Artificial Societies and Social Simulation*, 11(1), available at http://jasss.soc.surrey.ac.uk/11/1/5.html.

Moss, S. and B. Edmonds (2005), 'Sociology and Simulation: Statistical and Qualitative Cross-validation', *American Journal of Sociology*, 110(4): 1095–131.

Mount, D.W. (2004), *Bioinformatics: Sequence and Genome Analysis*, Second edition, Cold Spring Harbor, New York: Cold Spring Harbor Laboratory Press.

Myrdal, G. (1944), *An American Dilemma*, New York: Harper and Row.

Nelson, R.R. (ed.) (1993), *National Innovation Systems: A Comparative Analysis*, Oxford: Oxford University Press.

Nelson, R. (2005), *Technology, Institutions and Economic Growth*, Cambridge, MA: Harvard University Press.

Nelson, R. and S. Winter (1982), *An Evolutionary Theory of Economic Change*, Cambridge, MA: Harvard University Press.

Newman, M., A.-L. Barabási and D.J. Watts (eds) (2006), *The Structure and Dynamics of Networks*, Princeton, NJ: Princeton University Press.

Noble, D. (2006), *The Music of Life: Biology Beyond Genes*, Oxford: Oxford University Press.

North, D.C. (1990), *Institutions, Institutional Change and Economic Performance*, Cambridge: Cambridge University Press.

North, M.J. and C.M. Macal (2007), *Managing Business Complexity: Discovering Strategic Solutions with Agent-based Modeling and Simulation*, New York: Oxford University Press.

O'Neill, R.V., D.L. DeAngelis, J.B. Waide and T.F.H. Allen (1986), *A Hierarchical Concept of Ecosystems*, Princeton, NJ: Princeton University Press.

Obama, B. (2008), *Dreams from My Father*, Edinburgh: Canongate Books (first published 1995).

Odling-Smee, F.J., K.N. Laland and M.W. Feldmann (2003), *Niche Construction*, Princeton, NJ: Princeton University Press.

OECD (2000), *Learning to Bridge the Digital Divide*, Paris: OECD.

OECD (2001a), *Knowledge and Skills for Life: First Results for the OECD Programme for International Student Assessment (PISA)*, Paris: OECD.

OECD (2001b), *The New Economy: Beyond the Hype*, Paris: OECD.

OECD (2002a), *Dynamising National Innovation Systems*, Paris: OECD.

OECD (2002b), *OECD Information Technology Outlook*, Paris: OECD.

OECD (2003), *ICT and Economic Growth*, Paris: OECD.

OECD (2004), *The Economic Impact of ICT: Measurement, Evidence and Implications*, Paris: OECD.

OECD (2005), *Handbook on Economic Globalisation Indicators*, Paris: OECD.

Ormerod, P. and B. Rosewall (2009), 'Validation and Verification of Agent-based Models in the Social Sciences', in F. Squazzoni (ed.), *Epistemological Aspects of Computer Simulation in the Social Sciences*, Berlin: Springer: 130–40.

Orsenigo, L. (2000), 'Innovation, Organisational Capabilities and Competitiveness in a Global Economy', in K. Rubensen and H.G. Schuetze (eds), *Transition to the Knowledge Society*, Vancouver: University of British Columbia: 163–84.

Ostrom, E. (1990), *Governing the Commons: The Evolution of Institutions for Collective Action*, Cambridge: Cambridge University Press.

Ostrom, E. (2005), *Understanding Institutional Diversity*, Princeton, NJ: Princeton University Press.

Ouchi, W.G. (1980), 'Markets, Bureaucracies and Clans', *Administrative Science Quarterly*, 25: 129–41.

Palier, B. (ed.) (2010), *A Long Goodbye to Bismarck? The Politics of Welfare Reform in Continental Europe*, Amsterdam: Amsterdam University Press.

Palier, B. and C. Martin (eds) (2008), *Reforming the Bismarckian Welfare Systems*, Oxford: Blackwell.

Parker, D. and R. Stacey (1994), *Chaos, Management and Economics: The Implications of Non-linear Thinking*, London: Institute of Economic Affairs.

Pascale, R.T. (1999), 'Surfing the Edge of Chaos', *Sloan Management Review*, 40(3): 83–94.

Peitgen, H.-O., H. Jürgens and D. Saupe (1992), *Chaos and Fractals: New Frontiers of Science*, New York: Springer.

Penrose, E. (1959), *The Theory of the Growth of the Firm*, Oxford: Blackwell & Mott.

Perri 6 (1996), *Escaping Poverty*, London: Demos.

Peston, R. (2008a), 'The New Capitalism', available at http://www.bbc. co.uk/blogs/thereporters/robertpeston/16_12_09_new_capitalism1.pdf.

Peston, R. (2008b), *Who Runs Britain?*, London: Hodder and Stoughton.

Petmesidou, M. and E. Mossialos (eds) (2006), *Social Policy Developments in Greece*, Aldershot: Ashgate.

Pettigrew, A., R. Whittington, L. Melin et al. (eds) (2003), *Innovative Forms of Organising*, London: Sage.

Pierre, J. and B.G. Peters (2000), *Governance, Politics and the State*, Houndmills: Macmillan.

Pierson, P. (1994), *Dismantling the Welfare State*, Cambridge: Cambridge University Press.

Pierson, P. (2004), *Politics in Time*, Princeton, NJ: Princeton University Press.

Pochet, P. (2010), 'What's Wrong with EU2020?', ETUI Policy Brief, 2/2010, ETUI, Brussels.

Polanyi, K. (1944), *The Great Transformation*, New York: Rinehart.

Pollan, M. (1991), *Second Nature: A Gardener's Education*, New York: Grove Press.

Pollan, M. (1997), *A Place of My Own*, London: Bloomsbury.

Pollan, M. (2003), *The Botany of Desire*, London: Bloomsbury.

Pollan, M. (2006), *The Omnivore's Dilemma*, London: Bloomsbury.

Porter, M. (1990), *The Competitive Advantage of Nations*, London: Macmillan.

Porter, T. (2004), *Private Authority, Technical Authority and the Globalization of Accounting Standards*, Hamilton: McMaster University.

Potts, J. (2000), *The New Evolutionary Microeconomics: Complexity, Competence and Adaptive Behaviour*, Cheltenham, UK and Northampton, MA, USA: Edward Elgar Publishing.

Potts, J. (2001), 'Knowledge and Markets', *Journal of Evolutionary Economics*, 11: 413–31.

Potts, J. (2003), 'The *Prometheus* School of Information Economics', *Prometheus*, 21(4): 477–86.

Potts, J. (2006), 'How Creative are the Super-rich?', *Agenda*, 13(4): 339–50.

Potts, J. (2007a), 'Arts & Innovation: An Evolutionary Economic View of the Creative Industries', *Multi-disciplinary Research in the Arts*, 1, 1, Melbourne: University of Melbourne UNESCO Arts Education Observatory.

Potts, J. (2007b), 'Toward an Evolutionary Theory of Innovation and Growth in the Service Economy', *Prometheus*, 25(2): 147–59.

Potts, J. (2008a), 'Capitalism, Socialism and Culture: A Schumpeterian

Institutional Analysis of the Rise of the Creative Industries', unpublished manuscript, University of Queensland.

Potts, J. (2008b), 'Creative Industries and Cultural Science: A Definitional Odyssey', *Cultural Science*, 1, 1, available at http://cultural-science.org/journal/index.php/culturalscience/index.

Powell, J.H. and J.P. Bradford (1998), 'The Security-Strategy Interface: Using Qualitative Process Models to Relate the Security Function to Business Dynamics', *Security Journal*, 10: 151–60.

Powell, J.H. and J.P. Bradford (2000), 'Targeting Intelligence Gathering in a Dynamic Competitive Environment', *International Journal of Information Management*, 20: 181–95.

Power, S., T. Edwards, G. Whitty and V. Wigfall (2003), *Education and the Middle Class*, Buckingham: Open University Press.

Prete, F. (ed.) (2004), *Complex Worlds from Simpler Nervous Systems*, Cambridge, MA: MIT Press.

Prigogine, I. (1980), *From Being to Becoming: Time and Complexity in the Physical Sciences*, San Francisco, CA: W.H. Freeman and Co.

Prigogine, I. and I. Stengers (1984), *Order Out of Chaos*, London: Heinemann.

PriMetrica (2010), 'Global Internet Geography Database and Report', available at http://www.telegeography.com/product-info/gig/index.php.

Ramaswamy, S. (2000), 'Development Economics and Complexity', in D. Colander (ed.), *The Complexity Vision and the Teaching of Economics*, Cheltenham, UK and Northampton, MA, USA: Edward Elgar Publishing: 201–8.

Ramprakash, D. (1994), 'Poverty in the Countries of the European Union: A Synthesis of Eurostat's Statistical Research on Poverty', *Journal of European Social Policy*, 4(2): 117–28.

Ramprakash, D. (2004), *NESIS Summative Conference Proceedings Vol 1*, Athens: Informer S.A.

Rhodes, R.A.W. (1997), *Understanding Governance*, Buckingham: Open University Press.

Ridge, T. (2007), 'It's a Family Affair', *Journal of Social Policy*, 36(3): 399–416.

Ridge, T. and J. Millar (2008), *Work and Well-being Over Time: Lone Mothers and Their Children*, London: Department for Work and Pensions.

Robinson, J. (1964), *Economic Philosophy*, Harmondsworth: Penguin.

Robinson, P. (2007), 'Multi-agent Simulation of the Dynamics of Social Exclusion in School Choice', Department of Computer Sciences, University of Bath, available at http://opus.bath.ac.uk/16754/.

Rodrigues, M.J. (ed.) (2009), *Europe, Globalization and the Lisbon Agenda*, Cheltenham, UK and Northampton, MA, USA: Edward Elgar Publishing.

Rogers, E. (2003), *Diffusion of Innovations*, New York: Simon and Schuster, Fifth edition.

Room, G. (1979), *The Sociology of Welfare*, Oxford: Martin Robertson.

Room, G. (1986), *Cross-National Innovation in Social Policy*, London: Macmillan.

Room, G. (1990), *New Poverty in the European Community*, London: Macmillan.

Room, G. (1993), *Anti-poverty Action-Research in Europe*, Bristol: SAUS.

Room, G. (ed.) (1995), *Beyond the Threshold: The Measurement and Analysis of Social Exclusion*, Bristol: Policy Press.

Room, G. (2000), 'Commodification and Decommodification: A Developmental Critique', *Policy and Politics*, 28(3): 331–51.

Room, G. (2002), 'Education and Welfare: Recalibrating the European Debate', *Policy Studies*, 23(1): 37–50.

Room, G. (2004), 'Multi-tiered International Welfare Systems', in I.R. Gough, G.D. Wood, A. Barrientos, P. Bevan, P. Davis and G. Room (eds), *Insecurity and Welfare Regimes in Asia, Africa and Latin America*, Cambridge: Cambridge University Press: 287–311.

Room, G. (2005a), *The European Challenge: Innovation, Policy Learning and Social Cohesion in the New Knowledge Economy*, Bristol: Policy Press.

Room, G. (2005b), 'Policy Benchmarking in the European Union: Indicators and Ambiguities', *Policy Studies*, 26(2): 117–32.

Room, G. (2007), 'Challenges Facing the EU: Scope for a Coherent Response', *European Societies*, 9(3): 229–44.

Room, G. (2011), 'Social Mobility and Complexity Theory: Towards a Critique of the Sociological Mainstream', *Policy Studies*, 32(2): 109–26.

Room, G. and N. Britton (2006), 'The Dynamics of Social Exclusion', *International Journal of Social Welfare*, 15(4) (October): 280–89.

Rowlingson, K. (2008), 'Wealth', in T. Ridge and S. Wright (eds), *Understanding Poverty, Income and Wealth*, Bristol: Policy Press: 15–36.

Rowlingson, K. and S. Mackay (2005), *Attitudes to Inheritance in Britain*, Bristol: Policy Press.

Rubenson, K. and H.G. Schuetze (eds) (2000), *Transition to the Knowledge Society*, Vancouver: University of British Columbia.

Sanderson, I. (2006), 'Complexity, "Practical Rationality" and Evidence-based Policy Making', *Policy and Politics*, 34(1): 115–32.

Sankoff, D. and J.B. Kruskal (eds) (1983), *Time Warps, String Edits and*

Macromolecules: The Theory and Practice of Sequence Comparison, Reading, MA: Addison-Wesley.

Savage, M. and R. Burrows (2007), 'The Coming Crisis of Empirical Sociology', *Sociology*, 41: 885–99.

Schaaper, M. (2004), 'An Emerging Knowledge-based Economy in China?', STI Working Paper 2004/4, Paris: OECD.

Scharpf, F.W. (1997), *Games Real Actors Play: Actor-centred Institutionalism in Policy Research*, Boulder, CO: Westview Press.

Scheffer, M., J. Bascompte, W.A. Brock et al. (2009), 'Early Warning Signals for Critical Transitions', *Nature*, 461(3) (September): 53–9.

Scheinkman, J. (2004), 'Heterogeneous Beliefs, Speculation and Trading in Financial Markets', Paper delivered to the ESRC Seminar on Socio-Dynamics, London, 24 May.

Schelling, T.C. (1978), *Micromotives and Macrobehaviour*, London: W.W. Norton.

Schön, D.A. (1993), 'Generative Metaphor: A Perspective on Problem-setting in Social Policy', in A. Ortony (ed.), *Metaphor and Thought*, Cambridge: Cambridge University Press: 137–63.

Scott, J. (2000), *Social Network Analysis*, Second edition, London: Sage.

Seltzer, K. and T. Bentley (1999), *The Creative Age: Knowledge and Skills for the New Economy*, London: Demos.

Senge, P. (1990), *The Fifth Discipline*, London: Random Century.

Shubin, N. (2008), *Your Inner Fish*, Harmondsworth: Allen Lane.

Simon, H.A. (1996), *The Sciences of the Artificial*, Cambridge, MA: MIT Press.

Skidelsky, R. (2002), *John Maynard Keynes: Volume 3: Fighting for Freedom 1937–1946*, Harmondsworth: Penguin.

Skidelsky, R. (2009), *Keynes: The Return of the Master*, London: Allen Lane.

Sloane, D. and S.P. Morgan (1996), 'An Introduction to Categorical Data Analysis', *Annual Review of Sociology*, 22: 351–75.

Smithers, A. and P. Robinson (2010), *Worlds Apart: Social Variation Among Schools*, London: The Sutton Trust.

Snyder, D. and E.L. Kick (1979), 'Structural Position in the World System and Economic Growth, 1955–1970: A Multiple-Network Analysis of Transnational Interactions', *American Journal of Sociology*, 84(5): 1096–126.

Social Exclusion Unit (2004), *The Drivers of Social Exclusion*, London: Office of the Deputy Prime Minister.

Social Protection Committee (2008), *Child Poverty and Well-being in the EU: Current Status and the Way Forward*, Brussels: European Commission.

Solé, R. and J. Bascompte (2006), *Self-organization in Complex Ecosystems*, Princeton, NJ: Princeton University Press.

Solé, R. and R. Pasotor-Satorras (2003), 'Complex Networks in Genomics and Proteomics', in S. Bornholdt and H.G. Schuster (eds), *Handbook of Graphs and Networks*, Weinheim: Wiley-VCH: 145–67.

Sommer, R.J. (2003), 'Cells and Genes as Networks in Nematode Development and Evolution', in S. Bornholdt and H.G. Schuster (eds), *Handbook of Graphs and Networks*, Weinheim: Wiley-VCH: 131–44.

Sørensen, J.B. (1992), 'Locating Class Cleavages in Inter-generational Mobility: Cross-national Commonalities and Variations in Mobility Patterns', *European Sociological Review*, 8(3): 267–81.

Soros, G. (2008a), 'The Crisis and What to Do About It', *Guardian*, 22 November.

Soros, G. (2008b), *The New Paradigm for Financial Markets*, London: Perseus Books.

Squazzoni, F. (2006), 'Review of P. Hedström, *Dissecting the Social: on the Principles of Analytical Sociology*, Cambridge University Press (2005)', *Journal of Artificial Societies and Social Simulation*, 9(2), available at http://jasss.soc.surrey.ac.uk/9/2/reviews/squazzoni.html.

Squazzoni, F. (ed.) (2009), *Epistemological Aspects of Computer Simulation in the Social Sciences*, Berlin: Springer.

Stackelberg, H. v. (1952), *The Theory of the Market Economy (Grundlage der Theoretischen Volkswirtschaftslehre, 1948* (translated with an Introduction by Alan T. Peacock), London: William Hodge.

Statistics Canada (2004), *Workplace and Employee Survey Compendium 2001*, Ottawa: Statistics Canada.

Steinert, H. and A. Pilgram (eds) (2003), *Welfare Policy from Below: Struggles Against Social Exclusion in Europe*. Aldershot: Ashgate.

Stewart, I. (1997), *Does God Play Dice?*, Second edition, Harmondsworth: Penguin.

Stewart, M. (2001), *The Coevolving Organization: Poised Between Order and Chaos*, Rutland: Decomplexity Associates, available at http://www.decomplexity.com/.

Stewart, M. (2003), *The Robust Organization: Highly Optimised Tolerance*, Rutland: Decomplexity Associates, available at http://www.decomplexity.com/.

Streek, W. and K. Thelen (eds) (2005), *Beyond Continuity: Institutional Change in Advanced Political Economies*, Oxford: Oxford University Press.

Swift, A. (2003), *How Not To Be a Hypocrite: School Choice for the Morally Perplexed Parent*, London: Routledge.

Swiss Economic Institute (2010), 'KOF Index of Globalization', available at http://globalization.kof.ethz.ch/.

Tawney, R.H. (1931) [1964], *Equality*, London Unwin Books.

Tett, G. (2009), *Fool's Gold*, London: Little, Brown.

Thelen, K. (2003), 'How Institutions Evolve: Insights from Comparative Historical Analysis', in J. Mahoney and D. Rueschemeyer (eds), *Comparative Historical Analysis in the Social Sciences*, Cambridge: Cambridge University Press: 208–40.

Thelen, K. (2004), *How Institutions Evolve*, Cambridge: Cambridge University Press.

Thompson, G., J. Frances, R. Levacic and J. Mitchell (eds) (1991), *Markets, Hierarchies and Networks. The Coordination of Social Life*, London: Sage.

Tilman, H.W. (1987), *The Eight Sailing/Mountain-Exploration Books*, London: Diadem Books (distributed in Great Britan and Europe by Cordee).

Tily, G. (2007), *Keynes's General Theory, The Rate of Interest and 'Keynesian' Economics: Keynes Betrayed*, London: Palgrave Macmillan.

Tirole, J. (1988), *The Theory of Industrial Organization*, Cambridge, MA: The MIT Press.

Titmuss, R. (1973), *The Gift Relationship*, Hardmondsworth: Penguin.

Titmuss, R.M. (1963), *Essays on 'the Welfare State'*, Second edition, London: George Allen and Unwin.

Toner, P. (1999), *Main Currents in Cumulative Causation: The Dynamics of Growth and Development*, London: St Martin's Press.

Toulmin, S. (1972), *Human Understanding*, Oxford: Clarendon Press.

Toulmin, S. (2001), *Return to Reason*, Cambridge, MA: Harvard University Press.

Toulmin, S. and J. Goodfield (1967), *The Discovery of Time*, Harmondsworth: Penguin.

Toynbee, P. and D. Walker (2008), *Unjust Rewards*, London: Granta.

Treanor, J. and P. Inman (2009), 'Business as Usual for the Bankers', *Guardian*, 4 August.

Turing, A. (1952), 'On the Chemical Basis of Morphogenesis', *Philosophical Transactions of the Royal Society* B, 237: 37–72.

Turner, J.S. (2000), *The Extended Organism*, Cambridge, MA: Harvard University Press.

Urry, J. (2003), *Global Complexity*, Cambridge: Polity Press.

van der Heijden, K. (1996), *Scenarios: The Art of Strategic Conversation*, Chichester: John Wiley.

Veblen, T. (1898), 'Why is Economics Not an Evolutionary Science?', *Quarterly Journal of Economics*, 12(4): 373–97.

Veblen, T. (1899), *The Theory of the Leisure Class*, New York: Macmillan.

Vidgen, R. and J. Padget (2009), 'Sendero: An Extended, Agent-based Implementation of Kauffman's NKCS Model', *Journal of Artificial Societies and Social Simulation*, 12(4), available at http://jasss.soc.surrey.ac.uk/12/4/8.html.

Vidgen, R. and X. Wang (2004), *Adaptive Information System Development*, Proceedings of the 9th UK Association for Information Systems Conference, Glasgow, 5–7 March.

Vidgen, R., S. Henneberg and P. Naudé (2007), 'What Sort of Community is the European Conference on Information Systems?', *European Journal of Information Systems*, 16: 5–19.

Wack, P. (1985), 'Scenarios, Shooting the Rapids', *Harvard Business Review*, 63(6): 131–42.

Wagener, H.-J. and J.W. Drukker (eds) (1986), *The Economic Law of Motion of Modern Society: A Marx-Keynes-Schumpeter Centennial*, Cambridge: Cambridge University Press.

Waldrop, M.M. (1992), *Complexity: The Emerging Science at the Edge of Order and Chaos*, London: Viking.

Wasserman, S. and K. Faust (1994), *Social Network Analysis*, Cambridge: Cambridge University Press.

Watson, M. (2007), *The Political Economy of International Capital Mobility*, Houndmills: Palgrave Macmillan.

Watson, M. (2009), 'Headlong into the Polanyian Dilemma: The Impact of Middle-class Moral Panic on the British Government's Response to the Sub-prime Crisis', *British Journal of Politics and International Relations*, 11(3): 422–37.

Watts, D. (2003), *Six Degrees: The Science of a Connected Age*, London: Vintage.

Weber, M. (1930), *The Protestant Ethic and the Spirit of Capitalism*, London: George Allen and Unwin (first published in German 1905).

Weber, M. (1949), *The Methodology of the Social Sciences*, New York: Free Press.

Weber, M. (1965), *The Sociology of Religion*, London: Methuen (first published in German 1922).

White, H.C. (2008), *Identity and Control: How Social Formations Emerge*, Second edition, Princeton, NJ: Princeton University Press.

Whittard, D., M. Franklin, P. Stam and T. Clayton (2009), *Interviews with Firms on Innovation Investment (Final Report to NESTA)*, London: NESTA (National Endowment for Science Technology and the Arts).

Wilkinson, R. and K. Pickett (2009), *The Spirit Level: Why More Equal Societies Almost Always Do Better*, London: Allen Lane.

Williams, R. (1961), *The Long Revolution*, Harmondsworth: Penguin.

Williamson, O. (1975), *Markets and Hierarchies*, New York: Free Press.

Wilson, W.J. (1987), *The Truly Disadvantaged*, Chicago, IL: University of Chicago Press.

Windrum, P. and G.M.P. Swann (1999), *Networks, Noise and Web Navigation: Sustaining Metcalfe's Law through Technological Innovation*, Maastricht: University of Maastricht, MERIT.

Witt, U. (2003), *The Evolving Economy*, Cheltenham, UK and Northampton, MA, USA: Edward Elgar Publishing.

Wood, G.D. (2003), 'Staying Secure, Staying Poor: The "Faustian Bargain"', *World Development*, 31(3): 455–71.

World Economic Forum (2004), *The Global Information Technology Report 2003–2004: Towards an Equitable Information Society*, Oxford: Oxford University Press.

Wright, S. (1932), 'The Roles of Mutation, Inbreeding, Crossbreeding and Selection in Evolution', in D.F. Jones (ed.), *Proceedings of the Sixth International Congress on Genetics*, Vol. 1, Ithaca, NA: Genetic Society of America: 356–66.

Young, A. (1928), 'Increasing Returns in Economic Progress ', *Economic Journal*, 38(151): 527–42.

Zeitlin, J. and P. Pochet (2005), *The Open Method of Coordination in Action: The European Employment and Social Inclusion Strategies*, Brussels: P.I.E.-Peter Lang S.A.

Name index

Subject index